Contents

[v]

CONTENTS

Places of original publication are indicated at the foot of the opening page of each essay; where no such credit appears, the essay is previously unpublished.

Acknowledgements

My thanks to Ted Hughes for his help in putting this selection of his prose together; to Keith Sagar, who kindly gave me the run of his library, and valuable advice, at a moment's notice; to Sandy Brownjohn; and to Ekbert Faas and the Black Sparrow Press for permission to reprint two questions from an interview and the piece on Laura Riding.

W.S.

For reprinting articles and essays, acknowledgements are due to the following publishers: Carcanet Press: 'János Pilinszky', Introduction to *Selected Poems* (translated by Ted Hughes and János Csokits 1976, Anvil Press: 1989), 'Vasko Popa', Introduction to *Collected Poems* (1978, Anvil Press: 1989); Faber and Faber: *Poetry in the Making* (1967), Introduction to *A Choice of Shakespeare's Verse* (1971), Introduction to *A Choice of Emily Dickinson's Verse* (1968), Introduction to *Collected Poems of Sylvia Plath* (1981), Introduction to *Selected Poems: Keith Douglas* (1964), *A Dancer to God: Tributes to T. S. Eliot* (1992), extracts from *Shakespeare and the Goddess of Complete Being* (1992); *Grand Street* (Vol. 1 No. 3, Spring 1982): 'Sylvia Plath and Her Journals'; *Guardian* (14 May 1965): 'Music of Humanity'; Heinemann: 'Concealed Energies' from *Children as Writers* 2 (1975); 'Myth and Education' from *Writers, Critics and Children* (ed. Geoff Fox et al., 1976); Hodder and Stoughton: 'Fantastic Happenings and Gory Adventures', original draft of an article from *Meet and Write Book* 2 (ed. Sandy and Alan Brownjohn, 1987); Little, Brown & Co.: Introduction to *The Complete Prints of Leonard Baskin* (1984); *Listener*: 'Asgard for Addicts' (19 March 1964), 'Opposing Selves' (1 October 1964), 'Regenerations' (29 October 1964), 'National Ghost' (5 August 1965); Longman: 'Crow on the Beach' from *45 Contemporary Poems: The Creative Process* (ed. Alberta T. Turner, 1985); *London Magazine* (Vol. 1 No. 2): 'Context'; *New Statesman*: 'Quitting' (6 September 1963), 'Dr Dung' (4 September 1964), 'Superstitions' (2 October 1964), 'Heavenly Visions' (25 November 1966); *New York Review of Books*: 'The Genius of Isaac Bashevis Singer' (22 April 1965), 'Tricksters and Tar Babies' (9 December 1965); *New York Times Book Review*: 'Unfinished Business' (April 1964); *Observer*: 'Publishing Sylvia Plath' (21 November 1971); *Poetry Book Society Bulletin* No. 44, February 1965: 'Ariel'; Western

ACKNOWLEDGEMENTS

Education and Library Board, Northern Ireland: *The Pushkin Prizes Schools Prize Brochure* (1989): 'A Word about Writing in Schools'; *Vogue* (December 1971): 'Orghast'; *Your Environment I* (Summer 1970): 'The Environmental Revolution'.

Introduction

Ted Hughes has been a major presence in English poetry since the publication of *The Hawk in the Rain* in 1957. He has also made an important contribution to children's literature, and to the whole thorny problem of nurturing imagination and creativity in schools and in the community at large. Something of his originality was usefully characterized by Seamus Heaney in an interview given to John Haffenden in 1979:

Hughes's voice, I think, is in rebellion against a certain kind of demeaned, mannerly voice. It's a voice that has no truck with irony because his dialect is not like that . . . I mean, the voice of a generation – the Larkin voice, the Movement voice, even the Eliot voice, the Auden voice – the manners of that speech, the original voices behind that poetic voice, are those of literate English middle-class culture, and I think Hughes's great cry and call and bawl is that English language and English poetry is longer and deeper and rougher than that. That's of a piece with his interest in Middle English, the dialect, his insisting upon foxes and bulls and violence. It's a form of calling out for more, that life is more. And of course he gets back from that middle-class school the enmity he implicitly offers. Ted may be accused of violence, of grotesquerie, but there is tenderness and reverence and seriousness at the centre of the thing. That comes out clearly in many of the poems . . . I'm a different kind of animal . . . but I will always be grateful for the release that reading his work gave me . . . I find Ted personally powerfully creative, nurturing. I think he has understanding of people and creativity.*

It's about everything

Much of Hughes's achievement – the stream of books, the enabling presence behind the Arvon Foundation, the BBC's broadcasts for schools, the *Daily Mirror*'s and W. H. Smith's children's poetry competitions, the quiet but strong encouragement of other writers and teachers, the openness to diverse cultural influences, the collaborations with artists and theatre directors – is on record. So

---

* *Viewpoints: Poets in Conversation with John Haffenden* (London: Faber and Faber, 1981), pp. 73–4.

too is the exemplary manner in which he has led his writing life, avoiding all the fripperies and blandishments of contemporary literary fame. What is less well-known, perhaps, is that over the years, without deviating from his essential concerns, Hughes has also put together a major body of literary and cultural criticism, sometimes addressing particular writers and enthusiasms, sometimes the very largest social, aesthetic and metaphysical issues. This places him firmly in the tradition of poet-critics whose practical and theoretical meditations make up the canon of classic English literary criticism, from Sidney, Campion and Jonson down to Yeats, Pound, Eliot, Auden and Empson. In this long overdue selection I have tried to indicate something of the range and richness of his critical prose, from the early reviews and schools broadcasts (collected under the title *Poetry in the Making*, Faber 1967) to the brilliant essays on metre and on Coleridge, published here for the first time, and his recent re-engagement with Shakespeare. Each of the pieces is rewarding in its own right, quite often dense with intellectual excitement as Hughes grapples with the elusive stuff – verbal, social, physical, psychic – that goes to make up creation; and each, as well as throwing light on his own poems and habits of thought, marks a point in the larger trajectory of his own poetic 'myth', or schema, by means of which he positions himself in the modern chaos.

The power and subtlety of Hughes's mind, and the variousness of his wide-ranging concerns, are apparent in the essay-review of Isaac Bashevis Singer, in 'Myth and Education', in the short piece on the meta- or ur-language of *Orghast*, in his suicidal yet heroic condensation of Shakespeare's grand themes, in the pioneering brilliance and comprehensive sweep of the essay on Eliot's 'The Death of Saint Narcissus', and indeed in the penetrating remarks thrown off in the most casual of his early reviews. His empathy with such diverse talents as Emily Dickinson, Singer, Walter de la Mare, Owen, Douglas, Laura Riding, Dylan Thomas, János Pilinszky, Vasko Popa, and Sylvia Plath (one could deduce an even longer list from the poems, not to mention his engagement with the writers of 'primitive' cultures) is wonderfully acute, as is his absorption in those large and small issues that live in the nerve endings of twentieth-century men and women. His incisive overview of particularities and generalities, syntactical thumb-prints and entire civilizations, goes hand in hand with an engaging modesty, diffidence even, before the complexities every critic tangles with. 'I'm always aware, when I've "finished" a piece, of being utterly defeated and excluded – as if I'd been shoved aside by somebody I do not like one bit. Yet it seems to be the only way I can do it'.*

One of the things that emerges from an extended reading of Hughes's prose is that he has attacked and explored his themes and compulsions on all fronts, discursively and analytically as well as 'poetically', just as Coleridge and Eliot did. 'The characteristic of great works is exactly this: that in them the full presence of the inner world combines with and is reconciled to the full presence of the outer world'. 'Poetry has a warrant for the office of truth-teller only insofar as its music becomes a form of action'. Such observations can be directed back at Hughes's own criticism as it confronts Baskin's or Singer's or Dickinson's or Shakespeare's *daimon*, and the verbal or visual mechanisms brought to bear by those artists on its imperious commands. Similarly his accounts and partial explications of the genesis of *Crow*, and of *Orghast*, and of the power of the border ballads, and folk tales, show that he has an intellectual rationale available, when necessary, for the workings of intuition and magic. Whether or not the two modes are interdependent or mutually exclusive, and how much the explanation explains, are questions, no doubt, for further debate. There is a kaleidoscope of metaphors on offer too for the imagination, for the powers and necessities of storytelling, and for the uses of religion (understood in its widest sense), drawn from the whole spectrum of learning, and without privileging Eurocentrism.

Who am I, what am I, where am I going? asks Wodwo, Hughes's meditative spirit of the woods. What the essays insist on, time and again, is that the big questions don't and won't go away, however modern tacticians try to disarm them, however sophisticated our materialism grows, however technical our vocabulary; and that the

---

* Letter to the editor, 23 November 1990.

really interesting writers are those who address themselves directly to our naked selves. Whatever the 'laws of creation' might turn out to be they are not likely to be netted by, or simulated in, a computer, or simple behaviourism, or any of the various reductionisms practised by our age. In much of his thinking Hughes echoes Coleridge's notion that imagination is 'a dim analogue of creation',* and that poetry 'brings the whole soul of man into activity, with the subordination of its faculties to each other, according to their relative worth and dignity'.†

He also responds, as all good critics do, to that sort of truth Yeats invokes when he says 'God guard me from those thoughts men think / In the mind alone; / He that sings a lasting song / Thinks in a marrow-bone' ('A Prayer for Old Age'). The outriders and guarantors of such truths are likely to be purely verbal. Hence his alertness to new musics and new tracks in the sand, to the 'eternal delight' of those energies we find both in nature and in art. Hughes's radar picks up these energies in an astonishingly diverse number of places and persons, ancient and modern. Moreover he has a knack of conveying essences without fuss or pomposity. Has anyone summarized Emily Dickinson's enterprise better than Hughes does in the half dozen pages reprinted here; or the subterranean importance of the First World War to English political and social life; or Keith Douglas's fierce, self-incriminating honesty, and Dylan Thomas's naked hubris ('Every poem is an attempt to sign up the whole heavenly vision . . . in a static constellation of verbal prisms'); or been more usefully critical of English complacencies, social, intellectual, and spiritual? Hughes never wears his convictions on his sleeve, nor does he assume the lofty tones of the 'expert', but he does insist that there is more to life, as Seamus Heaney put it, than is comprehended in the chronic English tendency to look the other way, or see both sides of the question, or make disturbance cosy in a variety of codes and conventions.

Of course there are things to argue with here, as there are in all

* Letter to Richard Sharpe, 15 January 1804.
† *Biographia Literaria*, Chapter XIV.

writers of substance. The tendency to equate civilization with repression, for example, and reason with rationalization, might be countered by quoting Chekhov's observation that there is more love for humanity in electricity and a hygienic water supply than in any amount of spiritual breast-beating. (Chekhov had the later, fundamentalist Tolstoy in mind, and the nature of the peasants' working week.) Hughes might well assent to this and yet reply, with Pascal, Dostoevsky, and Lawrence that reason amounts to more than a tepid reasonableness and won't be accommodated in the utilitarian housing estates thrown up by the law of excluded middle. As the 'madman' hero of *Notes from Underground* says, 'If reason is against a man, man will be against reason'.

One might also grow uneasy, at times, with Hughes's 'cosmic' vocabulary, for instance in the Baskin essay, which whirls about between shamanism and sub-atomic physics, rabbinical theology and Greek tragedy, invoking Aeschylus, Einstein, Coatlicue, Prometheus, Christ, earth-goddesses and Aztec ritual with energetic abandon. The worry here is that in his desire to seize the ineffable Hughes may be left brandishing a fistful of resonant but opaque abstractions, to which the resounding proper names give only an illusory glow of substance. Perhaps this is merely to say that his imagination is essentially hyperbolical, like Dickens's – and similarly prolific. Where more circumspect critics (Eliot, for example) weave a critical snake-dance of precise understatement Hughes goes on the intellectual war-path, improvising whatever sort of ambush seems likely to capture the elusive soul-stuff we have no adequate vocabulary for.* The technique can be seen at its most impressive in the essays on Shakespeare and other poets, including that on our greatest Anglo-American modern. Of all the millions of words expended on Eliot's character and genius these are surely among the most penetrating and essential. Like his own thought-fox, Hughes's mind circles the relevant terrain then closes unerringly on the metaphysical and personal disturbances lying at the centre of Eliot's

---

* Hence in part, perhaps, the animal poems, ostensive definitions of that 'sharp hot stink' the mind can't close on, or file away in the dictionary. Cf. Dickens's 'types', which might be said to constitute a human bestiary.

life – hinted at by the poet himself, perhaps, in his reference to that 'acute personal reminiscence (never to be explicated, of course, but to give power from well below the surface)'* which animates *The Waste Land*, and which he is struggling to recapture in the *Quartets*.

The two words that always come to mind when one reads Hughes are 'imagination' and 'generosity'. The first he has called 'the original cauldron of wisdom'. The second is a function of his honesty as a man speaking to men, one who inspires by his own vibrant responsiveness to the primordial world in and around us, including its cloud-caps of literature, music, and art. It's worth remembering that he came to prominence at a time when Eliot's distinctive and powerful voice ruled the whole world of letters, and Larkin's plangent melancholy – which has its own fiercenesses – was sprinkling balm on the welfare state. To enter a new register of speech in the exclusive ledger of Anglo-American poetry, and to open up a way back into ordinariness and extraordinariness, after the dizzying rigours of Modernism on the one hand and post-war retrenchment on the other, was a very considerable achievement. One of the things Ted Hughes has given us to wonder at is ourselves, under a new, and a very ancient, aspect of vision. The fugitive reviews and considered essays that make up this book confirm his importance as one of the indispensable writers and critics of our time.

---

* Letter to John Hayward, quoted in *The Composition of the Four Quartets* by Helen Gardner (London: Faber and Faber, 1978).

Context

The poet's only hope is to be infinitely sensitive to what his gift is, and this in itself seems to be another gift that few poets possess. According to this sensitivity, and to his faith in it, he will go on developing as a poet, as Yeats did, pursuing those adventures, mental, spiritual and physical, whatever they may be, that his gift wants. Or he will lose its guidance, lose the feel of its touch in the workings of his mind, and soon be absorbed by the impersonal lumber of matters in which his gift has no interest, which is a form of suicide, metaphorical in the case of Coleridge, actual in the case of Mayakovsky.

Many considerations assault his faith in the finality, wisdom and sufficiency of his gift. Its operation is not only shadowy and indefinable, it is intermittent. It has none of the obvious attachment to publicly exciting and seemingly important affairs that his other mental activities have and in which all his intelligent contemporaries have such confidence, and so it receives no immediate encouragement – or encouragement only of the most dubious kind, as a flagellant, questioning his illuminations, might be encouraged by a bunch of mad old women and some other half-dead gory flagellant. It visits him when he is only half suspecting it, and he is not sure it has visited him until some days or months afterwards and perhaps he never can be sure, being a sensible person aware of the examples of earlier poets and of the devils of self-delusion and of the delusions of whole generations.

Coleridge himself is a good example of both the true poet and the false, the man trusting his gift and producing the real thing, and the man searching for his satisfaction among more popular and public causes. And his living poetry is a good example of how the significance of poetry depends on qualities of imagination, depth, breadth, intensity and accent in the spirit of it, rather than in reference to many matters.

From *London Magazine*, Vol. I No. 2, 1962.

The important issues of the two decades following the French Revolution were, in England, overwhelmingly social and political, one would say. Wordsworth and Coleridge and Blake were the great poets of that time, in English, and were as involved, intellectually, in those issues as anybody well could be, but that seems to have had very little to do, directly, with their poetry. From their surviving poetry alone one might suspect Wordsworth would have done better to leave his mountains and broaden his mind somewhat on life; that Coleridge ought to have wakened up to his time and come out of the dark ages and away from those fogs of the South Pole; that Blake needed friends of a more worldly and liberal conversation. This flower, this little girl, this bird, this old man paddling in a pool, this boat-stealing and woodcock-snaring, these soul-notes of a moun-tain-watcher, and these magical damsels in a magical forest and this dream flight with a dead bird, and these angels and black boys and roses and briars, all this infatuation with infancy and innocence, what did these have to do with the great issues of the time? Nothing whatsoever, till the spirit that worked through Wordsworth and Coleridge and Blake chose them for its parables. And looking back now, if we wish to see the important issues of those two decades, we find nothing so convincing and enlightening to so many of us, as the spirit which seems to touch us openly and speak to us directly through these poems.

Damon, quoted by Plato, says that the modes of music are nowhere altered without changes in the most important laws of the state. Is a musician to listen to his gift then, or study legislation? The poet who feels he needs to mix his poetry up with significant matters, or to throw his verse into the popular excitement of the time, ought to remember this strange observation.

His gift is an unobliging thing. He can study his art, experiment, and apply his mind and live as he pleases. But the moment of writing is too late for further improvements or adjustments. Certain memories, images, sounds, feelings, thoughts, and relationships between these, have for some reason become luminous at the core of his mind: it is in his attempt to bring them out, without impairment, into a comparatively dark world, that he makes poems. At the moment of writing, the poetry is a combination, or a resultant, of all that he is — unimpeachable evidence of itself and, indirectly, of himself — and for the time of writing he can do nothing but accept it. If he doesn't approve of what is appearing, there are always plenty of ways to falsify and 'improve' it, there are always plenty of fashions as to how it should look, how it can be made more acceptable, more 'interesting', his other faculties are only too ready to load it with their business, whereon he ceases to be a poet producing what poetry he can and becomes a cheat of a kind, producing confusion.

Fantastic Happenings and
Gory Adventures

For me, writing for pleasure began at school when I discovered that what I wrote amused my classmates, and sometimes my teacher. At that time I was eleven, living in an industrial town in South Yorkshire where my parents kept a newsagents shop. This shop was a large, busy, very interesting place. It also supplied me with every comic and boy's magazine available in that place at that time. I read them before they were sold.

My writing grew mainly out of my reading. I specialized in fantastic happenings and gory adventures. I set my tales, generally, North of the Great Divide, in the Wild West, in tropical jungles, and in Africa – places as far away as possible from the sooty town I lived in and the gloom of the War. At the same time, all I was really interested in was shooting, fishing and trapping, and birds, fish and animals. So I read about these things too, as much as I could find. Books about wild life were not as plentiful in those days as they are now, but I made do with weekly magazines such as *The Shooting Times* and *The Gamekeeper* (the only magazines I bought for myself), and various books from the town library. From eleven to thirteen I read *Tarka the Otter* over and over. So my writing drew on all this too, and on my experiences in the woods and fields where because of the war I had total freedom to wander as I pleased.

Some time during my first year at Grammar School, when I was eleven, it dawned on me that rhymes were more interesting than prose. In spite of the great numbers of poems that we read at school, I actually got the idea from a comic – where, one week, one of the characters sang a long rhymed song. I found that rhymes were more satisfying to write. They were more special. But for two or three years they were no more than an occasional game. Then at some point, when I was about fourteen, I borrowed Kipling's *Complete Poems* from the library. I don't know what drew me to Kipling.

Original draft of an article from *Meet and Write* Book 2, edited by Sandy and Alan Brownjohn (London: Hodder and Stoughton, 1987).

Perhaps *The Jungle Book*, his story of Mowgli, the boy among the animals, which our teacher had read aloud to us in class. But Kipling's poems were a revelation. Something about them, hard to define, appealed to me, but what took hold of me were his rhythms. They got into my head and evidently affected me greatly. From that point, I began to write all my verse tales in Kipling's lockstep rhythms and resounding deadlock rhymes:

And the curling lips of the five gouged rips in the bark of the
pine were the mark of the bear

was one of my lines. I began to search in poetry books for more poems in the same *tum – ti – ti – tum – ti – ti – tum* metre. For a year or two, my new interest in 'poetry' was limited to things written in that way: long lines, a rhythmical heavy beat, and deadlock rhymes. I remember the great expectations I had of the American poet, Walt Whitman, when I saw his book full of poems with long lines and the marvellous titles – 'Drum-Taps' and 'Leaves of Grass'. And then my dry disappointment when I found his lines had no metrical beat. In later years, those poems of his became as precious to me as any others. But then they seemed to me quite dead – as if written in a foreign language. Because they lacked that strongly marked rhythm. At the same time, the other book that took hold of me with its very different rhythms was the King James Bible. I read this through, like a novel, looking for the high moments and magical sentences: Job, The Song of Songs, Isaiah, Ecclesiastes, The Revelation of St John, with many scattered, briefer passages, gave me what I was looking for or rather listening for. Eventually, when I was flicking through a book of poetry in the school library, searching for poems with long lines and the right kind of metre, I came across the third part of a poem titled 'The Wanderings of Oisin', by W. B. Yeats.

Other books had been bombarding me, of course, through those years. And about this time, in my sixteenth year, I was awakening to the excitements of the books set for the exams: by a great stroke of luck we had *King Lear*, Hardy's *Woodlanders* and Shelley's *Adonais*. But there was another influence. When my craze for comics fizzled out – I was about thirteen – a craze for folktales took their place. The discovery of these things came as a deep shock. I began to collect them, noting them down in notebooks. In those days, books of folk tales, like books about wild life, were quite scarce. The rarity only made me keener. As it happens, one of the richest mines of folk tales, legends and myths in the world is the Irish. I fell under the powerful spell of these Irish tales. At the height of this craze, I came across the poem I mentioned above – 'The Wanderings of Oisin', by W. B. Yeats.

'The Wanderings of Oisin' is an Irish legend of the most magical sort, and the third part of Yeats's telling of it is written in the kind of metre I could respond to. Naturally, I went back to the beginning of the poem, to get the whole story. This was a new kind of spell. I searched other books by W. B. Yeats, and soon learned that all this writer's poems are saturated with Irish folk tales, legends and myths. I devoured his work whole, for the taste of those things. In return, his poetry digested me. I lost interest in the heavy metres. Simultaneously, my English teacher introduced me to Eliot and some of Hopkins's poems. I recognized in these something I very much wanted, and set about taking possession of both. Another influence got through to me without my being aware of it at the time. For reasons that had nothing to do with the language, I had set myself against Latin. Our Latin Master was an intense man with a strong Scots accent, and he loved to pace up and down the room intoning the long hexameter lines of Virgil's *Aeneid*. He seemed to hypnotize himself with the sound. But he must have hypnotized me too. In my own writing, as I tried to escape from Kipling into a 'free' combination of the wilder and more hauntingly varied (and often more biblical) rhythms of Yeats and Eliot, I fell without knowing it into Virgil's hexameter – or at least, into fragments of it. And sometimes, as in one line that I would have liked to salvage from those days:

The otter comes here in the winter but even the shells are empty

a pure hexameter.

But by that time, the magic door in metre and rhyme was opening to let me through into the underworld of strange goings on that we call poetic imagination. Everybody who gets into that underworld has to find their own way. In so far as books and authors led me, this roundabout route was mine.

The Burnt Fox

At Cambridge University in my third and final year I read *Archaeology and Anthropology*. But for my first two years, from 1951 to 1953, I read *English*. Like plenty of others, I had assumed that the course in English would help my own writing. Students of English were expected to produce a weekly essay. Though I felt a strong liking for my supervisor, and could not have been more interested in the subject, I soon became aware of an inexplicable resistance, in myself, against writing these essays. Perhaps many students experience this. With each week, the task was more of a struggle. The difficulty seemed to be quite separate from the actual business of having ideas. Towards the end of my second year, when I had recovered from the initial culture shock of University life, and was well on my way to developing my own route through it, in other words as I became happier, this resistance became much more serious. I say serious because it had a distressful quality, like a fiercely fought defence. In the end, it brought me to a halt.

As I recall, I had come to the last or all but the last essay before the exams for Part I of the degree. I had started it early in the week, hoping to get it out of the way quickly. But I had bogged down in the usual struggle and toiled on for three or four days. After several hours each day, usually on into the night, I had covered many pages, all torn up, and had retreated again and again to my opening sentence that I had rewritten and rearranged dozens of times. I thought I knew what I wanted to say – but to no avail.

Once again I had finished up at two a.m., exhausted, sitting in my college room at my table, bent over a page of foolscap that had about four lines written across the top of it – my opening sentence in its latest state. My desk lamp light fell on the paper. Close to my left was my high curtained window. In front of me, beyond my table, was my bed, the head at the far end. To my right, across the room, were the three wooden steps that climbed to my door, on which hung my gown. At last I had to give up and go to bed.

I began to dream. I dreamed I had never left my table and was still sitting there, bent over the lamplit piece of foolscap, staring at the same few lines across the top. Suddenly my attention was drawn to the door. I thought I had heard something there. As I waited, listening, I saw the door was opening slowly. Then a head came round the edge of the door. It was about the height of a man's head but clearly the head of a fox – though the light over there was dim. The door opened wide and down the short stair and across the room towards me came a figure that was at the same time a skinny man and a fox walking erect on its hind legs. It was a fox, but the size of a wolf. As it approached and came into the light I saw that its body and limbs had just now stepped out of a furnace. Every inch was roasted, smouldering, black-charred, split and bleeding. Its eyes, which were level with mine where I sat, dazzled with the intensity of the pain. It came up until it stood beside me. Then it spread its hand – a human hand as I now saw, but burned and bleeding like the rest of him – flat palm down on the blank space of my page. At the same time it said: 'Stop this – you are destroying us.' Then as it lifted its hand away I saw the blood-print, like a palmist's specimen, with all the lines and creases, in wet, glistening blood on the page.

I immediately woke up. The impression of reality was so total, I got out of bed to look at the papers on my table, quite certain that I would see the blood-print there on the page.

1993

Poetry in the Making:
Three Extracts

Capturing Animals

There are all sorts of ways of capturing animals and birds and fish. I spent most of my time, up to the age of fifteen or so, trying out many of these ways and when my enthusiasm began to wane, as it did gradually, I started to write poems.

You might not think that these two interests, capturing animals and writing poems, have much in common. But the more I think back the more sure I am that with me the two interests have been one interest. My pursuit of mice at threshing time when I was a boy, snatching them from under the sheaves as the sheaves were lifted away out of the stack and popping them into my pocket till I had thirty or forty crawling around in the lining of my coat, that and my present pursuit of poems seem to me to be different stages of the same fever. In a way, I suppose, I think of poems as a sort of animal. They have their own life, like animals, by which I mean that they seem quite separate from any person, even from their author, and nothing can be added to them or taken away without maiming and perhaps even killing them. And they have a certain wisdom. They know something special . . . something perhaps which we are very curious to learn. Maybe my concern has been to capture not animals particularly and not poems, but simply things which have a vivid life of their own, outside mine. However all that may be, my interest in animals began when I began. My memory goes back pretty clearly to my third year, and by then I had so many of the toy lead animals you could buy in shops that they went right round our flat-topped fender, nose to tail, with some over.

I enjoyed modelling and drawing, so when I discovered plasticine my zoo became infinite, and when an aunt bought me a thick green-backed animal book for my fourth birthday I began to draw the glossy photographs. The animals looked good in the photographs, but they looked even better in my drawings and were mine.

From *Poetry in the Making* (London: Faber and Faber, 1967).

I can remember very vividly the excitement with which I used to sit staring at my drawings, and it is a similar thing I feel nowadays with poems.

My zoo was not entirely an indoors affair. At that time we lived in a valley in the Pennines in West Yorkshire. My brother, who probably had more to do with this passion of mine than anyone else, was a good bit older than I was, and his main interest in life was creeping about on the hillsides with a rifle. He took me along as a retriever and I had to scramble into all kinds of places collecting magpies and owls and rabbits and weasels and rats and curlews that he shot. He could not shoot enough for me. At the same time I used to be fishing daily in the canal, with the long-handled wire-rimmed curtain mesh sort of net.

All that was only the beginning. When I was eight, we moved to an industrial town in South Yorkshire. Our cat went upstairs and moped in my bedroom for a week, it hated the place so much, and my brother for the same reason left home and became a gamekeeper. But in many ways that move of ours was the best thing that ever happened to me. I soon discovered a farm in the nearby countryside that supplied all my needs, and soon after, a private estate, with woods and a lake.

My friends were town boys, sons of colliers and railwaymen, and with them I led one life, but all the time I was leading this other life on my own in the country. I never mixed the two lives up. I still have some diaries that I kept in those years: they record nothing but my catches.

Finally, as I have said, at about fifteen my life grew more complicated and my attitude to animals changed. I accused myself of disturbing their lives. I began to look at them, you see, from their own point of view.

And about the same time I began to write poems. Not animal poems. It was years before I wrote what you could call an animal poem and several more years before it occurred to me that my writing poems might be partly a continuation of my earlier pursuit. Now I have no doubt. The special kind of excitement, the slightly mesmerized and quite involuntary concentration with which you make out the stirrings of a new poem in your mind, then the outline, the mass and colour and clean final form of it, the unique living reality of it in the midst of the general lifelessness, all that is too familiar to mistake. This is hunting and the poem is a new species of creature, a new specimen of the life outside your own.

I have now told you very briefly what I believe to be the origins and growth of my interest in writing poetry. I have simplified everything a great deal, but on the whole that is the story. Some of it may seem a bit obscure to you. How can a poem, for instance, about a walk in the rain, be like an animal? Well, perhaps it cannot look much like a giraffe or an emu or an octopus, or anything you might find in a menagerie. It is better to call it an assembly of living parts moved by a single spirit. The living parts are the words, the images, the rhythms. The spirit is the life which inhabits them when they all work together. It is impossible to say which comes first, parts or spirit. But if any of the parts are dead, if any of the words, or images or rhythms do not jump to life as you read them, then the creature is going to be maimed and the spirit sickly. So, as a poet, you have to make sure that all those parts over which you have control, the words and rhythms and images, are alive. That is where the difficulties begin. Yet the rules, to begin with, are very simple. Words that live are those which we hear, like 'click' or 'chuckle', or which we see, like 'freckled' or 'veined', or which we taste, like 'vinegar' or 'sugar', or touch, like 'prickle' or 'oily', or smell, like 'tar' or 'onion': words which belong directly to one of the five senses. Or words which act and seem to use their muscles, like 'flick' or 'balance'.

But immediately things become more difficult. 'Click' not only gives you a sound, it gives you the notion of a sharp movement such as your tongue makes in saying 'click'. It also gives you the feel of something light and brittle, like a snapping twig. Heavy things do not click, nor do soft bendable ones. In the same way, tar not only smells strongly, it is sticky to touch, with a particular thick and choking stickiness. Also it moves, when it is soft, like a black snake, and has a beautiful black gloss. So it is with most words. They belong to several of the senses at once, as if each one had eyes, ears and tongue, or ears and fingers and a body to move with. It is this little goblin in a word which is its life and its poetry, and it is this goblin which the poet has to have under control.

Well, you will say, this is hopeless. How do you control all that? When the words are pouring out how can you be sure that you do not have one of these side meanings of the word 'feathers' getting all stuck up with one of the side meanings of the word 'treacle', a few words later? In bad poetry this is exactly what happens, the words kill each other. Luckily, you do not have to bother about it so long as you do one thing.

That one thing is to imagine what you are writing about. See it and live it. Do not think it up laboriously, as if you were working out mental arithmetic. Just look at it, touch it, smell it, listen to it, turn yourself into it. When you do this, the words look after themselves, like magic. If you do this you do not have to bother about commas or full-stops or that sort of thing. You do not look at the words either. You keep your eyes, your ears, your nose, your taste, your touch, your whole being on the thing you are turning into words. The minute you flinch, and take your mind off this thing, and begin to look at the words and worry about them, then your worry goes into them and they set about killing each other. So you keep going as long as you can, then look back and see what you have written. After a bit of practice, and after telling yourself a few times that you do not care how other people have written about this thing, this is the way you find it; and after telling yourself you are going to use any old word that comes into your head so long as it seems right at the moment of setting it down, you will surprise yourself. You will read back through what you have written and you will get a shock. You will have captured a spirit, a creature.

After all that, I ought to give you some examples and show you some of my own more recently acquired specimens.

An animal I never succeeded in keeping alive is the fox. I was always frustrated: twice by a farmer, who killed cubs I had caught before I could get to them, and once by a poultry keeper who freed my cub while his dog waited. Years after those events I was sitting up late one snowy night in dreary lodgings in London. I had written

nothing for a year or so but that night I got the idea I might write
something and I wrote in a few minutes the following poem: the first
'animal' poem I ever wrote. Here it is:

The Thought Fox

I imagine this midnight moment's forest:
Something else is alive
Beside the clock's loneliness
And this blank page where my fingers move.

Through the window I see no star:
Something more near
Though deeper within darkness
Is entering the loneliness:

Cold, delicately as the dark snow
A fox's nose touches twig, leaf;
Two eyes serve a movement, that now
And again now, and now, and now

Sets neat prints into the snow
Between trees, and warily a lame
Shadow lags by stump and in hollow
Of a body that is bold to come

Across clearings, an eye,
A widening deepening greenness,
Brilliantly, concentratedly,
Coming about its own business

Till, with a sudden sharp hot stink of fox
It enters the dark hole of the head.
The window is starless still; the clock ticks,
The page is printed.

This poem does not have anything you could easily call a
meaning. It is about a fox, obviously enough, but a fox that is both a
fox and not a fox. What sort of a fox is it that can step right into my
head where presumably it still sits, smiling to itself when the dogs
bark. It is both a fox and a spirit. It is a real fox; as I read the poem I

see it move, I see it setting its prints, I see its shadow going over the irregular surface of the snow. The words show me all this, bringing it nearer and nearer. It is very real to me. The words have made a body for it and given it somewhere to walk.

If, at the time of writing this poem, I had found livelier words, words that could give me much more vividly its movements, the twitch and craning of its ears, the slight tremor of its hanging tongue and its breath making little clouds, its teeth bared in the cold, the snow-crumbs dropping from its pads as it lifts each one in turn; if I could have got the words for all this, the fox would probably be even more real and alive to me now, than it is as I read the poem. Still, it is there as it is. If I had not caught the real fox there in the words, I would never have saved the poem. I would have thrown it into the wastepaper basket as I have thrown so many other hunts that did not get what I was after. As it is, every time I read the poem the fox comes up again out of the darkness and steps into my head. And I suppose that long after I am gone, as long as a copy of the poem exists, everytime anyone reads it the fox will get up somewhere out in the darkness and come walking towards them.

Learning to Think

At school, I was plagued by the idea that I really had much better thoughts than I could ever get into words. It was not that I could not find the words, or that the thoughts were too deep or too complicated for words. It was simply that when I tried to speak or write down the thoughts, those thoughts had vanished. All I had was a numb blank feeling, just as if somebody had asked me the name of Julius Caesar's eldest son, or said '7,283 times 6,956 – quick. Think, think, think.' Now for one reason or another I became very interested in those thoughts of mine that I could never catch. Sometimes they were hardly what you could call a thought – they were a dim sort of feeling about something. They did not fit into any particular subject – history or arithmetic or anything of that sort, except perhaps English. I had the idea, which gradually grew on me, that these were the right sort of thoughts for essays, and yet probably not even essays. But for the most part they were useless to me because I could never get hold of them. Maybe when I was writing an essay I got the tail end of one, but that was not very satisfying. ⌒

Now maybe you can see what was happening. I was thinking all right, and even having thoughts that seemed interesting to me, but I could not keep hold of the thoughts, or fish them up when I wanted them. I would think this fact was something peculiar to me, and of interest to nobody else, if I did not know that most people have the same trouble. What thoughts they have are fleeting thoughts – just a flash of it, then gone – or, though they know they know something, or have ideas about something, they just cannot dig those ideas up when they are wanted. Their minds, in fact, seem out of their reach. That is a curious thing to say, but it is quite true.

There is the inner life, which is the world of final reality, the world of memory, emotion, imagination, intelligence, and natural common sense, and which goes on all the time, consciously or unconsciously, like the heart beat. There is also the thinking process by which we break into the inner life and capture answers and evidence to support the answers out of it. That process of raid, or persuasion, or ambush, or dogged hunting, or surrender, is the kind of thinking we have to learn, and if we do not somehow learn it, then our minds lie in us like the fish in the pond of a man who cannot fish.

Now you see the kind of thinking I am talking about. Perhaps I ought not to call it thinking at all – it is just that we tend to call everything that goes on in our heads thinking. I am talking about whatever kind of trick or skill it is that enables us to catch those elusive or shadowy thoughts, and collect them together, and hold them still so we can get a really good look at them. I will illustrate what I mean with an example: If you were told, 'Think of your uncle' – how long could you hold the idea of your uncle in your head? Right, you imagine him. But then at once he reminds you of something else and you are thinking of that, he has gone into the background, if he has not altogether disappeared. Now get your uncle back. Imagine your uncle and nothing else – nothing whatsover. After all, there is plenty to be going on with in your uncle, his eyes, what expression? His hair, where is it parted? How many waves has it? What is the exact shade? Or if he is bald, what does the skin feel like? His chin – just how is it? Look at it. As you can see, there is a great deal to your uncle – you could spend hours on him, if you could only keep him in your mind for hours; and when you have looked at him from head to foot, in your memory you have all the memories of what he has said and done, and all your own feelings about him and his sayings and doings. You could spend weeks on him, just holding him there in your mind, and examining the thoughts you have about him. I have exaggerated that, but you see straightway that it is quite difficult to think about your uncle and nothing but your uncle for more than a few seconds. So how can you ever hope to collect all your thoughts about him?

At the same time you obviously could not do that with everything that came into your head – grip hold of it with your imagination, and never let it go till you had studied every grain of it. It would not leave you any time to live. Nevertheless, it is possible to do it for a time. I will illustrate the sort of thing I mean with a poem called 'View of a Pig'. In this poem, the poet stares at something which is quite still, and collects the thoughts that concern it.

He does it quite rapidly and briefly, never lifting his eyes from the pig. Obviously, he does not use every thought possible – he chooses the thoughts that fit best together to make a poem. Here is the poem:

View of a Pig

The pig lay on a barrow dead.
It weighed, they said, as much as three men.
Its eyes closed, pink white eyelashes.
Its trotters stuck straight out.

Such weight and thick pink bulk
Set in death seemed not just dead.
It was less than lifeless, further off.
It was like a sack of wheat.

I thumped it without feeling remorse.
One feels guilty insulting the dead,

Walking on graves. But this pig
Did not seem able to accuse.

It was too dead. Just so much
A poundage of lard and pork.
Its last dignity had entirely gone.
It was not a figure of fun.

Too dead now to pity.
To remember its life, din, stronghold
Of earthly pleasure as it had been,
Seemed a false effort, and off the point.

Too deadly factual. Its weight
Oppressed me – how could it be moved?
And the trouble of cutting it up!
The gash in its throat was shocking, but not pathetic.

Once I ran at a fair in the noise
To catch a greased piglet
That was faster and nimbler than a cat,
Its squeal was the rending of metal.

Pigs must have hot blood, they feel like ovens,
Their bite is worse than a horse's –
They chop a half-moon clean out.
They eat cinders, dead cats.

Distinctions and admirations such
As this one was long finished with.
I stared at it a long time. They were going to scald it,
Scald it and scour it like a doorstep.

Now where did the poet learn to settle his mind like that on to one thing? It is a valuable thing to be able to do – but something you are never taught at school, and not many people do it naturally. I am not very good at it, but I did acquire some skill in it. Not in school, but while I was fishing. I fished in still water, in those days, with a float. As you know, all such a fisherman does is stare at his float for hours on end. I have spent thousands and thousands of hours staring at a float – a dot of red or yellow the size of a lentil, ten yards away. Those of you who have never done it, might think it is a very drowsy pastime. It is anything but that.

All the little nagging impulses, that are normally distracting your mind, dissolve. They have to dissolve if you are to go on fishing. If they do not, then you cannot settle down: you get bored and pack up in a bad temper. But once they have dissolved, you enter one of the orders of bliss.

Your whole being rests lightly on your float, but not drowsily: very alert, so that the least twitch of the float arrives like an electric shock. And you are not only watching the float. You are aware, in a horizonless and slightly mesmerized way, like listening to the double bass in orchestral music, of the fish below there in the dark. At every moment your imagination is alarming itself with the size of the thing slowly leaving the weeds and approaching your bait. Or with the world of beauties down there, suspended in total ignorance of you. And the whole purpose of this concentrated excitement, in this arena of apprehension and unforeseeable events, is to bring up some lovely solid thing, like living metal, from a world where nothing exists but those inevitable facts which raise life out of nothing and return it to nothing.

Words and Experience

Words are tools, learned late and laboriously and easily forgotten, with which we try to give some part of our experience a more or less permanent shape outside ourselves. They are unnatural, in a way, and far from being ideal for their job. For one thing, a word has its own definite meanings. A word is its own little solar system of meanings. Yet we are wanting it to carry some part of our meaning, of the meaning of our experience, and the meaning of our experience is finally unfathomable, it reaches into our toes and back to before we were born and into the atom, with vague shadows and changing features, and elements that no expression of any kind can take hold of. And this is true of even the simplest experiences.

For instance, that crow flying across, beneath the aeroplane – how are we going to give our account of it? Forgetting for a moment the aircraft, the sky, the world beneath, and our own concerns – how are we to say what we see in the crow's flight? It is not enough to say the crow flies purposefully, or heavily, or rowingly, or whatever. There are no words to capture the infinite depth of crowiness in the crow's flight. All we can do is use a word as an indicator, or a whole bunch of words as a general directive. But the ominous thing in the crow's flight, the barefaced, bandit thing, the tattered beggarly gipsy thing, the caressing and shaping yet slightly clumsy gesture of the down-stroke, as if the wings were both too heavy and too powerful, and the headlong sort of merriment, the macabre pantomime ghoulishness and the undertaker sleekness – you could go on for a very long time with phrases of that sort and still have completely missed your instant, glimpsed knowledge of the world of the crow's wingbeat. And a bookload of such descriptions is immediately rubbish when you look up and see the crow flying.

There are more important things than crows to try and say something about. Yet that is an example of how words tend to shut out the simplest things we wish to say. In a way, words are continually trying to displace our experience. And in so far as they are stronger than the raw life of our experience, and full of themselves and all the dictionaries they have digested, they do displace it.

But that is enough for the moment about the wilfulness of words. What about our experience itself, the stuff we are trying to put into words – is that so easy to grasp? It may seem a strange thing to say, but do we ever know what we really do know?

A short time ago, a tramp came to our door and asked for money. I gave him something and watched him walk away. That would seem to be a simple enough experience, watching a tramp walk away. But how could I begin to describe what I saw? As with the crow, words seem suddenly a bit thin. It is not enough to say 'The tramp walked away' or even 'The tramp went away with a slinking sort of shuffle, as if he wished he were running full speed for the nearest corner.' In ordinary descriptive writing such phrases have to suffice, simply because the writer has to economize on time, and if he set down everything that is to be seen in a man's walk he would never get on to the next thing, there would not be room, he would have written a whole biography, that would be the book. And just as with the crow, he would have missed the most important factor: that what he saw, he saw and understood in one flash, a single 1,000-volt shock, that lit up everything and drove it into his bones, whereas in so many words and phrases he is dribbling it out over pages in tinglings that can only just be felt.

What *do* we see in a person's walk? I have implied that we see everything, the whole biography. I believe this is in some way true. How we manage it, nobody knows. Maybe some instinctive and involuntary mimicry within us reproduces that person at first glance, imitates him so exactly that we feel at once all he feels, all that gives that particular uniqueness to the way he walks or does what he is doing. Maybe there is more to it. But however it works, we get the information.

It is one thing to get the information, and quite another to become conscious of it, to know that we have got it. In our brains there are many mansions, and most of the doors are locked, with the keys inside. Usually, from our first meeting with a person, we get some single main impression, of like or dislike, confidence or distrust, reality or artificiality, or some single, vivid something that we cannot pin down in more than a tentative, vague phrase. That little phrase is like the visible moving fin of a great fish in a dark pool: we can see only the fin: we cannot see the fish, let alone catch or lift it out. Or usually we cannot. Sometimes we can. And some people have a regular gift for it.

I remember reading that the novelist H. E. Bates was in the habit of inventing quick brief biographies or adventures for people he met or saw who struck his imagination. Some of these little fantasies he noted down, to use in his stories. But as time passed, he discovered that these so-called fantasies were occasionally literal and accurate accounts of the lives of those very individuals he had seen. The odd thing about this, is that when he first invented them, he had thought it was all just imagination, that he was making it all up. In other

[21]

words, he had received somehow or other accurate information, in great detail, by just looking – but hadn't recognized it for what it was. He had simply found it lying there in his mind, at that moment, unlabelled.

The great Swiss psycho-analyst Jung describes something similar in his autobiography. During a certain conversation, he wanted to illustrate some general point he was trying to make, and so just for an example he invented a fictitious character and set him in a fictitious situation and described his probable actions – all to illustrate his point. The man to whom he was speaking, somebody he had never met before, became terribly upset, and Jung could not understand why, until later, when he learned that the little story he had invented had been in fact a detailed circumstantial account of that man's own private life. Somehow or other, as they talked, Jung had picked it up – but without recognizing it. He had simply found it when he reached into his imagination for any odd materials that would make up a story of the kind he wanted.

Neither of these two men would have realized what they had learned if they had not both had occasion to invent stories on the spot, and if they had not by chance discovered later that what had seemed to them pure imagination had also somehow been fact. Neither had recognized their own experience. Neither had known what they really knew.

There are records of individuals who have the gift to recognize their experience at once, when it is of this sort. At first meeting with a stranger, such people sometimes see this person's whole life in a few seconds, like a film reeling past, in clear pictures. When this happens, they cannot help it. They simply see it, and know at once that it belongs to the person in front of them. Jung and Bates also saw it, but did not know – and they saw it only in an odd way, when they compelled themselves to produce a story at that very moment. And I believe we all share this sort of reception, this sort of faculty, to some degree.

There are other individuals who have the gift to recognize in themselves not simply experience of this sort, but even a similar insight into the past lives and adventures of objects. Such people are known as psychometrists, and have been used by the police. From some weapon or tool used in a crime, they can as it were read off a description of the criminal and often a great deal about him. They are not infallible. But the best of them have amazing records of successes. They take hold of the particular object and the knowledge they are after flashes across their imaginations. Again, it is said by some that this is a gift we all share, potentially, that it is simply one of the characteristics of being alive in these mysterious electrical bodies of ours, and the difficult thing is not to pick up the information but to recognize it – to accept it into our consciousness. But this is not surprising. Most of us find it difficult to know what we are feeling about anything. In any situation, it is almost impossible to know what is really happening to us. This is one of the penalties of being human and having a brain so swarming with interesting suggestions and ideas and self-distrust.

And so with my tramp, I was aware of a strong impression all right, which disturbed me for a long time after he had gone. But what exactly had I learned? And how could I begin to delve into the tangled, rather painful mass of whatever it was that stirred in my mind as I watched him go away?

And watching a tramp go away, even if you have just been subliminally burdened with his entire biography, is a slight experience compared to the events that are developing in us all the time: as our private history and our personal make-up and hour by hour biological changes, our present immediate circumstances and all that we know, in fact, struggle together, trying to make sense of themselves in our single life, trying to work out exactly what is going on in and around us, and exactly what we are or could be, what we ought and ought not to do, and what exactly did happen in those situations which, though we lived through them long since, still go on inside us as if time could only make things fresher.

And all this is our experience – the final facts, as they are registered on this particular human measuring instrument. I have tried to suggest how infinitely beyond our ordinary notions of what we know our real knowledge, the real facts for us, really is. And to live removed from this inner universe of experience is also to live removed from ourself, banished from ourself and our real life. The struggle truly to possess his own experience, in other words to regain his genuine self, has been man's principal occupation, wherever he could find leisure for it, ever since he first grew this enormous surplus of brain. Men have invented religion to do this for others. But to do it for themselves, they have invented art – music, painting, dancing, sculpture, and the activity that includes all these, which is poetry.

Because it is occasionally possible, just for brief moments, to find the words that will unlock the doors of all those many mansions inside the head and express something – perhaps not much, just something – of the crush of information that presses in on us from the way a crow flies over and the way a man walks and the look of a street and from what we did one day a dozen years ago. Words that will express something of the deep complexity that makes us precisely the way we are, from the momentary effect of the barometer to the force that created men distinct from trees. Something of the inaudible music that moves us along in our bodies from moment to moment like water in a river. Something of the spirit of the snowflake in the water of the river. Something of the duplicity and the relativity and the merely fleeting quality of all this. Something of the almighty importance of it and something of the utter meaninglessness. And when words can manage something of this, and manage it in a moment of time, and in that same moment make out of it all the vital signature of a human being – not of an atom, or of a geometrical diagram, or of a heap of lenses – but a human being, we call it poetry.

A Word about Writing in Schools

Years ago, I composed a short book about the teaching of writing in schools. It was actually a collection of programmes from the BBC series *Listening and Writing*. All that I had to say there boiled down to one idea. And I still could not add anything to it, except what has emerged from that idea. It is such an old-fashioned idea that it has been almost forgotten. It is certainly often forgotten in schools.

The idea is this: before the pen moves over the paper, the writer's imaginative re-creation of what is to be written must be (as near as this is possible) as if real. The life within words, the anatomy of sentences, and the music of narration or argument, can be taught, and must be taught. But how can such a thing as strength and steadiness of imagination be taught? Most teachers simply assume that the faculty is weak or strong by nature, and nothing can be done about it. Yet few teachers doubt that in writing, and in English Studies generally, a strong imagination is a pupil's greatest asset. It will do most of the English teacher's work spontaneously. If only it could be taught, and taught early, and strengthened and trained throughout school life, many a problem would be solved without much further effort.

And of course it can be taught. The most celebrated handbook of instructions on the training and strengthening of imagination is St Ignatius Loyola's book of Spiritual Exercises. These Exercises are, basically, gymnastics for the imagination. They are based on the understanding that the more powerfully real the imaginative grasp, the more accurate and lively and as-if-real will be the perceptions, feelings and experiences that flow from it. He evolved his method for training the priesthood. It demonstrates, as far as English teachers are concerned, that there is a method, and that the imagination can be trained. This faculty, with which we comprehend the reality and global intricacy of the world, and the reality and global intricacy of

From *The Pushkin Prizes Schools Prize Brochure* (Western Education and Library Board, Northern Ireland, 1989).

what goes on inside our neighbour's head, can be trained. Any teacher can adapt a rudimentary method for classroom use.

Without some training of this faculty, we waste most of our time teaching writing – except to the very few. With the help of this training, and a wise use of it, we find a surprising thing: a large proportion of any class have rich potential as writers. It turns out that those teachers who year after year produce a crop of outstanding young writers, are those who, one way or another, have devised a training of this sort for their pupils. This is what Children's Writing Competitions are beginning to discover.

Concealed Energies

The *Daily Mirror**** Children's Literary Competition was started as a parallel to the *Sunday Mirror* Children's Art Competition which is perhaps better known. Both were initiated largely by the late Sir Herbert Read, and he guided them through their first years. Their success has gone beyond what anybody imagined possible – and by success I mean the nearly incredible wealth of work and talent which they have uncovered.

The talent is so abundant, in fact, that it is difficult to stabilize one's attitude towards it. Ought we to think of it as something quite natural but also – as a rule – quite fleeting, like teenage beauty? Or ought we to think of it as an overwhelming supply of potential real ability, which somehow – because of educational and social conditions – we are failing to catch and develop? We resist this latter idea because it is too depressing.

Writing ability is not a freakish knack, connected to nothing in particular. In any social group, the imaginative writers are the most visible indicators of the level and energy and type of the imagination and other vital mental activities in the whole group. What everybody in the group shares in a hidden way, or needs to share, comes to expression in the writer. It is as if works of imaginative literature were a set of dials on the front of society, where we can read off the concealed energies. What happens in the imagination of those individuals chosen by the unconscious part of society to be its writers, is closely indicative of what is happening to the hidden energies of the society as a whole.

It is something to know, then, that the writing talents of children in the UK are phenomenally abundant, and, as a comparison with collections of children's writing made in other countries clearly

---

* Since 1976, this competition has been sponsored and managed by W. H. Smith Ltd.

From *Children as Writers* 2 (London: Heinemann, 1975).

shows, they are of exceedingly high quality. What one might call maximum gift is not at all uncommon. That is only a meaningful remark, of course, if the second of our possibilities is correct: that precocious abilities in writing are – potentially – real abilities, and are real indications of the general faculties in the group to which the writer belongs. If this is true, as I for one believe it is, then this competition bears witness to a fact of immense importance in English life, one which it might otherwise be easy to overlook.

This competition is now in its seventeenth year. During the last few years, the annual entry has topped 50,000. This material has to be reduced, each year, to an anthology of little more than one hundred pages, containing the work of selected prizewinners and their closest rivals. Out of the sixteen such anthologies which now exist, quite a few selections could be made, as long as this one, and each different – according to editorial taste.

The entries come from all over the UK – and mainly through schools. They are divided by age into three sections: under eight years; nine years to twelve; thirteen years to sixteen. This mass of entries are worked through by a large panel of selectors, who distil the number down to about 600 finalists. These are passed to a committee of judges who make the final choice. Each of the seven or eight people on this committee receives a copy of the whole 600, and picks out perhaps one hundred items – with degrees of preference. Finally the day comes when this committee meets and thrashes out the list of fifty or sixty winners on which all can pretty well agree. This is always a fascinating process.

Each year the entry is different. As in the painting competition, the most interesting things tend to appear in the youngest and the oldest sections. The middle section tends to be imitative and uncertain – with frequent startling exceptions. Usually, in the oldest bracket, there will be two or three or more entries of a brilliance everyone on the committee recognizes at once. Quite often, there are dark horses here and there, in which one or two of the committee divine some uniqueness that none of the others much care for. If the support is convinced enough, this sort of entry always gets included. Over the broad span, however, there is usually a large measure of agreement, with differences mainly in the order of preference.

It has often been said that children's writing is not simply adult writing in the larval stage. It is a separate literature of its own, to be judged – as Sir Herbert Read observed right at the outset of this competition – by the highest artistic standards. So these annual anthologies, and this present selection from them, display final products, accomplished works, to be enjoyed for what they are. Over and above that, however, children's writing provides one vital thing which adult literature never can.

The differences between children's sensibility and adult sensibility are obviously big and real. But not all the advantages lie with the adult. It may well be, as the Chinese sages declare, that the man in whom the child's heart and mind has died is no better than a dead man. Children's sensibility, and children's writing, have much to teach adults. Something in the way of a corrective, a reminder. Theirs is not just a miniature world of naïve novelties and limited reality – it is also still very much the naked process of apprehension, far less conditioned than ours, far more fluid and alert, far closer to the real laws of its real nature. It is a new beginning, coming to circumstances afresh. It is still lost in the honest amoebic struggle to fit itself to the mysteries. It is still wide open to information, still anxious to get things right, still wanting to know exactly how things are, still under the primeval dread of misunderstanding the situation. Preconceptions are already pressing, but they have not yet closed down, like a space helmet, over the entire head and face, with the proved, established adjustments of security. Losing that sort of exposed nakedness, we gain in confidence and in mechanical efficiency on our chosen front, but we lose in real intelligence. We lose in readiness to change, in curiosity, in perception, in the original, wild, no-holds-barred approach to problems. In other words, we start the drift away from the flux of reality and so from any true adaptation. We begin to lose validity as witnesses and participants in the business of living in this universe. Picasso knew what he was doing when he expended his tremendous energy to strip himself back to that child nakedness.

Each year, helping to judge this competition, one experience is the same: the frustration of having to leave so many good things out. At first reading, you make a rough selection. Your surprise – and annoyance – inevitably follows when on the second reading you find that apart from a few definite landmarks you now choose quite different pieces. In my own experience, three readings, and longish periods of incubation between them, are necessary before I begin to focus properly on this often very strange writing, and can assess its special honesties and discoveries. I'm not at all sure, even then. Over the years, heaps of these finalists have accumulated, all neatly typed by the *Daily Mirror's* secretaries. Almost any one I look at, from some earlier year, gives a genuine shock. I cannot imagine how it failed to get a prize or to be included in the annual anthology. Possibly this is because I see it – then, so much later, and perhaps by chance – in the context of adult writing and ordinary verbiage. It jumps out clear for what it is – something urgent, peculiar, real. But in the tunnel of judgement, where we are scrutinizing every detail and judging each one by the finest shades against hundreds of others, and hardly looking up, the average excellence becomes a norm. A very slight specialness of tone or subject can then decide a winner. It is not a completely satisfactory procedure – last minute shifts and arbitrary decisions lay siege on all sides. But there is no other way. And it is sufficient if we remember that most of our prizewinners are not all that different from a mass of runners-up. They are not so much 'winners' as successful representatives.

Looking over these pieces, anyone must wonder: What happens to all this talent? This is certainly a big question mark, and with every year it gets bigger. Because one of the curious facts about this competition, which has now been going for so long, is that out of all the precocious talent it has discovered, so very few have emerged in their adult life as writers. 'Very few' gives an exaggerated idea; 'almost none' seems to be nearer the truth. Perhaps it is still too early to make much of a generalization about this. Not all good writers are blazingly visible in their first ten years of apprenticeship. Some very fine writers hardly emerge in their first twenty. Perhaps it merely confirms that children's writing is, for one reason or another, a thing apart. One wonders, however, whether the reason might not be a sinister one. Which brings us back to where we started. If precocious writing ability is potentially real ability, and if, even more significant, it is a measure of the more general hidden abilities in the society, and if we can congratulate ourselves on the huge supply of such precocious abilities in the children of the UK, what are we to say about this fact: that almost without exception these abilities, according to that visible indicator of talent for imaginative writing, are somehow extinguished in the late teens?

The statistic becomes even more curious when we remember that among the individuals who do later become outstanding writers, very few show more than rudimentary talent up to their adolescence. Some form of compulsion seems to be far more important, in the making of a writer, than innate literary gifts. It is as if one grain of talent – in the right psychological climate – can become a great harvest, where a load of grains – in the wrong climate – simply goes off. The really unusual thing happens, no doubt, when the load of grains meets the right climate. Then, maybe, precocious abilities really do prove that they are convertible to real abilities. But the suspicion remains that we are talking about an unhappy not to say disastrous state of affairs, where this immense biological over-supply of precocious ability is almost totally annihilated, before it can mature. What is the future of a society, one wonders, that manages to lobotomize its talent in this way? Can anything at all be done about this?

Obviously, a competition for writing, even one as big as this, can do very little. What it does, perhaps, is promote the creative mood in schools. In this, it is part of a movement to which many teachers now belong. A creative mood can be induced in any group, just as a demoralized mood or a destructive mood can be induced. There are plenty of examples in the world of a mood being imposed on whole societies by a group of people with an idea and a method. Still, it is not very easy to imagine how the creative mood can be induced in any part of society outside schools. The inability of creative talent, at present, to survive leaving school, is perhaps one visible aspect of what must be a destructive mood in society as a whole. A self-destructive mood, that shuts down imagination and energy. It is not the only visible aspect, but it is, properly considered, the most horrifying – a massacre of the innocents, with a vengeance.

But if the creative mood can be fostered and strengthened in schools, that is something. Nobody knows when an opening will come.

Strong Feelings

We imagine primitives to possess some of the qualities of ideal poetry – full of zest, clairvoyantly sensitive, realistic, whole, natural, and passionate; and so we might well look at their songs hopefully. And since only a captious anthropologist could doubt that in broad human essentials the songs reproduce the features of our own literature's embryonic stage, we wonder if these earliest stirrings of the poetic impulse might show something analogous to the gills in the human embryo, something as revealing of the inmost buried nature of the thing.

Sir Maurice Bowra gets some control of the material, a mass of oddments, by treating all the songs as a single literature – the literature of Primitive Man. This generalization enables him to give his book an overall shape, outlining the subject roughly, and deploying the numerous songs almost one to a page. And, on the whole, the generalization is just. Life, to all primitive peoples, is pretty much the same, in so far as it forces them to think unremittingly about animals, herbage, weather, dependants and providers, and the inclination of the spirits which are everywhere and in everything. Sir Maurice can talk about the technique of the songs that spring out of this life, and indicate the characteristic human attitudes which they embody, and suggest their blood kinships with our civilized poetry, while still calling the songmaker 'primitive man'. But most of these songs are composed, as far as their subject-matter and motivations are concerned, of cryptics and particularities which open not into a world of common general ideas and familiar forms of life, as our poetry does, but into a world of rituals and objects unique to each tribe or group. Any analysis of this poetry that fails in its grasp of this substantive detail is going to be weaving about in a partial vacuum, just as would any analysis of a modern poem that failed to show a convincing grasp of the

Review of C. M. Bowra, *Primitive Song* (London: Weidenfeld and Nicolson, 1962) from the *Listener*, 3 May 1962.

intellectual and spiritual inheritance which all such poems must inevitably use. And so, for much of this book, Sir Maurice's prose has the appearance, at any given moment, of seeming a bit lost, circling, feeling for something recognizable, coming out at the same place, or just trudging along under the general drift. He is well equipped to deal with the subject in general, but not in detail, and yet he takes it on in detail. As a result, the book seems rather too long.

It stands, however, as an introduction to an excellent selection of the songs. There are over two hundred pieces here, most of them striking. We find much that we hoped to find. Poetry at its most primitive seems first to occur as a one-line chant of nonsense syllables in accompaniment to the rhythm of a stamping dance. Chimpanzees have got this far, and with them there is evidently not much before it. From that point, its development is moot, but among its early achievements are hints of the parallelism that becomes so powerful in Hebrew poetry and Shakespeare, a tendency to couplets, artful use of repetition and variations, and possibly rhyme. Its ultimate development, in this phase, is in the elaborately symbolic Australian song-cycles of the adventures of gods, which must be reckoned the stage before epic, and in the ritual dialogues of the Congo pygmies, which are a long step toward drama. Within that span, lyrics and laments attain great refinement. The bulk of the songs are power-charms, tools and practical agents in the business of gaining desired ends, or deflecting the spirits of misfortune from planting their larvae in the psyche.

It is an easy remove from such recipes to a more detached ritualizing in words of some exciting event, and the poems seem to gain in beauty and complexity as they lose in purpose. Most effective of all, perhaps, are the laments, where the poem's work is simply the humane relief of strong feeling:

> She has gone from us; never as she was will she return.
> Never more as she once did will she chop honey,
> Never more with her digging stick dig yams.
> She has gone from us; never as she was to return.

Mussels there are in the creek in plenty,
But she who lies here will dig no more.
We shall fish as of old for cod-fish,
But she who lies here will beg no more oil,
Oil for her hair, she will want no more.

Never again will she use a fire.
Where she goes, fires are not.
For she goes to the women, the dead women.
Ah, women can make no fires.
Fruit there is in plenty and grass seed,
But no birds nor beasts in the heaven of women.

There is enough here to make one want to see whatever there is of the same family elsewhere. The main body of civilized verse is a great deal duller.

Quitting

Because we know so little about him, the tramp is a free symbol, the shadow of the great prototype vagrants, Lear and Tolstoy in their final moments, and Christ who had nowhere to lay his head. Our common dream, as archetypal as any, of the two-way journey towards Reality – toward the objectless radiance of the Self, where the world is a composition of benign Holy Powers; and toward the objective reality of the world, where man is a virtuoso bacterium – goes in the aspect of a tramp, rejecting ego and possessions, claiming equality with all life, as Shakespeare went in the aspect of mad Lear and as Tolstoy went in person. There are no alternatives that are not compromises. And if you live that dream, and actually set out, you're going to look like a tramp, and you'll have to live like a tramp, which in our climate and society means Salvation Army hostels, Rowton Houses, demoralization in six weeks, and so perhaps on to alchoholism, to meths and surgical spirit, etcetera. What was a will modelled on Christ's own declines, through the sheer mental vaporization of such an existence, to the blankest kind of nihilism and the death of a yawning animal. But those are practical details. For the good citizen, tramps live in the region of a dream. Even after he's thoroughly investigated the lives those men lead, and knows what emptied wretches they mostly are, his dream persists in finding in them the symbol of the Holy Pilgrim, the Incorruptible Soul, the all-sufferer, the stone the builders reject again and again. Then the dream compromises his grip of the reality, and the reality confuses his dream.

The paradox is endlessly fascinating. And a would-be-fact-minded investigator, such as Mr O'Connor, who has lived as a vagrant from time to time and recently went back on the roads to collect notes, can devote a whole book to this belief: that though the tramp is as a rule feeble-minded, psychologically dismantled for good, and just scrounging along in despair between vague efforts to

Review of Philip O'Connor, *Vagrancy* (London: Penguin, 1963), from the *New Statesman*, 6 September 1963.

get back into society, he still holds the post of a kind of Social Messiah: the man of a too simple – albeit too stupid – integrity, too 'immune' a Christ-like non-competitive soul, to be capable of the perversities of social life as we now know it. 'The tramp stands at the end of the Christian ethos, embalming it, but no longer able to perform his old function.' O'Connor's book, in fact, only incidentally concerns itself with vagrancy in Britain in the sixties. Really, it's a Jeremiad. Our Ethic (i.e. Christian charity) and our survival (i.e. aggressive competition) 'have reached the stage of being incompatible,' says Mr O'Connor. And the tramp is a sort of dry seed: all that remains of the old hope, yet the beginning of a wholly new one.

This is his argument, and few people would deny that there is some metaphorical truth in it. Civilization is horribly sick, and vagrants undergo the hardest pains of it. But could anything growing as fast and on such a scale as mankind be much better than very sick, and in what kind of society would there be no individuals misfitting to the point of vagrancy? Mr O'Connor believes he has the answer. In his preface, he warns readers that he is arguing 'unequivocally from a personal socialist point of view'. But his 'unequivocal' tone is terribly hard to take, as it comes beating its way over you with every step begging a question. For instance, is it 'the Christian ethos' he means, when he says 'the man who is not good at keeping alive' may be closest to it? Is our society as competitive, so exclusively a rat-race and dog-fight, as he assumes? And is the spirit of competition picked up with such difficulty, and so against nature? Anyway, is it true that competition is as thoroughly evil in fact as it is in his imagination? When non-competition is enforced, what sort of genetic torpor ensues, and worse? Selfish instincts don't cease at a word, as we know. When Christ said 'get thee behind me', he both created Satan and set him free to experiment without supervision. And what if Mr O'Connor is wrong, and there actually *is* free will and self-responsibility? Or – to concede something – what if there is not much free will and self-responsibility, not much but a little, enough to qualify a starved crow to go feeding in the same field as a scarecrow? Then society is not entirely and to the last gasp responsible for the creation of vagrants, and Mr O'Connor has to find a new reason for writing about them. And if he is right, and all Will, and Absolute Will, is invested in society, then man is at the mercy of what? Whom? The great 'cooperatives' of non-competitive mutual parasitism, which Mr O'Connor visualizes as the lovely replacement of our present conditions, are presumably to be man-made, but surely that will take a lot of willing. Yet, again and again, Mr O'Connor will have no free will. It's not easy to see why he doesn't surrender to history.

This polemic passion of his confounds him at every point. Where he sees a selfish tendency in men, it's an unhuman enforcement of the Constitution. Where he feels a qualm, it's the still, small voice of man's final guidance. And the prose betrays the source of the confusion: this is 'wild' prose, a crazy flying-machine pieced together out of psychologist's and sociologist's and phrenologist's jargon, and driven by an irate blast of rhetorical poetry. In other words, his vision of society is symbolic, like a prophet's, but his method and style of exposition are supposedly scientific. In so far as he tries to present his vision as a piece of reasoning from factual evidence, everything is rancour and overstatement.

Of who these people are, where they come from and why they start, and how things are with them, he manages to give very little impression. His gallery of characters in close-up is interesting, but every other one seems to have appeared on TV, and his observations on them are peculiarly fine-drawn without being convincing. It is far from the sympathetic, responsible watchfulness, the objective open-minded style, that Orwell set up as a standard, and which has such tremendous persuasive effect. Much the best section is his account of his own tramping: he can talk well about himself, his words run smoothly and his remarks have weight. His description of the mental changes that followed on his quitting society is a piece of truly awful knowledge.

That modern western society has made an outcast of much in the human soul is credible enough, but maybe the abolition of horses says more about this than the continued, but greatly dwindling, presence of vagrants. Mr O'Connor never reserves a doubt that it may be an insoluble problem, this business of getting all man's soul happily into society. Maybe man's brain isn't big enough to manage it, now there are so many of us. Maybe all Mr O'Connor is offering is a change of party. And when he's ejected the great, perennial lusts, the bedevilled play of ingenuity, that have been the decisive creative forces in all societies so far, he'll just be creating more vagrants. The roads will be full of wandering symbols of Satan.

Asgard for Addicts

This is a survey of the worship of Odin, Thor and the rest of
Asgard, and the related myths and beliefs, according to a mainly
philological study of the old poems, sagas, and Eddas, and of
place-names, combined with the up-to-date findings of archaeology.
E. O. G. Turville-Petre is an exceedingly learned man, at present
Professor of Ancient Icelandic at Oxford. It is evident that little
speculation and research in the subject has outflanked him. For
students of religion, this book should be authoritative.

His method is much the same as Grimm's in his *Teutonic
Mythology*, which this largely replaces, though it confines itself
more to the central figures, and with references to Scandinavia and
the British Isles rather than to Germany. He takes the main gods,
heroes, and beliefs, and dismantles them into their component parts
– attributes, variants, developments, and so on. But he's more
readable than Grimm, and much more concerned to give a solid idea
of those contradictory, penumbral figures.

His book is hard going: there is inevitably a certain overwhelming
lifelessness about the philological approach for the casual reader.
But this book is for students, not casual readers. It gives information
in detail, not a past breathed to life. Yet this is a great opportunity
lost, or perhaps deferred, because Mr Turville-Petre would be the
perfect man to edit what this 'History of Religion' series ought, after
all, to provide – which would be a companion volume to this: the
original source-texts translated, and the myths and tales retold in
responsible detailed form. What a collection that could be! Because
at present, of the sources to which Mr Turville-Petre constantly
refers, only a small fraction has been done into English, and most of
these are inaccessible to the ordinary reader, while the myths and
tales are known, if at all, as emptily glossed children's fables.

This is a pity, because this particular mythology is much deeper in

Review of E. O. G. Turville-Petre, *Myth and Religion of the North*
(London: Weidenfeld and Nicolson, 1964), from the *Listener*, 19 March 1964.

us, and truer to us, than the Greek-Roman pantheons that came in
with Christianity, and again with the Renaissance, severing us with
the completeness of a political interdict from these other deities of
our instinct and ancestral memory. It is as if we were to lose *Macbeth*
and *King Lear,* and have to live on *Timon* and *Coriolanus*; or as if a
vocabulary drawn wholly from the Greek-Roman branch were to
take over absolutely from our Anglo-Saxon-Norse-Celtic: there's no
doubt which of these alternatives belongs to our blood. The
combination of the two is our wealth, but in the realm of mythologies, the realm of management between our ordinary minds and our
deepest life, we have had no chance to make a similar combination.
Even after Shakespeare, it is interesting to see what an infusion the
few artificial revivals of that lost inheritance have proved. William
Morris's Icelandic stories, the most genuine productions of the pre-
Raphaelite period, led directly to Yeats's whole-hearted attempt to
recover the pre-Christian imagination of Ireland, and the results
were a powerful source of the energy of the whole successful Irish
nationalist movement. But, as I say, one has only to look at our
vocabulary to see where our real mental life has its roots, where the
paths to and from our genuine imaginations run, clearly enough. It is
false to say these gods and heroes are obsolete: they are the better
part of our patrimony still locked up.

Unfinished Business

Wilfred Owen's twenty or so effective poems, all quite short, belong to a brief, abnormal moment in English history, and seem to refer to nothing specific outside it. That moment – the last two years of trench warfare in France, 1916–18 – was so privately English (ignoring what France and Germany made of it) and such a deeply shocking and formative experience for us that it is easy to see some of the reasons why Yeats (as an Irishman) dismissed Owen's verse, and why many discriminating American readers find it hard to account for his reputation, and why with the English his reputation is so high.

The particular pathos and heroism and horror of the fighting in France are not imaginable without a full sense of the deaf-and-blind tyranny of jingoism – the outraged rhetorical patriotism-to-the-death, the bluster and propaganda of England's unshaken imperial arrogance – of those who remained in England. These were the politicians, financiers, businessmen, all who found themselves too old, or too importantly placed, or too deeply embedded in business. They fastened like a lid over the men who were rubbished with such incredible pointless abandon into the trenches. For those men, Owen, who died in France a week before the Armistice, determined to become the Voice of Protest.

He had all the gifts ready for it. In 1911 he had started a year as pupil and lay assistant to the vicar of Dunsden, Oxfordshire, and there seems to have been an idea of his taking holy orders. This readiness to give his life to Christ was to be important, as was his talent for righteous wrath and quick sympathy for the socially oppressed that went with it. 'From what I hear from the tight-pursed lips of wolvish ploughmen in their cottages, I might say there is material here for another revolution', he noted.

His poetic talent was commonplace enough up to 1916 – but had

From *New York Times Book Review*, April 1964.

always displayed a precocious tendency to the monumental and elegiac on the one hand, and on the other a natural zest for orgies of sensation, carefully nursed in imitation of his idol Keats, that truly seems to have had a special taste for the horrible, a romantic lust for the Gothic and macabre. Then suddenly the unbelievable war was on him, mobilizing these inclinations in him, and in the name of a high, holy cause, and supplying the unique material, in the baldest reality, as nothing else could have done.

He worked within a narrow programme – not that his times or situation allowed him much alternative, but he did formulate it deliberately. He wanted to counter the propagandists in England with propaganda of a finally more powerful kind. He set himself to present the sufferings of the front line, with the youth and millions of deaths and smashed hopes of his generation behind him, as vividly and frighteningly as possible, not because they were piteous – in spite of all his talk about 'pity' – but because it was wrong, and the crime of fools who could not see because they would not feel.

The enemy was not Germany. The only German in his poems – in 'Strange Meeting' – is one he has been made to kill, who calls him 'my friend', and who turns out to be himself. The real enemy is the Public Monster of Warmongering Insensibility at home. For England, the Great War was, in fact, a kind of civil war (still unfinished – which helps to explain its meaning for modern England, its hold on our feelings, and why Owen's poetry is still so relevant). His poems had to be weapons. Nothing in them could be vivid enough, or sorrowful enough; words could never be terrible enough for the work he had set himself to do. He had an idea of helping his cause along with merciless photographs of the trenches that would be exhibited in London. Few poets can ever have written with such urgently defined, practical purpose. And it is this attitude of managing a vital persuasion which perhaps explains his extraordinary detachment from the agony, his objectivity. He is not saying, 'Ah, God, how horrible for us!' but, 'Look what you've done, look!', as he presses the reader's eyes into it.

The big thing behind these few short poems that makes them resound – as for instance Sassoon's similarly indignant poems do not

– is Owen's genius for immersing himself in and somehow absorbing that unprecedented experience of ghastliness, the reality of that huge mass of dumb, disillusioned, trapped, dying men. His every line is saturated with the vastness of it, a hallucinated telescope into the cluttered thick of it.

His work is a version of old-style prophecy: apocalyptic scenes of woe and carnage mingled with fulminations against the Godless oppressors, and somewhere at the bottom of the carnage, the Messiah struggling to be born – 'Christ is literally in no-man's land. There men often hear his voice', he wrote. It was Owen who showed what that war really meant, to us, in immediate suffering and general implication, as nobody else did.

Dr Dung

Prison-camps, brain-washers, recruitments of all sorts, have perfected a procedure for destroying a person's sense of his own
identity. Deprived of the outer security, inner security denied,
battered to exhaustion, the old self sooner or later capitulates. The
routed owner regresses to near-animal, a lump of ectoplasm desperate to get back into humanity by any means, ready to pour himself
into any new identity-mould, even into a workable madness sooner
than nothing, but soonest of all into the role that's safest in the new
conditions, the best-acknowledged and the most successful. So the
brainwasher's victim emerges grateful, the deathcamp number
becomes a strenuous Nazi. Professor Rokeach's working hypothesis
follows from this: that our sense of our own identity is rooted in
certain fundamental constancies, physical and social, and that these
'Primitive Beliefs,' as he calls them, cannot be disturbed without
finally disturbing our sanity. This is commonplace enough. But
Professor Rokeach concentrates his attention on one ingenious
inversion of the idea.

If all this is true, thought Professor Rokeach, then a paranoid
psychotic's idea of himself – i.e. his new, crazy identity of God, or
Caesar, or Jack the Ripper, or whatever he's chosen – must be a
'Primitive Belief', corresponding to a sane man's realistic idea of
himself. So to dislodge a psychotic from his delusory role would be
to collapse the whole psychosis, and to open the patient to cure – as
the brainwashed prisoner is open to 'cure' when his earlier 'political
insanity' has been collapsed. From there, it's a short but tortuous
step to gathering three claimants to Christhood at Ypsilanti State
Hospital, in Michigan, and supervising their disputations. This
might seem a cruel way to go about cracking their 'Primitive Beliefs',
but the Professor's justification is that a paranoid psychotic by
definition is fortressed against all reasonable negotiation, and has

Review of Milton Rokeach, *The Three Christs of Ypsilanti* (London: Barker, 1964),
from the *New Statesman*, 4 September 1964.

only one weak point – his conviction that he is the unique original of his particular role, which nothing can touch but the living evidence of a challenger to the same role. Rokeach quotes two examples, where a confrontation of that sort seemed to work according to his theory, but both seem a bit doubtful. And throughout this book the doubt grows.

It's a sinister book. The most sinister thing in it is Professor Rokeach's interested eye, coaxing his three psychotics to harder and harder head-on collisions with the intolerable. The main fascination – and it rarely lags – is provided by Leon, the youngest of the three, whose response seems at first to give the Professor hopes of success. Leon doesn't simply wall up and deny the sanity of his fellow Christs, as the other two do, but manoeuvres constantly to lower the pressure and live with the impossibility, by contriving that he be called Rex, for instance, instead of Christ or Leon, and by shifting his field of assertion to a wild, sad mythology, mainly the virtuoso development of his phantasmagoric bond with his mother, who seems to have been quite a psychotic herself. From being the 'Old Witch', a horrific sexual demoness, 'in with the arsenic and old lace gang', she becomes Woman Eve, seducer of Adam, then the Virgin Mary, Christ's (Leon's) wife. But under the Professor's relentless encirclement the strain of godhead in the open becomes too much, and he divorces her, announcing his marriage to Righteous Idealed Yeti Woman ('The highest form of blood genes are Yeti genes. The Yeti people are not stained with original sin'). Under the name of Dr Righteous Idealed Dung, he escapes with her, Christ-pride intact and incognito, into further developments and disappointments, crabbing away from the Professor's steady eye, till the experiment comes to a close, for lack of funds, leaving him married safely to himself, in the deepest cave of all, Dr R. I. Dung, God Morphodite, Potential Madame. It's a moving story, as well as horrible.

The Professor admits his defeat, but he doesn't altogether aban-don the hopes of his method, though it becomes clear enough that Leon's Christ, in his crazy system, is far from equivalent, in any way, to a sane man's idea of himself in his sane system, and that all the Professor has managed to do in the end is hammer Leon into a solid alloy ball of irreducible God, Wife and Dung, where before the elements were separate and more gracefully arranged.

Professor Rokeach's culminating suggestion is that a psychosis of this kind, generally, covers the patient's chronic uncertainty about his sexual identity. Considering this, rather than speculations about 'Primitive Beliefs', as the main thesis, the narrative leads up to it with clarity and force. The book as a whole says quite a lot about the modern epidemic alienation from society, from reality and from self – the vague dehumanization radiating from the violent religious, scientific and ideological contradictions of modern life, where every traditional impulse or assertion is an instant daylight casualty, where respectable societies can remain, at bottom, in a baffled condition of animal apathy and anarchy, or be overtaken by a sudden lunatic uniform, and where the only postures of confidence are to be dead, or God. — *Crow?*

Opposing Selves

Pushkin gives a peculiar impression of being something utterly different from his fellow-Russians – not just a genius, but different in kind, like some sort of changeling from outer space. By comparison, Byron's singularity looks like mere lordly English eccentricity; his club-foot, like Leopardi's hump, shrinks back into the normal run of things. When those two expose their sufferings, something slightly theatrical struts out. But Pushkin's plight is hopeless, right to the bottom, and his despair radiates more powerfully from these self-concealing letters than from anything in his works.

What a strange fate, after all, to be born into an aristocracy, in the half-frozen North, and forced to live at the glaring centre of it, among all those ferocious proprieties and discriminations, looking like an Abyssinian, and known most famously to be one. He defended his African blood by being proud of it, but at bottom it must have meant mainly humiliation, and a fixed idea of his separateness from other Russians, physiologically signed apart from their kind. His two languages helped to preserve, maybe even to nourish, this basic dilemma. He learned French, the language of polite society, from a tedious series of French tutors, whereas his Russian, his language of love and poetry, came from his grandmother and his peasant nanny. His parents more or less ignored his childhood, which fact no doubt fed his African thoughts. The whole predicament must have prepared him to see his difficulties clearly, and to manage them as brilliantly as he did, and to become such a representative specimen of revolutionary yet repressive times.

It amounted to supplying him with two antithetical poles of operation. Often he gives the impression of being two people. At one extreme, his deeper self, is the sufferer, solitary, outlawed from mankind somehow, with huge, gloomy reservoirs of romantic feeling (he liked to think of his private monopoly of primitive

Review of *The Letters of Alexander Pushkin*, edited and translated by
J. Thomas Shaw (Oxford: OUP, 1964), from the *Listener*, 1 October 1964.

African passion), susceptible to moods of oceanic desolation, an archaic, muzhik or life-prisoner sense of the nothingness and boredom and the mere playfulness of existence, a self that could pour its energies only into poetry and women. This is the self of the early poems. But after the first painful collisions with an exceedingly caustic and political society (at twenty-one he was exiled to southern Russia for the seditious air of his early poems and remarks – the beginning of a political persecution that got worse right up to his death), the other self came to his rescue and took over the practical guidance of his affairs. This self was a witty, shrewd man of the world, claiming descent not from Africa but from the French court, from Voltaire in particular. Pushkin's poetry thereafter is an account of the negotiations between these two opposing selves. Out of their antagonism he makes this third thing, his greatness, a powerful, mediating serenity, a unique blend of deeply-lit qualities. *Eugene Onegin* can be read as a description of the whole transaction, and its consequences. Pushkin would evidently have preferred a life where he could have lived out to the full the naïve, poetic potentialities of his character Lensky, but he woke up daily into the world (and mentality) of Onegin, who involves him finally in the marriage and the multiplying troubles that swamp his last years. And it is this Onegin whom we meet in the letters.

In other words, we meet a façade: not the artist, but the brilliant manager. So, in detail, the letters are disappointing, in spite of the clear and lively translation, since we inevitably come for confidences and a tour of the poetic works, as we do to Keats. Pushkin gives nothing away. He is always visiting you on brisk business. Or, if you visit him, he's always somehow showing you the door, in a delightful manner. Frank and direct, not meandering but seizing one thing after another and laying it cleanly open, yet playful. But brief; and nothing much has been said. Most of his troubles arose from one or two – only one or two – indiscreet remarks in his letters, which were censored from the beginning, and what we are reading are, in fact, letters to the censor. But the events come through, and as we work through the twenty years that the letters cover, something terrible begins to pervade.

The atmosphere of that society seems familiar – the Tsar's unpredictable favours and disfavours, personal spite of police supervision, extinction of all radical hopes and friends with them, censorship, social treachery – it all steams out of these letters like an up-to-date nightmare. But one sees too how, so long as he could debauch, he was happy enough; he could keep his inner freedom and flourish, secretly, in opposition, according to his genius. Marriage ended that – marriage to a court beauty and feather-brained favourite of the Tsar, which bound him at once to propriety on all fronts, and service at the court as an appendage. Expenses, debts, children, fears for the future, public and domestic humiliations which he was bound morally and financially to endure, plus ever-deepening bondage to the Tsar – all fell at once on to his pen, as well as the collapse of his parents' estate and for some reason his brother's debts, which found him at the same time. He was delivered over completely to the enemy. And the worst of it was he could blame himself. After his marriage, these letters reveal a changed man: he has compromised his genius, somehow. Thereafter, they read as a struggle not so much against odds as against his destruction and his own casting vote. It's easy to see how some modern Russians can make him a symbolic figure.

Superstitions

The major superstitions are impressive. They are so old, so unkill-able, and so few. If they are pure nonsense, why aren't there more of them? But they all keep on reviving with the perverse air of intuitions, never losing their central idea, no matter how richly they proliferate details. The worst thing against them is that they have no means of shedding their rubbish; every crazy development goes on hanging around them. Astrology's the most outlandishly draped, and the most disreputable. But what vitality! Louis MacNeice's historical survey is mostly a prodigious fleamarket of rubbish, kept on sale by many bookish astrologers, befogged by the complexities of their charts, trying to assemble something workable from the collapsed gazebos of the past. MacNeice seems to have moved from scepticism to wild laughter. Nevertheless he ended in curiosity.

To an outsider, astrology is a procession of puerile absurdities, a Babel of gibberish. It suffers by setting up as a science, and challenging the scientific eye. As it happens, statistics tend to support some of the general principles, but in a horoscope, cast according to any one of the systems, there are hundreds of factors to be reckoned with, each one interfering with all the others simultaneously, where only judgement of an intuitive sort is going to be able to move, let alone make sense. Some astrologers do make sense. A few, such as the American Evangeline Adams, produce results – under test conditions, and repeatedly – that seem to convince the most derisive. But these results are not material enough: they are verbal pronoun-cements, and elsewhere and afterwards they are indistinguishable from rumour, quickly overwhelmed by the manifest error and charlatanism of popular zodiackery.

Whether the genuine astrology works as an esoteric science, like advanced mathematics, as astrologers claim, or as an intuitive art, like throwing the bones, it doesn't matter, so long as it works. The

Review of Louis MacNeice, *Astrology* (Seattle: Aldus, 1964),
and of T. C. Lethbridge, *Ghost and Divining Rod*
(London: Routledge and Kegan Paul, 1963), from the *Listener*, 2 October 1964.

cloud of howlers that it advances on the public is no greater than what we'd see of science, if science hadn't the sense to conceal all but its successes, and if every decade of its history weren't littered with shed fantasts. The real resistance to astrology is a common-sense or moral one. Its great enemies, popular science and the Puritan strain of Christianity, come equally under this main objection – that it enslaves minds and interferes with free consideration, replacing natural response and observation with abstract rules. This is the deadly effect of popular astrology, however sensitive and useful it may prove in the hands of experts. But it's not likely to be restrained, and less than ever nowadays, when the other ancient occult loyalties are beginning to stir and show courage, thanks to physics.

The word 'rationality' is having a bad time. The laws of the Creation are the only literally rational things, and we don't yet know what they are. The nearest we can come to rational thinking is to stand respectfully, hat in hand, before this Creation, exceedingly alert for a new word. We no longer so readily make the grinding, funicular flight of cerebrations from supposed first principles. On all points of uncertainty, we give the Universe the benefit of the doubt. We'll stand to some claims: the moon is not green cheese, and birds lay eggs, and if we cross the room we reach the other side. But whether Gandhi's prayers affected European politics, whether Jehovah was or was not a highly irascible poltergeist laboriously constructed by the psychokinetic efforts of Moses and Aaron, and whoever else they could get to pray with them, we leave open. Whether or not an ill-wish gets up and walks the streets, or enemies' dreams meet, fight and mutilate each other, or unhuman electrical powers occasionally play a kind of witty or witless chess with men, there are no means to disprove such fantastic ideas; although they could conceivably at any moment come within the detection of new instruments. We reject them, if we do, because they inhabit a gulf where our careful civilization would disintegrate. Yet they are ancient ideas which from time to time men all over the world have found taking on power in their minds, just as they found the wild Heraclitean/Buddhist notion that the entire Universe is basically made of fire.

[52]

Modern physicists have reasserted this last one in civilized terms. Their 'rationality' has evaporated in an astonished watchfulness and the struggle to keep a grasp on the human dimension of things – evidently not easy, as we see in such men as Teller. They've landed themselves, and us, in a delicately balanced, purely electrical Creation, at the backdoor of the house of activities formerly called 'supernatural'. For a purely electrical Creation is one without walls, where everything, being an electrical power, can have an electrical effect on every other thing, and where electrical effects are vital effects. It is in this world that Lethbridge's book makes its sense.

It is well-known that all living creatures have a wide electrical aura. If you stroke a cat a few times, then bring your hand back over its fur, and a few inches above it, the cat's hair rises under your hand. What is not so easily demonstrated is that every single object, living or unliving, has a similar aura.

Lethbridge has the dowsing gift, a gift not to be questioned by those who possess it (and it's calculated that one in three do). If you try to hold the rod firm against the invisible power that pulls on it, the rod will be bent and perhaps broken. A more sensitive instrument, which nearly everybody (if not everybody) can use, is the pendulum. This is a tiny ball on the end of a length of thread, swung from the fingers. Lethbridge describes how he uses it in his archaeological digs to discover things in the ground. He not only divines where they are, but how deep they lie, and what they are made of: he describes his methods. With this device, he introduces us vividly to the forest of electrical fields in which we live, and which are all the time modifying our own field. The transmission of impulses full of complicated information, and the storing of impressions, among these fields, is not a matter of superstition but of electrodynamics.

He makes a logical application of these circumstances to the *couvade*, where the husband suffers the wife's childbirth pains, which is only one of the whole range of sympathetic illnesses, physical and mental, and which may be related to faith-healing, where as in some primitive medicine the healer takes over the illness of his patient or passes over some health. The key to this theory is the commonplace law that electrical potential flows from high tension to low. The person with the lower potential absorbs current from the one with higher, along with highly charged thought-forms, moods, colourings and so on as modifying waves. Certain conditions – high emotion in particular – seem to raise a person's potential, while depression, tiredness and fear seem to lower it. It's known, in support of Lethbridge's suggestion, that during a healing seance a faith-healer's static potential drops measurably. Another condition of the exchange is that the people involved share some sort of 'sympathy' – though a very little thing will suffice to establish this. Telepathy certainly works best between friends, and can be hair-raisingly intrusive between people who are really close. And the more practical operations of witchcraft, as well as long-distance magical healing (which works too well to be easily repudiated), require some scrap of the victim's or patient's body-hair, or a blood-drop.

All this opens onto a gulf – as Freud, for one, saw and feared. What are the limits of this involuntary transmission? What about the gift, recorded in several individuals (Jung cites an occasion where the gift visited him), of being able to read off, at first meeting, large stretches of the stranger's past life, seeing it unrolled like a cinema, and effortlessly, as Mozart heard his music. If that sort of reception occurs, it's quite as likely to be a common property of life's electrical constitution as a freakish personal talent. The possibilities of what a child might absorb from its lineage in this way are awesome, which is what alarmed Freud.

Other inhabitants of the gulf are ghosts. Many ghosts fall to psychological or medical explanations. But the ghosts or 'presences' which haunt one spot, where different people, and animals, react to them, are evidently part of the logic of the earth. Lethbridge's theory explains such a ghost as an impression – of terror, misery, hatred, or, it may be, happiness – projected into an electrical field by some individual in a state of intense emotion, and stored there as in a capacitor, or as our experience is stored in our own electrical field. When some person in a low state of potential, i.e. depressed or frightened or enfeebled in the early hours or ill, enters the same field, the impression is leaked back into their consciousness: they become 'aware' of it. In other words, all these electrical fields within the G-field of the earth store up experience, though perhaps fadingly, and the question of just what forms that experience may take confronts once more the swarming worlds of the religions.

These are only the shallows of Lethbridge's intriguing venture into the gulf. And if, by some spectacular development of sensitive recording equipment, all these refreshed but really very ancient and widely shared suppositions were proved, to the crassest incredulity, to be fact, what an entertaining place the world would become again! What a chaos! The only respectable sanities to survive undiscredited in all that would be physics and art.

Regenerations

Traces and variations of Shamanism are found all over the world, but it has developed its purest or most characteristic procedures in north-eastern and central Asia. The word 'shaman' comes from the Tungus. Shamanism is not a religion, but a technique for moving in a state of ecstasy among the various spiritual realms, and for generally dealing with souls and spirits, in a practical way, in some practical crisis. It flourishes alongside and within the prevailing religion. For instance, some Tibetan Lamas occasionally shamanize. And whereas religions may differ fundamentally, the inner experiences and techniques and application of Shamanism spring into shape everywhere similarly, as if the whole activity were something closer to biological inevitability than to any merely cultural tradition – though obviously cultural traditions influence it a good deal too, in detail. The Buddhist influence on Asiatic Shamanism is strong.

The vital function shamanizing can take on, even in a colossally formed religion like Buddhism, may be seen in the *Bardo Thodol*, the Tibetan 'Book of the Dead'. In the *Bardo Thodol* the geography and furnishings of the afterworld are Buddhist, but the main business of the work as a whole, which is to guide a dead soul to its place in death, or back into life – together with the principal terrific events, and the flying accompaniment of descriptive songs, exhortation to the soul, threats, and the rest – are all characteristically shamanic. This huge, formal work has long ago lost contact with any shaman, but its origins seem clear.

The shaman is 'chosen' in a number of ways. In some regions, commonly among the North American Indians, the aspirant inflicts on himself extraordinary solitary ordeals of fasting and self-mutilation, until a spirit, usually some animal, arrives, and becomes henceforth his liaison with the spirit world. In other regions, the tribe chooses the man – who may or may not, under the initiation

From the *Listener*, 29 October 1964.

ordeals, become a shaman. But the most common form of election comes from the spirits themselves: they approach the man in a dream. At the simplest, these dreams are no more than a vision of an eagle, as among the Buryats, or a beautiful woman (who marries them), as among the Goldi. But at the other extreme, the dreams are long and complicated, and dramatize in full the whole psychological transformation that any shaman, no matter how he has been initially chosen, must undergo. The central episode in this full-scale dream, just like the central episode in the rites where the transformation is effected forcibly by the tribe, is a magical death, then dismemberment, by a demon or equivalent powers, with all possible variants of boiling, devouring, burning, stripping to the bones. From this nadir, the shaman is resurrected, with new insides, a new body created for him by the spirits. When he recovers from this – the dream may hold him in a dead trance for several days – he begins to study under some shaman, learning the great corpus of mythological, medical, and technical lore of the particular cultural line of shamanism he is in: this stage takes several years.

Some shamans shamanize to amuse themselves, but usually the performance is public and to some public purpose. The preparations are elaborate, the shamanizing prolonged and spectacular, as the shaman dances, drums, leaps – in regalia hung with mirrors and iron emblems often weighing more than fifty pounds – and sings himself into ecstasy, entering the spirit realm. In this condition he can handle fire, be stabbed and not bleed, and perform incredible feats of strength and agility. His business is usually to guide some soul to the underworld, or bring back a sick man's lost soul, or deliver sacrifices to the dead, or ask the spirits the reason for an epidemic, or the whereabouts of game or a man lost. The structure of these spirit realms is universally fairly consistent, and familiar figures recur as consistently: the freezing river, the clashing rocks, the dog in the cave-entrance, the queen of animals, the holy mountain, and so on. The results, when the shaman returns to the living, are some display of healing power, or a clairvoyant piece of information. The cathartic effect on the audience, and the refreshing of their religious feeling, must be profound. These shamanizings are also entertainments, full of buffoonery, mimicry, dialogue, and magical contortions. The effect on the shaman himself is something to wonder about. One main circumstance in becoming a shaman, in the first place, is that once you've been chosen by the spirits, and dreamed the dreams, there is no other life for you, you must shamanize or die: this belief seems almost universal. The calling is not exclusively male: in some traditions (Japanese) women predominate.

And the initiation dreams, the general schema of the shamanic flight, and the figures and adventures they encounter, are not a shaman monopoly: they are, in fact, the basic experience of the poetic temperament we call 'romantic'. In a shamanizing society, *Venus and Adonis*, some of Keats's longer poems, *The Wanderings of Oisin*, *Ash Wednesday*, would all qualify their authors for the magic drum; while the actual flight lies perceptibly behind many of the best fairy tales, behind myths such as those of Orpheus and Herakles, and behind the epics of Gilgamesh and Odysseus. It is the outline, in fact, of the Heroic Quest. The shamans seem to undergo, at will and at phenomenal intensity, and with practical results, one of the main regenerating dramas of the human psyche: the fundamental poetic event. Mircea Eliade* carefully reviews all that is known about Shamanism in a scholarly, fascinating manner: it is a major survey of the subject.

But if Shamanism is such a personal, poetic, profound engagement with the miraculous forces of the universe, what is Sufism? After reading this astonishing book† by Idries Shah, Grand Chief of the Sufis, one would almost be inclined to say that Shamanism might well be a barbarized, stray descendant of Sufism. Among the scattered hypotheses of amateur mystics, theosophists, and dabblers in the occult, one often comes across reference to 'the secret doctrine', some mysterious brotherhood that is said to hold the keys to everything in the West, outside Christianity, that touches the occult: tarot cards, the witches (as distinct from the universal workings of magic), the secret societies, Rosicrucians, Masons, the

---

* Mircea Eliade, *Shamanism* (London: Routledge and Kegan Paul, 1964).
† Idries Shah, *Sufis* (London: W. H. Allen, 1964).

Kabbalah. This book makes it clear, and in no amateurish manner, that in fact all these things originated among the Sufis, and represent degenerate, strayed filterings of the doctrine. Their major poets – Hafiz, Rumi, Ibn El-Arabi – are not merely among the greatest poets in the world's history, but seem to have provided much of the material and inspiration for the greatest of the West. The 'romance' tradition, for instance, in its preoccupation with 'love' and the 'occult', was a Sufi bequest. As Robert Graves notes in his introduction, what is known of the Druidic tradition, like that of the early schools of poets in Ireland, shows surprising relationships to the outlook and training of the Sufis, who do not evangelize, have no established dogma, but wander all over the world planting schools, as at the root of Vedanta, and of Zen. The Sufi stream comes to the surface in the most unexpected places. Many forlorn puzzles in the world, which seemed to suggest that some great spiritual age somewhere in the Middle East had long since died and left indecipherable relics and automatisms to trouble our nostalgia, suddenly come into organic life in this book.

Candidates for Sufi-hood are selected for their natural aptitude to live the Sufi way: they undergo many years of rigorous mental and spiritual training in the Sufi schools, a highly refined course of moral self-development, annihilating themselves without heaven or hell or religious paraphernalia of any kind, and without leaving life in the world, to become the living substance of Allah, the power of Creation: a master Sufi lives this love, and performs therefore incredible miracles as a matter of course. His purpose is to lead others along the Sufi way, but only those who, coming to be led, are capable of being led. The Sufis, said to number fifty million strong, must be the only society of sensible men there has ever been on earth.

Revelations:
The Genius of Isaac Bashevis Singer

Isaac Bashevis Singer emigrated to the United States in 1935, which
was the year of his first novel *Satan in Goray*. Since then, he has
written more or less exclusively about the Jewish world of pre-war
Poland, or more exactly – it's a relevant qualification – about the
Hasidic world of pre-war Poland, into which he was born, the son of
a rabbi, in 1904. So not only does he write in Yiddish, but his chosen
subject is even further confined in place, and culture, and now to the
past. Nevertheless, his work has been lucky with its translators, and
he has to be considered among the truly great living writers, on
several counts.

He's produced three more novels, that have been translated, and
three volumes of short stories. Looking over his novels in their
chronological order (the stories are written in and among, but they
belong with the novels) the first apparent thing is the enormous and
one might say successful development of his vision. Vision seems to
be the right word for what Singer is conveying. The most important
fact about him, that determines the basic strategy by which he deals
with his subject, is that his imagination is poetic, and tends toward
symbolic situations. Cool, analytical qualities are heavily present in
everything he does, but organically subdued to a grasp that is finally
visionary and redemptive. Without the genius, he might well have
disintegrated as he evidently saw others disintegrate – between a
nostalgic dream of ritual Hasidic piety on the one hand and cosmic
dead-end despair on the other. But his creative demon (again, demon
is the right word) works deeper than either of these two extremes. It
is what involves him so vehemently with both. It involves him with
both because this demon is ultimately the voice of his nature, which
requires at all costs satisfaction in life, full inheritance of its natural
joy. It is what suffers the impossible problem and dreams up the
supernormal solution. It is what in most men stares dumbly through

From the *New York Review of Books*, 22 April 1965.

the bars. At bottom it is amoral, as interested in destruction as in creation. But being in Singer's case an intelligent spirit, it has gradually determined a calibration of degrees between good and evil, discovering which activities embroil it in misery, pain, and emptiness, and conjure into itself cruel powers, and which ones concentrate it towards bliss, the fullest possession of its happiest energy. Singer's writings are the account of this demon's re-education through decades that have been – particularly for the Jews – a terrible school. They put the question: 'How shall man live most truly as a human being?' from the centre of gravity of human nature, not from any temporary civic centre or speculative metaphysic or far-out neurotic bewilderment. And out of the pain and wisdom of Jewish history and tradition they answer it. His work is not discursive, or even primarily documentary, but a revelation – and we respect his findings because it so happens that he has the authority and force to compel us to do so.

Up to 1945, this demon in Singer's work shows itself overpowered. *Satan in Goray* and *The Family Moskat* give the story of its defeat. In some ways these two books belong together, though they are ten years apart. *Satan in Goray* seems to me the weaker book – important, and with a stunning finish, but for the most part confusingly organized. Perhaps we wouldn't notice this so much if we weren't comparing it with his later works, where the inspired rightness of his technical inventions are a study in themselves. *Satan in Goray* recounts the effects of the Sabbataí Zevi Messianic hysteria on a small Hasidic community in seventeenth-century Poland. Sabbatai Zevi's followers, who frequently appear in Singer's stories, effectually apotheosized the Evil One. They proclaimed salvation through an ecstasy of sinning, as if there were something purifying in the sheer intensity with which they surrendered to the forbidden, to the supercharged otherworld of disruptive powers and supernaturals which the Law, in its wandering history, had collided with and put under, and thereafter had to hold under. A terrific population was accumulated under the Cabala and on the Holy Fringes of everything, several entire religions and erstwhile creators screwed down under dots, letters, and ritual gestures. This isn't altogether ancient history. Something of it has been dogmatized in modern psychology and avant-garde literature. One could argue that the whole of modern Western life is one vast scientifically programmed surrender to what was formerly unknown and forbidden, as if salvation lay that way. The Sabbatai Zevi psychic epidemic is an accurate metaphor for a cultural landslide that has destroyed all spiritual principles and dumped an entire age into a cynical materialism emptied of meaning. Which is why the sufferings of Netchele, the bride of the leader of the Sabbatai Zevi sect in Goray, in whose brain the general eruption of infernal licence finally concentrates, belong to this century and not to the seventeenth. And why we can say her sufferings are perhaps an image of what Singer's own muse, representative of the Polish Jews, has undergone.

The key to Singer's works is an experience of the collapse of the Hasidic way of life under the pressure of all that it had been developed to keep out. Something like this is a usual moral position among poets who come at some revolutionary moment, but who need to respect order. Singer comes at the moment when the profound, rich, intense Hasidic tradition, with the whole Jewish tradition behind it, debouches into the ideological chaos of the mid-twentieth century. Visited with all that the old Law excluded, such poets are burdened with the job of finding new Law. But when the hosts of liberated instinct and passion and intellectual adventure and powers of the air and revelations of physical truth are symbolized by Satan, as they must be for a Hasidic Jew, and the old, obsolete order is symbolized by the devotion and ritual that are a people's unique spiritual strength and sole means of survival, the position must be a perilous one to manage. We can trace the workings of the whole conflict much more definitely – though without the symbolic impact of *Satan in Goray* – in Singer's next book, *The Family Moskat*.

Coming ten years later, *The Family Moskat* is radically different in style from the earlier book, cast in panoramic Tolstoyan mould, 600 pages long, covering the fates of the rich, patriarchal Moskat's large family and – in suggested parallel – of a whole people, from the beginning of this century up to the first Nazi bombs on Warsaw. The protagonist is one Asa Heshel, a young, precociously freethinking but, to begin with, outwardly orthodox Hasidic Jew, the son of a provincial rabbi, who arrives in Warsaw seeking life and the divine truths. He becomes entangled with Moskat's family. Thereafter, it is the story of the moral disintegration of the Polish Jews.

It is a monumental, seethingly real picture of Warsaw Jewish life, without a mistimed paragraph. In this city, the Jews are under the millstone of the west, and their inner coherence is breaking up. In the process, typical mutations appear. But the main current of the book flows through two men, Asa Heshel and Abram. Abram is a volcanic enjoyer of life. The gentile pressures have stripped him of all but the last nods towards orthodoxy, but they haven't frightened his energy: he keeps his Hasidic wholeness and joy. Though he lives more or less entirely in sin in every direction, collapsing finally on a whore's bed and dying in his mistress's, he remains 'a true Hasid' and 'biologically a Jew.' But it is all at a last gasp, it is all headlong into the new gentile age, into death, on the precarious foundations of a damaged, over-passionate heart. He is full-pressure Jewishness, making the leap, naïvely. He calls Asa Heshel, his protegé, a coward, and by superficial contrast Asa Heshel's behaviour is cowardly all right. But Asa Heshel has already recoiled. He made the leap early, without dying bodily, into the wilderness of Darwin and the physicists, the ceaseless covert battleground of Western civilization, and he has recoiled. He has no illusion that life lies that way. Yet he has allowed the wind off it to deprive him of his traditional faith, the meaning of his life. And that first treachery to God spreads a faithlessness, a heartlessness, into all his actions and thoughts. His two marriages founder and struggle on in torture. His grand intellectual ambitions fritter out in sterility and cynicism. He regards all the possibilities of life with frozen distrust. For him, God has died, yet he can't love anything else. The creation is a heap of atoms, a sterile promontory battered by blind appetites. His deep suspicion and perhaps hatred of women is equalled by his cold, desperate lust for their bodies. The great projected work of his youth, 'The Laboratory of Happiness', accompanies his pointless wanderings, decaying, finally lost. All the moral and intellectual consequences of his people's loss of faith, and their pursuit of the new, chaotic world, seem to have concentrated in his brain. Behind his coldness, he is suffering the mythic death Netchele suffered, in *Satan in Goray*, possessed and out of her mind, and perhaps this is the connection between the two books.

Adele, his second wife, on the point of leaving him to escape to Israel from the first rumours of Hitler, finds the words for Asa Heshel: 'He was one of those who must serve God or die. He had forsaken God and because of that he was dead – a living body with a dead soul.' It is from this situation of Asa Heshel's that the general moral implications of Singer's vision radiate. Asa Heshel, after all, is not only a Hasidic Jew. He is a typical modern hero. Remembering that Singer writes in Yiddish, for a primarily Jewish public, we can still see that he writes out of such essential imagination that he raises Jewishness to a symbolic quality, and is no longer writing specifically about Jews but about man in relationship to God. And his various novels and stories – with a few exceptions among the stories – describe the various phases and episodes of this relationship, though in concrete Jewish terms. This is near to saying that, in Singer, the Jew becomes the representative modern man of suffering, and understanding, and exile from his Divine inheritance, which isn't altogether Singer's own invention.

Asa Heshel ends up, hurrying under the Nazi bombers with his latest woman, Jewish also, but a determined Communist. He knows he has fallen the whole way. Communism is the ideological antithesis to the Holy Life, created by Jews living in defiance or denial of God, as Lucifer, fallen from praising in heaven, organized the abyss. In her company, Asa Heshel meets the philosopher, the bewildered genius, one-time hope of the gentilized Jewish intellectuals, who closes the book, among the falling bombs, with 'The Messiah will come soon . . . Death is the Messiah. That's the real truth.' This is the logical final point in Asa Heshel's progress, as death was the final point of Netchele's. The forsaking of God, the rejection of the life of Holy Disciplines, is a crime, as it turns out, without redemption, and, as history in this book seems to demonstrate, draws on itself the inevitable penalty: anonymous death – whether symbolic or actual hardly matters – in a meaningless wasteland of destruction and anguish.

Singer's vision arrived there, in despair in the absurd Universe, at a point where most comparable modern writers have remained, emotionally, despite their notable attempts to get beyond it. The Existential Choice, taken to its absolute limit of wholeheartedness, becomes inevitably a religion – because man is deeper and more complicated than merely rational controls can comprehend. Then his beliefs, disciplines, and prohibitions have to be cultivated against the odds, as in a world of poisons one chooses – sensibly after all – food that nourishes. Singer is at a point there, that is to say, where he has every sane and human reason to rebuild an appreciation of the Faith it was death for him to lose. So here again the Jewish Hasidic tradition takes on a Universal significance, as a paradigm of the truly practical Existential discipline, which perhaps it always has been. The core of the Jewish faith, unlike most larger persuasions, is one long perpetually-renewed back-to-the-wall Choice, one might say in this context, to affirm a mode of survival against tremendous odds. It has kept the Jewish heart in one piece through 3,000 years of such oppressions and temptations as dissolved other peoples in a few decades. So it is not surprising if Singer, in his books, gravitates back towards it as a way out of the modern impasse, salvaging at the same time the life of spirit and all the great human virtues.

The Family Moskat is the matrix from which Singer's subsequent work grows. His next two novels, *The Magician of Lublin* and *The Slave* are like dreams out of Asa Heshel's remorse. The Magician, Yasha Mazur, fallen from the Faith, is a kind of Satan, the opportunist of his own inspired ingenuity. But, unlike Asa Heshel's, his belief has not wholly died, it has (merely) been buried. It recovers him from the pit, and in a bricked-up cell in his yard he becomes an ascetic, a famous Holy man. In this, he has not rejected the world. He has accepted the only life that does not lead to misery for himself and for everybody he knows. *The Slave* goes a great step further in the same direction. Jacob – a slave of Polish peasants in the seventeenth century – is brutishly treated. He is stalled among the beasts. He is threatened with constant death. Yet he keeps his faith. He falls in love with the peasant daughter of his master, converts her, and returns with her to live in a Jewish settlement. It is a story of heroic dedication: no disappointment or persecution or obstacle can shake him – as Asa Heshel was so easily shaken – from the chosen way, and he becomes, again, a kind of Saint.

In this book, one of Singer's deep themes comes right to the surface. Singer implies – and seems to build his novels instinctively around the fact – that there is an occult equivalence between a man's relationship to the women in his life and his relationship to his own soul – and so to God. Netchele, in *Satan in Goray*, seems to bear a relationship to Singer himself. Hadassah, Adele, Barbara, and Asa Heshel's mother, precisely define the stages of Asa Heshel's fall. Esther, Masha and Emilia define the three Yasha Mazurs, in *The Magician*. Wanda and Sarah, two names of one woman, correspond to Jacob creating his soul out of chaos, and Jacob the Saint. These correspondences are subtle and revealing. On the mythical or symbolic plane, the women are always at the core of everything Singer is saying about his hero. And it's on this plane that we can best see what an achievement *The Slave* is, and perhaps why it comes to be such a burningly radiant, intensely beautiful book. Singer is answering his age like a prophet, though what he is saying may seem perverse and untimely. If the world is Gehenna, it is also the only 'Laboratory of Happiness', and in *The Slave* Jacob and Sarah achieve a kind of Alchemical Marriage, a costly, precarious condition, but the only truly happy one. So what are we to understand? The dynamics of man's resistance to demoralization and confusion, the techniques of 'creating' God and Holy Joy where there seemed to be only emptiness, never change, but they demand a man's whole devotion. And they can be abandoned in a day, whereon the world becomes, once more, Gehenna.

His stories fill out these guiding themes, or exploit situations suggested by them, in dozens of different ways, but they give freer play to his invention than the novels. At their best, they must be among the most entertaining pieces extant. Each is a unique exercise in tone, focus, style, form, as well as an unforgettable re-creation of characters and life. A comic note, a sort of savage enjoyment that scarcely appears in the novels, more or less prevails, though it is weirdly blended with pathos, simplicity, idyllic piety, horror. There is some connection here, in the actual intensity of the performance, and the impartial joy in the face of everything, with traditional Hasidic fervour. In substance, these stories recapitulate the ideas and materials of Jewish tradition. Intellectually their roots run into the high, conservative wisdom of the old Jewish sages. Yet it is only a slight thing that prevents many of them from being folk-tales, or even old wives' tales, narrated by a virtuoso. They all have the swift, living voice of the oral style. Some of them are very near a bare, point-blank, life-size poetry that hardly exists in English. 'The Black Wedding', in the volume titled *The Spinoza of Market Street*, is a more alive, more ferocious piece of poetic imagination than one can find, I think, in any living poet. Likewise 'The Fast', and 'Blood', in *Short Friday*. The stories often turn on almost occult insights – as the connection between blood-lust and sexual lust, in 'Blood'. It is his intimacy with this dimension of things that carries Singer beyond any easy comparison. Stories that are deadpan jokes, like 'Jachid and Jechidah', or fantasies like 'Shiddah and Kuziba', are not only brilliantly done, but are also moral/theological fables of great force, and direct outriders of Singer's main preoccupations. No psychological terminology or current literary method has succeeded in rendering such a profound, unified and fully apprehended account of the Divine, the Infernal, and the suffering space of self-determination between, all so convincingly interconnected, and fascinatingly peopled. There is a spherical completeness and internal consistency about his total hierarchy of psychological levels reminiscent of Kleist and Shakespeare. But it is in the plain, realistic tales, like 'Under the Knife' in *Short Friday*, that we can isolate his decisive virtue: whatever region his writing inhabits, it is blazing with life and actuality. His powerful, wise, deep, full-face paragraphs make almost every other modern fiction seem by comparison laboured, shallow, overloaded with alien and undigested junk, too fancy, fuddled, not quite squared up to life.

Music of Humanity

In his admirably clear and enlightening introduction to this anthology, in which he outlines the immense mongrel family of extant ballads, Mr Hodgart starts by distinguishing the ballad literature from the literature of the great tradition, the literature produced by sophisticated authors for a sophisticated audience. The cleavage between the two literatures in the British Isles is absolute. To ask why it should be so, and just what rules the cleavage, is to begin to isolate the special miraculous quality of the true ballads.

A ballad can be defined, in Mr Hodgart's words, as 'a song that comments on life by telling a story in popular style.' For the purposes of his anthology, which is meant as an introduction to the various modes, as well as a collection of the best monuments, he concentrates – quite rightly, since they are printed here without melodies – on their special kind of poetry. Some balladists would say that the poetry is of small importance and that the melodies are the great thing, but the fact remains – ballad poetry is impossible to imitate.

That hard core of 'true ballads' makes a body of literature that is valuable on the page or off. They are the model for all who wish – and who does not? – to tell their stories in words that live in the same dimension as life at its most severe, words that cannot be outflanked by experience.

All authors' literature, inevitably, exists in a dimension of imitation or substitute or rarefied life. But the true ballads touch a depth and breadth of life, a seriousness and summary finality, that belongs to the species rather than to individuals, and which shuts instantly against the author who separates himself, by name or by rôle or by motive, from the general dumb chorus of human evidence. It's with

Review of *The Faber Book of Ballads*, edited by Matthew Hodgart
(London: Faber and Faber, 1965), from the *Guardian*, 14 May 1965.

the words as with the melodies. Nobody knows how long ago, or out of what unfalsified depth of life, some of those supernatural airs first came into hearing.

National Ghost

The First World War goes on getting stronger – our number one national ghost. It's still everywhere, molesting everybody. It's still politically alive, too, in an underground way. On those battlefields the main English social issues surfaced and showed their colours. An English social revolution was fought out in the trenches.

The poetry of the war certainly suggests this. Sassoon's and Owen's poems were shaped and directed by ideas that were ultimately revolutionary in a political sense, no less than the more evidently committed poetry of the thirties. The enemy was not German. For four years, France was like England's dream world, a previously unguessed fantasy dimension, where the social oppressions and corruptions slipped into nightmare gear. Men had to act out the roles and undergo the extremes normally suffered only by dream shadows, but under just the same kind of sleep. If the poetry has one guiding theme it is: 'Wake up, we are what is really happening'. Or, perhaps: 'This is what you are doing to us'. The next step, logical but unimaginable, would have been a rising of the ranks, a purging of the mechanical generals, the politicians, the war-profiteers, everything brass-hat and jingoistic both civilian and military. The only German in Owen's poems is the ghost of one he has bayoneted and who calls him 'friend'. But France remained a dream-world, where everything could be suffered but no decision put into effect. In so far as the decisions made there have still not been put into effect, we are possessed by the dream, and find a special relevance in the poetry.

An extra fascination, that may well have disappeared in twenty years' time, radiates from the memories of the survivors. They gave their brain-scarred accounts and every generation since has grown up under their huge first-hand fairy-tale. And somewhere in the nervous system of each survivor the underworld of perpetual

Review of *Men Who March Away: Poems of the First World War*, edited by I. M. Parsons (London: Chatto and Windus, 1965), from the *Listener*, 5 August 1965.

Somme rages on unabated, ready to reabsorb the man completely at the right moment of alcohol or drug. We are still in the living thick of it, as well as being far out of it: so all the poems in this anthology have a circumstantial hold on us.

But on the whole, apart from Owen and Sassoon, the poets lost that war. Perhaps Georgian language wouldn't look nearly so bad if it hadn't been put to such a test. It was the worst equipment they could have had – the language of the very state of mind that belied and concealed the possibility of the nightmare that now had to be expressed. Yet these poems are evidence, in one way, of what one important aspect of the war was like, in that they record – as we find hardly anywhere else – the prevailing feeling of being, at that moment, well-educated, English, and conscripted. This collection is really an anthology of those typical feelings, rather than of objective recreations of the war. Those feelings changed, as the editor points out, during the four years, from 'Now God be thanked Who has matched us with His hour' to 'What more fitting memorial for the fallen / Than that their children / Should fall for the same cause?' They are stereotyped, familiar patterns, but it's these poems that have made them so.

After the first flush, the pattern settles to variations of the contrast between the battlefield in France and the rural beauties of England. Owen, Sassoon, Graves, and Thomas all use this in some of their best pieces. This simple strategy sharpens to something more serious later on, a bitter contrast between the landscape of dead bodies and the English-in-England complacency, which engages more urgent and more national feelings, and produces some of Owen's and Sassoon's best work. It might be said to have created Owen. We know that he intended his poems – as he intended those photographs of the trenches, emergency operations and the like, which he wanted to magnify and display in London – to drive the actuality of the front-line sufferings into the faces of those safe in England. His poems are partly substitutes or verbal parallels for those photographs. The main thing was that they could never be vivid or terrible enough. This immediate journalistic purpose was just what was needed to focus and mobilize his genius for absorbing suffering.

Perhaps what he called 'Pity' gave the depth, and the painful tenderness, to his experience, but it was indignation that turned it into poems – poems that were meant to frighten people, and to incite political action.

The war provided Owen and Sassoon with material their special gifts might not have found elsewhere, but it was disastrous for most of the others. Rosenberg seems grotesquely out of place in uniform. His imagination was bound to inner struggle, and seems to have found it hard to connect with the war, though 'Break of Day in the Trenches' is one of the best poems here. Two interesting survivors are Ivor Gurney and Osbert Sitwell. Both of them used a plain unpoetic language, which makes an impressive lesson in preservation among the other tainted fruit.

Perhaps what we would like from these poets is fuller descriptive and objective evidence. Except for Owen's pieces (of which the editor excludes half the best and perhaps the most graphic) there is very little. We have to remember how they were taken by surprise. It's that surprise which makes all the difference between the human measure of the first world war and of the second. Four years was not long enough, nor Edwardian and Georgian England the right training, nor stunned, somnambulist exhaustion the right condition, for digesting the shock of machine guns, armies of millions, and the plunge into the new dimension, where suddenly and for the first time Adam's descendants found themselves meaningless.

Tricksters and Tar Babies

In this context, we are not to quarrel with the term 'Literature'. It simply means what would be written down, in the way of imaginative verbal constructions, if the primitive authors could write and if their audience were also readers. We are to distinguish 'Primitive Literature' from folklore. Primitive Literature belongs to primitive peoples, who have no other kind of literature. When such a people acquires civilized techniques and associates, they develop a new sort of literature, in emulation of the most civilized, and their old oral literature degenerates into folklore, a process that can be seen happening now in parts of Africa. John Greenway, who is an Associate Professor of Anthropology at the University of Colorado, the editor of the *Journal of American Folklore*, is concerned with the original primitive thing, the imagination that still shares with its society the one centre of gravity.

He opens his *Literature Among the Primitives* with the question that has puzzled some others of us. Why is the literature of primitive peoples so disregarded? Even in the thriving litter of anthropological studies, it is the rickling. Current textbooks, he notes, give ten times as much space to potsherd analysis as they do to the literature. This volume of his, with its companion anthology of specimen pieces, *The Primitive Reader*, sets out to supply some of the deficit. He addresses himself to the general reader and to students in a popularizing style which his flexible combination of humour, eloquence, enthusiasm and thorough knowledge of the subject, is well-fitted to bring off.

Primitive literature has been unlucky. The recording of it began in earnest in the nineteenth century, but by just those individuals who had come to destroy – deliberately or otherwise – the unique conditions of its flourishing. Missionaries who emasculated all they heard, even when they were eager to hear, or who inspired

Review of John Greenway, *Literature Among the Primitives* (Folklore, 1964) and *The Primitive Reader* (Folklore, 1965), from the *New York Review of Books*, 9 December 1965.

automatic censorship in the narrators; lawmakers who had the same effect, and amateurs who were recording simply the outlines of something curious. When the anthropologists arrived, with few exceptions they were not much better, to begin with, since by cultural tradition and scientific bent they tended to despise these tales as infantile fantasies or – at best – fairytales fit (or unfit) for children. Poetasters and writers for the nursery fell on whatever material got through, and saturated it with nineteenth-century literary manners in which guise it was introduced to the civilized West, adjusted to the circle of Victorian ministers' daughters that corrupted Tennyson. Greenway's account of what happened to some of the North American Indian material illustrates what this meant. Even the popular presentations of the mythologies fared no better. Primitive literature hasn't yet recovered, among the non-specialist public, from this wretched début. That publishers still subscribe to the emasculations and and prettifications and denaturings can be seen from the popular selections that still come out plentifully.

As a result of all that, the mass of the literature has been lost. By the time modern recorders got down to it, with no squeamish reservations and with germanic faith (happily) in the great mystery of accurate detail, the primitives, with few exceptions, had been either wiped out or mentally reconstituted, their literatures dissolved with the natural circumstances and self-confidence that fostered them, and nothing remained but fragments. Still, these fragments amount to an immense and ever-increasing hoard – lying inert in the Departments of Anthropology and the Folklore Libraries. They are lying inert because the anthropologists do not know what to do with them. Nobody knows what to do with them.

There have been several attempts to work them up into interesting and perhaps useful studies, as, for instance, the scholarly speculations about the global travels of story-types and motifs. But these last don't much help the more germane speculation about the travels and contacts of the actual people. When the Bindibu were first discovered in the Australian desert they were using the word 'pudjikat' for a cat. 'Pussycat' had discovered them first. Wherever culture grows, the enigma of spontaneous archetypes and the banality of straight theft are inextricably meshed. *Patolli* was a Pre-Columbian Aztec game, played with flat discs, a scoreboard, a cross-shaped playing board, several men or counters, penalty and safety stations, and the idea of 'killing' your opponent's man when you landed on a square that he occupied. In ancient India the game *Parchisi* was played with the same six characteristics. The odds against spontaneous inventions separately of these two are high enough to force one to other explanations for their similarity. But tracing the paths of cultural diffusion is no more than a briefly amusing game. Frazer, Muller, Jane Harrison, Jung, Graves, Radin, and others that Greenway acknowledges, have put the material to bolder use, but their grand hypotheses proliferate like the tales themselves. Otherwise, those who come under the strong spell of this literature have to content themselves, like the folklorists, with scholarly conversation among scholars, or with the inexhaustible but useful task of codifying and collecting. From all this, the respectable anthropologist, sadly anxious for the scientific repu-tation of his discipline, holds back, as from a bundle of silly dreams. And when you consider that it's common for every primitive narrator to tell a different version of the same tale, and even a different version every time he tells it, there's no wonder the anthropologists have concentrated on other items in their vast Sargasso of miscellaneous unsorted cultural junk.

Still, the tales keep on teasing with all kinds of promises. They are generally regarded as useless for historical research, even where there's no other material. But occasionally historical details cling on surprisingly, as in the accurate accounts of the ancient cities of India that the Rig-Vedas preserved in oral tradition for well over 3,000 years, and which have been finally verified by recent excavations. Greenway mentions other examples. But anyone who tries the experiment of remembering a story, and writing down his memory of it, without reading his earlier versions, once a fortnight for five or six months, will have learned the best lesson possible about oral tradition and the folk memory and even more esteemed styles of history and will sympathize with the anthropologist who stands baffled about how to make scientific-looking contributions out of this literature, and with the Tuomotuan tribal scholar who being caught in an inconsistency stopped and sighed:

> Correct is the explanation, wrong is the lore.
> Correct is the lore, wrong is the explanation.
> Correct, correct is the lore.
> Ah, no!
> It is wrong, it is wrong, alas!

To yield anthropological fruits, these tales and poems call for a more imaginative approach than library anthropology permits. It takes a great tact, and that in an anthropologist who is actually on the spot, among the people who are telling the tales, to divine just how these tales do work for the society they are formed in, how they justify and fortify and explain the prevailing ethos, and just what they reveal that is otherwise secret, the deeper attitudes behind the ones that society sanctions openly. The trouble is, once the tale is brought away, into a book, we have lost that living context, no matter how good the notes are, whereupon that line of study – perhaps the most interesting possible, with this material, within the anthropological field – begins to look a little stale, and we are stymied again.

So what are we to do with them? In the end, there is a great and one would have thought obvious career on which these works have not yet started. Greenway's two books are a vigorous attempt to promote it. This literature is still, after all, what it primarily was – imaginative art, visionary accounts of profound psychological dramas, and entertainment. Life has not really stopped and the world is not really a museum, yet. These tales are as vital for our literature as they were for their own, alive with possibilities. And it is as such that Greenway wishes to introduce them to his readers.

He tours through the principal features of the literature, lingers on the chief protagonists – hero, trickster, tar-baby – and takes in the influences it comes under, and its peculiar reactions, in its ceaseless to and fro migrations through peoples, and the uses to which the various societies put it. All this is done with learning and brio, in a highly readable way not very common in this field. He ranges through all the published material and takes account of the main lines of commentary and theory (the bibliography of works he refers to runs to thirty-three pages), moving easily and even entertainingly through the complexities of the ethnological background, with a profusion of interesting detail and digression, fascinating sections on the Ghost Dance Religion and the relationship of words and music. And very properly – since he's advancing the literature itself, not some theory about it – he includes plenty of the tales and poems on the way. Altogether, this is a first rate introduction to just what is to be looked for in primitive literature, and incidentally covers a good history of anthropology's dealings with it.

But once he sets out to do what no other anthropologist or folklorist has done quite so deliberately – that is, treat this literature as a form of art – his thesis confines itself inevitably to his own standards of literary taste. And it is here, I feel, that with all his goodwill, he still doesn't quite do his subject justice. He is widely read in literature in English, and in his amusing survey of the translations of *Beowulf* he shows an enlightening penetration of the virtues of the original, and a learned impatience with the translators, which gives one great hopes for his personal choice of pieces in his anthology, *The Primitive Reader*. This selection is, in fact, good, and contains excellent things, like the Tongan shape-changing battle, the Dyak story of the origin of jungle leeches, the Ute story of how Trickster married his daughter, the variants on the snaring of the sun and the origin of the Pleiades, the superb West Indian Adam and Eve story, to mention only a few, and each tale is in a setting of copious notes. But it is not quite what I, for one, was hoping for. Somewhere in *Literature Among the Primitives* he makes a disparaging remark about Kafka, so perhaps it's natural that he excludes from his selection any of those tales which are, in my opinion, the most inspired and astonishing, and in a way the most concentratedly characteristic, in the entire literature, and which resemble nothing in Western Literature except Kafka. Paul Radin's collection *African*

Folk Tales and Sculpture contains quite a few of the sort of thing I mean; so does his Winnebago Trickster Cycle, and B. H. Chamberlain's collection of Ainu tales. It is in the elemental autonomy of these pieces that we can detect the seminal thing that in primitive sculpture and primitive music has already operated on us.

Primitive music has altered our world, maybe radically. Primitive sculpture has been one of the chief sources of modern sculpture; it certainly led the way out of the impasse. But somehow or other, primitive literature, of one spirit with the music and the sculpture, has not arrived, not fruitfully. The only instance I know was in the explosive transformation Radin's African collection worked on the poetry of Sylvia Plath.

For the time being, these two books are welcome, as is Greenway's implication that they should be required reading in any English course. If the Duende of Lorca's famous essay is to be found anywhere in a modern library, it is in the section on primitive literature.

Heavenly Visions

Start reading anywhere in this book and you'll find it hard to put down: it's his best comic work, both wilder and more tactfully managed than the comic stuff in *Under Milk Wood* or the stories. Thomas's ordinary personality, that same old self he kept being rueful about, was a comic genius and shared some of the language with his poetic one.

Whenever he turns on the tap, the ideas are there – same family as the ideas in the poems, intricately organic, jumping about in inspired phrases. Somewhere inside his head was a miniature replica of the world, with heavens and hells to match, in a brilliant radiance, slightly caricature, but quite real: it tumbles through his prose. For all his exaggerations, frequently rhetorical tone of voice, posing, the actual substance of Thomas's writing is very concrete. It's this weirdly alive, charmed, coherent world that is the magical attraction behind all he wrote. It shines through the seams of his most perverse and baffling phrases, just as through his occasional tired and mechanical ones. It is the mind behind the work: a very beautiful vision of a crooked, innocent creation.

Many of these letters, and paragraphs in all of them, are prose poems in comic vein. It could nearly be counted against them, this unflagging limelight of style they perform in. But 'literary' isn't the right word for them, even so – except maybe for those obvious purple donations, such as the late pieces to Princess Caetani. With all his highly polished acrobatics and mesmeric passes, he rarely loses the warm, intimate hold he has on his reader, as if he were responding to every flicker of reaction, more like a comedian than a careful writer.

No wonder he mismanaged things, considering the nature and the gifts and the guiding ideas he was stuck with. Assuming that his poetic genius was, for him, the most preoccupying fact of his life –

Review of *Selected Letters of Dylan Thomas*, edited by Constantine Fitzgibbon (London: Dent, 1966), from the *New Statesman*, 25 November 1966.

and I don't think that can be doubted – then the worst enemy was in himself. It was the demon of artistic or rather verbal self-consciousness, his super-ego stylist. He struggled against it, complained of it. At twenty-one he was already writing to Vernon Watkins (who always brings the best out of him):

I'm almost afraid of all the once-necessary artifices and obscurities, and can't, for the life or death of me, get any real liberation, any diffusion or dilution or anything, into the churning bulk of words. I seem, more than ever, to be tightly packing away everything I have and know into a mad doctor's bag, and then locking it all up.

Maybe he never did get out of that bag. The self-consciousness grew and consolidated itself around artistic standards that would make any poet sweat. The suddenly agog audience of *Deaths and Entrances*, and the relentless need, after his marriage, to make cash, and every delay, stepped up the voltage in that horrible spotlight over his worksheets. These letters tell the tale. In the eight years following *Deaths and Entrances* there come only six poems, in spite of his endless struggle to get down to writing. 'Lament' and 'Over Sir John's Hill' are masterpieces, as big as anything he did. But the other four are, for him, run-of-the-mill and weary, and coarse in a new way – one can see the old automatisms deadening against him. In those last poems, and in *Under Milk Wood* and the letters to Princess Caetani, he has been trapped under his carapace, finally immobilized. And the poetry which is, among other things, an escape from personality, was not to be written. The battle he fought with his steadily solidifying poetic style, pushing the adjectives for months at a time to and fro over those hundreds of worksheets, must be one of the keys to his demoralization.

Under Milk Wood was the inevitable and natural form for him. His everyday personality, that gift-of-the-lovely-gab comedian, seems to have been as much as anything else a cloud of surprising and busy voices. Maybe they are what made it so hard for him to listen through to the simple, single, final voice of the real poet. In the series of letters to Pamela Hansford Johnson, where he first settles into his recognizable self, the free-for-all monologue occasionally reminds one of the dogfighting voices in possessed medieval women. The only times he escapes this facetious theatre are when he speaks about poetry – his, hers, or in general. Then suddenly we hear the voice that polished the voices, the demon stylist, a cold, severe, even ruthless sort of person, a voice of settled, radical judgements and godly self-confidence: slightly pedagogue, freezingly objective, aggressively, almost witheringly critical, almost sarcastic, nearly cruel. Clearly enough, an abandoned surrealistic or therapeutic torrent was the last thing Thomas allowed his reservoirs to become.

The compulsive clowning never grows wearisome, not only because it's ring-mastered so artfully. Part of the comic effect is that it's always concealing something unusually serious – in the early years, his poetic gift, ambitions and ideals, and later on his struggle against the odds, the gruelling rearguard retreat towards the eighteen straight whiskies. This is what makes these letters the best introduction to the way his poetry ought to be read. Everything we associate with a poem is its shadowy tenant and part of its meaning, no matter how New Critical purist we try to be. Yeats's life is not the less interesting half of his general effort, and one wonders what his poetry would amount to if it could be lifted clear of the biographical matrix. Quite a lot, no doubt. But how much less than at present! With poets who set their poetic selves further into the third person, maybe the life is less relevant. But Thomas's life, letters and legends belong to his poetry, in that they make it mean more.

His poetic vision undid him. Or the sensitivity and psychic openness that showed him the vision also betrayed him in life. It was a vision of the total Creation, where everything, man and atom, life and death, was equal, and nothing could be ugly or bad, where everything was a vital member of a single infinite being, which he sometimes called God. It was sustained by the circulation of divine energy which he sometimes called love, sometimes joy. It was a morally undetermined, infinitely mothering creation. He had no comments or interpretations or philosophizings to add to it. His poetry was exclusively an attempt to present it. Every poem is an attempt to sign up the whole heavenly vision, from one point of vantage or other, in a static constellation of verbal prisms. It is this fixed intent, and not a rhetorical inflation of ordinary ideas, that gives his language its exaltation and reach.

In his life, the reflex of this vision was a complete openness toward both inner and outer worlds, denying nothing, refusing nothing, suppressing nothing. But the vision included the hells as well as 'the faces of a noiseless million in the busyhood of heaven.' The hells indeed were a favoured part of the task. Poetry, he said, was to drag into 'the clean nakedness of the light more even of the hidden causes than Freud could realise.' He made a half-conscious attempt to take on the underground life that the upper-crustish, militant, colonial-suppressive cast of the English intelligence excludes. It is apt that he seemed physically such a representative of the old Moorish strain of blood in South Wales. Much of his writing and general thinking was a perpetual invocation of the most hellish elementals. And as he said himself, when devils are called, they come. Maybe Yeats could have advised him how to confine their capers to his imaginative works, but it wasn't in Thomas to negotiate or protect himself on this or any other front. All life was one, and he was open to it all, and he'd 'be a damn fool' if he weren't. So the devils, the demands, the responsibilities, distractions, worries, worries and worries took over.

The crucifixion of his last years makes painful reading. Paralysis of the will, inside that circle of ever more rabidly demanding voices, and bedevilment, and the double bedevilments of his consequently frustrated genius, engrossment in his mythological pantheon of the human body – all gradually materialized in outer reality. And the whole lot was fuel to that terrible hot-spot of judgement over the pen on the page, the next word in the line. One wonders what a windfall could have done, or a patron, or an amnesty from the Inland Revenue. Probably not much. What he was really waiting for, and coaxing with alcohol, was the delicate cerebral disaster that demolishes the old self for good, with all its crushing fortifications, and leaves the *atman* a clear field.

Short of that, we can be glad about these letters, the wonderful autobiography in them and the comedy. And he emerges, from all the hunted corners, and from under his bedevilled behaviour, as a much nobler and more likeable character than the Thomas of

Fitzgibbon's biography, a man finally innocent, who had himself sized up quite a bit better, perhaps, than all those friends who found him so hard to take.

The Hanged Man and the Dragonfly

(Note for a Panegyric Ode on Leonard Baskin's
Collected Prints)

*The Sybil, with raving mouth, uttering her unlaughing,
unadorned words, reaches us over a thousand years with her
voice – through the inspiration of the god.* HERACLITUS

*The notion of some infinitely gentle
Infinitely suffering thing.*
T. S. ELIOT

Artistic form is, by definition, a lens, but Leonard Baskin's graphic images seem particularly lens-like. The typically rounded glass-blob outline, and the internal lattice of refracted, converging intensities, which lie there on the paper as a superbly achieved solidity of form and texture, in fact compose a web – a transparency, something to be looked through. The depths are focused right there at the surface – which directs our attention straight into the depths. And that deeper life, in all Baskin's work, is of a peculiar kind.

These images also resemble stained glass windows – not only physically (though they do that too, obviously enough, with their starkly subdivided interiors, their palimpsest of mapped inner regions behind and within each other), but in the way they process our attention. They place us within a sacred building, as if we were looking out through these icons and seeing the world's common light changed by them. Or else they place us outside looking in. Then we see through their symbols still further mysterious business going on round an altar. That deeper life, in other words, is not just deeper than ordinary life, or just more universal. It is elect and consecrated. One hesitates to call it religious. It is rather something that survives in the afterglow of collapsed religion.

This rich inwardness of Baskin's art has many components. Some of the more accessible of these, maybe, can be seen in his graphic style itself, which is so like a signature, so unique to him and so consistent, that it might well interest a graphologist. But the oddities

Introduction to *The Collected Prints of Leonard Baskin*
(Boston: Little, Brown & Co., 1984).

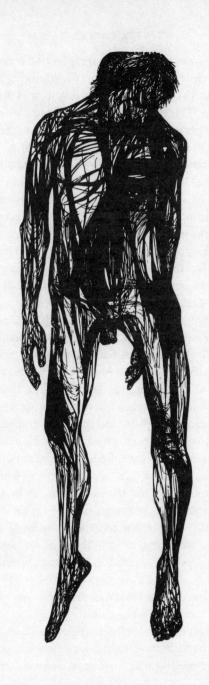

of it hint at other sources. As if a calligraphy had been improvised from the knotted sigils and clavicles used for conjuring spirits, those bizarre scratch-marks of the arcane powers, such as we can find in practical grimoires. This element in his draughtsmanship is no more than a trace, but it peers from every interstice, and suggests a natural psychic proclivity, enough to attune his operation, perhaps, to certain freedoms familiar in Jewish mysticism. A passport between worlds usually kept closed to each other. It is one of the essentials of his work's power to disturb, and of its weird beauty too.

At the same time more identifiably, his style springs from Hebrew script itself – all those Alephs, Bets, Lameds, Yods, crammed in a basketry of nerves, growing heads, tails, feelers, hair, mouths. And the typical lonely isolation of his figures both sharpens our sense of them as hieroglyphs, cryptograms, and intensifies that atmosphere of Cabala, where each image is striving to become a syllable of the world as a talismanic Word – or at least to become a Golem, bursting with extrasensory news, bulging the cage-mesh of lines.

This underswell of divination, which can be felt here and there almost as a pressure, produces wonderfully substantial, living shapes. The context of presentation, so to speak, is three-dimensionally objective – as it is throughout Baskin's art. He regards himself as first and foremost a sculptor, and in all his graphic images the 'wiry, bounding line', the sheer, physical definition, is sculptural. His imagination is innately kinaesthetic. It projects itself exclusively in tensile, organic forms, which are, moreover, whole forms – images of the whole being. At the same time, as he feels out the contours and balance of these forms, he receives an x-ray of their insides. His graphic image reproduces this complex of sensations as a blueprint: the translucent womb-life of an unborn sculpture, flattened onto the paper. Or, even more aptly, as a primitive hunter's x-ray drawing of a creature's essence – its soul or divine image – with vital centres, magical, mythical or astral or future real wounds and the life-mesh meridians all in plan.

As it happens, Baskin has no interest in the worlds of occultism, or in that plane of *participation mystique* which has produced the baffling records of natural man's parapsychological gifts. But this means no more than that he trusts only his own senses. It is unusual to find a pragmatic rationality so powerfully armed and so highly mobilized as his, in a modern artist. He abhors anything that strikes him as an evasion of the real. Most Baskin observers are eventually awed by his powers of destructive derision, and any facile artistic exploitation of the dream world receives his full barrage. Whatever comes under his aesthetic scrutiny is tested first and last for its 'reality'. And by 'reality' he means the ability to stand up in the highest, final court – 'the audit of ultimate reckoning'.

For Baskin, a work of art must have 'real content'. As he makes clear in his various writings, by 'real content' he means the 'physical presence of our common reality – the common experience of our common humanity.' And in the case of his own work he means, more specifically, the physical presence of 'our common suffering.' At this point, a captious critic might be alerted. He might say: 'Considering the nature of Baskin's forms, is this claim of his consistent?' And it is true, what Baskin makes, in his work, of this 'common reality' and 'common suffering', the scope he embraces, the depth he searches, the specific pain he locates, the light he casts on what he finds, and his treatment of it, presents us with what we might well call *uncommon* forms.

At the centre of his workshop stands the human figure, sure enough. But it is a figure in a perpetual flux of transmogrification. Other existences seem to compete for its substance. Owls, crows, angels, demons, mythical personages and half-monsters, see-ers, death apparitions – all press to assert themselves in that afflicted lump of ectoplasm at the heart of his opus. Their manifestations take up a goodly part of his output. He obviously feels compelled to give these *dramatis personae* their forms. But (remembering his own words) what sort of reality, what sort of content, can such entities deliver?

To understand the consistency which fastens his words and his images together, in this context, is to turn a key. Once that key is turned, the full psychological depth of his work can be explored.

And to turn it, perhaps, all we need is to bear in mind that Baskin is rabbinically trained, saturated with esoteric Jewish tradition. This tradition (which has indirectly supplied us, it could be argued, with the most extreme forms of scientific materialism) takes full account of all occult possibilities, and even gives most of them the benefit of the doubt. It is open, that is, on principle, to all that can happen on every imaginable level of human awareness. And it holds that what happens on one level affects all the other levels, with real consequences. It is a tradition in which the human body is the sole register, the only whole and adequate symbol, for the workings of an all-inclusive hierarchy of spirit life – an intricately organized universe of ghostly beings, conditions, powers, susceptibilities, attributes of every kind. As Jewish imagination has sustained it right up to the present, it serves as an accumulator of the full resonance of Jewish experience – an electronic archive of the inner life, as it has been lived out, and paid for, by Jews, such as no other nation possesses: a total system of coherent and workable signs. The goblins and spectres that crowd its magnetic fields are not the *ignes fatui* of folk superstition. They are minor functionaries in the oldest and most resolutely-fought court-case, still unfinished, in the judgements of God. This inheritance is as decisive in Baskin's work as it is in the achievement of that other giant among modern imaginations – Isaac Bashevis Singer. Baskin's sceptical eye, as I have said, is remarkably wide awake, but in fact it guards his inward, learned Jewishness, which is busy dreaming for him, in a rigorous, divining fashion, as it is also suffering for him. There is a patriarchal prophet among his hidden resources, as there was a Sufi master among those affable familiars of W. B. Yeats.

This tradition is the updated Witch of Endor's cave from which Baskin's forms rise. And what they soon tell us is – that they are drawn from the hard core of human pain. Each one embodies that compound of intimate, secret suffering and spiritual exultation which is Baskin's speciality. All his images, without exception, are precipitated out of this, as crystals out of a supersaturated solution. Even his birds and angels are solid and sharp with the salts and metals of it, they have the chemical composition and crystalline structure of it. Once absorbed through the eye into the nervous system they dissolve back into the real knowledge and presence of it.

[88]

Without any doubt, this is 'real content'. But it is not all. His images bear witness to the 'horror' within the created 'glory' (two terms much employed in Baskin's lexicon), as our common humanity undergoes it. But there is still much more to them. Above all, and before anything else, they are beautiful. This is the first and last fact about Baskin's art: it has a peculiarly intense kind of beauty.

It is an odd paradox. He records, in what we feel to be a coolly objective way, a shocking experience of life, as it occurs somewhat behind the face, as it might return at night to one who thought he had escaped and blessedly forgotten it – returning intact, worse, more dangerously connected, more deeply involved with friend and enemy, more open to things beyond the soul's reach, but in some symbolic form, as a distorted mask simply, a sidelong look, a blank, deadpan face, or a dream shout that stays in the waking mind as a lumpish humanoid crouched there on the threshold. Yet this is the very figure he makes beautiful.

This startling, sinister beauty, characteristic of all his works, cannot easily be called 'content'. Yet it is something more than style, something other than the masterful technical expertise that gives his image the foot-poundage of its striking power and penetration. The subject matter of his image may shock us, and his phenomenal technique may overpower us, but this other thing does not attack in any way. It summons us very quietly. But more and more strongly. In the end it makes us seek his work out as if we needed it, and makes us cherish it, as some source of elixir, long after more documentary or photographic evidence of 'our common suffering' has become a sad blur.

Again remembering Baskin's own criterion, we should ask, perhaps, just what sort of 'reality' this beauty has. What weight of 'necessity' – another favourite word of his – presses behind it? And being so paradoxical anyway, as a beauty created so openly and directly out of pain, it challenges us to examine it more closely.

Baskin writes of his ideal image as one that seems to have lain in the earth for generations, re-emerging now with all its temporary cultural superficies corroded away, so that only some core of

Sketch of the Aztec sculpture of Coatlicue
in the Anthropological Museum in Mexico City

elemental artistic substance remains. It is interesting to put one of his own images to this test, in imagination, so far as one can, and to superimpose a typical Baskin figure, say 'The Hanged Man', on a related image from another culture. In my own mind I associate that giant woodcut with the statue of Coatlicue, the colossal, horrendous Aztec mother and earth goddess, which stands in the Museum of Anthropology, in Mexico City.

'The Hanged Man' holds a special place among Baskin's graphic works. It was his first fully mature, large-scale piece (1954), and it was like the herald of everything he has done since. One might say, it was the whole new thing itself, like a tight-wrapped seed.

Once we bring these two forms together, a lively field of force springs into place between them and round them, uniting them. And the Hanged Man becomes the archetypal victim of the Mother Earth Goddess in her most horrifying aspect – as a Death Goddess in fact. He becomes, like crucified Jesus, a figure nailed to his mother, sucked empty by his mother, paralysed by the clasp of her extraordinary gravity, borne through timelessness in a trance of mother-possession, in death-like communion with the goddess of the source, a figure rooted in the womb, as if rooted in the earth or death. The cadenza on these themes develops itself.

But there is something through and beyond that. Something that both the Hanged Man and Coatlicue carry equally, neither male nor female, common to both, which is as well symbolized by a dangling, flayed man's corpse as by that contained eruption, that nuclear Aztec war-head.

Baskin himself might say: It is the *horror*. (And he would quote his favourite line from Conrad: 'The horror! The horror!'). But what exactly is it, here, that horrifies us?

It isn't only the gruesome pain of the flayed man, or the macabre grotesquerie of the divinity that requires it. 'The Hanged Man' is certainly an image of pain. Even – of absolute pain, pain beyond flesh: ineffable, infinite affliction of being, from the dumb mouth of which the foetus hangs like some roping coagulation.

There is something beyond that pain of the Hanged Man and beyond the fact that Coatlicue is one hundred and fifty tons of rattlesnakes and skulls in a symmetrical, molecular combination.

New art awakens our resistance in so far as it proposes changes and inversions, some new order, liberates what has been repressed, lets in too early whiffs of an unwelcome future. But when this incidental novelty has been overtaken or canonized, some other unease remains. At least, where the art is serious and real (one supposes, major) it remains. An immanence of something dreadful, almost (if one dare say it) something unhuman. The balm of great art is desirable and might even be necessary, but it seems to be drawn from the depths of an elemental grisliness, a ground of echoless cosmic horror.

The mystery of music opens this horror as often as we properly hear it. Perhaps music holds the key to it. If, as we are told, mathematical law is the tree of the original gulf, rooted outside the psychological sphere, outside the human event-horizon, and if music is a sort of nest, the consolingly-shaped soul-nest, that we feathery and hairy ones weave out of the twigs of that tree (audial nerve sunk in the mingling chorales of the body's chemistry), then the horror which wells up out of music is also the sap of mathematical law, a secretion of the gulf itself – the organizing and creative energy itself.

In all art, everything that isn't the music rides on the music. Without that inner musicality of every particle, art ceases to do the work and have the effect and retain the name of art. And so the very thing that makes it art, that gives it the ring of cosmic law and grips us to itself and lifts us out of our egoistic prison and connects, as it seems, everything to everything, and everything to the source of itself – is what makes it unpleasant.

Whatever this musical influx may be, human societies are apparently not too sure about it. A capricious cycle of opening to let it in, and closing to shut it out, shapes the history of every culture. It is as if it were some ambiguous substance, simultaneously holy and anathema, some sort of psychological drug flourishing in the bloodstream. Lorca gave it a name, calling it the Duende, when he described how even in one person, in one half-minute, it irrupts from the faintest titillation to the soul-rending. In his Arab-Andalusian setting he shows how naturally it can be taken for God – a divine horror – a thunderbolt beautiful and terrible.

And he makes the suggestive point – that it seems to come from 'beyond death'. As if he meant that it comes from 'beyond life'.

Yet it is the core of life, like the black, ultimate resource of the organism. Maybe that is why it rouses itself only in an atmosphere of crisis, at extreme moments. Or in the individual, it may be, who somehow lives a perpetual 'extreme moment' – not of heightened powers of life, but of dead man nakedness, dead man last ditch helplessness, dead man exposure to the crowding infinities, getting to his feet only as a Lazarus, having had life stripped off him, as in those skinned figures of Baskin's, and the ego and personal life plucked out of him, through the strange wound in the chest.

This Duende-music, or music within music, or ectoplasmic essence or whatever it is, has a more familiar role as *mana*.

Mana comes to the sufferer, it is said. Maybe *mana* is the body's natural response to grave hurt – a healing. Which would make it, more than metaphorically, redemption incarnate. And all historical cultures agree, it is purchased by suffering. And it has to be paid for. Some people seem to get it – or take it – and pay later. Or pay invisibly, perhaps. Normally, payment comes first. It is a curious circumstance, a technical discovery, that deliberately self-inflicted suffering will buy *mana*. The sufferer suffers till *mana* can't hold off any longer – and so surrenders and heals the sufferer – and remains, it seems, at his, or her, disposal. Like those Indian gods who play deaf to the mortifications and ordeals and cries of the suppliant, till they can't stand it any longer – the stones of their heaven begin to sweat, their thrones begin to tremble – whereupon they descend and grant everything. And the suppliant becomes Holy, and a Healer.

Or they descend earlier and grant not quite so much.

However it is obtained, and in whatever intensity, *mana*, and the roots of music, and healing, are all mixed up in the same medicine, which oozes from that tree in the gulf.

We can only guess at the significance Coatlicue held for the men who carved her. She is a giant, composite word of Aztec hiero-glyphs, a monstrous *quipu* of religious and mythological conun-drums for anthropologists. But her power speaks for itself. She is a daemonic lump of *mana*, a petrified mass of grotesque music, like an irruption of dancing electrons into our sensual world – a titanic snake of solar magma, knotting a likeness of limbs and face to itself as it congealed.

It is the very image of *mana*, the embodiment of pure *mana*. *Mana* as the goddess of the source of terrible life, the real substance of any art that has substance, in spite of what we might prefer.

The Hanged Man is also an image of *mana*: all hanged gods, hung on a single rope, strung from a single hook, in the flesh of a skinned man. Not quite Coatlicue. Though she is crusted with the flayed and the self-flaying – with skulls and serpents – Coatlicue is obviously neither flayed nor strung up. She is a solid plug of magma shouldering through the basalt.

If the Hanged Man is also an image of *mana*, it is *mana* with a difference.

Other parts of Baskin's oeuvre help to define what is going on within 'The Hanged Man'. Among the varied range of his images, there is a quite large and notable category that bears no taint of the supernatural, no evident burden of the symbolic. Among these are the etched insects, in the book *Diptera*, which close the present collection. If we imagine 'The Hanged Man' at one pole, then the opposite pole might be occupied by one of these insects – maybe by the 'Dragonfly.' It is very relevant, in any interpretation of 'The Hanged Man', to ask how this Dragonfly fits into the global wholeness of Baskin's work.

The Dragonfly does seem beautiful in an undisturbed way – at first sight. Precisely observed, densely moulded, solidly realized, compactly beautiful. As an expressive image, does the Dragonfly say more than that it is very beautiful? Is paradise all around and inside dragonflies? Or has Baskin himself escaped, for a while, from that consciousness where his other images suffer – into this little redoubt of precarious bliss?

And the Dragonfly isn't alone. Baskin's later work is richer and richer in the flora and fauna of the natural world delineated just as objectively as the 'Dragonfly,' and always with marvellous, luminous intensity. How do such things fit into the single organism of his work? Because it *is* a single organism. I have called it global in its wholeness, but it is also organically articulated, and that *mana* circulates through every cell of it, and the whole creature has a single purpose.

The clue to the role of the Dragonfly, in his work – and of every other image in that class – is in the palpable fullness of *mana*. In the daemonic intensity – one might say, the daemonic beauty – of the object. Without any distortion of symbolic intent, the Dragonfly nevertheless performs the heroic role in this Mystery Drama. And that is, the protagonist as a consecrated being – as *the* consecrated being. What brings it into relationship with the Hanged Man is the peculiar sacramental act, the beatification, which it has undergone.

At their opposite poles, the Hanged Man and the Dragonfly can be seen as the beginning and end of a process of transformation. But the whole process is there at the beginning inside the Hanged Man, and it is still there at the end inside the Dragonfly. As if one examined these two images made of light through opposite facets of the one crystal. The same might be said for every other image that Baskin has created. Each one resonates with this same process as if they were all clones – which cells of a single organism are. And that sacramental process, which culminates in that dark radiance, which we recognize as the beauty of his art, is the essential task of his genius.

We can look into this task more narrowly, perhaps more deeply, and can come maybe to some sense of the biological weight of necessity behind it, if we think of his graphic line as an image in itself – his fundamental image.

Does this line attack, as it seems to, or does it suffer under attack, as again it seems to – or with subtle sleight of hand does it manage both simultaneously?

As a thing in itself it has a certain glamour of deadliness. An uncanny sort of grace, raptorial. Maybe all those massively-taloned birds fly up out of the line's exultation in its own hawkish-owliness.

At the same time, the line is above all delicate. And a real wound. At one moment a sensor, alert for floating particles. At the next – a deep astonished cut just about to bleed. A pain-diviner, and a pain-fathomer. The spirit of the blade of the burin, but also of the scalpel – operating, as a rule, on a naked torso, a face.

The blade and the wound: simultaneously male and female. It is a common mythological and folklore motif that the wound, if it is to be healed, needs laid in it the blade that made it.

As if the blade might cut to a depth where blood and cries no longer come – only *mana* comes.

Baskin writes, somewhere, that his subject is the wound. One could as truly say that his subject is *mana*. His real subject is the healing of the wound.

Throughout Baskin's artistic life, he has drawn strength from the kinship he feels with William Blake. One clue to this link is their preoccupation with the Book of Job. Both artists share a biblical concern for what Blake called the human form divine. It is prophetic concern. Since Blake's day, the disasters of the human condition have become more explicit, maybe more inescapable. To the apocalyptic eye (and all Baskin's work assumes an apocalyptic eye), the human form divine – formerly the responsibility of religion – is now a universal casualty. He tries to get to his feet after the nuclear shock-wave – the atomization of all supportive beliefs – and responsibility for him is blowing in the solar wind.

That ravaged, emptied figure appears everywhere in contemporary art. But directly abreactive art is one thing, redemptive art quite another. Baskin's jeremiads against contemporary artists are notorious. He sees most of them as little more than fragmented, convulsive reflexes, after the explosion. Or as zoologically primitive forms after some disruption of the ozone layer: a teeming of random mutations in the genetic melt-down, a forlorn hope of irradiated chromosomes scrabbling for the new terms of adaptation, in the new conditions of maelstrom firestorm.

But these holocaust conditions are the very ones within which Baskin's art has evolved. Like the fourth figure in the burning, fiery furnace, it has become visible to the human eye, at the side of the condemned, only in this degree of spiritual catastrophe.

What Baskin has done could seem to be inevitable – if the resurgence of Nature's powers is inevitable. He has salvaged that responsibility for the human form divine, and bestowed it again – on art. An art that has been qualified by a course in surgery. What religion once did is now, it appears, the work of an improvised field hospital. And the Hanged Man, the century's flayed victim, lies there on the operating table.

The human form divine has become the wound. The biggest wood-engraving ever made up to that point in the history of Western art ('The Hanged Man' is nearly six feet high), is the portrait of a total wound – head to foot one wound.

And it is here, in this woodcut, in the actual work of the blade, that we can find the meaning of Baskin's line. With deep labour, he is delivering his form from the matrix. He is liberating a body from the death that encloses it. Inevitably, one imagines a surgeon's tranced sort of alertness, as he cuts. Baskin's electrocardiograph, and the surgeon's, at the moment of incision, must be very alike. And as the scalpel cuts, *mana* flows. That is, seen from our point of vantage, beauty flows. As if the blade, in prayer, were less a honed edge, more a laying on of hands – a blessing – a caress – and a glorification. The steel, under Baskin's care, is a balm flowing into the wound.

It really is very like worship. Do you worship a wound, or rather, what is wounded, to heal it? Yet the healing does happen. We are talking about an art, after all, that has consummated its purpose. Is it less of a miracle, if it happens in art, than when it happens under the hands of the rural healer – the rough hands that pass over the wound without touching it and send a shiver through the human form, while all who witness it, when it succeeds, want to laugh and weep with amazed feeling?

And the Hanged Man really is healed. When we acknowledge the beauty, so complete, in that delineation of agony and death, we have recognized the triumph of *mana*, the musical release and emanation of *mana*, that lifts this corpse into the force-field of cosmic law – which only incidentally, and to our unaccustomed eyes, wears the illusion of horror. It is as if Coatlicue, or her equivalent, had lifted up this hanged, flayed god-man. And her *mana* suffuses him. From whichever side we look, it is a pietà. In the religion, with the dead, everliving god, it is *the* religious moment. In the woodcut 'The Hanged Man', it is *the* aesthetic moment. As if the Muse of this art were only another aspect of the mother of that god.

But in Baskin's imagination the Hanged Man is evolving further, and becoming something else too. That moment of redemption, where healing suddenly wells out of a wound that had seemed fatal, is not enough. The beauty of it has to blossom. The dead man has to flower into life. And so this skinned carcass, so wrapped and unwrapped in its pain, is becoming a strange thing – a chrysalis. A giant larva. And under Baskin's continuous concentration – the labour of his arduous life – it emerges, at last, as a Dragonfly.

This completes the cyclic process within Baskin's art.

The Hanged Man is a symbol of the first phase: mana nursed from agony. And the Dragonfly is a symbol of the last phase: the agony wholly redeemed, healed – and transformed into its opposite, by *mana*. The old terms of suffering have become the new terms of grace. The Hanged Man has become the Dragonfly without having ceased to be the Hanged Man. This is the healing operation of *mana*, in front of our eyes. Of a very great, concentrated density of *mana*.

There is a miracle in this, and the work seems to me miraculous, in the sense that healing is miraculous. And again, if one says: 'But it's only in art', what is that 'only'? The operation of art comes to the same thing, whichever way we describe it. Whether we say that it enacts, in a home-made Mystery Drama, the most important event of all – the birth, in 'hard and bitter agony', of the creative, healing spirit, the nativity of the redemptive divine gift, or that it demonstrates the biological inevitability of art, as the psychological component of the body's own system of immunity and self-repair.

So when we question the peculiar beauty of Baskin's art, and ask what order or 'reality', what degree of 'necessity' there is behind it, the answer is to be found here: in this act of consecration made perfect.

The Hanged Man himself is in some way exultant, even jubilant. He's almost ribald, the gallows joke to end all gallows jokes.

His figure is a parable. All Baskin's figures are, in one way or another, parables – reminiscent of those Hasidic or Sufi parables: each simple-seeming confrontation is a *trompe l'oeil* of perspectives, at a crossroads between different planes of experience. And in this parable of the Hanged Man, after the judges have stopped laughing, and the torturers, the hangman, the skinners, the soldiers and the survivors, after they have all stopped laughing, their ears prick. The corpse, the skinless cadaver itself, has begun to laugh. Lorca did not find a more satisfying image of the Duende.

And then – in this revelatory parable – the judges cry out and fall in the dust, like Saul on the road, while the torturers, the hangman, the skinners, the soldiers and the rest, roll on the ground and grind their teeth and cry out like those tribesmen the astounded archaeologist Layard describes, hearing the epic song of the Bedouin poet in the tent.

The impact of the Hanged Man, on his own wavelength, is like a sacred shout. In some shrine, some underground chamber of the religious mystery beloved by Aeschylus, one imagines a stunning, end-of-all-things cry at the death of the god – which is also the cry of incredulity, the ecstatic outcry at his simultaneous resurrection.

Those feelings actually do flash through. The step-down transformers we've installed in our frontal lobes, at such cost, still register the input. The nerves have looked in a mirror, and the experience whizzes just past the skull, leaves a faint sweat over the brow, probably measurable electrostatic changes, even as the observer says: 'I don't like it.'

The Hanged Man's laughter, that flinging off of everything, deep down among the roots of the unkillable thing in nature, is the voice of *mana*.

Baskin's work in sculpture is monumental. Monumentality, as he has said himself, is one of his sculptural preoccupations, and it affects many of his prints. The facial expression of all his figures, for instance, tends to be monumental. Typically, his large figures embody an Egyptian burden, the mass of indestructible matter, after some harrowing Aztec initiation. Humanoid, emerging out of Einstein's shadow, out of a cauldron of atoms – like a projectile from space, flayed and half-molten, some sort of cry arrested before it reaches the paralysed lips, the eyes catatonic with the shock of arrival into the skull – but taking the first human step, materializing there on the threshold, begging for a name.

This figure has immensity. The bronze-like or stony fragment of the universe, its mantle of substance, gives it immensity. And it has glory. It clutches, like some perilous crumb of radium, immortal flames of Eros. And it has tragic pathos. Its planetary physical mass, so loaded with fate and momentum, and that draughty, flamey sun-scrap of glory, are exacting their price. The pinched, stricken face is fully aware of the price. And as the features become more human, the cosmic loneliness becomes more frostily awful, and the pathos more acute.

Nevertheless this figure insists it is a Prometheus, a Job. And if it could speak, or more likely sing, we would hear the full, balanced chord of epic.

Epic is the story of *mana*. The morphology of epic, its recurrent pattern of recognizable episodes, emerges wherever the saga tells, in one metaphor or another, of the search for and the finding of *mana*.

To a surprising degree, when one examines it, Baskin's imagery can be seen to revolve around the epic archetypes. If epic has three historically familiar forms, with religious quest as the most civilized form, and heroic epic as the barbaric form, and the shaman's dream of his flight as the prototypical and, as it were, biological form, then Baskin's imagery derives abundantly from all three. Everything in his gallery of images belongs to epic's adventurous, imaginative penetration through suffering into the land of death, or into a land beyond life. The infernal or purgatorial circumstances of so many of his figures, souls in carnal torment, bodies in spiritual torment, plentiful officers of heaven and hell, mutilated torsos, terrible warriors, glimpses of Paradise, supernatural women, monstrous beings, personalities from sacred and mythical history, herbs of everlasting life, hallucinatory apparitions of death – all these obsessive themes of his are epic stock. And his most favoured images, his most personal, the forms he returns to as if to renew his energies – the birds, the bird-men, the vatic figures, and not least the death-trance as a portrait of the communion with ultimate reality, truth and the divine – all these come straight from the shaman's dream-journey, from his difficult take-off and flight, through obstacles and ordeals, to the source of renewal. In fact, these particular items have no other cultural context – except maybe for that transcendental role of the corpse, which has been requisitioned by all sacrificial religions.

All this is inevitable, since what Baskin's work has in common with all three forms of epic is that fundamental scenario of the quest for *mana*. By confining his procedure to a detailed surgery of organisms, in the spirit of the immediate crisis, he has kept his operation hard-edged and hard-headed, ironic, usually witty even when he pries deepest among the nerves. But *mana*, meanwhile, has carried him away on a long journey, down the archaic lines of the palm, and he has returned with all the traditional experiences of the shaman's entranced flight, which has always recurred, and presumably will go on recurring, spontaneously, wherever individuals are overloaded with private pain or tribal calamity. It is no coincidence that Baskin belongs to the very people which, in his generation, met the full ferocity of our mid-twentieth century head on, and rising out of their own ashes mastered it, and after two thousand years restored Israel.

The pattern of unity in Baskin's art, or that part of it which I have been able to glimpse and to sketch out, as I understand it, finds its fullest, most poignant verbal expression in the Book of Job. The fullest in our culture, at least. I say, our culture. I should say, Baskin's culture. And the Book of Job is like the hidden masterplan behind everything he produces. It aligns all his images in their right relationships to each other and to the source of his inspiration. And it sustains the grand dimension of feeling and statement in which he casts his forms.

This kinship to the Book of Job suggests what part his art performs in the contemporary drama of Western spiritual morale, and gives us some bearing on the scale of his endeavour. As the sacerdotal trappings and hangings and dogmas melt, or evaporate, in the enlightenment of holocaust, Christianity burns down to its root in the aboriginal Jewish rock. As if the soul, which was for so long, in Western terms, 'naturally Christian', had fallen from that dream of the Cross. Coming to consciousness in the ashes it finds itself to be, after all, Jewish too, and cognate with naked Job, if not Job himself. Job, the human form divine, pure and simple. The naked child of an infinitely glorious, infinitely terrible Creator.

By just such shifts as these, maybe, Baskin, a healer and an Elihu of the modern cataclysm of Jewishness, comes to find, lying under his blade, the casualty of a revelation that seems universal – the 'human form divine' of all men and women.

The Great Theme:
Notes on Shakespeare

The reasons for not reading Shakespeare's Complete Works seem to be many. Few of us ever get beyond the seven or eight popular plays, and when we feel like more Shakespeare we re-read these. So most of his vast following meet:

> Time hath, my lord, a wallet at his back . . .

or

> With fairest flowers
> While summer lasts and I live here, Fidele . . .

as if their greatest poet had suddenly up and published a new volume. This selection is intended mainly for their pleasure.

It might be asked, whether these passages do not just collapse, like pulses plucked from the body, when we lift them out of their context.

It is true, the play binds the words magnetically, decides their meaning and polarity, seals them off from ordinary life, consecrates and inspires them. Reading them in context, we look through them into the action and life of the play, a wonderfully well organized circuit of interior illuminations, to which all the complexities of the words are aligned with such subtle accuracy it seems miraculous, and which is a bigger poem in bigger language and of greater beauty than any brief isolated passage of verse could possibly bring into focus. Out of context, we have to admit, they are different words. Fallen from the visionary world of the play, they have to make their meaning out of the rubbish-heap and more or less chaotic half-digested turnover of experience, the flux of half-memories and broken glimpses, in their reader at the moment of reading. And suddenly we notice what densely peculiar verbal poetry they are. We

Introduction to *A Choice of Shakespeare's Verse* (London: Faber and Faber, 1971).

see quite new things in them, a new teeming of possibilities, as we look through them into our own darkness.

So in separating these passages from the plays, we lessen their poetry but we liberate something in the activity of the language. Entering the world of ordinary poets and poetry, they become more common to the language in general and more personal to us.

And so in a way we gain a poet, a whole poet where before we had only one of his hands – i.e. the smaller and different poetry of the sonnets, which is the early or marginal work of this worldly, one might almost say devilish, Shakespeare, whom now we draw a little out of the heavenly one, where he wasn't so visible and where he was spellbound. And we leave the higher poet unimpaired after all. Reacquaintance with his lesser self here opens directly to his greater self there. The Complete Works are still intact.

In selecting, I have kept to passages of top pressure poetry which are also long enough and self-contained enough to strike up a life on their own. This has cut my choice down quite a bit. I doubt if many passages could be added (at least from the plays after *Measure for Measure*) without moving out into what is more diffuse (plenty of that), or less self-contained (the great passages in the death-scenes of *Antony and Cleopatra* for instance) or more fragmentary (*passim*, overwhelming abundance). As it is, several of the plays have supplied nothing at all.

In spite of its Elizabethan ruff, Shakespeare's language is somehow nearer to the vital life of English, still, than anything written down since. One reason for this is that it is a virtuoso development of the poetic instincts of English dialect. Even his famous pincer movement, where he contains an idea with a latinate word on one wing and an Anglo-Saxon on the other, is an innate trick of fluent dialect. The air of wild, home-made poetry which he manages to diffuse through a phenomenally complicated and intellectualized language, and which makes the work of almost any other poet seem artificial, derives also from another dialect instinct, which is the instinct to misuse latinisms, but in an inspired way. This is really a primitive, unconscious but highly accurate punning. A familiar example would be the notorious 'aggravate'. In its vulgar use, this means 'to goad beyond endurance', which is not merely a Joycean fusion of irritate, anger, exaggerate, but a much deeper short circuit to the concrete Anglo-Saxon 'gr' core of growl, grind, eager, grief, grate etc. The word inherits a much more powerful meaning by this wrenching misuse in English than by its precise use in its Latin sense. Shakespeare is doing this, just slightly, constantly, and it is this, as I say, more than anything else, which gives his language the air of being invented in a state of crisis, for a terribly urgent job, a homely spur-of-the-moment improvisation out of whatever verbal scrap happens to be lying around, which is exactly what real speech is. The meaning is not so much narrowly delineated as overwhelmingly suggested, by an inspired signalling and hinting of verbal heads and tails both above and below precision, and by this weirdly expressive underswell of a musical neargibberish, like a jostling of spirits. The idea is conveyed, but we also receive a musical and imaginative shock, and the satisfaction of that is unfathomable. Just as in real speech, where what is being said is not nearly so important as the exchange of animal music in the voices and expressions. In so far as he is a master of this, Shakespeare's language is not obsolete so much as futuristic: it enjoys a condition of total and yet immediate expressiveness that we hope sooner or later to get back to, or forward to, without the incidental archaisms.

Such considerations are what prompted me to make this selection in the first place, to bring the verse from under the dramas and their funereal pyramid of theatre conventions, and to present some of the best of it straight.

The fragment of a long poem does not become a short poem. It remains a fragment, its elements are not balanced within itself, and so it excites a sense of unease. In a selection such as this, that sensation will have to be allowed for. The devilishness of many of the greatest passages (most of those, in the later plays, which are not spoken by somebody possessed by some murderous wickedness or illusion, or spoken by somebody just exorcized – such as Othello's, 'Soft, you, a word or two before you go . . .' and Macbeth's, 'Tomorrow and tomorrow and tomorrow . . .' and so on) is, in the context, controlled and usually balanced (though not always, not in *Macbeth*, for instance) by the rest of the play. We are here plucking out Shakespeare's heart, and if it has a black look it is as well to remember that most readers have decided the plays are healthy.

Selecting, as I have done, for poetic intensity, length and completeness, has had one result that might surprise some readers. The passages that answer these requirements nearly all have a strong family likeness, especially those coming from *Hamlet* and the plays after. It is impossible not to recognize what looks more and more like a simple fact: whenever Shakespeare wrote at top intensity, at unusual length, in a burst of unusually self-contained completeness, he was almost invariably hammering at the same thing – a particular knot of obsessions.

In other words, the scope and variety of the plays conceals what a selection of this sort makes nakedly plain (so naked that one almost has doubts about the propriety of it) – that the poetry has its taproot in a sexual dilemma of a peculiarly black and ugly sort. And when we look further, we see that whatever else the plays take account of, they are also doggedly bent on analysing and exploring that same dilemma.

This might be thought belittling and a disappointment, a pointless thing to do, to bring Shakespeare down to a single fundamental idea. However, singleness can be all-inclusive. In this case, the singleness is the plan Shakespeare made of his own nature, as he unearthed it. And even he had only one nature. Even Shakespeare, finally, was stuck with himself.

His single fundamental idea, then, is the symbolic fable which nearly all his greatest passages combine to tell, and which each of his plays in some form or other tells over again. This was the way his imagination presented the mystery of himself to himself. It was his great recurrent dream. And it so happened that his nature was such and the time was such and the place was such that this symbolic form of his nature – his deeply divided nature – appeared to him, when he exploited it for drama, as a problem – the posing of a chronic sexual dilemma, a highly dramatic and interesting collision of forces.

It might be said – every poet does no more than find metaphors for his own nature. That would only be partly true. Most poets never come anywhere near divining the master-plan of their whole make-up and projecting it *complete*. The majority cling to some favoured corner of it, or to remotely transmitted Reuters-like despatches, or mistranslate its signals into the language of a false nature. Shakespeare is almost unique in having unearthed the whole original thing, learned its language, and then found it such a cruel riddle that he could not rest from trying to solve it. Dramatists in those days were prolific, but it was evidently something more than commissions that roused him to mount thirty-eight or more such tremendous and tormented campaigns.

The fragments of this skeleton-key fable are visible enough in the early plays. *Titus Andronicus* has all the elements but cannot quite fit them together. They provide the great things in the Histories and gradually dominate the essential shape of those plays (the shape we remember) in the polar opposition of Falstaff and Prince Hal. A curious thing happened when he turned aside to write the two long poems, *Venus and Adonis* and *The Rape of Lucrece* – in 1592 and 1593. Here, where nothing but poetry concerned him, he immediately produced the whole fable beautifully intact and very precisely analysed. Then again it went underground. The Comedies toy with fragments of it – fragments which gradually become too awful to toy with. Such plays as *The Merchant of Venice*, *Julius Caesar*, *Romeo and Juliet* and *Troilus and Cressida* seem to be holding it off – as if its magnetic shape were trying to overpower their shape. It can be seen clearly enough through them.

This fable was evidently Shakespeare's poetic powerhouse. He was able to reveal it in full in the poems, but in the plays only in so far as he managed to poeticize the dramatic action. But then, with *Hamlet*, some sort of mental revolution occurred. Suddenly he discovered the difference between a poetic drama and a dramatic poem. Instead of using the poetry to explore the drama he discovered how to use the drama to explore his poetry – to explore, that is, his poetic fable.

Probably a truer way of saying that would be to say that this poetic fable which was the groundplan or blueprint of his imagination came to such importance that instead of allowing itself to be exploited any further by formal dramatic subjects, it commandeered all the means, took the centre of the stage and expressed first and foremost itself. With *Hamlet*, in other words, this fable becomes the main subject. And it remains so for all the subsequent plays. There is every sign in *Hamlet* that the fable surfaced before Shakespeare was ready for it, and that he rewrote it over a longish period, as it kept bursting his controls at every point. Nevertheless, it is here in *Hamlet* that his poetic and dramatic interests converged. At the same time all the elements of his poetic style converged: the great mature style, on which he was to work all his later modulations, was suddenly there full-fledged.

What the arrival of this fable amounted to can be judged if we imagine Shakespeare dying in the middle of writing *Troilus and Cressida*. If that had happened, a play like *Hamlet* would be inconceivable. But once we have *Hamlet*, we can see how every subsequent Shakespeare play has all its work cut out to consolidate or rearrange or take to the limit something of what appears in that work.

I have made this fable sound very private to Shakespeare. Fortunately, we cannot know what the private aspect of it was. But the public aspect is wide open. With the dynamo of any poet – any unusual poet – it is impossible to tell which is decisive, whether the peculiar forces of his time or his own peculiar make-up. One imagines that it is only those poets whose make-up somehow coincides with the vital impulse of their times who are able to come to real stature – when poets apparently more naturally gifted simply wither away. This was evidently enough the case with Shakespeare. As will be seen, I trust, when I come to outline it, this fable of his, this very private assembly of his deepest obsessions, reflected perfectly the prevailing psychic conflict of his times in England, the conflict which exploded, eventually, into the Civil War.

Elizabeth's reign seems to have been overwhelmed with events, with turmoils of all kinds, at every level, as hardly before or since, and it is easy enough to show how any of these influenced Shakespeare. But the strongest single determinant of a person's poetic imagination is the state of negotiations between that person and their idea of the Creator. This is natural enough, and everything else is naturally enough subordinate to it. How things are between man and his idea of the Divinity determines everything in his life, the quality and connectedness of every feeling and thought, and the meaning of every action. So we needn't be surprised if the ground-plan of Shakespeare's imagination very closely fits the groundplan of the religious struggle which – history tells us convincingly – embroiled every fibre of Elizabethan life.

In this struggle between radical Calvinism and the Reformed Church (at the head of which stood the Queen), the Calvinists, or Puritans, intensified their efforts throughout Shakespeare's life (their first real demonstrations occurred in 1564, and in Warwickshire of all places), claiming that the Reformation in England had been mismanaged, that it had done no more than replace the Pope with the Queen, and that all the old evils remained.

Things were further complicated for Elizabeth and her subjects, by the circumstance that the Queen of England was already, automatically, the representative of the old goddess – the real deity of Medieval England, the Celtic pre-Christian goddess, with her tail wound round those still very much alive pre-Christian and non-Christian worlds. That goddess had been naturalized into the old Catholicism as Mother Mary and Satan. Mary Tudor had been the first to inherit the double burden – the goddesses of both religions. The fusion of the two in one person happened all the more naturally in that the Isis behind the Virgin Mary and the Celtic goddess behind Medieval England had originally been one. Mary Tudor's bad luck was that she came at a moment when the opposition of the Nonconformists, pushing to complete the Reformation, drove her to react from the Satanic side of the old goddess, earning the name Bloody Mary, and making the identification of the Catholic Crown and the old Mediterranean serpent goddess, the Anathema of the Old Testament, all the more obvious and terrible and unforgettable in the Puritan mind.

From this complex of accidental but nonetheless deeply symbolic circumstances, the Reformation in England, as it defined itself from the 1560s in the gradual rise of Puritanism, together with its accompanying materialist and democratizing outlook and rational philosophy, had very specific consequences. But the most important of these, as far as Shakespeare's poetry is concerned, was the drastic way the Queen of Heaven, who was the goddess of Catholicism, who was the goddess of Medieval and Pre-Christian England, who was the divinity of the throne, who was the goddess of natural law and of love, who was the goddess of all sensation and organic life – this overwhelmingly powerful, multiple, primaeval being, was dragged into court by the young Puritan Jehovah. It was a gigantic all-inclusive trial: the theology of it was merely the most visible face of the social revolution included behind it. Throughout Shakespeare's lifetime, this was the Civil War within every citizen, as the two fought it out. They brought up every resource. Everything had to be remembered, every argument tried, every scrap of evidence displayed. This grand spiritual courtcase is one chief source of the ferocious Elizabethan energy. And Shakespeare's plays are the fullest record of the opening collisions. And just as fully they predict the close.

Sometimes Revolutions explode too quickly for poets to get much out of them. The forces that make the Revolution make the poet, then explode and disperse into changed circumstances, leaving the poet either dead or obsolete. Shakespeare was luckier. Queen Elizabeth held off the explosion as long as she lived. Managing to keep herself from being too closely identified with the Satanic side of the old goddess, and encouraging her identification with the Heavenly Gloriana side, she held a balance of indecision right up to her death in 1603, by which time Shakespeare was thirty-nine. This suspended conflict, intensifying all the time, forming the minds of all her subjects, formed him too. Long before she died fears of religious Civil War were common, and the steady advance of the Puritan sympathy was as evident among the best of the courtiers – Sidney,

Bacon, Essex, for instance – as among those crazy visionary extremists who proclaimed William Hackett 'the new Messiah and King of Europe' in 1591, in Cheapside.

When Elizabeth died and James her successor openly threw his weight against the old goddess and all her idolatrous witcheries, we can imagine how in a real sense the conflict within individuals went out of control. On the level of such events, every man is a microcosm of the nation he belongs to, whether he likes it or not. A divine representative of Jehovah, a Jehovah in fact, had actually and symbolically displaced the goddess. The job of suspending civil war now devolved on each individual. Everybody went to right or left. Or, if they were simultaneously too deep in both worlds – the old medieval goddess's world and the world of the new Jehovah – they could do something imaginative. They could create a provisional *persona*, an emergency self, to deal with the crisis. They could create a self who would somehow hang on to all the fragments as the newly throned god and the deposed goddess tore each other to pieces behind his face. And this is where Shakespeare's hero comes staggering in. Mother-wet, weak-legged, horrified at the task, boggling – Hamlet.

Very much as in Ancient Greece, it was the moment for tragedy: the agonies of an ancient Dionysus in a world of suddenly hardening sceptical intellect and morality.

To see how Shakespeare's fable is shaped by this battle between these two, and to see how in turn it shapes the plays and supplies the greatest moments of the poetry, we need to look first at the two long poems – *Venus and Adonis*, 1592, and *The Rape of Lucrece*, 1593.

At first glance, each of these is the obverse of the other. In the first a love-goddess – *the* love-goddess – tries to rape Adonis, a severely puritan youth. In the second, the lust-possessed king, Tarquin, rapes the severely puritan young wife, Lucrece.

The puritans here are simple figures – simply excessively puritan: and their arguments against the world of lust take up much of the length of these very long poems. The other figures are more mysterious. Venus is not only the goddess of love, she is the Queen of

Heaven, whose doves are the original ministers of grace. The kinships of mythology came as naturally to Shakespeare as the kinships of all other forms of metaphor. She is also the Queen of Hell, in which aspect her wild boar is the demon of destruction and death. In that form she is also Hecate, goddess of witchcraft, all magical operations, the underworld, spirits, the moon, darkness, hounds etc. As Venus, again, she is also Isis, mother of all the gods, and all living things: she is Nature.

Tarquin is as complicated, but of slightly different dimension. He is of course a Divine King – but he is not really the rightful King. His divinity is therefore suspect. He is a King by regicide: he got his throne by killing the rightful King. Moreover, the King he killed was his father-in-law, which brings him close to patricide. In raping Lucrece he kills her, in that his action destroys her. In destroying her, he effectively destroys the divine kingship within himself.

Once we have seen that the two poems are each other's obverse, in the fairly mechanical way common in mythology, we can see that they are also, in a deeper sense, complementary. In the first, the Divine Power in female form offers her love with such fullness and intensity that ordinary defensive humanity does not know how to accept it. In the second, the Divine Power, enraged after rebuff, in male and destructive form (Mars is the Shiva behind the boar and behind Tarquin), completes the visitation fatally. This shift from loving female to angry male is a regular sequence or oscillation in religions, and very relevant here.

Now perhaps we can see how the two poems are, in fact, the two unjoined halves of a single story. And the story these two halves make is Shakespeare's fable – his major discovery, the equation on which all his work is based. But the most inspired piece of intuition in the whole assembly, the mechanism on which the dramatic development depends, is still absent. It occurs in the gap between the two poems. If there were no plays, that gap would be a problem. But from the evidence of the plays we can see that the gap corresponds to a strange sudden transformation, a frightening psychic event. It is not only – in a sense – the key to the madness of the Civil War, a madness which bewildered all participants, it is the mainspring of every play, from *Hamlet* on in the Complete Works.

Shakespeare himself seems not to have understood exactly what it was until *Measure for Measure*. After his fable had surfaced so violently in *Hamlet*, and overpowered him, he got his discovery at a distance, and put it on ice, and analysed it as coolly as possible in detail – with evident horror – in *Measure for Measure*. And it is in *Measure for Measure* that we see most clearly what is missing from the broken joint between the two long poems.

In this play, Angelo, the chronic puritan, polices a city which is a stew of sexual corruption – wholly given over to rampant Venus. Isabella, a perfect Lucrece figure, about to enter a nunnery, pleads with him for her brother's life, whose sin has been innocent lust. In other words, the chaste puritan pleads for the natural sin of her own blood. This situation, where the beauty descended from doings near heaven pleads the cause of physical love with the critical puritan, closely corresponds, obviously enough, with the situation in *Venus and Adonis*. The arguments are the same, and carried on with the same almost repulsively obsessive zest. Angelo, like Adonis, rejects her, and Isabella, like Venus, persists.

At this point in the play, Shakespeare shifts his gaze a little, and we see that something is happening to Angelo. Virtually only one big thing happens in *Measure for Measure*, the whole play is a device for focusing our attention upon it, and it is now happening to Angelo. A demon has arrived. Angelo is suddenly, and dead against his will, 'inflamed by Venus'. Angelo is no longer Angelo. His brittle puritan mask is split – and another being emerges. At the same point, in the parallel story of the long poem, Adonis has ceased to be Adonis. In his case, Shakespeare is younger and things occur at a more mythical remove. The dream still stands in its symbols uninterpreted. But a demon has arrived there too – in the shape of a boar. Adonis is suddenly destroyed by Venus in her infernal aspect, as a mythographer might say – he is taken possession of by Venus as the Queen of Hell. The brittle puritan gentleman ceases to be. In his place we have a flower. This blood-splashed flower is what stands in the gap between *Venus and Adonis* and *The Rape of Lucrece*.

Meanwhile, Angelo, destroyed only in his mask, has emerged as a lust-mad tyrant. His affinity to Tarquin is close. He rules – but he is not the rightful ruler. And now his lust has usurped the place of rule. As with Tarquin, it is the woman's very purity, her chastity, her freedom from lust and her opposition to it, combined with the dumb appeal of her physical beauty, which have inflamed him. Like Tarquin, he is ready to do murder, if she will not submit. Like Tarquin, he wants everything to be performed in dead secret, under cover of darkness. And like Tarquin, as it turns out, satisfaction will leave him quite a different person, a stranger to what he has done.

The boar that demolished Adonis was, in other words, his own repressed sexuality – crazed and bestialized by being separated from his intelligence and denied. The Venus which he refused became a demon and supplanted his consciousness. The frigid puritan, with a single terrible click, becomes a sexual maniac – a destroyer of innocence and virtue, a violator of the heavenly soul, of the very thing he formerly served and adored. Adonis has become Tarquin.

This metamorphosis is triggered by a simple and one might think academic factor: namely, Adonis's Calvinist spectacles, which divide nature, and especially love, the creative force of nature, into abstract good and physical evil. Nature's attempts to recombine, first in love, then in whatever rebuffed love turns into, and the puritan determination that she shall not recombine under any circumstances, are the power-house and torture-chamber of the Complete Works.

And the vital twist, the mysterious chemical change that converts the resisting high-minded puritan to the being of murder and madness, is that occult crossover of Nature's maddened force – like a demon – into the brain that had rejected her. Hamlet, looking at Ophelia, sees his mother in bed with his uncle and goes mad; Othello, looking at his pure wife, sees Cassio's whore, and goes mad; Macbeth, looking at the throne of Scotland, and listening to his wife, hears the witches, the three faces of Hecate, and the invitation of Hell, and goes mad; Lear, looking at Cordelia, sees Goneril and Regan and goes mad; Antony, looking at his precious queen, sees the ribaudred nag of Egypt betraying him 'to the very heart of loss' and goes – in a sense – mad; Timon, looking at his loving friends, sees the wolfpack of Athenian creditors and greedy whores and goes mad; Coriolanus, looking at his wife and mother, sees the Roman mob who want to tear him to pieces, and begins to act like a madman; Leontes, looking at his wife, sees Polixenes's whore and begins to act like a madman; Posthumous, looking at his bride, who of his 'lawful pleasure oft restrained' him, sees the one Iachimo mounted 'like a full-acorned boar' and begins to act like a madman.

Shakespearean lust, this boar of blackness, emerging to do murder, accompanied – as a rule – by various signs of a hellish apparition, and leagued with everything forbidden,

> Perjured, murderous, bloody, full of blame,
> Savage, extreme, rude, cruel, not to trust. . . .

combines with the puritan mind – a mind desensitized to the true nature of nature – and produces this strange new being: Richard III, Tarquin, Hamlet, Angelo, Othello, Macbeth – men of chaos.

The peculiar fact is, that it is just this man of chaos – from Aaron to Caliban – who is the mouthpiece of the poetry. Looking through the great passages, one sees that the mass of them belong to this possessed homicide – either in his full rage, or just after. If he does not speak them, they describe him.

This man of chaos is the killer of the King or the murderer of the woman, or both. As can already be seen in the long poem, the Lucrece figure, throughout the plays, is identical with the figure of the Kings – with the divinity of the Kingship, in the sense that these two, the angel maiden of pure love and truth, and the Divine Hero of perfect order and justice, are the inner and outer of a single principle. The Tarquinized figure murders both: killing either, he destroys the other. Destroying one in principle, he destroys the other in fact, and vice versa. Throughout the plays, the rapes or murders of the maiden are simultaneous regicides – destroying the divine rule of order. The regicides are all simultaneous rapes – destroying the divine principle of love, truth and innocence.

This is the secret of one of Shakespeare's greatest strokes of genius. When this suppressed Nature goddess erupts, possessing the man who denied her, and creating this regicidal man of chaos, Shakespeare has conducted what is essentially an erotic poetry into an all-inclusive body of political action – especially that action in which a rightful ruler is supplanted by a half-crazed figure who bears in some form the mark of the beast.

In those two long poems, then, Shakespeare established his four poles of energy – Lucrece, Venus, Tarquin, Adonis – as phases in a narrative cycle: Venus confronts Adonis, whereupon Adonis dies through some form of destroying tempest and is reborn, through a flower death, as Tarquin, whereupon Tarquin destroys Lucrece (and himself and all order). The plays rearrange these four poles in all manner of combinations, in what looks like Shakespeare's attempt to reverse the decision – pronounced so emphatically in the two long poems and in each subsequent play up to *Timon* – against Adonis and Lucrece. Each play represents an increasingly desperate effort to lift an increasingly ideal spirit of Lucrece from an increasingly infernal cauldron of sexual evil. Parallel to that runs a steady effort to save Adonis, somehow or other, from the boar. It is interesting to watch how – after *King Lear* and its equally horrible afterbirth *Timon* – Shakespeare suddenly steps back and relaxes the pressure. *Coriolanus* is the first play where the Tarquinized Adonis finally refuses to go through with it. From that point, Shakespeare begins to modify the crime, and we begin to call what he then writes 'romances'. In these plays the young women, murdered by madmen or tempest, do not actually die – they reappear to forgive the criminal and make him happy.

What Shakespeare records, apart from the agony of all parties, is the gradual defeat of Venus and the Boar. Behind him, as he progresses from play to play, the relentless alchemy of the puritan elements are defining and refining themselves in the spirit of the whole nation. His tragic hero, the puritan Adonis possessed by the demon he rejects, and thereby suffering some bond of allegiance to all four principles – Adonis, Tarquin, Venus and Lucrece – struggles to reconcile them and is unfailingly torn apart.

Hamlet is Adonis, half-possessed by Venus (his black suit), refusing to become Tarquin complete. His madness is the first fear of the rip in his mind – through which the boar will enter. When Ophelia dies her flower-death, we know it has happened: Hamlet must now act out his Tarquin destiny – but in full consciousness, and resisting all the way, and never quite ceasing to be Adonis. It is the death of Adonis in very slow motion.

He reappears, greatly fortified on the military side (after the impressive lesson of Fortinbras) as Othello. Othello, man of decision, is in a much more critical condition of possession by Venus, the blackness by now having penetrated his skin and changed his nature to primitive African under a Christian veneer. In other words, he is an over-ripe Adonis, at the point of splitting and becoming Tarquin. He is Tarquin contained by the thinnest skin of Adonis. This play enacts a much closer analysis of that moment of changeover. Othello is going to prove, with enormous care and concentration, that Desdemona actually is Lucrece. But the critical, cynical puritan argument (which Hamlet still had *inside* his head) is outside of Othello, yet still not completely shed, in the person of Iago – in the last moments of goading Othello to explode into Tarquin and be torn to pieces.

He reappears, almost at once, as Macbeth. Shakespeare limits this play to a close-up of that vital moment – the switch from Adonis to Tarquin, a magnified, slow motion close-up of what happened in the gap between the two long poems, a microscopic analysis of that flower springing from the blood of Adonis, a continuous explosion, Macbeth emerging from the rags of a former Adonis in a cloud of bloody blackness. The blackness, too, is analysed and it turns out to be Macbeth's state of possession by demons – actually by his wife, behind whom stand the three witches, behind whom stands no other than Hecate herself – Venus in the underworld. This is the full-length portrait of the Shakespearean moment. Adonis, fully conscious, and dead against his will, understanding just what it means to become Tarquin. Macbeth's horror at himself, as the change works, is the greatest horror in the plays.

In *King Lear*, Lear, after his transformation in the first act, gives up the struggle to reconcile the warring fragments. He simply leaves everything to them, delegates the responsibility, and blows away empty from the resulting explosion. This play is an immensely magnified close-up analysis of the inevitable destruction of Tarquin.

If Shakespeare's fictions were experiments with certain forces, it must be admitted that his results stood the test of actuality. From this collision of Puritan and Medieval goddess he found this consistent third figure emerging, performing consistent actions, in an upheaval of imageries of Civil War and murdered women. The history of the time was not an experiment, yet in the generation of Shakespeare's children a man did emerge, in an upheaval of Civil War and an epidemic of murders of women, one who killed the King and usurped his rule – an Adonis who, confronting the Old Goddess, became a Tarquin. Cromwell's horror at what Divine Possession compelled him to do is amply recorded. The cunning historical passage between him and Shakespeare's nightmarish upstart is perhaps even more direct. About the time of the first production of *Macbeth* a little boy dreamed he would be King of England. He told his puritan schoolmaster and was flogged for it. Was the juvenile Cromwell enjoying Shakespeare's revelation by telepathy, or was it simply a breakthrough of the national dream that everybody except Shakespeare and the little boy Cromwell was trying not to dream? Was it the spirit of that third being, emerging from the deadlock of religious oppositions, trying to get into life, first through Shakespeare, then – frustrated by mere fictions – through Cromwell?

Such correspondences are as intriguing as they are mysterious. Whatever else they mean, they give some hint of the depth and seriousness of the forces that were putting the pressure on Shakespeare, as they struggled to rehearse their roles in imagination, before they possessed men and stepped into life.

Cromwell took up the fable. The goddess who appeared to the young Shakespeare, *passim*, as Venus, ended up as Sycorax, banished from Setebos, or rather, as Delilah and Satan and the female spirit in general, thrown into the bottom of hell by the puritans, as the Protectorate's Secretary Milton faithfully recorded. The Shakespearean fable, in other words, is really the account of how, in the religious struggle that lasted from the middle of the sixteenth century to the middle of the seventeenth, England lost her soul. To call that event a 'dissociation of sensibility' is an understatement. Our national poems are tragedies for a good reason.

What sealed the disaster, as far as later ages are concerned, was the flukish character of the Restoration. The King's return to the throne, when it occurred, restored a court that imposed the mid-century tastes of the French Court on the literacy and manners of a nation whose radical Englishness it had every reason to fear. The success and really amazing suddenness of that takeover can be seen well enough, where the prose of Milton was replaced overnight (the same night that Urquhart, translator of Rabelais, died of laughter – one can imagine that laugh, which he thought was joy) by the prose of Addison, which in all essentials is still our cultivated norm.

It was even worse bad luck for Shakespeare's language that the crippled court-artifice of Restoration speech should have been passed on to the military garrison of the Empire, where the desirable ideal of speech for all Englishmen became the officers' mess and parade-ground system of vocal controls which we inherit as Queen's English.

Shakespeare's persistence has to be admired. After all his experience of the odds against the likelihood, he did finally succeed in salvaging Lucrece from the holocaust and Adonis from the boar. He rescued the puritan abstraction from the gulf of Nature. He banished Venus, as Sycorax, the blue-eyed hag. He humbled Tarquin as Caliban, the poetry crammed half-beast. And within an impenetrable crucible of magic prohibitions, he married Lucrece (Miranda) to Adonis (Ferdinand). But what a wooden wedding! What proper little Puritan puppets! And what a bitter expression on Prospero's punished face. We know why he wants to drown his book in the sea (where Venus was born – the lap of Creation) – it contains the tragedies, with their evidence.

After Shakespeare's treatment of it, we can more easily see why the religious conflict did embroil every fibre of ordinary life. The plays demonstrate how it became, at bottom, a sexual dilemma. A historical development that worked itself out in theology as a war over metaphysical symbols, worked itself out in the imagination and nervous systems of individuals as a war over 'the dark and vicious place', a struggle over the fallen body, and a final loss of the creative soul. When the physical presence of love has been degraded to lust, and forbidden lust has combined with every other forbidden thing to become a murderous devil, life itself has become a horror, the maiden has become a whore and a witch, and the miraculous source of creation has become the empty hole through into Nothing. The extremes oscillate, in the treacherous lens of those puritan spectacles, like an agonizing optical illusion. And it is in striving to hold them steady, and measure them one against the other, that Shakespeare finds his greatest moments of poetry.

Inevitably, his fable takes account of other parallel worlds of experience, besides the state of religious feeling in his day. It is a perfect example of the ancient Universal shamanistic dream of the call to the poetic or holy life. It embodies the groundplan of major religions. It dramatizes the biological polarity of the life of the body and archaic nervous system and the life of the reflective cortex. In more concrete form, the fable contains hints of atavistic memories from earlier times, resurfacings of rituals and symbols of which Shakespeare cannot have heard or read. Knowing how deep a not especially gifted schizophrenic can dive for material, one would not readily set limits to Shakespeare's secret flights. It may be, that all these are the valuable and timeless things, and the religious confrontations of his own time are irrelevant, except in so far as they sensitized him to these deeper patterns, for which he found, in his fable, the master skeleton-key, opening energies and illuminations that make him seem, compared to other poets, a species on his own.

I would have felt happier as an editor if the Shakespeare who wrote at top poetic pressure, and at length, and in form suitable for this selection, had ranged over a greater variety of subjects and moods. If the Shakespeare, for instance, who wrote the great speech 'Be absolute for death' had gone on giving us similarly ripe, leisurely digressions, ranging over the abundance he had shown himself master of in *Troilus and Cressida*. But *Hamlet* was already written, or was being written. The great theme had surfaced: the pressure was on: digressions were over.*

* The 'great theme' of this Introduction was later developed into the full-length study: *Shakespeare and the Goddess of Complete Being* (London: Faber and Faber, 1992). The new, enlarged edition of *A Choice of Shakespeare's Verse*, published by Faber in 1991, carries a different Introduction which examines more closely and at length the characteristics of Shakespeare's poetic language and verse.

Orghast:
Talking without Words

In the summer of 1971 I worked with Peter Brook and Geoffrey Reeves and the actors of the International Centre of Theatre Research, based in Paris, on making a dramatic production, which used archaic and invented language, out of Prometheus Bound, *the Manichean cosmology, Persian and Japanese folktales, Calderon's* Life is a Dream, *and several other elements. The final play was titled* Orghast *– which was a word meaning, among other things, 'sun' in the invented language. It was performed at the tomb of Artaxerxes II and the cliff-tombs of Xerxes and Darius at Persepolis, in Persia, as part of the Fifth Festival of Arts of Shiraz which opened on 29 August 1971.*

We can define truth baldly as 'what is and what happens'. But when a man tells a lie, it actually does happen that he tells it, and that is a truth. His awareness of telling the lie is another truth. The truth he conceals, but knows about, is another truth. The consequences of his lie, which follow mechanically in his conscience, which he perhaps doesn't know about, are another truth. Other hidden feelings of the moment, which used the material of the lie to express themselves slyly yet perhaps quite boldly, are another truth. And so on. In one lie, there speaks a whole family of truths. His words shape the lie, but the truths speak through distortions of his vocal chords, his expression, his gestures, and by some electrical flash that we call telepathy.

Bigger truths speak just as surely, and just as oddly. A strange quality of truth is that it is reluctant to use words. Like Cordelia, in *King Lear*. Perhaps the more sure of itself a truth is, the more doubtful it is of the adequacy of words. This struck me forcibly once when I was collecting material for what I hoped would be a long poem about the campaign on Gallipoli during the First World War.

From *Vogue*, December 1971.

I read memoirs and histories, eloquent and detailed. But however eloquent and detailed such writings are, one always half dismisses them, because they are inevitably false. The actuality must always have been different – in every way that really matters.

I had an enlightening experience talking to two of the survivors – one eloquent, one taciturn, both unsophisticated serious men, and they talked about the war in general. The eloquent one had been badly wounded, the other one only slightly. Yet from the eloquent one I seemed to get very little, merely anecdotes. From his mono-syllabic friend something so frightening and terrible came over, that even now I remember that man's memories with caution. Both had lived through and registered the same terrific events. Yet words and natural, narrative, dramatic skill concealed everything in the one. While in the other, exclamations, hesitating vague words, I don't know what, just something about his half movements and very dumbness released a world of shocking force and vividness.

The same principle works in all sorts of situations. At every point, a man's deeper sufferings and experiences are almost impossible for him to express by deliberate means. The immense literature of such things is almost totally unreal. For a man even to know what he really wants, is beyond him. He tries to be sincere, and he sounds falser than ever. He swears he will dig out his real true feeling, and he flounders from shape to shape in a fog. He gets hold of what seems like the real thing, and he vows 'this *is* it' – and he might even start building a life round it, to fortify it, to make sure of it. But then another contrary feeling snakes up and says 'what about me?' and another 'what about me?' and another 'and me?' and 'we're all you, too.' In the end maybe he sits despairing under a brawl of voices – all falsehoods, but all ringingly sincere, and all absolutely serious, so alarmingly serious, one of them might even control a pistol. Yet none of these is 'it'. None of them is the 'real' him. Then some stranger comes along and hears his voice in the next room, or sees him coming in through the door, or getting up smiling to shake somebody's hand – and in a flash they know him perfectly, as if they knew what to expect of him in every situation. It happens like that. And almost inevitably closer acquaintance proves sooner or later just how accurate that first flash vision was. The real self, the one the man himself could not find, spoke loud and clear through his whole being. Or maybe just through a flicker in his voice. And this man, composed entirely of life-size truth, managing these incomprehensible, concrete, final circumstances of life, survivor of incomprehensible birth, life-prisoner of incomprehensible death, he might write a fearless novel or a hardgoing philosophical treatise or a heart-searching book of poems every two or three years for thirty years without setting down one live or true word.

He is just like the rest of us. His real life, with all its real knowledge, is somehow locked up in him. It is responsible for everything he does, and it suffers the consequences, yet he's shut out from it, in an effective way. And the mind he has, no matter how clever, seems to be no key to the door. Then most action becomes some sort of attempt to smash a way in to the locked up life. Psychoanalysis becomes a popular liberation front, and art (and particularly drama) a specialized one. And society is in perpetual turmoil with the efforts of this huge suffering lump of vital shut-away truths to escape and speak, and with our efforts to release it and hear it.

Yet this creature of truths, which provides most of the excitement in our lives, is only halfway to the truth we really need. There is another person, another being, much more important, of much greater truth, beyond this one. If this one finds it so difficult to speak his truth, what about the further, deeper one? And if this one is so hard to get to grips with, how far away from us is that other, hidden beyond and beneath?

And in fact this other rarely speaks or stirs at all, in the sort of lives we now lead. We have so totally lost touch, that we hardly realize he is absent. All we know is that somehow or other the great, precious thing is missing. And the real distress of our world begins there. The luminous spirit (maybe he is a crowd of spirits), that takes account of everything and gives everything its meaning, is missing. Not missing, just incommunicado. But here and there, it may be, we hear it.

It is human, of course, but it is also everything else that lives.

When we hear it, we understand what a strange creature is living in this Universe, and somewhere at the core of us – strange, beautiful, pathetic, terrible. Some animals and birds express this being pure and without effort, and then you hear the whole desolate, final actuality of existence in a voice, a tone. There we really do recognize a spirit, a truth under all truths. Far beyond human words. And the startling quality of this 'truth' is that it is terrible. It is for some reason harrowing, as well as being the utterly beautiful thing. Once when his spirits were dictating poetic material to Yeats, an owl cried outside the house, and the spirits paused. After a while one said: 'We like that sort of sound.' And that is it: 'that sort of sound' makes the spirits listen. It opens our deepest and innermost ghost to sudden attention. It is a spirit, and it speaks to spirit.

Sometimes singers have this elemental, bottomless, impersonal, perfect quality, which seems open to the whole Creation, but they are usually old men, singing very ancient songs, or women who sing like mediums, possessed. Children acting sometimes have it, and it is the distinctive thing in the recorded chanting of religious texts, where they are distinctive at all, or in the recorded singing of primitive holy men. In all these, that lost spirit being opens a door to a world of spirit – nothing else, it simply opens a door, and that other world is present. And it is as if the whole Creation were suddenly present.

And sometimes actors have it. It not only speaks, it moves – a particular quality of movement, or of action, can announce its presence as distinctly as a sound. The sole original purpose of the sound and action of poetic drama was to engage that world, open it, and act out its pressures and puzzle over its laws. In a play of that sort, properly performed, the poetry of the words is unimportant. What is important about them is that they should speak with everything else, where everything is speaking together, every muscle, every inflection, every position. The incidental verbal poetry of true poetic drama is the least poetic thing about it.

At least, that is the sort of drama I have always imagined as an ideal. I never thought I would see it in English, because it would need such ideal, unlikely actors, and above all a director who not only wanted what I wanted, but knew how to get it. And I could never imagine what language would carry it.

In this kind of special drama, the real poetic potential would lie in the physical events, which would be of a special sort, and in the pattern of their sequence, but above all in the actor. That actor is the problem. It has never been my illusion that the theatre should belong to the writer. The theatre belongs to the actor. Perhaps that means, given the necessary nature of actors, that it also belongs to the director who trains them. But an inspired director is helpless if the actor is closed. Finally everything depends on what the actor finds, and how purely he can release it. If he is empty, or just full of ordinary stage vanity, then the greatest text in the world becomes empty, or just full of ordinary stage vanity. To sensitize an actor to the poetic reality of a situation, so that he can open it wide and release it purely, is a matter of immensely arduous psychic tempering, because no actor alive retains the selfless innocence that would enable him to do it naturally. To teach him to do what almost nobody can do, to teach him to become the vehicle for a spirit, not for a bundle of repressed passions, but for those powers much closer to the source, that speak and move so strangely, but who supply everything finally that we really want and need, and who once we have met them threaten to make our whole life seem trivial and false, that is almost impossible. But not quite. It is possible, because here and there for seconds at a time, on this stage or that, we have seen it done, or something so close to it that it is better than anything else.

When Peter Brook invited me to join him in the experimental production that eventually became *Orghast*, I knew he thought much as I did about these particular things. It soon became clear that he had been preparing his actors for months to explore just the sort of acting I have been describing. But not only that. His strong hermetic drive towards a spiritual intensity is counterbalanced by an instinct for the all-inclusive, Shakespearean style of dramatic world, a giant rag-bag of everything possible, a colliding place of all human energies and all polarities. And his experimental imagination and skill, which open away out of sight in all directions, are also, in the final reckoning, completely pragmatic. He would correct my statement about the theatre belonging to the actor. He would probably say the theatre at any given moment during a performance belongs to the momentary combination of everything in the theatre, and a good deal of what's outside the theatre also, and a good deal of what's gone before the moment and what's coming after: and that combination has to work at that moment.

How my thoughts mingled with his, in the text we gradually produced for *Orghast*, how we deprived the actors of every source of facile verbal association, facile verbal concealment of the deeper kind of truth that we wanted to release, and how we plunged them in a sequence of events that put the special training – for some of them – literally through the test of fire, and how we hammered it all into one and a quarter hours of what came repeatedly and for long minutes very close to what we were after, that riveting near-holy or unholy experience where, as the Bible says, 'a spirit passed before my face, the hair of my flesh stood up' – all that is a more complicated story.

The Environmental Revolution

Perfectly timed, and with an unusually qualified author, *The Environmental Revolution* manages to be several things – and all of them are important.

Basically, it is a history of Conservation, worldwide and from the beginning. It includes a detailed survey of the movement in modern times in the US and in Britain, where most of the pioneering work was done. The author goes on to a wider account of the largely successful attempts to make the movement international. He gives a full picture of how things stand at the moment, and projects vivid panoramas of the earth's alternative futures, which are now within the power of man to choose. The earlier phases were comparatively simple – in England the enlightened care of the land by pre-nineteenth century landowners, and in the States the setting up of the first National Parks. The later phase has become vastly complicated, and involves the salvaging of all nature from the pressures and oversights of our runaway populations, and from the monstrous anti-Nature that we have created, the now nearly-autonomous Technosphere. From being the high-minded vision of a few rich and powerful men, Conservation has become the desperate duty of everybody. Max Nicholson is the perfect authority on all this. He was the Director General of the Nature Conservancy from 1952 to 1966, and the list of International Commissions, Projects, Committees, Research Programmes, Councils, Conferences and the rest, in which he has taken a frequently leading part, makes a reader wonder how one man could ever have fitted it all in. He reveals a world of Conservationists which is enormously active and energetic, involving great numbers of people. Yet why does his account come as a surprise?

This surprise is a measure of two things – the ordinary public ignorance of the issues at stake, and the failure of the Conservation-

Review of Max Nicholson, *The Environmental Revolution* (London: Hodder and Stoughton, 1970), from *Your Environment I*, Summer 1970.

ists to make those issues known. The public ignorance is also a deep resistance, of course. We have a biologically inbuilt amnesia against the fears of extinction. And hunger and greed will always sacrifice almost anything. And most people have already more than enough to worry about. The failure of Conservationists to publicize their anxieties, nevertheless, is not so easy to understand. To most of the world, Rachel Carson's *Silent Spring* came as an absolute shock. What has followed it, in the same vein, has been mainly the work of casual journalists. After ten years, the evidence of that book has not reached the average gardener, and it has changed the doings of the average farmer only so far as it changed the laws which in turn have forced him to change. The colossal mass of evidence simply has not been marshalled and sent to the one front that counts: the ear of the public. But there is more to it.

The fundamental guiding ideas of our Western Civilization are against Conservation. They derive from Reformed Christianity and from Old Testament Puritanism. This is generally accepted. They are based on the assumption that the earth is a heap of raw materials given to man by God for his exclusive profit and use. The creepy crawlies which infest it are devils of dirt and without a soul, also put there for his exclusive profit and use. By the skin of her teeth, woman escaped the same role. The subtly apotheosized misogyny of Reformed Christianity is proportionate to the fanatic rejection of Nature, and the result has been to exile man from Mother Nature – from both inner and outer nature. The story of the mind exiled from Nature is the story of Western Man. It is the story of his progressively more desperate search for mechanical and rational and symbolic securities, which will substitute for the spirit-confidence of the Nature he has lost. The basic myth for the ideal Westerner's life is the Quest. The quest for a marriage in the soul or a physical reconquest. The lost life must be captured somehow. It is the story of spiritual romanticism and heroic technological progress. It is a story of decline. When something abandons Nature, or is abandoned by Nature, it has lost touch with its creator, and is called an evolutionary dead-end. According to this, our Civilization is an evolutionary error. Sure enough, when the modern mediumistic artist looks into his crystal, he sees always the same thing. He sees the last nightmare of mental disintegration and spiritual emptiness, under the super-ego of Moses, in its original or in some Totalitarian form, and the self-anaesthetising schizophrenia of St Paul. This is the soul-state of our civilization. But he may see something else. He may see a vision of the real Eden, 'excellent as at the first day', the draughty radiant Paradise of the animals, which is the actual earth, in the actual Universe: he may see Pan, whom Nietzsche, first in the depths, mistook for Dionysus, the vital, somewhat terrible spirit of natural life, which is new in every second. Even when it is poisoned to the point of death, its efforts to be itself are new in every second. This is what will survive, if anything can. And this is the soul-state of the new world. But while the mice in the field are listening to the Universe, and moving in the body of nature, where every living cell is sacred to every other, and all are interdependent, the Developer is peering at the field through a visor, and behind him stands the whole army of madmen's ideas, and shareholders, impatient to cash in the world.

The history of Conservation is also the history of this opposition against it. Nobody understands the enemy better than Max Nicholson. For much of his life, his task must have seemed impossible. What good is 1,000 miles of preserved coastline, when the sea is a stew of poisons and nuclear waste? He probably knows the wage of the contractor who dumps the poisons and the waste. He knows the kitchen-gardener who finds it easier to scatter poison for the slugs – poison which goes into the soil, the water and the birds – than to kill them with sunken saucers of sugared beer. He knows the ordinarily pig-headed Civil Servant who will see thousands of acres destroyed because he is playing his ill-informed pet idea like a hand of cards, and cannot bear to lose. He knows the mindless greed of big industry, and the shameless dealing of the government departments who promote and protect it. The book is crammed with his knowledge of such things, and with the evidence he piles against them, yet his comments – though they are cautious – are anything but hopeless.

Inevitably, the main obstacle to his work in Conservation has been Government opposition, in all its forms. He has collected his experience of Government mismanagement into his now-famous book, *The System*, but such things can never be publicized enough. The collisions must have been bitter for him. He was, after all, defending the earth's life from its murderer. In so far as the earth's life is being murdered, it is in the hands of Government and departmental committees. If Government could feel the crisis of it, or if the public could make Government feel the experience of it, the industrial poisoning of the water-systems in and around England, for instance, could be cut to something negligible very quickly. A crash programme of legislation and subsidies, of applying technological means already well researched, would cost no more than a few strikes, and would not require much more Government time and attention than did Rhodesia. It could be dealt with, as it should be dealt with, as a war. It would transform England, and the example would go a long way to alter the world. In the end, it would be a national investment on a grand scale. It is well-known that if it is not done soon the consequences will be a disaster worse than anything we suffered in the last war. Yet it is beyond us.

Max Nicholson moves over such things patiently in this book, which is a constructive book, more concerned to call the hits than the misses. He drops quite heavily on education, though he understands that for our schools to teach – as their most essential lesson – a proper knowledge of the sacred wholeness of Nature, and a proper alignment of our behaviour within her laws, is something that is only just becoming possible. He blames the education of economists, who wield such enormous power in the shaping of industrial society, for the fact that they are so utterly ignorant of the importance for all life of the nature they have done so much to contaminate and destroy. He emphasizes the urgent need to educate farmers. Not just our food, but the life of that nine inches of soil, and of much else, is in their care. The opportunism of some farmers, who act as if history were finished, and their soil would not be needed after another thirty years, and as if the public who buy what they grow were a species better killed off quickly and profitably, has to be seen to be believed.

The plain gullible ignorance of many others is just as bad. It equals the cynicism of the chemical industries that hold them all by the nose.

He has some hard words for the Forestry Commission, though one wonders if they are having such an effect on the land as the happy power-sawyer who will fell our trees free just for the joy of gliding through the great trunks. His deadly buzz is the new song of rural England. Wherever the Forestry Commission has not planted its impenetrable sour parallelograms, the power saw is scraping the skylines. All those things wait only for a little legislation. Even the one great problem, which is behind every other, and which brings Max Nicholson's powerful hopes to a stop again and again, the explosion of world population (now doubling every thirty-five years), rests with legislation.

He presses on past all this. His hopeful, positive drive is one of the admirable things in the book. You can feel everywhere the pressure of his opening sentence: '. . . one thing in the world is invincible, an idea whose time has come'.

The time for Conservation has certainly come. But Conservation, our sudden alertness to the wholeness of nature, and the lateness of the hour, is only the crest of a deeper excitement and readiness. The idea of nature as a single organism is not new. It was man's first great thought, the basic intuition of most primitive theologies. Since Christianity hardened into Protestantism, we can follow the underground heretical life, leagued with everything occult, spiritualistic, devilish, over-emotional, bestial, mystical, feminine, crazy, revolutionary, and poetic. Suddenly, within the last few years, it has re-emerged, presenting scientific credentials through the voice of the Computer. And that is nature's only hope: the Computer's phenomenal power of assessment, and mankind's awed respect for it. Science, it has often been said, which began by deposing every primitive idea, will end by reinstating them as the essential conditions for life and as true descriptions of the Universe. It is like the old-fashioned dynasties of the gods. Christianity deposes Mother Nature and begets, on her prostrate body, Science, which proceeds to destroy Nature, but which in turn, on its half-destroyed mother's body, begets the Computer, a god more powerful than its Father or its Grandfather, who reinstates Nature, its Mother and Grandmother and Great Grandmother, as the Holy of Holies, mother of all the gods. Because this is what we are seeing: something that was unthinkable only ten years ago, except as a poetic dream: the re-emergence of Nature as the Great Goddess of mankind, and the Mother of all life. And her oracle, speaking the language to which everybody, even Technology itself, has agreed to listen, is the Computer.

By this timely publication of his book, and by the position he has achieved in public life, Max Nicholson becomes one of the prophets and chief publicists of this revolution. In the past, Conservation's main weakness has lain in the over-specialization of its experts, so that Geophysics, Physiography, Hydrology, Botany, Zoology, Genetics, Biometrics, Ecology, Meteorology and the rest worked on in nearly complete insulation from each other. And none of them had a vision of where they were going. And none of them had a public voice. Conservation lay scattered like the dry bones. They are now assembling at great speed. Max Nicholson is outstanding because he saw from the start that a total knowledge was essential. From his older generation of specialists, he is one of the very few who combines in himself several of the vital specializations, and a good knowledge of the others. He is the only one who adds to these advantages a great talent for administration, an inclusive vision, and a formidable voice.

In an early chapter of the book he describes in detail the surface of the whole earth, most of which he has examined at close quarters, as if on a flight round and round the earth in a spiral from North to South. Throughout the book, in the many fascinating photographs and their long descriptive comments, and in the charts of the appendix, he builds this model into a living miniature of the earth, seen from the Conservationist's point of view – which is to say, from Nature's point of view. The effect is unforgettable. He is not only showing us the wholeness of this living globe. He is showing us the extreme intricacy and precision of its interconnected working parts – winds, currents, rocks, plants, animals, weathers, in all their swarming and yet law-abiding variety. At the same time he is showing us the extreme smallness of it. The final impression of its finiteness and frailty is alarming – the tiny area of usable land, the fragility of the living cell. Moreover, with this model he puts the whole globe into our hands, as something now absolutely in our care. It is novel to look at it in this way – both frightening and exhilarating. The whole description – though he writes as always more for thoroughness than for entertainment – has a lasting imaginative impact. One's imagination is altered. And what alters the imagination, alters everything. We hold this globe in our hands, and all the inherited ideas vanish: the evidence is too plain. This miniature earth has our stomach, our blood, our precarious vital chemistry, and our future.

Looking at this image of global unity, so prehistoric and yet so actually present, we see how far ahead of its time Conservation has been. While Politicians, Sociologists, Economists, Theologians, Philosophers and the rest pick over the stucco rubble of a collapsed civilization, the Conservationists are nursing a new global era. It seems right that Max Nicholson should sub-title his book 'A Guide for the New Masters of the Earth'. And in contrast to the hopeless gloom of all comment on our civilization, it is right that his tone should be so hopeful, and his will so purposeful. He makes it very clear that we may well be too late, that our civilization may be too strong for us for too long. In spite of that, he leaves the reader feeling that the wonderful thing might be possible, that the earth can be salvaged, that we are not hopelessly in the grip of our abstractions, our stupidity and greed, and our shiftless, imbecile governments. He makes it seem possible that we can come to our senses in time.

Max Nicholson writes as a scientist. Throughout his life, from his earliest days as a naturalist and birdwatcher, he has stuck to scientific methods and scientific evidence. He has kept his faith in Technology, even when it seemed the worst enemy. Yet he actually is a prophet, and all this dedication has been based on a sure intuition of what language would finally carry the weight, when he came to tell his vision. Beneath the doggedly objective exposition, the juggernaut grinding through masses of fact, there is a real vision. As if he had managed to set every abstraction or bias aside, he writes from an imagination constructed out of the actualities of the earth's life, and at times his otherwise omnivorous administrator's prose rises to riveting eloquence. His pages about the inter-relationship of Nature and the inmost psychology of man, beginning on page 259, go beyond all sciences, and leave most modern theology in a vacuum. They display tremendous imaginative grasp of the true life of the earth, the inner spiritual unity of nature. And they give some glimpse into the depths of the *geist* which is now taking a grip on us.

Nature's obsession, after all, is to survive. As far as she is concerned, every new baby is a completely fresh start. If Westernized civilized man, the evolutionary error, is still open to correction, presumably she will correct him. If he is not open enough, she will still make the attempt. This book leaves one more than ever convinced that the moment has come.

Myth and Education

Somewhere in *The Republic*, where he describes the constitution of his ideal State, Plato talks a little about the education of the people who will live in it. He makes the famous point that quite advanced mathematical truths can be drawn from children when they are asked the right questions in the right order, and his own philosophical method in his dialogues is very like this. He treats his interlocutors as children and by small, simple, logical, stealthy questions gradually draws out of them some part of the Platonic system of ideas – a system which has in one way or another dominated the mental life of the Western world ever since. Nevertheless he goes on to say that a formal education – by which he means a mathematical, philosophical and ethical education – is not for children. The proper education for his future ideal citizens, he suggests, is something quite different: it is to be found in the traditional myths and tales of which Greece possessed such a huge abundance.

Plato was nothing if not an educationalist. His writings can be seen as a prolonged and many-sided debate on just how the ideal citizen is to be shaped. It seemed to him quite possible to create an élite of philosophers who would also be wise and responsible rulers, with a perfect apprehension of the Good. Yet he proposed to start their training with the incredible fantasies of these myths. Everyone knows that the first lessons, with human beings just as with dogs, are the most important of all. So what would be the effect of laying at the foundations of their mental life this mass of supernatural figures and their impossible antics? Later philosophers, throughout history, who have come near often enough to worshipping Plato, have dismissed these tales as absurdities. So how did he come to recommend them?

They were the material of the Greek poets. Many of them had been recreated by poets into works that have been the model and

From *Writers, Critics and Children*, edited by Geoff Fox et al.
(London: Heinemann, 1976).

despair of later writers. Yet we know what Plato thought about poets. He wanted them suppressed – much as it is said he suppressed his own poems when he first encountered Socrates. If he wanted nothing of the poets, why was he so respectful of the myths and tales which formed the imaginative world of the poets?

He had no religious motives. For Plato, those Gods and Goddesses were hardly more serious, as religious symbols, than they are for us. Yet they evidently did contain something important. What exactly was it, then, that made them in his opinion the best possible grounding for his future enlightened, realistic, perfectly adjusted citizen?

Let us suppose he thought about it as carefully as he thought about everything else. What did he have in mind? Trying to answer that question leads us in interesting directions.

Plato was preceded in Greece by more shadowy figures. They are a unique collection. Even what fragments remain of their writings reveal a cauldron of titanic ideas, from which Plato drew only a spoonful. Wherever we look around us now, in the modern world, it is not easy to find anything that was not somehow prefigured in the conceptions of those early Greeks. And nothing is more striking about their ideas than the strange, visionary atmosphere from which they emerge. Plato is human and familiar; he invented that careful, logical step-by-step style of investigation, in which all his great dialogues are conducted, and which almost all later philosophers developed, until it evolved finally into the scientific method itself. But his predecessors stand in a different world. By comparison they seem like mythical figures, living in myth, dreaming mythical dreams.

And so they were. We find them embedded in myth. Their vast powerful notions are emerging, like figures in half-relief, from the massif of myth, which in turn is lifting from the human/animal darkness of early Greece.

Why did they rise in Greece and not somewhere else? What was so special about early Greece? The various peoples of Greece had created their own religions and mythologies, more or less related but with differences. Further abroad, other nations had created theirs, again often borrowing from common sources, but evolving separate

systems, sometimes gigantic systems. Those supernatural seeming
dreams, full of conflict and authority and unearthly states of feeling,
were projections of man's inner and outer world. They developed
their ritual, their dogma, their hierarchy of spiritual values in a
particular way in each separated group. Then at the beginning of the
first millennium they began to converge, by one means or another,
on Greece. They came from Africa via Egypt, from Asia via Persia
and the Middle East, from Europe and from all the shores of the
Mediterranean. Meeting in Greece, they mingled with those rising
from the soil of Greece itself. Wherever two cultures with their
religious ideas are brought sharply together, there is an inner
explosion. Greece had become the battleground of the religious and
mythological inspirations of much of the archaic world. The conflict
was severe, and the effort to find solutions and make peace among
all those contradictory elements was correspondingly great. And
the heroes of the struggle were those early philosophers. The
struggle created them, it opened the depths of spirit and imagination
to them, and they made sense of it. What was religious passion in the
religions became in them a special sense of the holiness and
seriousness of existence. What was obscure symbolic mystery in the
mythologies became in them a bright, manifold perception of
universal and human truths. In their works we see the transformation from one to the other taking place. And the great age which
immediately followed them, in the fifth century BC, was the
culmination of the activity.

It seems proper, then, that the fantastic dimension of those tales
should have appeared to Plato as something very much other than
frivolous or absurd. We can begin to guess, maybe, at what he
wanted, in familiarizing children with as much as possible of that
teeming repertoire.

To begin with, we can say that an education of the sort Plato
proposes would work on a child in the following way.

A child takes possession of a story as what might be called a unit
of imagination. A story which engages, say, earth and the underworld is a unit correspondingly flexible. It contains not merely the
space and in some form or other the contents of those two places; it

Atomic thinking - imagineme?

reconciles their contradictions in a workable fashion and holds open the way between them. The child can re-enter the story at will, look around him, find all those things and consider them at his leisure. In attending to the world of such a story there is the beginning of imaginative and mental control. There is the beginning of a form of contemplation. And to begin with, each story is separate from every other story. Each unit of imagination is like a whole separate imagination, no matter how many the head holds.

If the story is learned well, so that all its parts can be seen at a glance, as if we looked through a window into it, then that story has become like the complicated hinterland of a single word. It has become a word. Any fragment of the story serves as the 'word' by which the whole story's electrical circuit is switched into consciousness, and all its light and power brought to bear. As a rather extreme example, take the story of Christ. No matter what point of that story we touch, the whole story hits us. If we mention the Nativity, or the miracle of the loaves and fishes, or Lazarus, or the Crucifixion, the voltage and inner brightness of the whole story is instantly there. A single word of reference is enough – just as you need to touch a power-line with only the tip of your finger.

The story itself is an acquisition, a kind of wealth. We only have to imagine for a moment an individual who knows nothing of it at all. His ignorance would shock us, and, in a real way, he would be outside our society. How would he even begin to understand most of the ideas which are at the roots of our culture and appear everywhere among the branches? To follow the meanings behind the one word Crucifixion would take us through most of European history, and much of Roman and Middle Eastern too. It would take us into every corner of our private life. And before long, it would compel us to acknowledge much more important meanings than merely informative ones. Openings of spiritual experience, a dedication to final realities which might well stop us dead in our tracks and demand of us personally a sacrifice which we could never otherwise have conceived. A word of that sort has magnetized our life into a special pattern. And behind it stands not just the crowded breadth of the world, but all the depths and intensities of it too.

Those things have been raised out of chaos and brought into our ken by the story in a word. The word holds them all there, like a constellation, floating and shining, and though we may draw back from tangling with them too closely, nevertheless they are present. And they remain, part of the head that lives our life, and they grow as we grow. A story can wield so much! And a word wields the story.

Imagine hearing, somewhere in the middle of a poem being recited, the phrase 'The Crucifixion of Hitler'. The word 'Hitler' is as much of a hieroglyph as the word 'Crucifixion'. Individually, those two words bear the consciousness of much of our civilization. But they are meaningless hieroglyphs, unless the stories behind the words are known. We could almost say it is only by possessing these stories that we possess that consciousness. And in those who possess both stories, the collision of those two words, in that phrase, cannot fail to detonate a psychic depth-charge. Whether we like it or not, a huge inner working starts up. How can Hitler and Crucifixion exist together in that way? Can they or can't they? The struggle to sort it out throws up ethical and philosophical implications which could absorb our attention for a very long time. All our static and maybe dormant understanding of good and evil and what opens beyond good and evil is shocked into activity. Many unconscious assumptions and intuitions come up into the light to declare themselves and explain themselves and reassess each other. For some temperaments, those two words twinned in that way might well point to wholly fresh appraisals of good and evil and the underground psychological or even actual connections between them. Yet the visible combatants here are two stories.

Without those stories, how could we have grasped those meanings? Without those stories, how could we have reduced those meanings to two words? The stories have gathered up huge charges of reality, and illuminated us with them, and given us their energy, just as those colliding worlds in early Greece roused the philosophers and the poets. If we argue that a grasp of good and evil has nothing to do with a knowledge of historical anecdotes, we have only to compare what we felt of Hitler's particular evil when our knowledge of his story was only general with what we felt when we learned more details. It is just details of Hitler's story that have changed the consciousness of modern man. The story hasn't stuck onto us something that was never there before. It has revealed to us something that was always there. And no other story, no other anything, ever did it so powerfully. Just as it needed the story of Christ to change the consciousness of our ancestors. The better we know these stories as stories, the more of ourselves and the world is revealed to us through them.

The story of Christ came to us first of all as two or three sentences. That tiny seed held all the rest in potential form. Like the blueprint of a city. Once we laid it down firmly in imagination, it became the foundation for everything that could subsequently build and live there. Just the same with the story of Hitler.

Are those two stories extreme examples? They would not have appeared so for the early Greeks, who had several Christs and several Bibles and quite a few Hitlers to deal with. Are Aesop's fables more to our scale? They operate in exactly the same way. Grimm's tales are similar oracles.

But what these two stories show very clearly is how stories think for themselves, once we know them. They not only attract and light up everything relevant in our own experience, they are also in continual private meditation, as it were, on their own implications. They are little factories of understanding. New revelations of meaning open out of their images and patterns continually, stirred into reach by our own growth and changing circumstances.

Then at a certain point in our lives, they begin to combine. What happened forcibly between Hitler and the Crucifixion in that phrase, begins to happen naturally. The head that holds many stories becomes a small early Greece.

It does not matter, either, how old the stories are. Stories are old the way human biology is old. No matter how much they have produced in the past in the way of fruitful inspirations, they are never exhausted. The story of Christ, to stick to our example, can never be diminished by the seemingly infinite mass of theological agonizing and insipid homilies which have attempted to translate it into something more manageable. It remains, like any other genuine story, irreducible, a lump of the world, like the body of a new-born child. There is little doubt that, if the world lasts, pretty soon someone will come along and understand the story as if for the first time. He will look back and see two thousand years of somnolent fumbling with the theme. Out of that, and the collision of other things, he will produce, very likely, something totally new and overwhelming, some whole new direction for human life. The same possibility holds for the ancient stories of many another deity. Why not? History is really no older than that new-born baby. And every story is still the original cauldron of wisdom, full of new visions and new life.

What do we mean by 'imagination'? There are obviously many degrees of it. Are there different kinds?

The word 'imagination' usually denotes not much more than the faculty of creating a picture of something in our heads and holding it there while we think about it. Since this is the basis of nearly everything we do, clearly it's very important that our imagination should be strong rather than weak. Education neglects this faculty completely. How is the imagination to be strengthened and trained? A student has imagination, we seem to suppose, much as he has a face, and nothing can be done about it. We use what we've got.

We do realize that it can vary enormously from one person to the next, and from almost non-existent upwards. Of a person who simply cannot think what will happen if he does such and such a thing, we say he has no imagination. He has to work on principles, or orders, or by precedent, and he will always be marked by extreme rigidity, because he is after all moving in the dark. We all know such people, and we all recognize that they are dangerous, since if they have strong temperaments in other respects they end up by destroying their environment and everybody near them. The terrible thing is that they are the planners, and ruthless slaves to the plan – which substitutes for the faculty they do not possess. And they have the will of desperation: where others see alternative courses, they see only a gulf.

Of the person who imagines vividly what will happen if he acts in a certain way, and then turns out to be wrong, we say he is dealing with an unpredictable situation or else, just as likely, he has an inaccurate imagination. Lively, maybe, but inaccurate. There is no innate law that makes a very real-seeming picture of things an accurate picture. That person will be a great nuisance, and as destructive as the other, because he will be full of confident schemes and solutions, which will seem to him foolproof, but which will simply be false, because somehow his sense of reality is defective. In other words, his ordinary perception of reality, by which the imagination regulates all its images, overlooks too much, or misinterprets too much. Many disturbances can account for some of this, but simple sloppiness of attention accounts for most of it.

Those two classes of people contain the majority of us for much of the time. The third class of people is quite rare. Or our own moments of belonging to that class are rare. Imagination which is both accurate and strong is so rare, that when somebody appears in possession of it they are regarded as something more than human. We see that with the few great generals. Normally, it occurs patchily. It is usually no more than patchy because accurate perceptions are rarely more than patchy. We have only to make the simplest test on ourselves to reconfirm this. And where our perceptions are blind, our speculations are pure invention.

This basic type of imagination, with its delicate wiring of perceptions, is our most valuable piece of practical equipment. It is the control panel for everything we think and do, so it ought to be education's first concern. Yet whoever spent half an hour in any classroom trying to strengthen it in any way? Even in the sciences, where accurate perception is recognizably crucial, is this faculty ever deliberately trained?

Sharpness, clarity and scope of the mental eye are all-important in our dealings with the outer world, and that is plenty. And if we were machines it would be enough. But the outer world is only one of the worlds we live in. For better or worse we have another, and that is the inner world of our bodies and everything pertaining. It is closer than the outer world, more decisive, and utterly different. So here are two worlds, which we have to live in simultaneously. And because they are intricately interdependent at every moment, we can't ignore one and concentrate on the other without accidents. Probably fatal accidents.

But why can't this inner world of the body be regarded as an extension of the outer world – in other words why isn't the sharp, clear, objective eye of the mind as adequate for this world as it is for the other more obviously outer world? And if it isn't, why isn't it?

The inner world is not so easily talked about because nobody has ever come near to understanding it. Though it is the closest thing to us – though it is, indeed, us – we live in it as on an unexplored planet in space. It is not so much a place, either, as a region of events. And the first thing we have to confess is that it cannot be seen objectively. How does the biological craving for water turn into the precise notion that it is water that we want? How do we 'see' the make-up of an emotion that we do not even feel – though electrodes on our skin will register its presence? The word 'subjective' was invented for a good reason – but under that vaguest of general terms lies the most important half of our experience.

After all, what exactly is going on in there? It is quite frightening, how little we know about it. We can't say there's nothing – that 'nothing' is merely the shutness of the shut door. And if we say there's something – how much more specific can we get?

We quickly realize that the inner world is indescribable, impenetrable, and invisible. We try to grapple with it, and all we meet is one provisional dream after another. It dawns on us that in order to look at the inner world 'objectively' we have had to separate ourselves from what is an exclusively 'subjective' world, and it has vanished. In the end, we acknowledge that the objective imagination, and the objective perceptions, those sharp clear instruments which cope so well with the outer world, are of very little use here.

By speculating backwards from effects, we can possibly make out a rough plan of what ought to be in there. The incessant bombardment of raw perceptions must land somewhere. And we have been able to notice that any one perception can stir up a host of small feelings, which excite further feelings not necessarily so small, in a turmoil of memory and association. And we do get some evidence, we think, that our emotional and instinctive life, which seems to be

Myth and Education

on a somewhat bigger scale and not so tied to momentary perceptions, is mustering and regrouping in response to outer circumstances. But these bigger and more dramatic energies are also occasionally yoked to the pettiest of those perceptions, and drive off on some journey. And now and again we are made aware of what seems to be an even larger drama of moods and energies which it is hard to name – psychic, spiritual, cosmic. Any name we give them seems metaphorical, since in that world everything is relative, and we are never sure of the scale of magnification or miniaturization of the signals. We can guess, with a fair sense of confidence, that all these intervolved processes, which seem like the electrical fields of our body's electrical installations – our glands, organs, chemical transmutations and so on – are striving to tell about themselves. They are all trying to make their needs known, much as thirst imparts its sharp request for water. They are talking incessantly, in a dumb radiating way, about themselves, about their relationships with each other, about the situation of the moment in the main overall drama of the living and growing and dying body in which they are assembled, and also about the outer world, because all these *dramatis personae* are really striving to live, in some way or other, in the outer world. That is the world for which they have been created. That is the world which created them. And so they are highly concerned about the doings of the individual behind whose face they hide. Because they are him. And they want him to live in the way that will give them the greatest satisfaction.

This description is bald enough, but it is as much as the objective eye can be reasonably sure of. And then only in a detached way, the way we think we are sure of the workings of an electrical circuit. But for more intimate negotiations with that world, for genuine contact with its powers and genuine exploration of its regions, it turns out that the eye of the objective imagination is blind.

We solve the problem by never looking inward. We identify ourselves and all that is wakeful and intelligent with our objective eye, saying, 'Let's be objective'. That is really no more than saying 'Let's be happy'. But we sit, closely cramped in the cockpit behind the eyes, steering through the brilliantly crowded landscape beyond the lenses, focused on details and distinctions. In the end, since all our attention from birth has been narrowed into the outward beam, we come to regard our body as no more than a somewhat stupid vehicle. All the urgent information coming towards us from that inner world sounds to us like a blank, or at best the occasional grunt, or a twinge. Because we have no equipment to receive it and decode it. The body, with its spirits, is the antennae of all perceptions, the receiving aerial for all wavelengths. But we are disconnected. The exclusiveness of our objective eye, the very strength and brilliance of our objective intelligence, suddenly turns into stupidity – of the most rigid and suicidal kind.

That condition certainly sounds extreme, yet most of the people we know, particularly older people, are likely to regard it as ideal. It is a modern ideal. The educational tendencies of the last three hundred years, and especially of the last fifty, corresponding to the rising prestige of scientific objectivity and the lowering prestige of religious awareness, have combined to make it so. It is a scientific ideal. And it is a powerful ideal, it has created the modern world. And without it, the modern world would fall to pieces: infinite misery would result. The disaster is, that it is heading straight towards infinite misery, because it has persuaded human beings to identify themselves with what is no more than a narrow mode of perception. And the more rigorously the ideal is achieved, the more likely it is to be disastrous. A bright, intelligent eye, full of exact images, set in a head of the most frightful stupidity.

The drive towards this ideal is so strong that it has materialized in the outer world. A perfect mechanism of objective perception has been precipitated: the camera. Scientific objectivity, as we all know, has its own morality, which has nothing to do with human morality. It is the morality of the camera. And this is the prevailing morality of our time. It is a morality utterly devoid of any awareness of the requirements of the inner world. It is contemptuous of the 'human element'. That is its purity and its strength. The prevailing philosophies and political ideologies of our time subscribe to this contempt, with a nearly religious fanaticism, just as science itself does.

Some years ago in an American picture magazine I saw a

collection of photographs which showed the process of a tiger killing a woman. The story behind this was as follows. The tiger, a tame tiger, belonged to the woman. A professional photographer had wanted to take photographs of her strolling with her tiger. Something – maybe his incessant camera – had upset the tiger, the woman had tried to pacify it, whereupon it attacked her and started to kill her. So what did that hero of the objective attitude do then? Among Jim Corbett's wonderful stories about man-eating tigers and leopards there are occasions when some man-eater, with a terrifying reputation, was driven off its victim by some other person. On one occasion by a girl who beat the animal over the head with a digging stick. But this photographer – we can easily understand him because we all belong to the modern world – had become his camera. What were his thoughts? 'Now that the tiger has started in on her it would be cruelty to save her and prolong her sufferings', or 'If I just stand here making the minimum noise it might leave her, whereas if I interfere it will certainly give her the death bite, just as a cat does when you try to rescue its mouse', or 'If I get involved, who knows what will happen, then I might miss my plane,' or 'I can't affect the outcome of this in any way. And who am I to interfere with the cycles of nature? This has happened countless millions of times and always will happen while there are tigers and women,' or did he just think 'Oh my God, Oh my God, what a chance!'? Whatever his thoughts were he went on taking photographs of the whole procedure while the tiger killed the woman, because the pictures were there in the magazine. And the story was told as if the photographer had indeed been absent. As if the camera had simply gone on doing what any camera would be expected to do, being a mere mechanical device for registering outer appearances. I may be doing the photographer an injustice. It may be I have forgotten some mention that eventually when he had enough pictures he ran in and hit the tiger with his camera or something else. Or maybe he was just wisely cowardly as many another of us might be. Whatever it was, he got his pictures.

The same paralysis comes to many of us when we watch television. After the interesting bit is over, what keeps us mesmerized by that bright little eye? It can't be the horrors and inanities and killings that jog along there between the curtains and the mantel-piece after supper. Why can't we move? Reality has been lifted beyond our participation, behind that very tough screen, and into another dimension. Our inner world, of natural impulsive response, is safely in neutral. Like broiler killers, we are reduced to a state of pure observation. Everything that passes in front of our eyes is equally important, equally unimportant. As far as what we see is concerned, and in a truly practical way, we are paralysed. Even people who profess to dislike television fall under the same spell of passivity. They can only free themselves by a convulsive effort of will. The precious tool of objective imagination has taken control of us there. Materialized in the camera, it has imprisoned us in the lens.

In England, not very long ago, the inner world and Christianity were closely identified. Even the conflicts within Christianity only revealed and consolidated more inner world. When religious knowledge lost the last rags of its credibility, earlier this century, psychoanalysis appeared as if to fill the gap. Both attempt to give form to the inner world. But with a difference.

When it came the turn of the Christian Church to embody the laws of the inner world, it made the mistake of claiming that they were objective laws. That might have passed, if Science had not come along, whose laws were so demonstrably objective that it was able to impose them on the whole world. As the mistaken claims of Christianity became scientifically meaningless, the inner world which it had clothed became incomprehensible, absurd and finally invisible. Objective imagination, in the light of science, rejected religion as charlatanism, and the inner world as a bundle of fairy tales, a relic of primeval superstition. People rushed towards the idea of living without any religion or any inner life whatsoever as if towards some great new freedom. A great final awakening. The most energetic intellectual and political movements of this century wrote the manifestos of the new liberation. The great artistic statements have recorded the true emptiness of the new prison.

The inner world, of course, could not evaporate, just because it no longer had a religion to give it a visible body. A person's own inner world cannot fold up its spirit wings, and shut down all its tuned circuits, and become a mechanical business of nuts and bolts, just because a political or intellectual ideology requires it to. As the religion was stripped away, the defrocked inner world became a waif, an outcast, a tramp. And denied its one great health – acceptance into life – it fell into a huge sickness. A huge collection of deprivation sicknesses. And this is how psychoanalysis found it.

The small piloting consciousness of the bright-eyed objective intelligence had steered its body and soul into a hell. Religious negotiations had formerly embraced and humanized the archaic energies of instinct and feeling. They had conversed in simple but profound terms with the forces struggling inside people, and had civilized them, or attempted to. Without religion, those powers have become dehumanized. The whole inner world has become elemental, chaotic, continually more primitive and beyond our control. It has become a place of demons. But of course, in so far as we are disconnected anyway from that world, and lack the equipment to pick up its signals, we are not aware of it. All we register is the vast absence, the emptiness, the sterility, the meaninglessness, the loneliness. If we do manage to catch a glimpse of our inner selves, by some contraption of mirrors, we recognize it with horror – it is an animal crawling and decomposing in a hell. We refuse to own it.

In the last decade or two, the imprisonment of the camera lens has begun to crack. The demonized state of our inner world has made itself felt in a million ways. How is it that children are so attracted towards it? Every new child is nature's chance to correct culture's error. Children are most sensitive to it, because they are the least conditioned by scientific objectivity to life in the camera lens. They have a double motive, in attempting to break from the lens. They want to escape the ugliness of the despiritualized world in which they see their parents imprisoned. And they are aware that this inner world we have rejected is not merely an inferno of depraved impulses and crazy explosions of embittered energy. Our real selves lie down there. Down there, mixed up among all the madness, is everything that once made life worth living. All the lost awareness and powers and allegiances of our biological and spiritual being.

The attempt to re-enter that lost inheritance takes many forms, but it is the chief business of the swarming cults.

Drugs cannot take us there. If we cite the lofty religions in which drugs did take the initiates to where they needed to go, we ought to remember that here again the mythology was crucial. The journey was undertaken as part of an elaborately mythologized ritual. It was the mythology which consolidated the inner world, gave human form to its experiences, and connected them to daily life. Without that preparation a drug carries its user to a prison in the inner world as passive and isolated and meaningless as the camera's eye from which he escaped.

Objective imagination, then, important as it is, is not enough. What about a 'subjective' imagination? It is only logical to suppose that a faculty developed specially for peering into the inner world might end up as specialized and destructive as the faculty for peering into the outer one. Besides, the real problem comes from the fact that outer world and inner world are interdependent at every moment. We are simply the locus of their collision. Two worlds, with mutually contradictory laws, or laws that seem to us to be so, colliding afresh every second, struggling for peaceful coexistence. And whether we like it or not our life is what we are able to make of that collision and struggle.

So what we need, evidently, is a faculty that embraces both worlds simultaneously. A large, flexible grasp, an inner vision which holds wide open, like a great theatre, the arena of contention, and which pays equal respects to both sides. Which keeps faith, as Goethe says, with the world of things and the world of spirits equally.

This really is imagination. This is the faculty we mean when we talk about the imagination of the great artists. The character of great works is exactly this: that in them the full presence of the inner world combines with and is reconciled to the full presence of the outer world. And in them we see that the laws of these two worlds are not contradictory at all; they are one all-inclusive system; they are laws that somehow we find it all but impossible to keep, laws that only the greatest artists are able to restate. They are the laws, simply, of human nature. And men have recognized all through history that the restating of these laws, in one medium or another, in great works of art, are the greatest human acts. They are the greatest acts and they are the most human. We recognize these works because we are all struggling to find those laws, as a man on a tightrope struggles for balance, because they are the formula that reconciles everything, and balances every imbalance.

So it comes about that once we recognize their terms, these works seem to heal us. More important, it is in these works that humanity is truly formed. And it has to be done again and again, as circumstances change, and the balance of power between outer and inner world shifts, showing everybody the gulf. The inner world, separated from the outer world, is a place of demons. The outer world, separated from the inner world, is a place of meaningless objects and machines. The faculty that makes the human being out of these two worlds is called divine. That is only a way of saying that it is the faculty without which humanity cannot really exist. It can be called religious or visionary. More essentially, it is imagination which embraces both outer and inner worlds in a creative spirit.

Laying down blueprints for imagination of that sort is a matter of education, as Plato divined.

The myths and legends, which Plato proposed as the ideal educational material for his young citizens, can be seen as large-scale accounts of negotiations between the powers of the inner world and the stubborn conditions of the outer world, under which ordinary men and women have to live. They are immense and at the same time highly detailed sketches for the possibilities of understanding and reconciling the two. They are, in other words, an archive of draft plans for the kind of imagination we have been discussing.

Their accuracy and usefulness, in this sense, depend on the fact that they were originally the genuine projections of genuine understanding. They were tribal dreams of the highest order of inspiration and truth, at their best. They gave a true account of what really happens in that inner region where the two worlds collide. This has been attested over and over again by the way in which the imaginative men of every subsequent age have had recourse to their basic patterns and images.

But the Greek myths were not the only true myths. The unspoken definition of myth is that it carries truth of this sort. These big dreams only become the treasured property of a people when they express the real state of affairs. Priests continually elaborate the myths, but what is not true is forgotten again. So every real people has its true myths. One of the first surprises of mythographers was to find how uncannily similar these myths are all over the world. They are as alike as the lines on the palm of the human hand.

But Plato implied that all traditional stories, big and small, were part of his syllabus. And indeed the smaller stories come from the same place. If a tale can last, in oral tradition, for two or three generations, then it has either come from the real place, or it has found its way there. And these small tales are just as vigorous educational devices as the big myths.

There is a long tradition of using stories as educational implements in a far more deliberate way than Plato seems to propose. Steiner has a great deal to say about the method. In his many publications of Sufi literature, Idries Shah indicates how central to the training of the sages and saints of Islam are the traditional tales. Sometimes no more than small anecdotes, sometimes lengthy and involved adventures such as were collected into the Arabian Nights.

As I pointed out, using the example of the Christ story, the first step is to learn the story, as if it were laying down the foundation. The next phase rests with the natural process of the imagination.

The story is, as it were, a kit. Apart from its own major subject – obvious enough in the case of the Christ story – it contains two separable elements: its pattern and its images. Together they make that story and no other. Separately they set out on new lives of their own.

The roads they travel are determined by the brain's fundamental genius for metaphor. Automatically, it uses the pattern of one set of images to organize quite a different set. It uses one image, with slight variations, as an image for related and yet different and otherwise imageless meanings.

In this way, the simple tale of the beggar and the princess begins to

Myth and Education

transmit intuitions of psychological, perhaps spiritual, states and relationships. What began as an idle reading of a fairy tale ends, by simple natural activity of the imagination, as a rich perception of values of feeling, emotion and spirit which would otherwise have remained unconscious and languageless. The inner struggle of worlds, which is not necessarily a violent and terrible affair, though at bottom it often is, is suddenly given the perfect formula for the terms of a truce. A simple tale, told at the right moment, transforms a person's life with the order its pattern brings to incoherent energies.

And while its pattern proliferates in every direction through all levels of consciousness, its images are working too. The image of Lazarus is not easily detached by a child from its striking place in the story of Christ. But once it begins to migrate, there is no limiting its importance. In all Dostoevsky's searching adventures, the basic image, radiating energies that he seems never able to exhaust, is Lazarus.

The image does not need to be so central to a prestigious religion for it to become so important. At the heart of *King Lear* is a very simple Fairy Tale King in a very simple little tale – the Story of Salt. In both these we see how a simple image in a simple story has somehow focused all the pressures of an age – collisions of spirit and nature and good and evil and a majesty of existence that seemed uncontainable. But it has brought all that into a human pattern, and made it part of our understanding.

working myth into one's life

Emily Dickinson

Though she had a reputation among her friends for the occasional verses and poems which she enclosed in letters, Emily Dickinson's phenomenal secret output was unsuspected until after her death, in 1886, when her sister found the mass of manuscripts in her bureau. Some of it was neatly copied in her headlong, simplified script, and sewn loosely together in little booklets. The rest was in every possible state of mid-composition – a great problem for her editors, Mrs Mabel Loomis Todd and Millicent Todd Bingham, who prepared for the public eye successive selections of the poems, which came out between 1890 and 1945. Emily Dickinson's niece brought out other selections, so that by 1945 all the poems had been published, but in more or less heavily edited form. Apart from the frequent obscurity of Emily Dickinson's script and her habit of listing – at the crucial point in a poem – several alternative words or lines without clearly indicating which she finally preferred, the greatest problem for these editors lay in reducing her punctuation of simple dashes to something more orthodox. They acted boldly, but not to everybody's satisfaction. The subsequent experiments in this line by such sensitive and sympathetic critics as John Crowe Ransom have not checked the growing opinion that Emily Dickinson's eccentric dashes are an integral part of her method and style, and cannot be translated to commas, semicolons and the rest without deadening the wonderfully naked voltage of the poems.

Accordingly, T. H. Johnson re-edited the Complete Poems, in a variorum edition, retaining everything – as closely as possible – just as the poet left it. And so in 1955 Emily Dickinson's poetry appeared for the first time without editorial adjustments, and complete. In 1960, T. H. Johnson made an edition for the ordinary reader in which he reduced the manuscript variants of the poems to a single text of each, again following the poet's directives as far as he could

Introduction to *A Choice of Emily Dickinson's Verse*
(London: Faber and Faber, 1968).

determine them, a feat of taste and tact to which this present selection is indebted. On the final count, the collected poems number 1,775. Emily Dickinson only ever saw six of these in print, and then they had been so heavily corrected, by editorial hands, to the taste of the day, that she seems to have resigned herself after that to posterity or nothing.

She is one of the oddest and most intriguing personalities in literary history. She was born in 1830, in Amherst, Massachusetts. As a girl she was notorious for her comic wit and high-spirited originality, among her friends and within her family. But she showed little inclination to venture into the world, and less and less as time went on. Even at twenty four she was saying, 'I don't go from home, unless emergency leads me by the hand.' Eventually, and by degrees, she developed this into nearly complete self-imprisonment in her father's house, avoiding all visitors. Her father was a leading citizen of the small town, a popular lawyer, active in local affairs, political and social, with a wide circle of friends, some of whom had a notable part in the public life of the State. To Emily in particular he appeared as a stern, awe-inspiring man. 'His heart was pure and terrible and I think no other like it exists', she wrote later, but he had a large library, and it was perhaps through his concerns and acquaintances that his intense daughter eavesdropped on the world.

When she did meet visitors, she gave no impression of a person timid or withdrawn. One T. W. Higginson, to whom she had written asking for criticism of her poems, visited her in 1870, and though their long correspondence had prepared him for something unusual he was astounded and overwhelmed by the barrage of extravagant intensities and imagery and epigrams that met him. He afterwards described the conversation of his 'half-cracked poetess' as 'the very wantonness of overstatement' and said 'I was never with anyone who drained my nerve power so much.' She made no attempt to conceal her ecstatic delight in life. 'My Business is to love . . . my Business is to sing,' and 'I find ecstasy in living . . . the mere sense of living is joy enough.' One can imagine how her retreat from the world must have stepped this temperament up to terrific pressure, till any excitement at all became explosive. 'Friday I tasted life. It was a vast morsel. A circus passed the house – still I feel the red in my mind.' It was to Higginson that she described herself as 'small, like the Wren, and my hair is bold, like the Chestnut bur – and my eyes, like the Sherry in the Glass, that the Guest leaves.' In her poems she presents herself as 'freckled' and 'Gypsy'.

Around 1860, something decisive happened to Emily Dickinson. How far it was the natural point of maturation of many things in herself, and how much it was triggered by some outer event, is not known, though the possibilities have been endlessly discussed. But the effect was a conflagration within her that produced just about one thousand poems in six years, more than half her total. In 1862 alone it has been calculated that she wrote 366 poems. Those years coincided with the national agitations of the Civil War, with her own coming to mental maturity, and with the beginning of her thirties – when perhaps she realized that her unusual endowment of love was not going to be asked for. But the central themes of the poems have suggested to many readers that the key event was a great and final disappointment in her love for some particular person, about this time. There are two or three likely candidates for the role, and some evidence in letters. This theory supposes that the eruption of her imagination and poetry followed when she shifted her passion, with the energy of desperation, from this lost person onto the only possible substitute – the entire Universe in its Divine aspect. She certainly describes this operation in her poems several times, and it's hard not to believe that something of the sort happened. Thereafter, the marriage that had been denied in the real world, went forward in the spiritual – on her side – as dozens of her poems witness:

> Title divine—is Mine!
> The Wife—without the Sign!

The forces which now came together in the crucible of her imagination decided her greatness. One of the most weighty circumstances, and the most interesting, was that just as the Universe in its Divine aspect became the mirror-image of her 'husband', so the whole religious dilemma of New England, at the most critical moment in its history, became the mirror-image of her relationship to 'him' – of her 'marriage', in fact. And so her spiritualized love and its difficulties became also a topical religious disputation on the grandest scale.

At that time, the old Calvinism of the New England States was in open battle against the spirit of the new age – the Higher Criticism that was dissolving the Bible, the broadening, liberalizing influence of Transcendentalism, the general scientific scepticism which, in America, was doubly rabid under the backlash of the ruthless, selective pragmatism of the frontier and the international-scale hatreds smuggled in by the freedom-grabbers. While radical Puritan revivals were sweeping Emily Dickinson's friends and relatives away from the flesh and the world, like epidemics which she was almost alone among her friends in resisting, she quarantined herself in Jonathan Edwards's faith that the visible Universe was 'an emanation of God for the pure joy of Creation in which the creatures find their justification by yielding assent to the beauty of the whole, even though it slay them.' Beyond this, the Civil War was melting down the whole Nation in an ideological gamble of total suicide or renewal in unity. The Indian tribes and the great sea of buffalo waited on the virgin plains, while Darwin wrote his chapters. The powers that struggled for reconciliation in Emily Dickinson were no less than those which were unmaking and remaking America.

In all this, as her poems testify, she kept her head. Whether the divine 'You', to which her poems are regularly addressed, be a Pan-Christ or the absconded Rev. Charles Wadsworth, a Jehovah/ Nature or the inaccessible Mr Otis P. Lord, Judge of the Supreme Court of Massachusetts, or an altogether darker enigma, it is impossible to tell, but whichever it was, they had a difficult spiritual 'wife' in her. She was devoted, she led the life of a recluse and she wore white, proper for a bride of the spirit, and she daily composed poems that read like devotions. But she was first of all true to herself and her wits. Whether from Church or Science, she would accept nothing by hearsay or on Authority, though she was tempted every way. She reserved herself in some final suspension of judgement. So her poems record not only her ecstatic devotion, but the drama of her sharp, sceptical independence, her doubt, and what repeatedly opens under her ecstasy – her despair.

However important for her poetry her life of love, with all its difficulties, may have been, there is another experience, quite as important, which seems to have befallen her often, and which had nothing to do with her outer life. It is the subject of some of her greatest poems, and all her best poems touch on it. It is what throws the characteristic aura of immensity and chill over her ideas and images. She never seems to have known quite what to think of it. It seems to have recurred to her as a physical state, almost a trance state. In this condition, there opened to her a vision – final reality, her own soul, the soul within the Universe – in all her descriptions of its nature, she never presumed to give it a name. It was her deepest, holiest experience: it was also the most terrible: timeless, deathly, vast, intense. It was like a contradiction to everything that the life in her trusted and loved, it was almost a final revelation of horrible Nothingness –

> Most—like Chaos—stopless—cool
> Without a chance—or spar—
> Or even a Report of Land
> To justify Despair

– and as such, it was the source of the paradox which is her poetic self, and which proliferates throughout her feelings, her ideas, her language, her imagery, her verse technique, in all kinds of ways. At any moment she is likely to feel it ushering itself in, with electrical storms, exalted glimpses of objects, eerie openings of the cosmos –

> A wind that rose, though not a leaf
> In any forest stirred—

Remaining true to this, she could make up her mind about nothing. It stared through her life. Registering everywhere and in everything the icy chill of its nearness, she did not know what to think. The one thing she was sure about, was that it was there, and that its speech was poetry. In its light, all other concerns floated free of finality, became merely relative, susceptible to her artistic play. It was a mystery, and there was only one thing she relied on to solve it, and that was death. Death obsessed her, as the one act that could take her the one necessary step beyond her vision. Death would carry her and her sagacity clean through the riddle. She deferred all her questions to death's solution. And so these three – whatever it was that lay beyond her frightening vision, and the crowded, beloved Creation around her, and Death – became her Holy Trinity. What she divined of their Holiness was what she could divine of their poetry. And it is in her devotion to this Trinity, rather than in anything to do with the more orthodox terminology which she used so freely and familiarly, that she became 'the greatest religious poet America has produced'.

In a way, it was the precision of her feeling for language, which is one department of honesty, that kept her to the painful short-coming of her suspended judgement, and saved her from the easy further step of abstraction into philosophy and shared religion. And it is in her verbal genius that all her gifts and convulsive sufferings came to focus. She was able to manage such a vast subject matter, and make it so important to us, purely because of the strengths and ingenuities of her poetic style.

There is the slow, small metre, a device for bringing each syllable into close-up, as under a microscope; there is the deep, steady focus, where all the words lie in precise and yet somehow free relation-ships, so that the individual syllables seem to be on the point of slipping into utterly new meanings, all pressing to be uncovered; there is the mosaic, pictogram concentration of ideas into which she codes a volcanic elemental imagination, a lava flood of passions, an apocalyptic vision; there is the tranced suspense and deliberation in her punctuation of dashes, and the riddling, oblique artistic strate-gies, the Shakespearian texture of the language, solid with meta-phor, saturated with the homeliest imagery and experience; the freakish blood-and-nerve paradoxical vitality of her latinisms, the musical games – of opposites, parallels, mirrors, chinese puzzles, harmonizing and counterpointing whole worlds of reference; and everywhere there is the teeming carnival of world-life. It is difficult to exhaust the unique art and pleasures of her poetic talent. With the hymn and the riddle, those two small domestic implements, she grasped the 'centre' and the 'circumference' of things – to use two of her favourite expressions – as surely as human imagination ever has.

To select the poems in this volume has not been easy. Her unique and inspired pieces are very many, and very varied. In the limits of this 'selection' it was not possible to be representative. Finally, I chose the pieces I liked best at the time of choosing, well aware that among so many poems of such strong charm this choice must be far from final, for me or for any reader.

Sylvia Plath: *Ariel*

In her earlier poems, Sylvia Plath composed very slowly, consulting her Thesaurus and Dictionary for almost every word, putting a slow, strong line of ink under each word that attracted her. Her obsession with intricate rhyming and metrical schemes was part of the same process. Some of those early inventions of hers were almost perverse, with their bristling hurdles. But this is what she enjoyed. One of her most instinctive compulsions was to make patterns – vivid, bold, symmetrical patterns. She was fond of drawing – anything, a blade of grass, a tree, a stone, but preferably something complicated and chaotic, like a high heap of junk. On her paper this became inexorably ordered and powerful, like a marvellous piece of sculpture, and took on the look of her poems, everything clinging together like a family of living cells, where nothing can be alien or dead or arbitrary. The poems in *Ariel* are the fruits of that labour. In them, she controls one of the widest and most subtly discriminating vocabularies in the modern poetry of our language, and these are poems written for the most part at great speed, as she might take dictation, where she ignores metre and rhyme for rhythm and momentum, the flight of her ideas and music. The words in these odd-looking verses are not only charged with terrific heat, pressure and clairvoyant precision, they are all deeply related within any poem, acknowledging each other and calling to each other in deep harmonic designs. It is this musical almost mathematical hidden law which gives these explosions their immovable finality.

Behind these poems there is a fierce and uncompromising nature. There is also a child desperately infatuated with the world. And there is a strange muse, bald, white and wild, in her 'hood of bone', floating over a landscape like that of the Primitive Painters, a burningly luminous vision of a Paradise. A Paradise which is at the same time eerily frightening, an unalterably spot-lit vision of death.

From the *Poetry Book Society Bulletin* No. 44, February 1965.

And behind them, too, is a long arduous preparation. She grew up in an atmosphere of tense intellectual competition and Germanic rigour. Her mother, first-generation American of Austrian stock, and her father, who was German-Polish, were both University teachers. Her father, whom she worshipped, died when she was eight, and thereafter her mother raised Sylvia and her brother single-handed. Whatever teaching methods were used, Sylvia was the perfect pupil: she did every lesson double. Her whole tremendous will was bent on excelling. Finally, she emerged like the survivor of an evolutionary ordeal: at no point could she let herself be negligent or inadequate. What she was most afraid of was that she might come to live outside her genius for love, which she also equated with courage, or 'guts', to use her word. This genius for love she certainly had, and not in the abstract. She didn't quite know how to manage it: it possessed her. It fastened her to cups, plants, creatures, vistas, people, in a steady ecstasy. As much of all that as she could, she hoarded into her poems, into those incredibly beautiful lines and hallucinatory evocations.

But the truly miraculous thing about her will remain the fact that in two years, while she was almost fully occupied with children and house-keeping, she underwent a poetic development that has hardly any equal on record, for suddenness and completeness. The birth of her first child seemed to start the process. All at once she could compose at top speed, and with her full weight. Her second child brought things a giant step forward. All the various voices of her gift came together, and for about six months, up to a day or two before her death, she wrote with the full power and music of her extraordinary nature.

Ariel is not easy poetry to criticize. It is not much like any other poetry. It is her. Everything she did was just like this, and this is just like her – but permanent.

Publishing Sylvia Plath

Some months ago, in his *Observer* review of Sylvia Plath's recently published collections of poetry, *Crossing the Water* and *Winter Trees*, A. Alvarez speculated about the general history of the publication of Sylvia Plath's writings since her death. Now that there seems to be, as he says, 'a vast potential audience' (after the success of her novel in the States) for her poetry, he supposes her literary executors must be undergoing 'overwhelming temptation' to linger out new publications in a deliberately artful way, exploiting both the work (with the inferior audience) and the audience (with the inferior work), and in fact he all but questions whether this hasn't been happening right from the start, whether this isn't the strangeness of the 'strange' manner in which the work has appeared so far. This is nothing to what has been wafting from some corners of the Universities in the US. Possibly Mr Alvarez doesn't know what a crazy club his article belongs to.

All these people are basically telling Sylvia Plath's executors just what their editorial obligations are and were. It seems her complete opus should be published (should have been published long ago) in complete detail, preferably with all the fragments and variants and cancellations of her bristling manuscripts – some of these being otherwise a loss to literature. To a scholar, it is a simple business, and merely needs his/her diligence and care.

As I am aware of them, my obligations are not so simple as a scholar's would be. They are, first, towards her family, second, towards her best work. Just like hers, in fact – a point to be considered, since I feel a general first and last obligation to her.

For her family, I follow her principle and try to manage the writing in ways that will earn as much income as possible. If that worries Mr Alvarez, I only wish there were more to worry him with. For her work, I have tried to publish it in ways that would help the

From the *Observer*, 21 November 1971.

best of it make its proper impact and take its proper place, uncompromised by weaker material. And that has not been such a simple business as her admirers might think.

Towards what he calls 'the Plath industry throbbing with busyness in the Universities', and towards that 'vast potential audience', I feel no obligations whatsoever. The scholars want the anatomy of the birth of the poetry; and the vast potential audience want her blood, hair, touch, smell, and a front seat in the kitchen where she died. The scholars may well inherit what they want, some day, and there are journalists supplying the other audience right now. But neither audience makes me feel she owes them anything.

I agree the publication of her work might seem to have been odd. But not really odd. The speculations about it have had to strain and warp in order to miss the obvious, natural reasons. The literary history of it is more or less as follows.

The Colossus in 1961 had been a moderate success with reviewers and a moderate failure, financially, for her publishers, who saw nothing there to persuade them that they could be handling a genius who might some day become an asset. Her novel *The Bell Jar*, published in England only, and under a pseudonym, in January 1963, was very moderately reviewed by reviewers who noticed it at all. I remember only one (by Anthony Burgess) that seemed to have any inkling of the qualities that became obvious ten years later, when the author was known and her poetry famous. When she died in February 1963, her audience was quite small. Many more editors were rejecting than were accepting the *Ariel* poems, which were beginning to appear here and there. Among magazine editors, a clear recognition of her talent seemed confined to only two or three. But they would publish everything she wrote (Alan Ross at the *London Magazine*, Brian Cox and Tony Dyson at the *Critical Quarterly*, and Alvarez himself). She kept a neat list of what she sent out, where to, what was bought, by whom, when, how much for, and what was sent back. That list makes interesting reading now.

She left behind a carbon typescript, its title altered from *Daddy* to *Ariel*, its pages littered with minor corrections, containing about thirty-five poems, beginning as now with 'Morning Song' and ending with the Bee poems (without 'Stings'). It began with the word 'love' and ended with 'spring', as she pointed out. She avoided answering the question of when she was going to publish it, which I repeatedly asked her, or she made deliberately mysterious answers which gave me the impression that she did not quite know what to do. This was very different from her usual eagerness to circulate her book manuscript at every stage of its development.

The last of the poems in that manuscript had been written on 2 December 1962. After writing nothing for nearly two months she began again on 28 January 1963 and writing on five days up to 5 February produced twelve more poems. Of these she showed me 'Totem' and 'The Munich Mannequins'. These seemed to me, and to her too, even finer than the *Ariel* poems (of which she had shown me a selected few). It may seem odd to say she was pleased with them. After her death, these last pieces lay separate and loose, together with the poems not included in the *Ariel* manuscript though written at the same time, and with those written in the longish interval between the last of the *Colossus* and the first of *Ariel*. All these poems were either already published, or were on their way to and from magazines, except the last dozen. She was always scrupulous or unscrupulous about selling every line she wrote, preferably in both England and the States. But when she was assembling a book her self-criticism went up a gear. Enthusiasts, like scholars, feel the need to see every word of their poet, but only a ninny imagines that the poor doesn't ultimately confuse the effect of the good. Art's whole purpose is to recognize the good and bring it clear of the not so good, and keep it there. That's what all the work is about.

The poetry of the *Ariel* poems was no surprise to me. It was at last the flight of what we had been trying to get flying for a number of years. But it dawned on me only in the last months which way it wanted to fly.

As I have said, she herself was a little afraid of her poems, of what the consequences might be in the long run, a little baffled about what to do. After her death they presented me with complications that were absolutely baffling, absolutely without precedent. Everything she and her family feared at that time has since come to pass, and more. And there is no doubt more to come, since some of the victims of those consequences haven't yet entered the arena. But when I finally stopped trying to foreweigh all that, there were still many delaying obstacles.

Alvarez has noticed that '*Ariel* was not published until two and a half years after her death'. Others have complained, some of them in fantasies that are nearly incredible. In those days, I admit, I wasn't the briskest executor, or the most alert guardian of her family's interests. But her public wasn't in such great voice at the time, either. This is evidently hard for people to believe. Even Alvarez, after only eight years, seems to have forgotten it. When I finally got a typescript of her manuscript to her publishers, in England and the States, neither of them wanted it. James Michie, who had taken on *The Colossus* at Heinemann, and was one of her keenest supporters, had left. And Knopf, her publisher in the States, seemed nonplussed. Part of their reluctance was probably connected to the terms I was asking – highish but not that high. I knew what I was offering, and I knew it was the last. A deadlock dragged on. The paralysis of circumstances surrounding her poems cannot be imagined by anybody who was not at the centre of it.

In the end, I offered the book to my own publishers in the States, with strong backing from both inside and outside the firm, but nothing accelerated. And even its most ardent and vocal supporters wanted the manuscript cut by half, or at least to 'about twenty poems'. They felt the full collection might provoke some outraged backlash. This introduced new hesitations because it touched my own uncertainties. They seemed like real questions: ought I to publish only a few poems to begin with? Was the whole book simply unacceptable, did it overdo itself? I was anxious that the collection should not falter in any way, and that her work should be recognized, yet I saw quite plainly that very few knew what to make of it. And I know what a person becomes while writing a review. So I had already started rearranging the collection, cutting out some pieces that looked as if they might let in some facile attacker, cutting out one or two of the more openly vicious ones, and a couple of others that I thought might conceivably seem repetitive in tone and form. Two or three I simply lost for a while in the general fog of those days. I would have cut out 'Daddy' if I'd been in time (there are quite a few things more important than giving the world great poems). I would have cut out others if I'd thought they would ever be decoded. I also kept out one or two that were aimed too nakedly (I kept them out in vain, as it happened. They were known and their work is now done.) I added two pre-*Ariel* poems, 'Little Fugue', because I think it is good enough to stand with the others, and belongs, and 'Hanging Man' not because it is good – though it is – but because it describes with only thin disguise the experience that made *Ariel* possible – a definite event at a definite moment (like everything in her poems). Also, I added about nine of the last poems, because they seemed to me too important to leave out. The uncertainties around this cutting and adding were naturally very thick. I'm still not sure whether *Ariel* would not be a better book if I had kept out everything that followed the Bee poems, as in her version. She herself regarded those last poems as the beginning of a new book. But I no longer remember why I did many things – why the US edition is different from the English, for example. But again, I think most of it was concern for certain people. I don't think I over-estimated the possible injuries.

Eventually contracts were signed, in England and the States, but even after that formality, as every writer knows, many months can pass before the public sees the book. I forget how long *Ariel* took – what was left of the two and a half years. Bearing everything in mind, that seems to me now quite a short time.

It left me with a wad of poems I had no particular thought of publishing, beyond the fact that I had no intention of destroying them. This wad wasn't exactly the 'mass' that some people seem to have been expecting, though it depends how you look at it. Considering the quality, I suppose it was a 'mass'. What made it look more was the fact that from the first *Ariel* poem she suddenly started saving all the draft pages, which she had never bothered about before. She not only saved them, she dated them carefully. I don't know how grossly she might have exaggerated, but there certainly were days when she wrote three poems, or rather finished three. There must have been quite a few more days when she worked on three or more without finishing them.

Winter Trees contains all but about six of the *Ariel* and after poems that were not in *Ariel*. *Crossing the Water* contains the poems she wrote between *The Colossus* and the first *Ariel* – I think all of them. The material is published in two separate volumes because it is so distinctly two separate bodies of work. In spite of Alvarez's implications, whether two thin volumes will coax along that 'that vast potential audience' or earn more income than one thicker volume at a higher price seems to me moot. They might, and I hope they do, but I doubt if it will be enough to justify anybody's concern. These are the first collections of her poems to appear since *Ariel*, six years ago, except for two small limited editions the Turret Press brought out around the time of the earlier book. What has persuaded me to publish this other material now is sure enough her fame. But this fame, here in 1971, is quite recent. Even now, it isn't her poems that have made her famous, but her novel in the US – sensationalized by the editorial apparatus. I did waken to the commercial opportunities of this situation just in time to publish the material in two limited editions, but if I'd found the temptations as overwhelming as Alvarez fears they might be, I could well have deployed the material over five or six.

I wish I could follow his suggestion and go on in this way, producing another volume of her work every two or three years, and really farm the market that he tells us has now appeared. Alas, I've wakened up too late. All that remains, besides those half dozen or so poems which will probably go into her *Collected* edition sooner or later, is her stories and short prose pieces. Some of these are good and I hope will be published. Only scholars more concerned for their own theses, etc., than for her achievement would want to publish her juvenilia. The 'second novel', that Alvarez mentions, got lost – along with quite a few other things – in the traffic terminal confusion, with which he was familiar, just after her death.

As it is, I'm not sure that I haven't compromised her best work, in producing these last two volumes. The response to them, so far,

[168]

would suggest that I definitely have. English reviewers have been puzzled by the poems, pitifully eager – like the 'base man' at the archery butts in the Chinese proverb – to call out what they imagine are her misses. After such fantasy expectations, I suppose any actual poems must appear anticlimactic, even such exercises of genius as her weakest pieces undoubtedly are. But such a response would persuade nobody about the desperate need for a *Collected Poems*.

Collecting Sylvia Plath

By the time of her death, on 11 February 1963, Sylvia Plath had written a large bulk of poetry. To my knowledge, she never scrapped any of her poetic efforts. With one or two exceptions, she brought every piece she worked on to some final form acceptable to her, rejecting at most the odd verse, or a false head or a false tail. Her attitude to her verse was artisan-like: if she couldn't get a table out of the material, she was quite happy to get a chair, or even a toy. The end product for her was not so much a successful poem as something that had temporarily exhausted her ingenuity. So this book contains not merely what verse she saved, but – after 1956 – all she wrote.

From quite early she began to assemble her poems into a prospective collection, which at various times she presented – always hopeful – to publishers and to the judging committees of contests. The collection evolved through the years in a natural way, shedding old poems and growing new ones, until by the time the contract for *The Colossus* was signed with Heinemann, in London, on 11 February 1960, this first book had gone through several titles and several changes of substance. 'I had a vision in the dark art lecture room today of *the* title of my book of poems,' she wrote in early 1958. 'It came to me suddenly with great clarity that *The Earthenware Head* was the right title, the only title.' She goes on to say, 'Somehow this new title spells for me the release from the old crystal-brittle and sugar-faceted voice of *Circus in Three Rings* and *Two Lovers and a Beachcomber*' (the two immediately preceding titles). Two months later she had replaced *The Earthenware Head*, briefly, with *The Everlasting Monday*. A fortnight later the title had become *Full Fathom Five*, 'after what I consider one of my best and most curiously moving poems, about my father-sea god-muse . . . "[The Lady and] The Earthenware Head" is out:

Introduction to *Collected Poems of Sylvia Plath* (London: Faber and Faber, 1981).

once, in England, my "best poem": too fancy, glassy, patchy and rigid – it embarrasses me now – with its ten elaborate epithets for head in five verses.'

During the next year *Full Fathom Five* was replaced by *The Bull of Bendylaw*, but then in May 1959 she wrote: 'Changed title of poetry book in an inspiration to *The Devil of the Stairs* ... this title encompasses my book and "explains" the poems of despair, which is as deceitful as hope is.' This title lasted until October, when she was at Yaddo, and now on a different kind of inspiration she noted: 'Wrote two poems that pleased me. One a poem to Nicholas' [she expected a son, and titled the poem 'The Manor Garden'] 'and one the old father-worship subject' [which she titled 'The Colossus']. 'But different. Weirder. I see a picture, a weather, in these poems. Took "Medallion" out of the early book and made up my mind to start a second book, regardless. The main thing is to get rid of the idea that what I write now is for the old book. That soggy book. So I have three poems for the new, temporarily called *The Colossus and other poems*.'

This decision to start a new book 'regardless', and get rid of all that she'd written up to then, coincided with the first real break-through in her writing, as it is now possible to see. The actual inner process of this quite sudden development is interestingly recorded, in a metaphysical way, in 'Poem for a Birthday', which she was thinking about on 22 October 1959: 'Ambitious seeds of a long poem made up of separate sections. Poem on her birthday. [Her own birthday fell on 27 October.] To be a dwelling on madhouse, nature: meanings of tools, greenhouses, florists' shops, tunnels, vivid and disjointed. An adventure. Never over. Developing Rebirth. Despair. Old women. Block it out.' Then on 4 November she wrote: 'Miraculously I wrote seven poems in my "Poem for a Birthday" sequence, and the two little ones before it, "The Manor Garden" and "The Colossus", I find colorful and amusing. But the manu-script of my [old] book seems dead to me. So far off, so far gone. It has almost no chance of finding a publisher: just sent it out to the seventh. ... There is nothing for it but to try to publish it in England.' A few days later she noted: 'I wrote a good poem this week on our walk Sunday to the burnt-out spa, a second-book poem. How it consoles me, the idea of a second book with these new poems: "The Manor Garden", "The Colossus", the seven birthday poems and perhaps "Medallion", if I don't stick it in my present book.' But then she realized: 'If I were accepted by a publisher . . . I would feel a need to throw all my new poems in, to bolster the book.'

This last is exactly what happened. With time running out at Yaddo, which had suddenly become so fruitful for her, followed by the upheaval of returning to England in December, she was able to add very little to her 'second' book. So it was this combination of the old poems, which she had inwardly rejected, and the few new ones that seemed to her so different, that James Michie told her – in January 1960 – Heinemann would like to publish, under the title of *The Colossus*.

Once that contract had been signed, she started again, though with a noticeable difference. As before, a poem was always 'a book poem' or 'not a book poem', but now she seemed more relaxed about it, and made no attempt to find an anxious mothering title for the growing brood, over the next two years, until she was overtaken by the inspiration that produced the poems of the last six months of her life.

Some time around Christmas 1962, she gathered most of what are now known as the 'Ariel' poems in a black spring binder, and arranged them in a careful sequence. This collection of hers excluded almost everything she had written between *The Colossus* and July 1962 – or two and a half years' work. She had her usual trouble with a title. On the title-page of her manuscript *The Rival* is replaced by *A Birthday Present* which is replaced by *Daddy*. It was only a short time before she died that she altered the title again, to *Ariel*.

The *Ariel* eventually published in 1965 was a somewhat different volume from the one she had planned. It incorporated most of the dozen or so poems she had gone on to write in 1963, though she herself, recognizing the different inspiration of these new pieces, regarded them as the beginnings of a third book. It omitted some of the more personally aggressive poems from 1962, and might have omitted one or two more if she had not already published them herself in magazines – so that by 1965 they were widely known. The collection that appeared was my eventual compromise between publishing a large bulk of her work – including much of the post-*Colossus* but pre-*Ariel* verse – and introducing her late work more cautiously, printing perhaps only twenty poems to begin with. (Several advisers had felt that the violent contradictory feelings expressed in those pieces might prove hard for the reading public to take. In one sense, as it turned out, this apprehension showed some insight.)

A further collection, *Crossing the Water* (1971), contained most of the poems written between the two earlier books; and the same year the final collection, *Winter Trees*, was published, containing eighteen uncollected poems of the late period together with her verse play for radio, *Three Women*, which had been written in early 1962.

The aim of the present complete edition, which contains a numbered sequence of the 224 poems written after 1956 together with a further 50 poems chosen from her pre-1956 work, is to bring Sylvia Plath's poetry together in one volume, including the various uncollected and unpublished pieces, and to set everything in as true a chronological order as is possible, so that the whole progress and achievement of this unusual poet will become accessible to readers.

The manuscripts on which this collection is based fall roughly into three phases, and each has presented slightly different problems to the editor.

The first phase might be called her juvenilia and the first slight problem here was to decide where it ended. A logical division occurs, conveniently, at the end of 1955, just after the end of her twenty-third year. The 220 or more poems written before this are of interest mainly to specialists. Sylvia Plath had set these pieces (many of them from her early teens) firmly behind her and would certainly never have republished them herself. Nevertheless, quite a few seem worth preserving for the general reader. At their best, they are as distinctive and as finished as anything she wrote later. They can be intensely artificial, but they are always lit with her unique excitement. And that sense of a deep mathematical inevitability in the sound and texture of her lines was well developed quite early. One can see here, too, how exclusively her writing depended on a supercharged system of inner symbols and images, an enclosed cosmic circus. If that could have been projected visually, the substance and patterning of these poems would have made very curious mandalas. As poems, they are always inspired high jinks, but frequently quite a bit more. And even at their weakest they help chart the full acceleration towards her final take-off.

The greater part of these early poems survive in final typed copies; some others have been recovered from magazines, and still others, not in the typescript and not appearing in any magazine, have turned up in letters and elsewhere. Presumably there may be more, still hidden. The chronological order of the work of this period is often impossible to determine, except in its broadest outlines. A date can sometimes be fixed from a letter or from the date of magazine publication, but she occasionally took poems up again – sometimes years later – and reworked them.

From this whole pre-1956 period, I have selected what seem to be the best, some fifty pieces, and these are printed – as nearly as possible in the order of their writing – at the back of the book, as an appendix. Also given there is a complete list, alphabetically by title, of all the pre-1956 poems that survive, with dates where these can be assigned.

The second phase of Sylvia Plath's writing falls between early 1956 and late 1960. Early 1956 presents itself as a watershed, because from later this year come the earliest poems of her first collection, *The Colossus*. And from this time I worked closely with her and watched the poems being written, so I am reasonably sure that everything is here. Searching over the years, we have failed to unearth any others. Final typescripts exist for all of them. The chronological order, also, is less in doubt here, though the problem does still linger. Her evolution as a poet went rapidly through successive moults of style, as she realized her true matter and voice.

Each fresh phase tended to bring out a group of poems bearing a general family likeness, and is usually associated in my memory with a particular time and place. At each move we made, she seemed to shed a style.

So the sequence of the groups of poems through this period is fairly certain. But I am rarely sure now which poem comes before which in any particular group. In among them, the odd poem will pop up that looks like a leftover from long before. Occasionally, she anticipated herself and produced a poem ('Two Lovers and a Beachcomber by the Real Sea', for instance, in the pre-1956 selection, or 'The Stones' from her 1959 'Poem for a Birthday') which now seems to belong quite a bit later. In several cases I can fix poems precisely to a date and place. (She was writing 'Miss Drake Proceeds to Supper' on a parapet over the Seine on 21 June 1956.) Then again, in one or two cases the dates she left on the manuscripts contradict what seem to me very definite memories. So I have nowhere attempted to affix a date where none appears on the manuscript. Fortunately, after 1956 she kept a full record of the dates on which she sent her poems off to magazines, and she usually did this as soon as possible after writing them, which sets one limit to my approximations of order.

The third and final phase of her work, from the editorial point of view, dates from about September 1960. Around that time, she started the habit of dating the final typescript of each poem. On the two or three occasions when she modified a poem later, she dated the revision as well. From early 1962 she began to save all her handwritten drafts (which up to that time she had systematically destroyed as she went along), and provisional final versions among these are usually dated as well. So throughout this period the calendar sequence is correct, and the only occasional doubt concerns the order of composition among poems written on the same day.

I have resisted the temptation to reproduce the drafts of these last poems in variorum completeness. These drafts are arguably an important part of Sylvia Plath's complete works. Some of the handwritten pages are aswarm with startling, beautiful phrases and lines, crowding all over the place, many of them in no way less remarkable than the ones she eventually picked out to make her final poem. But printing them all would have made a huge volume.

Sylvia Plath and Her Journals

Sylvia Plath's journals exist as an assortment of notebooks and bunches of loose sheets, and the selection just published here contains about a third of the whole bulk. Two other notebooks survived for a while after her death. They continued from where the surviving record breaks off in late 1959 and covered the last three years of her life. The second of these two books her husband destroyed, because he did not want her children to have to read it (in those days he regarded forgetfulness as an essential part of survival). The earlier one disappeared more recently (and may, presumably, still turn up).

The motive in publishing these journals will be questioned. The argument against is still strong. A decisive factor has been certain evident confusions, provoked in the minds of many of her readers by her later poetry. *Ariel* is dramatic speech of a kind. But to what persona and to what drama is it to be fitted? The poems don't seem to supply enough evidence of the definitive sort. This might have been no bad thing, if a riddle fertile in hypotheses is a good one. But the circumstances of her death, it seems, multiplied every one of her statements by a wild, unknown quantity. The results, among her interpeters, have hardly been steadied by the account she gave of herself in her letters to her mother, or by the errant versions supplied by her biographers. So the question grows: how do we find our way through this accompaniment, which has now become almost a part of the opus? Would we be helped if we had more first-hand testimony, a more intimately assured image, of what she was really like? In answer to this, these papers, which contain the nearest thing to a living portrait of her, are offered in the hope of providing some ballast for our idea of the reality behind the poems. Maybe they will do more.

Looking over this curtailed journal, one cannot help wondering whether the lost entries for her last three years were not the more important section of it. Those years, after all, produced the work that made her name. And we certainly have lost a valuable appendix to all that later writing. Yet these surviving diaries contain something that cannot be less valuable. If we read them with understanding, they can give us the key to the most intriguing mystery about her, the key to our biggest difficulty in our approach to her poetry.

That difficulty is the extreme peculiarity in kind of her poetic gift. And the difficulty is not lessened by the fact that she left behind two completely different kinds of poetry.

Few poets have disclosed in any way the birth circumstances of their poetic gift, or the necessary purpose these serve in their psychic economy. It is not easy to name one. As if the first concern of poetry were to cover its own tracks. When a deliberate attempt to reveal all has been made, by a Pasternak or a Wordsworth, the result is discursive autobiography – illuminating enough but not an X-ray. Otherwise poets are very properly bent on exploring subject matter, themes, intellectual possibilities and modifications, evolving the foliage and blossoms and fruit of a natural cultural organism whose roots are hidden, and whose birth and private purpose are no part of the crop. Sylvia Plath's poetry, like a species on its own, exists in little else but the revelation of that birth and purpose. Though her whole considerable ambition was fixed on becoming the normal flowering and fruiting kind of writer, her work was roots only. Almost as if her entire oeuvre were enclosed within those processes and transformations that happen in other poets before they can even begin, before the muse can hold out a leaf. Or as if all poetry were made up of the feats and shows performed by the poetic spirit Ariel. Whereas her poetry is the biology of Ariel, the ontology of Ariel – the story of Ariel's imprisonment in the pine, before Prospero opened it. And it continued to be so even after the end of *The Colossus*, which fell, as it happens, in the last entries of this surviving bulk of her journal, where the opening of the pine took place and was recorded.

This singularity of hers is a mystery – an enigma in itself. It may be that she was simply an extreme case, that many other poets' works nurse and analyse their roots as doggedly as hers do, but that she is distinguished by an unusually clear root system and an abnormally clear and clinically exact system of attending to it. It may have something to do with the fact the she was a woman. Maybe her singularity derives from a feminine bee-line instinct for the real priority, for what truly matters – an instinct for nursing and repairing the damaged and threatened nucleus of the self and for starving every other aspect of her life in order to feed and strengthen that, and bring that to a safe delivery.

The root system of her talent was a deep and inclusive inner crisis which seems to have been quite distinctly formulated in its chief symbols (presumably going back at least as far as the death of her father, when she was eight) by the time of her first attempted suicide, in 1953, when she was twenty-one.

After 1953, it became a much more serious business, a continuous hermetically sealed process that changed only very slowly, so that for years it looked like deadlock. Though its preoccupation domin-ated her life, it remained largely outside her ordinary consciousness, but in her poems we see the inner working of it. It seems to have been scarcely disturbed at all by the outer upheavals she passed through, by her energetic involvement in her studies, in her love affairs and her marriage, and in her jobs, though she used details from them as a matter of course for images to develop her X-rays.

The importance of these diaries lies in the rich account they give of her attempts to understand this obscure process, to follow it, and (in vain) to hasten it. As time went on, she interpreted what was happening to her inwardly, more and more consciously, as a 'drama' of some sort. After its introductory overture (everything up to 1953), the drama proper began with a 'death', which was followed by a long 'gestation' or 'regeneration', which in turn would ultimately require a 'birth' or a 'rebirth,' as in Dostoevsky and Lawrence and those other prophets of rebirth whose works were her sacred books.

The 'death', so important in all that she wrote after it, was that almost successful suicide attempt in the summer of 1953. The mythical dimensions of the experience seem to have been deepened, and made absolute, and illuminated, by two accidents: she lay undiscovered, in darkness, only intermittently half-conscious, for 'three days'; and the electric shock treatment which followed went wrong, and she was all but electrocuted – at least so she always claimed. Whether it did and she was, or not, there seems little doubt that her 'three day' death, and that thunderbolt awakening, fused her dangerous inheritance into a matrix from which everything later seemed to develop – as from a radical change in the structure of her brain.

She would describe her suicide attempt as a bid to get back to her father, and one can imagine that in her case this was a routine reconstruction from a psychoanalytical point of view. But she made much of it, and it played an increasingly dominant role in her recovery and in what her poetry was able to become. Some of the implications might be divined from her occasional dealings with the Ouija board, during the late fifties. Her father's name was Otto, and 'spirits' would regularly arrive with instructions for her from one Prince Otto, who was said to be a great power in the underworld. When she pressed for a more personal communication, she would be told that Prince Otto could not speak to her directly, because he was under orders from the Colossus. And when she pressed for an audience with the Colossus, they would say he was inaccessible. It is easy to see how her effort to come to terms with the meaning this Colossus held for her, in her poetry, became more and more central as the years passed.

The strange limbo of 'gestation/regeneration', which followed her 'death', lasted throughout the period of this journal, and she drew from the latter part of it all the poems of *The Colossus*, her first collection. We have spoken of this process as a 'nursing' of the 'nucleus of the self', as a hermetically sealed, slow transformation of her inner crisis; and the evidence surely supports these descriptions of it as a deeply secluded mythic and symbolic inner theatre (sometimes a hospital theatre), accessible to her only in her poetry. One would like to emphasize even more strongly the weird autonomy of what was going on in there. It gave the impression of being a secret crucible, or rather a womb, an almost biological process – and just as much beyond her manipulative interference. And like a pregnancy, selfish with her resources.

We can hardly make too much of this special condition, both in our understanding of her journal and in our reading of the poems of her first book. A reader of the journal might wonder why she did not make more of day-to-day events. She had several outlandish adventures during these years, and interesting things were always happening to her. But her diary entries habitually ignore them. When she came to talk to herself in these pages, that magnetic inner process seemed to engross all her attention, one way or another. And in her poems and stories, throughout this period, she felt her creative dependence on that same process as subjection to a tyrant. It commandeered every proposal. Many passages in this present book show the deliberate – almost frantic – effort with which she tried to extend her writing, to turn it toward the world and other people, to stretch it over more of outer reality, to forget herself in some exploration of outer reality – in which she took, after all, such constant, intense delight. But the hidden workshop, the tangle of roots, the crucible, controlled everything. Everything became another image of itself, another lens into itself. And whatever it could not use in this way, to objectify some disclosure of itself, did not get onto the page at all.

Unless we take account of this we shall almost certainly misread the moods of her journal – her nightmare sense of claustrophobia and suspended life, her sense of being only the flimsy, brittle husk of what was going heavily and fierily on, somewhere out of reach inside her. And we shall probably find ourselves looking into her poems for things and qualities which could only be there if that process had been less fiercely concentrated on its own purposeful chemistry. We shall misconstrue the tone and content of the poetry that did manage to transmit from the centre, and the psychological exactness and immediacy of its mournful, stressful confinement.

A Jungian might call the whole phase a classic case of the alchemical individuation of the self. This interpretation would not tie up every loose end, but it would make positive meaning of the details of the poetic imagery – those silent horrors going on inside a glass crucible, a crucible that reappears in many forms, but always glassy and always closed. Above all, perhaps, it would help to confirm a truth – that the process was, in fact, a natural and positive process, if not the most positive and healing of all involuntary responses to the damage of life: a process of self-salvation – a resurrection of her deepest spiritual vitality against the odds of her fate. And the Jungian interpretation would fit the extraordinary outcome too: the birth of her new creative self.

The significant thing, even so, in the progress she made, was surely the way she applied herself to the task. Her battered and so-often-exhausted determination, the relentless way she renewed the assault without ever really knowing what she was up against. The serious-ness, finally, of her will to face what was wrong in herself, and to drag it out into examination, and to remake it – that is what is so impressive. Her refusal to rest in any halfway consolation or evasive delusion. And it produced some exemplary pieces of writing, here and there, in her diaries. It would not be so impressive if she were not so manifestly terrified of doing what she nevertheless did. At times, she seems almost invalid in her lack of inner protections. Her writing here (as in her poems) simplifies itself in baring itself to what hurts her. It is unusually devoid of intellectual superstructures – of provisional ideas, theorizings, developed fantasies, which are all protective clothing as well as tools. What she did have, clearly, was character – and passionate character at that. One sees where the language of *Ariel* got its temper – that unique blend of courage and vulnerability. The notion of her forcing herself, in her 'Japanese silks, desperate butterflies', deeper into some internal furnace, strengthens throughout these pages, and remains.

But she was getting somewhere. Late in 1959 (toward the end of the surviving diaries) she had a dream, which at the time made a visionary impact on her, in which she was trying to reassemble a giant, shattered, stone Colossus. In the light of her private myth-ology, we can see this dream was momentous, and she versified it, addressing the ruins as 'Father', in a poem which she regarded, at the time, as a breakthrough. But the real significance of the dream emerges, perhaps, a few days later, when the quarry of anthropomorphic ruins reappears, in a poem titled 'The Stones'. In this second poem, the ruins are none other than her hospital city, the factory where men are remade, and where, among the fragments, a new self has been put together. Or rather an old shattered self, reduced by violence to its essential core, has been repaired and renovated and born again, and – most significant of all – speaks with a new voice.

This 'birth' is the culmination of her prolonged six-year 'drama'. It is doubtful whether we would be reading this journal at all if the 'birth' recorded in that poem, 'The Stones', had not happened in a very real sense, in November 1959.

The poem is the last of a sequence titled 'Poem for a Birthday'. Her diary is quite informative about her plans for this piece, which began as little more than an experimental poetic idea that offered scope for her to play at imitating Roethke. But evidently there were hidden prompters. As a piece of practical magic, 'Poem for a Birthday' came just at the right moment. Afterward, she knew something had happened, but it is only in retrospect that we can see what it was. During the next three years she herself came to view this time as the turning point in her writing career, the point where her real writing began.

Looking back further, maybe we can see signs and portents before then. Maybe her story 'Johnny Panic and the Bible of Dreams' was the John the Baptist. And in her own recognition of the change, at the time, she spread the honours over several other poems as well – 'The Manor Garden' (which is an apprehensive welcome to the approaching unborn), 'The Colossus' (which is the poem describing the visionary dream of the ruined Colossus), and 'Medallion' (which describes a snake as an undead, unliving elemental beauty, a crystalline essence of stone). But this poem, 'The Stones', is the thing itself.

It is unlike anything that had gone before in her work. The system of association, from image to image and within the images, is quite new, and – as we can now see – it is that of *Ariel*. And throughout the poem what we hear coming clear is the now-familiar voice of *Ariel*.

In its double focus, 'The Stones' is both a 'birth' and a 'rebirth'. It is the birth of her real poetic voice, but it is the rebirth of herself. That poem encapsulates, with literal details, her 'death,' her treatment, and her slow, buried recovery. And this is where we can see the peculiarity of her imagination at work, where we can see how the substance of her poetry and the very substance of her survival are the same. In another poet, 'The Stones' might have been an artistic assemblage of fantasy images. But she was incapable of free fantasy, in the ordinary sense. If an image of hers had its source in a sleeping or waking 'dream', it was inevitably the image of some meaning she had paid for or would have to pay for, in some way – that she had lived or would have to live. It had the *necessity* of a physical symptom. This is the objectivity of her subjective mode. Her internal crystal ball was helplessly truthful, in this sense. (And truthfulness of that sort has inescapable inner consequences.) It determined her lack of freedom, sure enough, as we have already seen. But it secured her loyalty to what was, for her, the most important duty of all. And for this reason the succession of images in 'The Stones', in which we see her raising a new self out of the ruins of her mythical father, has to be given the status of fact. The 'drama', in which she redeemed and balanced the earlier 'death' with this 'birth/rebirth', and from which she drew so much confidence later on, was a great simplification, but we cannot easily doubt that it epitomizes, in ritual form, the main inner labour of her life up to the age of twenty-seven.

And this is the story her diaries have to tell: how a poetic talent was forced into full expressive being, by internal need, for a purpose vital to the whole organism.

'Birth', of the sort we have been talking about, is usually found in the context of a religion, or at least of some mystical discipline. It is rare in secular literature. If 'The Stones' does indeed record such a birth, we should now look for some notable effects, some exceptional flowering of energy. It is just this second phase of her career that has proved so difficult to judge in conventional literary terms. But whatever followed November 1959, in Sylvia Plath's writing, has a bearing on our assessment of what is happening in this journal.

Shortly after the date of the last poems of *The Colossus*, and the last date of her diary proper, a big change did come over her life. It took a few weeks to get into its stride.

When she sailed for England in December with her husband, though she had her new, full-formed confidence about her writing to cheer her, her life still seemed suspended, and all her ambitions as far off as ever. In a poem she wrote soon after, 'On Deck', she mentions that one of her fellow passengers on the S.S. *United States*, an American astrologer (he was physically a double for James Joyce), had picked that most propitious date for launching his astrological conquest of the British public. His optimism did not rub off on her. With her last college days well behind her, and only writing and maternity ahead, the December London of 1959 gave her a bad shock – the cars seemed smaller and blacker and dingier than ever, sizzling through black wet streets. The clothes on the people seemed even grubbier than she remembered. And when she lay on a bed in a basement room in a scruffy hotel near Victoria, a week or two later with *The Rack*, by A. E. Ellis, propped open on her pregnant stomach, it seemed to her she had touched a new nadir.

Yet within the next three years she achieved one after another almost all the ambitions she had been brooding over in frustration for the last decade. In that first month her collection of poems, *The Colossus*, was taken for publication in England by James Michie at Heinemann. In April she produced a daughter. In early 1961, at high speed, and in great exhilaration, she wrote her autobiographical novel *The Bell Jar*, and though both Harper and Knopf rejected it in the States, Heinemann took it at once for publication in England. One important part of her life-plan was to acquire a 'base', as she called it, somewhere in England, from which she hoped to make her raids on the four corners of the earth, devouring the delights and excitements. And accordingly, later in 1961, she acquired a house in the west of England. In January of 1962, she produced a son. In May of that year *The Colossus* was published in the States by Knopf.

Meanwhile, she went on steadily writing her new poems. After the promise of 'The Stones', we look at these with fresh attention. And they *are* different from what had gone before. But superficially not very different. For one thing, there is little sign of *Ariel*. And she herself seemed to feel that these pieces were an interlude. She published them in magazines, but otherwise let them lie – not exactly rejected by her, but certainly not coaxed anxiously toward a next collection, as this journal shows her worrying over her earlier poems. The demands of her baby occupied her time, but this does not entirely explain the lull in her poetry. The poems themselves, as before, reveal what was going on.

Everything about her writing at this time suggests that after 1959, after she had brought her death-rebirth drama to a successful issue, she found herself confronted, on that inner stage, by a whole new dramatic situation – one that made her first drama seem no more than the preliminaries, before the lifting of the curtain.

And in fact that birth, which had seemed so complete in 'The Stones', was dragging on. And it went on dragging on. We can follow the problematic accouchement in the poems. They swing from the apprehensions of a woman or women of sterility and death at one extreme, to joyful maternal celebration of the living and almost-born foetus at the other – with one or two encouraging pronouncements from the oracular foetus itself in between. But evidently much had still to be done. Perhaps something like the writing of *The Bell Jar* had still to be faced and got through. It is not until we come to the poems of September, October, and November of 1961 – a full two years after 'The Stones' – that the newborn seems to feel the draught of the outer world. And even now the voice of *Ariel*, still swaddled in the old mannerisms, is hardly more than a whimper. But at least we can see what the new situation is. We see her new self confronting – to begin with – the sea. Not just the sea off Finisterre and off Hartland, but the Bay of the Dead, and 'nothing, nothing but a great space' – which becomes the surgeon's 2 a.m. ward of mutilations (reminiscent of the hospital city in 'The Stones'). She confronts her own moon-faced sarcophagus, her mirror clouding over, the moon in its most sinister aspect, and the yews – 'blackness and silence'. In this group of poems – the most chilling pieces she had written up to this time – what she confronts is all that she had freed herself from.

Throughout the *Colossus* poems, as we have seen, the fateful part of her being, the part – a large, inclusive complex – that had formerly been too much for her, had held her, as a matrix, and nursed her back to new life. Death, in this matrix (and in one sense the whole complex, which had tried to kill her and had all but succeeded, came under the sign of death), had a homeopathic effect on the nucleus that survived.

But now that she was resurrected, as a self that she could think of as Eve (as she tried so hard to do in her radio play *Three Women*), a lover of life and of her children, she still had to deal with everything in her that remained otherwise, everything that had held her in the grave for 'three days', The Other. And, it was only now, for the first time, at her first step into independent life, that she could see it clearly for what it was – confronting her, separated from her at last, to be contemplated and, if possible, overcome.

It is not hard to understand her despondency at this juncture. Her new Ariel self had evolved for the very purpose of winning this battle, and much as she would have preferred, most likely, to back off and live in some sort of truce, her next step was just as surely inescapable.

From her new position of strength, she came to grips quite quickly. After *Three Women* (which has to be heard, as naïve speech, rather than read as a literary artifact) quite suddenly the ghost of her father reappears, for the first time in two and a half years, and meets a daunting, point-blank, demythologized assessment. This is followed by the most precise description she ever gave of The Other – the deathly woman at the heart of everything she now closed in on. After this, her poems arrived at a marvellous brief poise. Three of them together, titled 'Crossing the Water', 'Among the Narcissi', and 'Pheasant', all written within three or four days of one another in early April 1962, are unique in her work. And maybe it was this achievement, inwardly, this cool, light, very beautiful moment of mastery, that enabled her to take the next step.

Within a day or two of writing 'Pheasant,' she started a poem about a giant wych elm that overshadowed the yard of her home. The manuscript of this piece reveals how she began it in her usual fashion, as another poem of the interlude, maybe a successor to 'Pheasant' (the actual pheasant of the poem had flown up into the actual elm), and the customary features began to assemble. But then we see a struggle break out, which continues over several pages, as the lines try to take the law into their own hands. She forced the poem back into order, and even got a stranglehold on it, and seemed to have won, when suddenly it burst all her restraints and she let it go.

And at once the *Ariel* voice emerged in full, out of the tree. From that day on, it never really faltered again. During the next five months she produced ten more poems. The subject matter didn't alarm her. Why should it, when Ariel was doing the very thing it had been created and liberated to do? In each poem, the terror is encountered head on, and the angel is mastered and brought to terms. The energy released by these victories was noticeable. According to the appointed coincidence of such things, after July her outer circumstances intensified her inner battle to the limits. In October, when she and her husband began to live apart, every detail of the antagonist seemed to come into focus, and she started writing at top speed, producing twenty-six quite lengthy poems in that month. In November she produced twelve, with another on 1 December, and one more on 2 December, before the flow stopped abruptly.

She now began to look for a flat in London. In December she found a maisonette, in a house adorned with a plaque commemorating the fact that Yeats had lived there, near Primrose Hill. She decorated this place, furnished it prettily, moved in with her children before Christmas, and set about establishing a circle of friends.

By this time she knew quite well what she had brought off in October and November. She knew she had written beyond her wildest dreams. And she had overcome, by a stunning display of power, the bogies of her life. Yet her attitude to the poems was detached. 'They saved me', she said, and spoke of them as an episode that was past. And indeed it was blazingly clear that she had come through, in Lawrence's sense, and that she was triumphant. The impression of growth and new large strength in her personality was striking. The book lay completed, the poems carefully ordered. And she seemed to be under no compulsion to start writing again. On 31 December she tinkered with a poem that she had drafted in October but had not included in the *Ariel* canon, and even now she did not bother to finish it.

In January 1963 what was called the coldest freeze-up in fifteen years affected her health and took toll of her energy. She was in resilient form, however, for the English publication of *The Bell Jar* on 23 January. If she felt any qualms at the public release of this supercharged piece of her autobiography, she made no mention of it at the time, either in conversation or in her diary. Reading them now, the reviews seem benign enough, but at the time, like all reviews, they brought exasperation and dismay. But they did not visibly deflate her.

Then on 28 January she began to write again. She considered these poems a fresh start. She liked the different, cooler inspiration (as she described it) and the denser pattern, of the first of these, as they took shape. With after-knowledge, one certainly looks at something else – though the premonitory note, except maybe in her very last poem, is hardly more insistent than it had seemed in many an earlier piece.

But in that first week of February a number – a perverse number – of varied crises coincided. Some of these have been recounted elsewhere. No doubt all of them combined to give that unknowable element its chance, in her final act, on the early morning of Monday, 11 February.

All her poems are in a sense by-products. Her real creation was that inner gestation and eventual birth of a new self-conquering self, to which her journal bears witness, and which proved itself so overwhelmingly in the *Ariel* poems of 1962. If this is the most important task a human being can undertake (and it must surely be one of the most difficult), then this is the importance of her poems, that they provide such an intimate, accurate embodiment of the whole process from beginning to end – or almost to the end.

That her new self, who could do so much, could not ultimately save her, is perhaps only to say what has often been learned on this particular field of conflict – that the moment of turning one's back on an enemy who seems safely defeated, and is defeated, is the most dangerous moment of all. And that there can be no guarantees.

Sylvia Plath:
The Evolution of 'Sheep in Fog'

Written for Roy Davids, of Sotheby's Manuscripts Department, to be given as an illustrated lecture to the Wordsworth Trust, Grasmere, 25 February 1988.

Because we have all the manuscripts, all dated, of all her late poems, we can trace the course of the two amazing surges of inspiration that produced them – two waves of excitement like two successive waves on a graph. The first of these surges produced three poems in July of 1962, one in August, then twenty-seven between the end of September and the end of October, ten in November, two on the first day of December, ending abruptly with a final poem, 'Sheep in Fog', on 2 December.

She collected most of these, with a few others from just before, and called the volume *Ariel*. Without going into detailed analysis it is possible to point out that the *Ariel* poems document Plath's struggle to deal with a double situation – when her sudden separation from her husband coincided with a crisis in her traumatic feelings about her father's death which had occurred when she was eight years old (and which had been complicated by her all but successful attempt to follow him in a suicidal act in 1953). Against these very strong, negative feelings, and others associated with them, her battle to create a new life, with her children and with what she regarded as her new, reborn self, supplies the extraordinary positive resolution of the poems that she wrote up to 2 December 1962.

After that, (2 December), she wrote nothing at all for two months. On only one occasion, on 31 December, did she take up a poem to revise during this period. That was 'The Eavesdropper', first written on 15 October. She shortened this piece, corrected it quite heavily, but left it without any final draft (it is the only poem that to my knowledge she never finished). The dated manuscripts tell us this, and enable us to be sure that she did not start writing again until 28 January 1963. On that day she revised the very last poem of the earlier outburst, 'Sheep in Fog', and went on, the same day, to write three new ones. This was the beginning of the second wave. By the time she died, two weeks later, she had written twelve poems towards a new collection, and the revised 'Sheep in Fog' lay among them.

The final group of poems is very different in mood from the earlier group. And yet this poem, 'Sheep in Fog', belongs to both groups: the last poem of the first group, in its first version, and the first poem of the last group, in its final version.

[*see* PAGE A] Here is the poem leading its double life. The typed lines, dated at the top, belong to 2 December 1962. The revision in pen, which as you can see involves only the last three-line verse, is dated at the bottom, 28 January 1963.

She then typed out the revised version [*see* PAGE B] and gave it those two dates at the top, as if she recognized some particular significance in the different character of the two versions. As I recall, she did this with no other poem. However, if we look at these three lines closely we see that the change she made in them, on 28 January, reveals just what that peculiar significance was. The new version amounts to a full, perfect realization of the calamitous change of mood, the sinister change of inspiration, between the two groups of poems.

Looking first at the first version of 2 December, we see in those last three lines her main *Ariel* themes tangled in a strange fashion. They are nothing like so ominous as the three she replaced them with, two months later on 28 January 1963. They are ambiguous – but leaning strongly towards the positive. 'Patriarchs' give a sense of something fatherly in a benign, protective even biblically protective way. And though these Patriarchs move away from her – as stones or clouds – yet they have babies' faces. In Plath's mythology babies are always intensely positive creatures, of new life, fresh beginnings, vital and innocent force etc., so this too presses towards a positive emphasis,

Dec. 2
1962

Sylvia Plath
Court Green
North Tawton
Devonshire, England

~~Fog~~ Sheep in A fog

The hills step off into whiteness.
People or stars
Regard me sadly, I disappoint them.

The train leaves a line of breath.
O slow
Horse the color of rust,

Hooves, dolorous bells---
All morning the
Morning has been blackening,

A flower left out.
My bones hold a stillness, the far
Fields melt my heart,

Patriarchs till now immobile
In heavenly wools
Row off as stones or clouds with the faces of babies.

The ~~white~~ ~~most~~ my heaven
~~Threatens~~ to let me through ~~to~~ a ~~star~~ heaven
Starless & fatherless, ~~a~~ dark water.

Jan. 28
1963

Revised Dec. 2, 1962
Jan 28, 1963

Sylvia Plath
23 Fitzroy Road
London N.W.1

Sheep in Fog

The hills step off into whiteness.
People or stars
Regard me sadly, I disappoint them.

The train leaves a line of breath.
O slow
Horse the color of rust,

Hooves, dolorous bells---
All morning the
Morning has been blackening,

A flower left out.
My bones hold a stillness, the far
Fields melt my heart.

They threaten
To let me through to a heaven
Starless and fatherless, a dark water.

PAGE B The typescript finalized on 28 January 1963.

Fog Sheep   (1)

The hills step off into whiteness.
People or stars
Regard me sadly, I disappoint them.

~~Wrapped in their wool like patriarchs~~
The train leaves a line of breath.
~~Thighs clamping my animal~~
O slow
Horse, ~~the same your color~~ we are one color,
~~And the~~ ~~My~~ world   the color of rust—
~~My world rusts around us~~
~~Ribs, spokes, a scrapped chariot~~

The train leaves a line of breath.
O slow
Horse, the color of rust,
~~I am a scrapped chariot~~
O hooves, O dolorous bells—
~~All morning the~~
Morning has been blackening
like a dead man left out.
Why do I find them so beautiful,
~~the souls of witches~~
~~the faces of sheep, like patriarchs~~
these sheep with the faces of babies—

Old as the tors, & furious.
I am not the one, ~~this~~ disquiets them.
~~With my four hooves~~ &

PAGE C The first draft page of the manuscript.

Fog Sheep

(2)

The hills step off into whiteness.
People or stars
Regard me sadly, I disappoint them.
The train leaves a line of breath.
O slow
Horse, the color of rust,
~~O~~ hooves, dolorous bells —
All morning the
Morning has been blackening

~~A~~ flower left out.
Why do I find them so beautiful,
These sheep with the faces of babies —

Old as the hills, o furious.
I am not the one, this disquiets them.
~~They will effectually continue~~

Stones, ~~clouds~~, transformations.
So I have seen the ~~and~~ serious

Faces of aunts in photographs
The color of rust, the world
Rusting the rings, ~~the daisies~~ the faces
Met poke, pale peaks under glass.
Now ~~even your kisses stiffen~~
~~But the~~ sheep are stones, they are blessed.
~~The hill is indestructible.~~
Little saints, they inhabit an absence

PAGE D The second draft page of the manuscript.

Fog Sheep

    The hills step off into whiteness.
    People or stars
    Regard me sadly, I disappoint them.
    The train leaves a line of breath.
    O slow
    Horse the color of rust,
    Hooves, dolorous bells —
    all morning the
    Morning has been blackening,
    A flower left out.
    My bones hold a stillness, the far
    Fields melt

My heart ~~the patriarchs~~ ~~all~~ ~~using~~ immobile
~~Immobile In~~ heavenly walls
Row off as stones or clouds with the faces of babies.

My heart.
Patriarchs til now immobile
In heavenly wools

Row off as stones or clouds with the faces of babies

Dec. 2
1962   ③

PAGE E The third and final page of the manuscript as finished on
2 December 1962.

and 'babies' as the last word ends the poem forcefully upbeat. These Patriarchs which are protective fathers which are the babies of life which (in their 'heavenly wools') are also perhaps cherubic angels – though they move off a little, are still close and have not entirely withdrawn their good and familiar magic. In fact, the title seems to tell us that the whole point of the poem is to invoke their protective benediction.

In other words, this final three-line image is still trying to stay in the *Ariel* world of hope and a triumphant outcome. And we remember that this was 2 December and had been preceded by weeks of fierce inspiration and confidence.

Yet the three lines don't quite work. They don't ring true, somehow. They can't finally reverse the mood of the 'hooves, dolorous bells' or the 'Morning . . . blackening like a flower left out' – the whole heavy, grieving momentum of the preceding four verses. And we begin to feel an eerie, afterlife feeling – a uniquely Plath sensation – about the Patriarchs and their baby faces. A little like figures in Dante's Purgatorio – the babies are perhaps too much like cherubs, as if a soul just after death were seeing these figures, and not quite understanding. In spite of this, she seems as I say to cling to the hopeful possibility, that these baby faces promise and might even ensure life.

Even so, we can't help seeing, I think, how with this poem, quite suddenly, the *Ariel* inspiration has changed. The astonishing, sustained, soaring defiance of the previous eight weeks has suddenly failed. Or rather has reversed. Or rather, maybe, has revealed what was always there. It is still inspiration. Those first four verses still supply four fifths of one of her most beautiful poems. But the rage, which was also a kind of joy, has evaporated. What remains is mourning.

So now we see why those last three lines don't work. In them, she makes a convulsive effort to switch this poem onto the *Ariel* tracks, with magical images of divine help and rebirth. But the new kind of inspiration refuses to be coerced. This last image remains mechanical and unconvincing. It was still too early, evidently, for her to face the real conclusion – the foregone conclusion on which the poem was insisting. And so she denied and suppressed it with these three artificial lines.

All this can be said simply from that 2 December version of the poem, which on that date she had thought was final. To see what was really happening, however, we have to look not only at that final 28 January version, but at all drafts of the poem, from the beginning. And they do tell everything.

One of Plath's most famous poems is the title poem – 'Ariel' itself. This poem describes and almost apotheosizes a dawn ride, on Dartmoor, on her horse which was called Ariel. It is the quintessential Plath *Ariel* poem in that the speaker, the I, hurls herself free from all earthly confinement and aims herself and her horse – as the poem says, 'suicidal' directly into the red, rising sun. The overt sense here is that the liberation from earthly restraints (earthly life) is a rebirth into something greater and more glorious but which is still some kind of life – a spiritual rebirth perhaps. She wrote it on her thirtieth birthday.

The only other poem about her morning ride, in the same place and on the same horse, Ariel, is the poem we have been looking at, 'Sheep in Fog'. First written about a month later.

As we see, 'Sheep in Fog' has the same theme – a dawn ride towards a kind of death. But here all the values of the earlier poem are inverted. Instead of hurtling towards the rising, patriarchal sun, in triumph, as a spiritual hero, she is now the failed one, the one who disappoints, trudging towards a mournful dissolution in bottomless, starless, fatherless darkness.

In other words, the connection between these two horse-riding poems reveals the crucial, dangerous extreme polarity, the precarious dynamics, of Plath's inspiration, and achievement, and fate.

To see even more vividly just how she experienced this we only have to turn right back to the beginning of her working drafts of 'Sheep in Fog' and then go through them in order. (After what I've said, you'll be able to make very good sense of the main points.)

See her very first draft [PAGE C].

The first three lines come out limpid and clear – exactly as she wanted them and as they would always be.

But then, immediately, she reaches out towards those Patriarchs. However, she realizes it's too soon, and sends them off.

In that next moment of hovering uncertainty, the train line emerges, perfect and unalterable.

Then we see her trying to unite with her horse. 'Thighs clamping my animal'. This is almost a direct memory of the Ariel lines:

> God's lioness
> How one we grow
> Pivot of heels and knees!

and also recalls another line, later in the same poem, 'At one with the drive'. But though she has now made the inner connection with the earlier poem, she realizes that the connotations of striving ecstatic energy no longer apply. And she has already seen a more appropriate and expressive way of blending with her beast. So she rejects the old, used-up *Ariel* muscular connection and finds their new identity in their common colour.

It is as though she is aware of something very undesirable coming up at this point, something she is not ready for. The phrases of cancellation and revision wrestle on the page. Then we see it is not so much their common colour, hers, her horse's or her hair's or even the world's – it isn't this that confuses her so much as the idea of 'rust'.

'Rust'. Why should this word disturb her? But now we are told immediately what the rust is. And in two lines she shows us the full complexity of the relationship between this poem and the poem 'Ariel'. The rust belongs to the wreckage of a chariot. Her horse, herself, and the world, just for a glimpse, are the rusty iron wreckage of a chariot.

We know where this chariot comes from. Not Ariel, but Phaeton, son of a mortal woman and Apollo (the god of the Sun and of Poetry), took his father's Sun-chariot for a run, and the solar horses, under his half-mortal hands, ran out of control through the heavens. The chariot, it might be supposed, was wrecked and he was killed. As an image of her Ariel flight in the chariot of the God of Poetry, which was also her attempt to soar (plunge) into the inspirational form of her inaccessible father, to convert her former physical suicide into a psychic rebirth, that myth is the parable of the book *Ariel* and of her life and death. In the poem 'Ariel', though it is so very present in the situation and drama of the poem, the myth shows no sign of having broken into her consciousness. And here, in 'Sheep in Fog', when it makes the attempt, she shoves it out.

Nevertheless, from somewhere behind that earlier poem 'Ariel' it insists on pushing through:

> The world rusts around us
> Ribs, spokes, a scrapped chariot.

And yet this image is somehow out of place. It is too indefinite. It brings up a whole world of meanings that are too large and mythic (and raw) for this particular poem – the cool realism of this delicate lament.

We then see how much of it she is willing to accept, as she condenses it into an image where the line:

> O slow

fuses the train and its line of breath, with her horse, as if the essence of the fallen chariot, instead of lying around the countryside as a gigantic, lumpish ruin, had now secreted itself within the iron train and the rust-coloured horse as two aspects of the vehicle's stricken condition.

But the chariot still tries to make a come-back, and suddenly she has identified its technology with her own body – no longer the 'arrow, at one with the drive', but:

> I am a scrapped chariot

As before it is too much to handle. She pushes it out again and for a while it has to be content with the word 'rust' and the ghostly after-image of a train.

And now a totally new idea, and another perfect three line verse, as if it had slipped through her temporary exhaustion – after her struggle to get rid of her chariot. In the finished poem we might well ask: What are these dolorous bells? But knowing as we now do about the disastrously fallen sun-chariot which is the catastrophe behind this poem, we know they are bells for a dead Phaeton – mourning bells. Just to drive this home, the word 'morning' is twice and mournfully repeated as if the morning – which in the poem 'Ariel' was the rising red eye of the new day, the 'cauldron' of rebirth – were now a funeral, no longer red but black.

And then with a real shock we come to the actual body of the fallen charioteer, lying there on the moors: the day itself –

Like a dead man left out.

With this dead man, the truth is out, too. A reader of Plath immediately thinks of the shattered, landscape *Colossus*, the great dead man who appears here and there in her earlier poems, the unburiable body, as she interpreted it, of her father. But the voice of the *Ariel* poems was the voice that had been buried with him, identified with him, and that had struggled into rebirth, in those *Ariel* poems, to tell its story. The re-emergence of that body, in one of the last of the *Colossus* poems, had been like the re-emergence of that voice in *Ariel* – as if the body of her father were also the Chrysalis of the voice. But where the rider in the poem 'Ariel' drove straight into God's eye, here in 'Sheep in Fog' God's eye, the day itself, the light of the sun, is blackened with mourning, and the rider, the charioteer of the sun, the spirit that was also her resurrected father, is dead on the earth.

But immediately she tries to escape the implications: in so far as that dead charioteer is the spirit of *Ariel* it is also herself. She reaches out for her old comforters, the sheep, mysteriously beautiful. But they have already metamorphosed (as if in fright, at sight of that revealing corpse) into 'the souls of worms'. At once she tries to re-convert them into something more reassuring – as one tries to force an image in a dream to become something more propitious – whereupon the 'Patriarchs' re-enter. Yet still she feels she needs something more reliable. Cancelling the Patriarchs she wards off those souls of worms with her often tried and tested crucifix magic – the faces of babies. But the old *Ariel* reflex is obsolete. The babies turn in her hands into terrible cherubs –

Old as the tors, and furious.

('Tors' are the granite piles or 'buttes' that stick up from the top of the granite hills on Dartmoor, the cores of ancient mountains.) She knew she needed the help of fiery angels, but again these are too much to handle, her attempt to rescue herself disintegrates and she starts afresh [*see* PAGE D].

In this second page, the first three verses have emerged, in their own strong, inevitable music. The scene of disaster has been set. And the corpse of the charioteer, still too savagely mythical, has been naturalized to the poem as 'A flower left out'. But (like the flower which replaces the body of Adonis, in Shakespeare's *Venus and Adonis*) this metamorphosed flower now has a lively, coded meaning for us. Because of these manuscript drafts we know (and without them we could not possibly know) what a frightful psychological event, and for the poet what a truly fateful event, lies behind it and is enclosed within it. This dead flower, or rather not yet expressly dead but 'blackening' because it has been 'left out', is nothing less than the spirit that rode Ariel in the earlier poem, and that composed the *Ariel* poems. It is all that remains of that heroic effort. It is the seal of the wild endeavour of the *Ariel* inspiration.

But still she tries to use what she had learned in those *Ariel* poems to rescue the situation. She now reaches back into the *Ariel* world for more of the kind of imagery that once helped her. Taking up the first verse's idea of Mankind's and Heaven's disappointment with her, and now finding a similar attitude in the sheep, she explores first of all a possibility that 'they are expecting', intensifies it to 'they are wanting', as if she hoped to find something positive there – but fails to see that they want, in truth, anything but stones, clouds and transformations, which lead straight back to desolation. Scrapping this, she looks through the sheep's faces and seizes on the faces of Aunts in photographs – heirlooms that were formerly, in *Ariel*, vibrant with intimate life. But these now collapse back, remorselessly, into that insuppressible rusted chariot, which suddenly re-emerges yet again, now loaded with photographs, rings, diaries, mysterious beaked faces under glass and even, it seems, kisses.

Everything in her life and marriage had been with her in that chariot – and the rust now corrodes it all. Again it drags her towards something she cannot manage, and again she separates herself forcibly from it, returning to her baby-faced sheep, which are now:

saner, they are blessed.

And 'Like saints, they inhabit an absence'. We now see why these sheep were important enough to give the poem its title. At this point they represent her desperate effort to bring the poem to a close in a positive, sacred, talismanic image that can float on the darkening current of the poem and protect her from it. She makes a single bid, a magical gesture, to reinforce this image, and give it a barbed, defended permanence, with the sudden appearance, out of nowhere, of:

The holly is indestructible

On 2 December, maybe, those Saints were approaching Christmas like the Magi, and this Holy Holly probably came with them – for the rebirth of the soul, the baby-faced Sheep, the Lamb. All this would be stirring behind there. Magi, Holly and Lamb had all featured in the victorious drama of *Ariel*. But though the line about the Saints and the line about the Holly are thoroughbred *Ariel* phrases, beautiful in themselves, even as she writes them she realizes they won't do, as we can see. And she goes back to the beginning, on a third sheet, to take another run at the mysterious barrier [*see* PAGE E].

Copying out the first three perfected verses gives her focus and tuning to slip between the clashing rocks and press on through a perfect verse four – which introduces two decisive new ideas. The Chariot and Charioteer were as we saw first separated and secreted, the one into the rust-coloured horse and the train that leaves a breath, the other into the 'flower left out'; she then made another attempt to identify herself, rider and vehicle, with the 'scrapped chariot'. Now, in her first new idea, both dead rider and ruined chariot dissolve into an image less defined but more potent than either:

My bones hold a stillness . . .

Dead man, flower, and scrapped chariot, are all in this stillness. Following immediately, comes the second new idea:

> the far
> Fields melt
> My heart.

This opens directly towards what will be, two months later, when she gives the poem its final shape, the inevitable ending. The decisive word here will turn out to be 'melt'. 'Melt' reaches through to another myth. It 'dissolves' one here who flew too recklessly into the sun with another who did the same, as will be clear in a minute, or rather in two months.

But now, on 2 December, she tries to save the situation and give herself a hopeful outcome, rather than obey the inexorable inner laws of the poem. She does this by acting ruthlessly. Instead of wading deeper into the tangle of the rusty chariot, and perhaps unearthing a whole, other, different poem – the poem that has been so persistently trying to force its way through this one – she abandons her baffled struggle with that doom-laden vehicle and ties the four verses that she has into a neat parcel, making a formal and perfunctory though decorative knot out of her sacred images of sheep that are both Patriarchs and cherub-faced babies (the beatific disguises of her Father and his Daughter, her Husband and her Children). And there she leaves it, on 2 December, under this *Ariel* seal which, as now seems clear, is makeshift and inadequate.

Realizing perhaps that this ending is not quite right, and also, no doubt, that the mood and 'story' of the body of the poem contradicts the generally masterful programme of *Ariel*, she keeps the poem out of that collection. It is not until two months later, as we have seen, that she is able to accept the poem's inevitable true conclusion. This acceptance then releases the inspiration of the final eleven poems that chart her final breakthrough – into the real meaning of 'dark water'.

So on 28 January taking up the poem again she removes the false ending. She then looks through that word 'melt' and sees, now, in perfect focus, the myth behind it. Brueghel's painting of Icarus falling out of the sky and into the sea was a favourite of hers: a print of it hung on her wall at university, and she referred to him as a figure frequently. Auden's poem about the same painting, 'Musée des Beaux Arts', was, I think her favourite Auden poem. From the northern edge of Dartmoor, where she was riding, the whole panorama of North Devon seems to lie below like a different land – a sea undulating softly away to the Northern skyline, behind which lies the true sea. As the rider looks out over this landscape in its dawn mists, those far fields both 'melt' their undulations and 'melt' her heart into themselves. In the poem 'Ariel' she had fused her heart – her whole being – into the sun's red eye, as a triumphant Phaeton reaching her Father. Here that word 'melt' has metamorphosed the sun's chariot and horses into the wax of the wings of Icarus – who also flew (against his father's warning) too near the sun. Instead of climbing, as Phaeton, into the 'cauldron of morning' (having fallen, secretly, earlier in this poem's scrapped drafts, as Phaeton) she now falls as Icarus into 'a heaven' that is the opposite of the sun's paternal 'cauldron of morning.' This other 'heaven' is that 'dark water', 'starless' and 'fatherless'.

The 'melting' of the 'Phaeton myth' behind Ariel into the 'Icarus myth' behind this (and the last eleven poems) is done with beautiful, extremely powerful effect, yet without overt mention of either. And one can see how any mention of either would have killed the suggestive power of the mythic ideas.

What these drafts reveal, then, is more than the working out of a famous poem. They reveal what is essentially a parallel body of poetry. They are a transparent exposure of the poetic operations to which the finished work is – well, what is it? In one sense, that final version conceals all these operations. It exploits them, plunders them, appropriates only what it can use, and then, finally for the most part, hides them. But having seen these drafts, we do not respect the poem less. We understand it far better, because we have learned the peculiar meanings of its hieroglyphs. These drafts are not an incidental adjunct to the poem, they are a complementary revelation, and a log-book of its real meanings.

They have revealed the nature and scope of the psychological crisis that gives the poem its weird life, sonority, its power to affect us. In other words, they are, as the final poem is not, an open window into the poet's motivation and struggle at a moment of decisive psychological change.

We now know the precise significance of that single word 'rust', of that simple noun 'flower', of the mysteriously affecting adjectives 'starless' and 'fatherless'. Behind these bald glyphs, we now understand, there lies a submerged, struggling and certainly terrible large-scale psycho-mythological drama.

If it were not for the surviving manuscripts, we would never guess that the 'dark water', those last words of the final version, is in fact swallowing up the fallen chariot of the sun and the reckless charioteer who fell with it, or that this small cool poem is the epitaph and funeral cortège of the whole extraordinary adventure drama-tized in the poems of *Ariel* – the endeavour that, as far as she was concerned, failed.

*

Finally, this full sequence of drafts reveals, in a highly interesting form, the beginning, middle and end of a phenomenon to which no poem's final printed version can give any clue. It is common to the experience of all poets, at various times, and works as follows:

The first 'inspiration' of a poem can be, and often is, without words, without images, without any clear 'idea' of any sort. It need be no more than a dimly sensed mood or tone. Many poets confirm this.

At the moment of writing, one of four things can happen.

First, the 'inspiration' can suddenly rise to the surface, somehow in the process (and as if instantaneously, or even as if pre-formed) finding its own perfect words, images, rhythms and shape. The poem seems to write itself, and takes the poet completely by surprise, as if he had no idea where it came from. Once on the page, it cannot be altered. A famous example would be 'Kubla Khan'. This sort of poem is for most poets quite rare.

Or, secondly, the poem can half rise. The poet then struggles to help it, offering it words, images, anything from his bag of tricks, trying to anticipate and coax it, taking every slightest suggestion from the bits that have appeared. He has actually little idea whether he is really helping or not, in most of this busy midwifery. This is where many promising poems are ruined. It could be that while he hopes he is helping his inspiration, he is actually suppressing it – suppressing a perfect and preformed but not yet fully emerged poem of that first kind, and supplanting it with one of another kind, concocted out of officious interference from other parts of his brain that want to get in on the act. But if he is receptive and submissive enough (suspending his routine ego), and if his technique and imagination and mind generally are flexible enough, he may find himself gradually unearthing something unlike anything he or anybody else has ever written before – something that surprises him just as much, and seems just as strange to him, as the poem that arrives complete and ready made from nowhere. A famous example of this sort of poem would be *The Waste Land*. Most poets' best pieces are of this sort.

But a third process accounts for most of the poems that most poets write. Here, the inspiration offers only the odd phrase, or line, and the poet goes after it with a technique that is maybe very resourceful but is essentially fixed and predetermined by his own earlier writings and by his regular practice, by his aesthetic prejudices, by his conscious desire to write a certain kind of poetry. In this case, a scrap of inspiration is really no more than the occasion for a routine display of the poet's prosody. The finished versions of this type of poem can often enough carry a strong poetic charge, striking phrases, lines and felicities, and at the very least can be admirable pieces of verbal dressage and pleasing craftsmanship. But they nevertheless stand as monuments to the unique originals that died in the womb – and were reabsorbed. When you sense that this happened – and it is sometimes possible to sense a unique, beautiful poem behind the patented finish – you naturally ask whether there was a special reason for it to be suppressed, some reason for the nerve to fail, other than that the poet has somehow, through mere force of habit, perhaps, gone into partnership with the substitute.

There is a fourth kind of poem, a more interesting variant of the third. Here the final poem is not so much a display of the poet's accomplished style, and a suppression of the unorthodox event behind it, but a sort of hard-fought treaty – some kind of provisional reconciliation between the inspiration and other parts of the poet's character, a precarious, jagged, touchy kind of agreement. These can be exciting pieces of writing even when they are anything but what you would call a perfect poem.

The successive drafts of 'Sheep in Fog' demonstrate something of all these procedures.

To begin with, the first verse is very pure inspiration. This suggests that the whole poem was prepared and ready to glide out without a pang. But something alerted the writer – a premonition. So straight-away, for that special reason, she interferes. Her nerve flinches, and she grabs for the protective Patriarchal sheep – a proven sort of Ariel staple. This means that she breaks the thread of her inspiration, which, as we eventually see, has nothing at all to say about sheep. (They remain only in the title.)

She realizes her mistake, corrects her tack, and manages to find the broken thread end – with that next perfect line. But again anxiety spoils her concentration, and again she tries to lift everything into the successful mode of her earlier poem 'Ariel', in that line 'Thighs clamping my animal'.

So she goes on, trying to tune in on that first inspiration of the poem that is pressing to be written but that for some reason frightens her, and at the same time trying to write the old *Ariel* type of poem that will save her from what this frightening inspiration is about to say. It is as if she were trying to force this poem's horse, with its hooves like 'dolorous bells', to be the horse that in her earlier poem flew with her into the sun.

Then when she reaches 'rust' she is taken by surprise. She is thrown off balance, as we saw, by another poem altogether. Suddenly we – and she – are stumbling among the wreckage of that chariot.

This is a difficult moment and it takes her quite a while to get past it. She is now trying to write three different poems simultaneously. The first is the poem of the original inspiration – lucid, realistic, and perfectible, perhaps already perfected and only waiting to be found, though it will take her two months to find it. The second is the poem she wants to write – the poem about the biblical Patriarchal sheep, the *Ariel* style of poem that knows how to deal with terrible news about her father and her fateful bond with him (such as she feels stirring again here more frighteningly than ever), a style that will hoist her as before into defiant transcendence. The third is this other inchoate poem about the rusted chariot, the poem out of the depths of her 'suicidal' ride into the sun's eye. This third poem has somehow risen – 'like a terrible fish' – into the occasion of this poem, probably invoked by the simple fact that she is once again in the saddle of Ariel, her real horse on which last time she flew to the sun.

From this point while taking down, from inner dictation, her inspired lament, she never relaxes her attempt to write the self-protective poem she consciously wants to write, using the techniques and apparatus that had worked in the *Ariel* poems. At the same time, she cannot disengage herself from the deeper, much bigger, mythical poem that in fact tells the true story, and foretells the end of the story, behind those *Ariel* poems. At no point does she show any awareness that this material of the chariot might be an altogether different poem, and a different kind of poem, trying to emerge. But at last her defensive tactics win. She does manage to disengage herself from the chariot and its freight. In this way, the two other poems combine to suppress and do away with the third poem – the great story from behind the scenes.

If, at this point, the poet had had more energy, or more time, it could be she would have turned wholly towards this deeper more difficult mythic poem, and tried to excavate it. When she did this once before, with some bigger suggestions pushing through a constricted, suppressive group of lines about an elm tree, she made one of her biggest breakthroughs, transformed her whole technique, and located her true subject matter.

But here, finally, she suppresses the intruder, and banishes it into the depths – where it remains, peering out obliquely from 'rust', through the train's breath, the blackening flower, and the 'stillness' held in her bones.

The situation is still quite complicated: two poems are still fighting for the single final draft. Her plans for the sheep are still trying to suppress the other – the inspired poem with the bad news. The drafts show what a struggle she put up, with her tried and tested technique. Finally, when the unwanted newcomer had almost taken over, she allowed the *Ariel* squad to go in as a police force, imposing the three final lines – like martial law.

So here four kinds of poem show their paces. As I say, the first kind of poem – the effortless inspiration, was probably there from the start. Even though she keeps disrupting the flow, all the final wording of the poem does arrive, wherever it arrives, fully-formed – the phrases do not have to be hammered visibly out of some cruder ore. Maybe the only hesitation is a slight mishearing in the last two lines. At the same time, you could say the perfect poem was delivered with difficulty, and obvious struggle – as with the second kind of poem. And at every point, what is obvious is the obstinate interference of that other, suppressive routine, trying to hijack the occasion for a display of the already established style, as in the third kind of poem. Finally, it could be said that the poem she was left with, on 2 December, was a Treaty – a formal truce maintained under tension between opposed and mutually hostile interests: the fourth kind of poem. Meanwhile, of course, we have glimpsed another kind of poem altogether, a fifth kind, a massive complex of images, of the kind that rises into the 'total statements' of epic and drama – the mythic poem of the chariot, the full subjective drama of her fate, that was pushed under, and sank away, and never did get written. Although, in a sense, the effort of this fifth poem to come into existence determined every word of the poem we have, and provided the final three lines by metamorphosing the myth of Phaeton into that of Icarus, it remains unknown. Just as those last three lines, and the final complete perfect form, of 'Sheep in Fog' would have remained unknown if she had died two weeks earlier.

All this, which that final copy conceals, is revealed only because the full sequence of drafts was saved.

Keith Douglas

Keith Douglas was born in 1920 and killed in Normandy in 1944. This selection contains not quite half of his surviving poetry.

When his Collected Poems were first published in 1951, by Editions Poetry London Ltd, with notes and introduction, edited by John Waller and G. S. Fraser, he appeared primarily interesting, to most of his readers, as a 'war-poet', and as such seems to have been largely forgotten. Now, twelve years later and twenty years after his death, it is becoming clear that he offers more than just a few poems about war, and that every poem he wrote, whether about war or not, has some special value. His poetry in general seems to be of some special value. It is still very much alive, and even providing life. And the longer it lives, the fresher it looks.

The first poem printed here, 'Encounter with a God', is dated 1936. It is quite limited in scope, and comes properly into the category of Juvenilia, but it accomplishes its job, not an easy one, as brilliantly and surely as anything Douglas ever did. And the qualities that create and distinguish his most important later work are already there.

It is not enough to say that the language is utterly simple, the musical inflection of it peculiarly honest and charming, the technique flawless. The language is also extremely forceful; or rather, it reposes at a point it could only have reached, this very moment, by a feat of great strength. And the inflexion of the voice has a bluntness that might be challenging if it were not so frank, and so clearly the advance of an unusually aware mind. As for the technique, in so far as it can be considered separately, there is nothing numb or somnambulist in it, nothing tactless, and such swift subtlety of movement, such economy of means, such composition of cadences, can hardly be matched in the work of any poet living. And behind that, ordering its directions, the essentially practical cast of his energy, his impatient, razor energy.

Introduction to *Selected Poems: Keith Douglas* (London: Faber and Faber, 1964).

In his nine years of accomplished writing, Douglas developed rapidly. Leaving his virtuoso juvenilia, his poetry passed through two roughly distinguishable phases, and began to clarify into a third. The literary influences on this progress seem to have been few. To begin with, perhaps he takes Auden's language over pretty whole, but he empties it of its intellectual concerns, turns it to the practical experience of life, and lets a few minor colours of the late 1930s poetry schools creep in. But his temperament is so utterly modern he seems to have no difficulty with the terrible, suffocating, maternal octopus of English poetic tradition.

The first phase of his growth is typified in the poem titled 'Forgotten the Red Leaves'. He has lost nothing since 'Encounter with a God', but gained a new freedom of imagination, a new ease of transition from image to image. Yet in this particular poem the fairyland images are being remembered by one still partly under their spell, indulging the dream, and this mode of immaturity is the mark of this first phase, which lasts until he leaves Oxford in 1940.

Before he leaves, a poem titled 'The Deceased' heralds the next stage. Here, the picturesque or merely decorative side of his imagery disappears; his descriptive powers sharpen to realism. The impression is of a sudden mobilizing of the poet's will, a clearing of his vision, as if from sitting considering possibilities and impossibilities he had stood up to act. Pictures of things no longer interest him much: he wants their substance, their nature, and their consequences in life. At once, and quite suddenly, his mind is whole, as if united by action, and he produces poetry that is both original and adult. Already, in this poem 'The Deceased', we can see what is most important of all about Douglas. He has not simply added poems to poetry, or evolved a sophistication. He is a renovator of language. It is not that he uses words in jolting combinations, or with titanic extravagance, or curious precision. His triumph lies in the way he renews the simplicity of ordinary talk, and he does this by infusing every word with a burning exploratory freshness of mind – partly impatience, partly exhilaration at speaking the forbidden thing, partly sheer casual ease of penetration. The music that goes along with this, the unresting variety of intonation and movement within his patterns, is the natural path of such confident, candid thinking.

There is nothing studied about this new language. Its air of improvisation is a vital part of its purity. It has the trenchancy of an inspired jotting, yet leaves no doubt about the completeness and subtlety of his impressions, or the thoroughness of his artistic conscience. The poem titled 'Egypt', for instance, could be a diary note, yet how could it be improved as a poem?

The war brought his gift to maturity, or to a first maturity. In a sense, war was his ideal subject: the burning away of all human pretensions in the ray cast by death. This was the vision, the unifying generalisation that shed the meaning and urgency into all his observations and particulars: not truth is beauty only, but truth kills everybody. The truth of a man is the doomed man in him or his dead body. Poem after poem circles this idea, as if his mind were tethered. At the bottom of it, perhaps, is his private muse, not a romantic symbol of danger and temptation, but the plain foreknowing of his own rapidly-approaching end — a foreknowledge of which he becomes fully conscious in two of his finest poems. This sets his writing apart from that of Hemingway, with which it shares certain features. Hemingway tried to imagine the death that Douglas had foresuffered. Douglas had no time, and perhaps no disposition, to cultivate the fruity deciduous tree of How To Live. He showed in his poetry no concern for man in society. The murderous skeleton in the body of a girl, the dead men being eaten by dogs on the moonlit desert, the dead man behind the mirror, these items of circumstantial evidence are steadily out-arguing all his high spirits and hopefulness.

Technically, each of the poems of this second phase rests on some single objective core, a scene or event or thing. But one or two of them, and one in particular, start something different: the poems are 'On a Return from Egypt' and 'Simplify me when I'm Dead'. Their inner form is characterized not by a single object of attraction, but a constellation of statements. In the second of these poems, more liberated than the first, Douglas consummates his promise. Here he has invented a style that seems able to deal poetically with whatever it comes up against. It is not an exalted verbal activity to be attained for short periods, through abstinence, or a submerged dream treasure to be fished up when the everyday brain is half-drugged. It is a language for the whole mind, at its most wakeful, and in all situations. A utility general-purpose style, as, for instance, Shakespeare's was, that combines a colloquial prose readiness with poetic breadth, a ritual intensity and music of an exceedingly high order with clear direct feeling, and yet in the end is nothing but casual speech. This is an achievement for which we who come after can be grateful.

Postscript 1: Douglas and Owen
Letter to the editor, 2 February 1988

I'd be interested to know what's been said about the relationship between Owen and Douglas. That symmetrical inversion of some of their salient features, which I chew over,* seems to exist (maybe it's a current cliché!), yet I can see why it presented itself to me as it did. After I'd written that piece I realized I'd drawn something from my father and brother. When my elder brother joined up in 1939 my permanent preoccupation became – praying that he wouldn't be dragged into what our father had been dragged through from 1914–18. I expect he contemplated it even more fatefully than I did. Owen, when I came to know his poems, grew to represent my father's experience, and later on Douglas my brother's (who was in North Africa through the same period). So that pattern of antithetical succession was prefigured, for me, and quite highly charged.

As a character in my piece, Owen offered himself as the familiar ground to set off the less familiar (?) contrasting article.

I'm sure you're right about Rosenberg.† Douglas must have recognized the less dated, more serviceable components in his attitude to the business.

What you say about Art Artifice and distancing makes me feel I must have left bigger holes in my fabric than I thought. If I seem to

---

* Introduction to a new impression of *The Complete Poems of Keith Douglas*, edited by Desmond Graham (Oxford: OUP, 1988).
† In William Scammell, *Keith Douglas: A Study* (London: Faber and Faber, 1988).

neglect that aspect, it must be because I took it so naturally for granted as the starting point of whatever I wanted to say. I didn't go into detail, but for me the question that circumscribes all my thoughts about Douglas is – how did he manage to make such final and in their way archetypal and manifestly indestructible designs sound so spontaneous, so much like the thought of a moment?

My whole piece is striving to define something slightly different – something which in the end it fails, maybe, even to suggest. This something is whatever it is that inhabits the curious electrified inflection of his each line. It's that imprint of intimate presence – a naked activism of a very essential, irreducible self. It's not the unique identity that makes every line of Auden's obviously an Auden line and so on. Most poets don't have any suggestion of it. So it's obviously not a very necessary quality – Milton none, Wordsworth none, Eliot none. The only poet who seems to have something of the same is Wyatt. I'm always feeling I find it too in R. S. Thomas. It's personal, because it bears the tones of private anguish and struggle, but mainly it is a unique sort of essence, spiritual and hard come by. Less a talent, or faculty, than a quality of being – that's what brought me to Gurdjieff. It's rare and different the way instant healing flows from the hands of just the odd rare individual, while nobody else, even celebrated doctors, has any touch of it. Or if one could believe in mediums, it's rare and different the way one or two of them, here and there, produce a real foxglove in January – something of that sort. I'm not going to define it here either. This is what I meant by the poetry being somehow the naked presence of the inmost being of the man – the innermost creature, the decisive, most truthful spirit control of his nature. The poems formulate the terms this creature comes to with his predicament – with its unpredictable jagged edges and reality.

Do I suggest that this formulation was an easy business? This essence I'm failing to pin down doesn't emerge in the drafts till the very last moment. I agree with you, the poems come from far down – from some place of final resolutions. So the documentary bent, and opportunity, and as I say motivation, provided the external means. So 'Vergissmeinicht' moves from being a sharp journal entry, through psychic turmoil, to the crystalline poem – reconciling every phase of its transformation, never altogether ceasing to be documentary.

Postscript 2: 'Adams' and 'The Sea Bird'
Letter to the editor, 8 May 1988

Looking at 'The Sea Bird' again, through your lens, I found myself reading 'Adams' as a gloss on the shorter version. An attempt to drag into the light and confront point blank and separately the double vision that is all but fused in the single image of the bird alone. Don't you think there's something about

> Adams is like a bird
>
> he does not hear you, someone said
>
> in appearance he is bird-eyed

reminiscent of

> He is a jailer.
> Allows me out on parole
> brings me back by telepathy
> is inside my mind

That stolid sort of deliberation seems to be Douglas's mode of squaring up to and coming to grips with essentials of something painfully real but impalpable, something a bit too close to him (for artistic control) but impalpable. ('sitting down to describe it I have sensations of physical combat'.)

Again through your lens, I see the impalpable painfully real thing, in 'The Sea Bird', as the real identity of the live bird and the dead one – an image of his sense of his own death having somehow already happened, of himself alive being already his own death and corpse in some abnormal degree of awareness. In 'The Sea Bird' so many of the lines superimpose the two

> a dead bird and a live bird

not differentiated in place

>   the dead eyeless, but with a bright eye

(the empty eyesocket has a bright eye in it)

>   the live bird discovered me

(rumbled me as an eyeless corpse) – (as Adams, in fact even)

>   and stepped from a black rock into the air

(stepped out of a sarcophagus – like a ghost)

>   I turn from the dead bird to watch him fly

(I shift focus from the vision of him as a corpse to the vision of him as a live bird, though still watching the same bird)

>   electric, brilliant blue

(is equally live and dead, electron life, high-voltage ghost and healthy plumage – and a symbol too, simply of existence, 'truth alone', i.e. dead or alive, simply 'in being', in so far as for Douglas death is such a vibrant touchstone condition. But then contrasted with

>   beneath he is orange, like flame

the blue takes a charge of Death in Life (electric fatality, sinister beauty) and the orange a charge of Life in Death (combustion of carbon, fatality, life-glory) which

>   colours I can't believe are so

defines as the simultaneous mutual-exclusives of the dead-alive paradox against which he is beating his brains.

Interesting to see how the same binary system strobes away down through almost all the lines – fascinating how tightly and precisely he brings it off.

I imagine Adams loomed up into near-focus as he concentrated the implications. Then the physical combat that follows does seem to engage his real concerns. Maybe he felt the bird image refracted them too obliquely, exploited them too merely aesthetically. Strange figure, that Adams. If he's a real officer, plus Douglas himself, don't you think he's also something of the beast on Douglas's back – a Frankenstein monster sort of bird man, trying to achieve real existence, 'come back to tell you all, I shall tell you all' etc? Odd how he sticks in the mind, so jagged and disturbing – Douglas's old Adam! The creature with the vision of Death in Life.

That Death In Life double vision is almost like a mystical experience in Douglas. Painfully vivid and beautiful life – Universe of nothingness. I think it's in the pressure of this sort of big preoccupation, behind the nimble physical engagement of his language, that we sense he's something more than a good poet – he's an important one.

Vasko Popa

Vasko Popa was born in 1922 in Grebenats, Banat, in Northern Yugoslavia. He studied at the Universities of Belgrade, Vienna and Bucharest, and was a Corresponding Member of the Serbian Academy of Sciences and an editor of the publishing house Nolit. He died in 1991.

Popa's work has been translated into many languages. In English, apart from separate poems in journals (notably *Modern Poetry in Translation*) three volumes have so far appeared: *Selected Poems*, translated by Anne Pennington with an introduction by Ted Hughes (Penguin Books, 1969); *The Little Box*, translated by Charles Simic (The Charioteer Press, Washington, 1970 – a limited edition of 350 copies); and *Earth Erect*, translated and with notes by Anne Pennington (Anvil Press Poetry, 1972).

The present volume includes all that was in the Penguin volume and in *Earth Erect*, plus the poems from *Bark* that the Penguin volume omitted, plus the three volumes that Popa has published since. This is virtually a complete collection, therefore, of all that Popa himself has published so far in volume form.

He is one of a generation of Mid-European poets – Holub of Czechoslovakia, Herbert of Poland and Amichai of Germany/Israel are perhaps others of similar calibre – who were caught in mid-adolescence by the war. Their reaction to the mainly surrealist principles that prevailed in Continental poetry in the inter-war years was a matter of personal temperament, but it has been reinforced by everything that has since happened, to their countries in particular and in some measure (more than ever before) to human beings everywhere. Circumstantial proof that man is a political animal, a state numeral, as if it needed to be proved, has been weighed out in dead bodies by the million. The attempt these poets have made to

Introduction to *Collected Poems* (London: Penguin, 1969;
London: Anvil Press Poetry, 1978; Manchester: Carcanet Press, 1989).

record man's awareness of what is being done to him, by his own institutions and by history, and to record along with the suffering their inner creative transcendence of it, has brought their poetry down to such precisions, discriminations and humilities that it is a new thing. It seems closer to the common reality, in which we have to live if we are to survive, than to those other realities in which we can holiday, or into which we decay when our bodily survival is comfortably taken care of, and which art, particularly contemporary art, is forever trying to impose on us as some sort of superior dimension. I think it was Milosz, the Polish poet, who when he lay in a doorway and watched the bullets lifting the cobbles out of the street beside him realized that most poetry is not equipped for life in a world where people actually do die. But some is. And the poets of whom Popa is one seem to have put their poetry to a similar test.

We can guess at the forces which shaped their outlook and style. They have had to live out, in actuality, a vision which for artists elsewhere is a prevailing shape of things but only brokenly glimpsed, through the clutter of our civilized liberal confusion. They must be reckoned among the purest and most wide awake of living poets.

In a way, their world reminds one of Beckett's world. Only theirs seems perhaps braver, more human and so more real. Beckett's standpoint is more detached, more analytical, and more the vision of an observer, or of the surgeon, arrived at through private perseverance. Their standpoint, in contrast, seems that of participants. It shows the positive, creative response to a national experience of disaster, actual and prolonged, with endless succession of bitter events. One feels behind each of these poets the consciousness of a people. At bottom, their vision, like Beckett's, is of the struggle of animal cells and of the torments of spirit in a world reduced to that vision. But theirs contains far more elements than his. It contains all the substance and feeling of ordinary life. And one can argue that it is a step or two beyond his in imaginative truth, in that whatever terrible things happen in their work happen within a containing passion – Job-like – for the elemental final beauty of the created world. Their poetic themes revolve around the living suffering spirit, capable of happiness, much deluded, too frail, with doubtful and provisional senses, so undefinable as to be almost silly, but palpably existing, and wanting to go on existing – and this is not, as in Beckett's world, absurd. It is the only precious thing, and designed in accord with the whole universe. Designed, indeed, by the whole universe. They are not the spoiled brats of civilization disappointed of impossible and unreal expectations and deprived of the revelations of necessity. In this they are prophets speaking somewhat against their times, though in an undertone, and not looking for listeners. They have managed to grow up to a view of the unaccommodated universe, but it has not made them cynical, they still like it and keep all their sympathies intact. They have got back to the simple animal courage of accepting the odds.

In another way, their world reminds one of the world of modern physics. Only theirs is more useful to us, in that while it is the same gulf of unknowable laws and unknowable particles, the centre of gravity is not within some postulate deep in space, or leaking away down the drill-shaft of mathematics, but inside man's sense of himself, inside his body and his essential human subjectivity. They refuse to sell out their arms, legs, hair, ears, body and soul and all it has suffered with them, in order to escape with some fragmentary sense, some abstract badge of self-estrangement, into a popular membership safety. In their very poetic technique – the infinitely flexible, tentative, pragmatic freedom with which they handle their explorations – we read a code of wide-openness to what is happening, within or without, a careful refusal to seal themselves off from what hurts and carries the essential information, a careful refusal to surrender themselves to any mechanical progression imposed on them by the tyranny of their own words or images, an endless scrupulous alertness on the frontiers of false and true. In effect, it is an intensely bracing moral vigilance. They accept in a sense what the prisoner must accept, who cannot pretend that any finger is at large. Like men come back from the dead they have an improved perception, an unerring sense of what really counts in being alive.

This helplessness in the circumstances has purged them of rhetoric. They cannot falsify their experience by any hopeful effort to change it. Their poetry is a strategy of making audible meanings without disturbing the silence, an art of homing in tentatively on vital scarcely perceptible signals, making no mistakes, but with no hope of finality, continuing to explore. In the end, with delicate manoeuvring, they precipitate out of a world of malicious negatives a happy positive. And they have created a small ironic space, a work of lyrical art, in which their humanity can respect itself.

Vasko Popa uses his own distinctive means. Like the others, he gives the impression of being well-acquainted with all that civilization has amassed in the way of hypotheses. Again, like the others, he seems to have played the film of history over to himself many times. Yet he has been thoroughly stripped of any spiritual or mental proprietorship. No poetry could carry less luggage than his, or be freer of predisposition and preconception. No poetry is more difficult to outflank, yet it is in no sense defensive. His poems are trying to find out what does exist, and what the conditions really are. The movement of his verse is part of his method of investigating something fearfully apprehended, fearfully discovered. But he will not be frightened into awe. He never loses his deeply ingrained humour and irony: that is his way of hanging on to his human wholeness. And he never loses his intense absorption in what he is talking about, either. His words test their way forward, sensitive to their own errors, dramatically and intimately alive, like the antennae of some rock-shore creature feeling out the presence of the sea and the huge powers in it. This analogy is not so random. There is a primitive pre-creation atmosphere about his work, as if he were present where all the dynamisms and formulae were ready and charged, but nothing created – or only a few fragments. Human beings, as visibly and wholly such, rarely appear in Popa's land-scapes. Only heads, tongues, spirits, hands, flames, magically vitalized wandering objects, such as apples and moons, present themselves, animated with strange but strangely familiar destinies. His poetry is near the world of music, where a repository of selected signs and forms, admitted from the outer world, act out fundamental combinations that often have something eerily mathematical about their progressions and symmetries, but which seem to belong deeply to the world of spirit or of the heart. Again like music, his poems turn the most grisly confrontations into something deadpan playful: a spell, a riddle, a game, a story. It is the Universal Language behind language, and when the poetic texture of the verbal code has been cancelled (as it must be in translation, though throughout this volume the translations seem to me extraordinary in poetic rightness and freshness) we are left with solid hieroglyphic objects and events, meaningful in a direct way, simultaneously earthen and spiritual, plain-statement and visionary.

He arrived at this freedom and inevitability gradually. His earliest manner often owes a lot to a familiar kind of mildly surrealist modern poesy, though it is charming in Popa, and already purposeful, as in the poem entitled 'In Forgetting', which is from a series of landscapes:

> From the distant darkness
> The plain stuck out its tongue
> The uncontrollable plain
>
> Spilt events
> Strewn faded words
> Levelled faces
>
> Here and there
> A hand of smoke
>
> Sighs without oars
> Thoughts without wings
> Homeless glances
>
> Here and there
> A flower of mist
>
> Unsaddled shadows
> More and more quietly paw
> The hot ash of laughter

That is from his first book, *Kora*, but 'Acquaintance', the first poem in the same book, already sketches out the essential method and universe of his later and more characteristic work:

Don't try to seduce me blue vault
I'm not playing
You are the vault of the thirsty palate
Over my head

Ribbon of space
Don't wind round my legs
Don't try to entrance me
You are a wakeful tongue
A seven-forked tongue
Beneath my steps
I'm not coming

My ingenuous breathing
My breathless breathing
Don't try to intoxicate me
I sense the breath of the beast
I'm not playing

I hear the familiar clash of dogs
The clash of teeth on teeth
I feel the dark of the jaws
That opens my eyes
I see

I see
I'm not dreaming

It is all there, the surprising fusion of unlikely elements. The sophisticated philosopher is also a primitive, gnomic spellmaker. The desolate view of the universe opens through eyes of childlike simplicity and moody oddness. The wide perspective of general elemental and biological law is spelled out with folklore hieroglyphs and magical monsters. The whole style is a marvellously effective artistic invention. It enables Popa to be as abstract as man can be, yet remain as intelligible and entertaining and as fully human as if he were telling a comic story. It is in this favourite device of his, the little fable or visionary anecdote, that we see most clearly his shift from literary surrealism to the far older and deeper thing, the surrealism of folklore. The distinction between the two seems to lie in the fact that literary surrealism is always connected with an extreme remove from the business of living under practical difficulties and successfully managing them. The mind, having abandoned the struggle with circumstances, and consequently lost the unifying focus that comes of that, has lost morale and surrendered to the arbitrary imagery of the dream flow. Folktale surrealism, on the other hand, is always urgently connected with the business of trying to manage practical difficulties so great that they have forced the sufferer temporarily out of the dimension of coherent reality into that depth of imagination where understanding has its roots and stores its X-rays. There is no sense of surrender to the dream flow for its own sake or of relaxation from the outer battle. In the world of metamorphoses and flights the problems are dismantled and solved, and the solution is always a practical one. This type of surrealism, if it can be called surrealism at all, goes naturally with a down-to-earth, alert tone of free inquiry, and in Popa's poetry the two appear everywhere together.

The air of trial and error exploration, of an improvised language, the attempt to get near something for which he is almost having to invent the words in a total disregard for poetry or the normal conventions of discourse, goes with his habit of working in cycles of poems. He will trust no phrase with his meaning for more than six or seven words at a time before he corrects his tack with another phrase from a different direction. In the same way, he will trust no poem with his meaning for more than fifteen or so lines, before he tries again from a totally different direction with another poem. Each cycle creates the terms of a universe, which he then explores, more or less methodically, with the terms. And one of the attractions of all Popa's poems is that one cannot set any limit to how deeply into the substance of the universe his intuitions may penetrate. They are often reminiscent of Kekulé's whirling dream snake. The cycle called 'Games', for instance, is close to mankind as we know it. Nothing prevents these poems from being merely ingenious, or virtuoso pieces of phrasing and timing, except the shock of recognition they impart, and the universe of grim evil which they evoke. It could as well be protozoa, or mathematical possibilities, playing these games, as anything in humanity. They are deeper than our reality as puppets are deeper than our reality: the more human they look and act the more elemental they seem.

In *Secondary Heaven* (1968), the total vision has become vast and one understands why he has been called an epic poet. His cosmos is more mysteriously active and dreadful but his affection for our life is closer than ever. The infinite terrible circumstances that seem to destroy man's importance, appear as the very terms of his importance. Man is the face, arms, legs, etc., grown over the infinite, terrible All. Popa's poems work in the sanity and fundamental simplicity of this fact, as it might appear to a man sitting in a chair.

Earth Erect, published in 1972, is a poetic commentary on the historical folk-memory of the Serbs, a poem of pilgrimage through sacred national places and events, and revolving around St Sava, the patron saint of Serbia and mythical shepherd of the wolves. Applied to such material, Popa's methods produce a marvellously rich busily-working pattern of associations, with large, sudden openings through history and weird resonances of tribal feelings. At the same time the whole sequence operates, with even greater intensity, as an organic sequence of dream-visions, drawing on many sources, charged with personal feeling, an alchemical adventure of the soul through important changes. It is a unique display of his art, to produce a national poem, a psychological adventure, a tribal dream of mythical density, and a private commentary on history, all in the same brief words, and simultaneously create a chain of such intensely beautiful artefacts.

In 1975 he published three long cycles. *Wolf-Salt* drew on the same lode of material as *Earth Erect*, but in a slightly different way. This is surely one of the most fascinating collections. The lame wolf is the modern Serb, and the Lame Wolf is the spirit of the Serbs. The poems are lame-wolf psalms addressed – in many moods and with much shape-shifting – to the mythical Lame Father or Mother of all Serb-Wolves. It is the real thing, a call to a whole people, in the profoundest kind of language. And a call to the Ancestral Spirit of a whole people. The way to read it, perhaps, is as something in the same category of literary production as David's Psalms. But the motive, and the serious weight of the work, is by the way. Whatever else it may be, it is for us a book of Popa's poems at their best – entertaining, infinitely inventive, and beautiful.

A few wolf-poems spill over into *Raw Flesh*, another group of poems published in 1975 and written during the same period as *Wolf-Salt*. These are unlike anything Popa has published before: simple direct jottings evoking memories of the poet's childhood and youth, memories of the war years and the town of Vershats. Except for the poems relating to his earliest childhood and forebears, where the wolves appear, these poems are without mythical dimension. But unfailingly they stretch wings towards the wider legendary worlds of the other books, setting themselves into the bigger settings.

All Popa's collections are now beginning to echo among each other. One begins to feel the large consistent wholeness behind the swarming parts. The third collection published in 1975, *The House on the Highroad*, was written over the preceding twenty years. None of his tightly consistent cycles seems to have been written at one go, on a single inspiration. They smoulder along through years, criss-crossing each other, keeping the character of their own genes, working out their completeness, until the cycles themselves, which are already made up of smaller cycles, begin to look like members of greater cycles. As Popa penetrates deeper into his life, with book after book, it begins to look like a Universe passing through a Universe. It has been one of the most exciting things in modern poetry, to watch this journey being made.

János Pilinszky

Hungarians consider János Pilinszky to be one of their best poets. Sándor Weöres, a towering poet, and nobody's lipserver, called him 'our greatest'. He died in 1981.

His special quality is not easy to define. He recognizably belongs to that generation of East European poets which includes Herbert, Holub and Popa, but his differences draw any discussion of him into quite another context. Hungarians tend to set him a little outside their ordinary writers, and his poetry a little outside ordinary poetry. The reason for this is something essential to Pilinszky's character. Critical judgement cannot rest in the aesthetic excellence of his work: it inevitably ends up arguing the ethical-religious position of Pilinszky himself, not at all a simple one in modern Hungary or anywhere else, but one which his poems and other writings and his life define with such poignancy and authority that it confronts the critic with a problem – a private, existential challenge. His 'greatness', then, unlike Weöres's, is not a greatness of imaginative and linguistic abundance. It has more to do with some form of spiritual distinction. The weight and unusual temper of his imagination and language derive from this.

The total volume of his poetry is quite slight. Up to 1970 the forms he used were traditional, varying only between tightness and looseness. Thereafter, his forms became externally free, and he became much more productive, though the poems themselves became more brief. The quality of his actual style is an essence, from the heart of his vision. It is direct, simple, even 'impoverished', but all Hungarians agree that it is a marvel of luminosity, unerring balance, sinuous music and intensity – a metal resembling nothing else. Through translation we can only try to imagine that (though working as closely with the originals as I have worked, one soon picks up a very distinct idea of it). But even a rough translation

Introduction to *Selected Poems* (Manchester: Carcanet Press, 1976; London: Anvil Press Poetry, 1989).

cannot completely blanket Pilinszky's unique vision of final things, or the urgency and depth and complexity of his poetic temperament.

He was born in Budapest in 1921. Certain known factors which have had a vital influence on the mature form of his work, are worth mentioning. Perhaps one of the most decisive has been what might seem the most trivial. His syntax, for all its classical finish, is quite idiosyncratic. This can be felt clearly in a word-for-word crib – though it is less easy to translate further. Something elliptical in the connections, freakishly home-made, abrupt. It would not be going too far to say there is a primitive element in the way it grasps its subject. Yet this peculiarity is deeply part of its most sophisticated effects, and its truth. His own words give the best idea of it:

Should someone ask, what after all is my poetic language, in truth I should have to answer: it is some sort of lack of language, a sort of linguistic poverty. I have learned our mother-tongue from my mother's elder sister, who met with an accident, was ill, and got barely beyond the stage of childlike stammering. This is not much. No doubt the world has added this and that, completely at random, accidentally, from very different work-shops. This I *received*. And because the nice thing about our mother-tongue is exactly this fact, that we receive it, we do not want to add anything to it. We would feel it detrimental to do so. It would be as if we tried to improve our origin. But in art even such a poor language – and I must say this with the pride of the poor – can be redeemed. In art the deaf can hear, the blind can see, the cripple can walk, each deficiency may become a creative force of high quality. (*from an interview* – 1969)

This 'mother-tongue' and especially his attitude towards it, as he describes it here, is a revealing clue to Pilinszky's whole poetic character.

Another pervading factor, which almost every word he writes forces us to take into account, has been his Catholic upbringing and education. His continuing allegiance to certain aspects of Catholicism is evident in small things – his publishing many of his poems in Catholic journals, his joining the staff of the Catholic weekly *Új Ember* in 1957. The poems demonstrate, however, that his inner relationship to Catholicism is neither simple nor happy. He has been called a Christian poet, even a Catholic poet, and the increasing density of Catholic terminology and imagery in his work provides argument for this. But he rejected those labels absolutely. There is no doubt that he was above all a religious poet. A rather dreadful sun of religious awareness, a midnight sun, hangs over all his responses. But his loyalty to a different order of revelation – which at first seems a directly opposite and contradictory order – came first.

In 1944 he was conscripted for military service – just in time to be scooped up by the retreating German army. His last year of the war was spent moving from prison camp to prison camp in Austria and Germany.

Whatever he met in those camps evidently opened the seventh seal for Pilinszky. It was a revelation of the new man: humanity stripped of everything but the biological persistence of cells. After this experience there emerges, at the heart of his poems, a strange creature, 'a gasping, limbless trunk', savaged by primal hungers, among the odds and ends of a destroyed culture, waiting to be shot, or beaten to death, or just thrown on a refuse heap – or simply waiting in empty eternity. The shock of this initiation seems to have objectified and confirmed something he had known from childhood: the world of the camps became the world of his deepest, most private, poetic knowledge.

His first collection of poems appeared in 1946. It was a literary event in Hungary. He became leader, with Ágnes Nemes Nagy, of a new school of poets, and co-edited their magazine. Silence soon descended, however, and ten years had to pass before his poems began to emerge again. His second book, containing eighteen poems reprinted from his first, and thirty-four new poems, came out in 1959. It was acclaimed, at once, as the major achievement of a major writer.

Those comparatively few poems have gradually established his international reputation. It was recognized, from the start, that he spoke from the disaster-centre of the modern world. What was also clear, though, was that his words escaped, only with great effort, from an intensifying, fixed core of silence. The bleak, lonely, condemned one, at the heart of his poems, spoke less and less.

The next thirteen years added only sixteen new poems. Then in 1971 and 1974 two new collections, projecting a new line of development from what had seemed impossible to alter, contained ninety-seven fresh pieces. Yet these pieces, if anything, only deepened the fixity and silence. All are short, fragmentary. Some are hardly more than a sentence or couplet. The first of these collections was titled *Splinters* – splinters, that is, from the cross. The title of the second can be translated *Denouement*. The change, however, was there. The mood and imagery of his earlier work survived through an inner transformation which seemed uncompleted until, in 1975, he published *Space and Relationship*, a collection of poems interspersed with photographs of the sculptures of Erzsébet Schaár.

'I would like to write,' Pilinszky said, 'as if I had remained silent.' He is not alone among modern poets, particularly those of his generation and experience, in his obsession with personal silence. As it is used by those Indian saints who refuse to speak at all until the ultimate truth speaks through them, or as Socrates used it before his judges, or as Christ used it before his accusers, silence can be a resonant form of speech. Pilinszky, who is rarely ironic and never Messianic, makes us aware of another silence.

It is impossible not to feel that the spirit of his poetry aspires to the most naked and helpless of all confrontations: a Christ-like posture of crucifixion. His silence is the silence of that moment on the cross, after the cry.

The silence of artistic integrity 'after Auschwitz' is a real thing. The mass of the human evidence of the camps, and of similar situations since, has raised the price of 'truth' and 'reality' and 'understanding' beyond what common words seem able to pay. The European poets who have been formed by this circumstance are well known. They have only continued to write, when at all, with a seasoned despair, a minimal, much-examined hope, a special irony. But because he was as he was, consumed with religious awareness, Pilinszky shifted the problem into other dimensions – which are more traditional but also, perhaps, broader and older, more intimately relevant, more piercing.

This is not to suggest that his poetry is in its inmost spirit necessarily Christian. The poems are nothing if not part of an appeal to God, but it is a God who seems not to exist. Or who exists, if at all, only as he exists for the stones. Not Godlessness, but the immanence of a God altogether different from what dogmatic Christianity has ever imagined. A God of absences and negative attributes, quite comfortless. A God in whose creation the camps and modern physics are equally at home. But this God has the one Almightiness that matters: He is the Truth.

We come to this Truth only on the simplest terms: through what has been suffered, what is being suffered, and the objects that participate in the suffering. The mysterious thing is that in Pilinszky the naked, carnal, helpless quality of this truth is fused with the utmost spiritual intensity. The desolate furnishings of his vision are revealed by their radiance. The epiphany of this peculiarly bleak and pitiless God is the flash-point in all these psalms.

In each poem, we find the same diamond centre: a post-apocalyptic silence, where the nail remains in the hand, and the wound cannot speak. All the light of Pilinszky's religious feeling radiates from the fixity of that crystal. The only possible direction of movement is away from the nailed wound – out of the flesh, and that he rejects.

In this final biological humiliation and solitude, say the poems, nothing can help. Sexual love becomes a howl, or a dumbness groping for somebody – anybody – in the dazzling emptiness. In his love poems, 'he' is separated from 'her' as the flesh is separated from meaning and hope, and as the spirit is separated from any form of consolation. Yet Pilinszky's horror at the physicality and wretchedness of this trap is without any taint of disgust.

And how is it, we might well ask, that this vision of what is, after all, a Universe of Death, an immovable, unalterable horror, where trembling creatures still go uselessly through their motions, how is it that it issues in poems so beautiful and satisfying? How do his few poor objects, his gigantic empty vistas, come to be so unforgettably alive and lit? The convict's scraped skull, the chickens in their wooden cages, the disaster-blanched wall, which recur like features of a prison yard – all have an eerie glowing depth of hieratic beauty, like objects in an early religious painting.

They reveal a place where every cultural support has been torn away, where the ultimate brutality of total war has become natural law, and where man has been reduced to the mere mechanism of his mutilated body. All words seem obsolete or inadequate. Yet out of this apparently final reality rise the poems whose language seems to redeem it, a language in which the symbols of the horror become the sacred symbols of a kind of worship.

These symbols are not redeemed in an unworldly sense. They are redeemed, precariously, in some all-too-human sense, somewhere in the pulsing mammalian nervous system, by a feat of homely consecration, a provisional, last-ditch 'miracle' achieved by means which seem to be never other than 'poetic'.

By this route, Pilinszky's poetry proves itself to be almost a religious activity. But once we have said this we realize it is also a by-product. The main task is something else, deepening a certain kind of attention, refining his submission to his vision of things, which involved Pilinszky's whole life at every moment. And it is true, his personality and his life were as exemplary, for Hungarians, as his poems: they were a single fabric. This insistence of Pilinszky's on paying for his words with his whole way of life attested the authority of his poems. And this is how they come to be an existential challenge to whoever is deeply drawn into them.

It is characteristic that his affinities are not with other poets, but with such figures as Van Gogh, certain of Dostoevsky's characters and above all, perhaps, with Simone Weil. (He translated the *Complete Works* of Simone Weil into Hungarian.) These extreme individuals, the nature of their inner struggles, the temperament verging on the saintly or the suicidal, zigzag like naked lightning through the magnetic atmosphere of Pilinszky's writings. They personify the most vital element, the electrified steely strength under his passivity and gentleness.

If the right hand of his poetic power is his sure grasp of a revealed truth of our final condition, then his left hand, so much more human and hurt, is his mystically intense feeling for the pathos of the sensual world. The intensity is not forceful or strenuous, in any way. It is rather a stillness and at the same time an ecstasy of affliction, a glare of inner exposure, a passivity of transfiguration. At this point, when all the powers of the soul are focused on what is final, and cannot be altered, even though it is horrible, the anguish, it seems, is indistinguishable from joy. The moment closest to extinction turns out to be *the* creative moment.

The result is not comforting. But it is healing. Ghastliness and bliss are weirdly married. The imagery of the central mysteries of Catholicism and the imagery of the camps have become interdependent.

In trying to articulate my impression of the key sensations in Pilinszky's poetry, I realize I have ignored important things, and no doubt missed others completely. 'Poems of such symbolic vitality, like cut jewels, draw their light from every direction.' But after eight or nine years of acquaintance, it seemed worth the attempt to indicate something of the temper and truth of the vision behind these superficially plain and open poems, which our translation has directed itself towards.

Nevertheless, this translation is as close as I could make it. Several Hungarian writers were extremely willing to supply all the word-for-word cribs I needed, and I would like to thank them. It proved most convenient for me, finally, to work with the poet János Csokits, a close friend of long standing, who introduced me to the work of Pilinszky years ago. He has guided me strictly. This translation is really every bit as much his as mine. Very many lines of his rough draft have been impossible to improve, as far as I could judge, and besides that odd inevitability and 'style' which a poet's translation into a language other than his own often seems to have, he retained naturally an unspoiled sense of the flavour and the tone of the originals – that very intriguing quality which is the translator's will-o'-the-wisp, the foreignness and strangeness. That most important thing was something I developed a feeling for, wherever János Csokits captured it, but I could not begin to reinvent it where he did not, or where I had to re-align his wording. The very thing that attracted me to Pilinszky's poems in the first place was their air of simple, helpless accuracy. Nothing conveys that so well as the most literal crib, and I suppose if we had the audacity that is what we should be printing here. As it is, we settled for literalness as a first principle.

One poem in particular which baffled my efforts was 'Apocrypha'. This could well be Pilinszky's summary, ultimate statement. For quite a while I despaired of translating it at all – the eerie splendour of the original is so evident, even in the roughest literal, that any solution seemed tame. János Csokits's word-for-word version, in all its rawness and bracketed shades of meaning, conveyed a vivid sense of this atmosphere and power. In the end I let it rest as printed here, with only the slightest verbal adjustments.

In general, wherever I took a liberty, János Csokits corrected me with infinite pains and lexicographical toil. These translations, then, in the sense of being word for word are close to the originals, and will have served their purpose if they serve as pointers, to help a reader re-imagine what those originals must be.

Laura Riding

The problem of any poet writing at present is how not to be overwhelmed by the influences of the great period now just ended. The bequest of that generation is too rich. At the same time, as far as its usefulness to a living poet goes, it seems obsolete. The huge poetic account they amassed is somehow – without ever having been really spent – bankrupt. Perhaps the world has changed too quickly. Now among the greater number who go on presenting dud cheques, one sees poets preferring to accept total poverty – as a more honest alternative.

But the real alternative, which Laura Riding's poetry exemplifies like nobody else's, is for the poet to do what is perhaps easier at the beginning of a good period than at the end, to ignore all influences and mine his way back to the source of poetry inside his own head. This, which one imagines ought to be the distinctive labour that makes a poet a poet, is what poets almost never manage to keep up: given our social natures, and our instinctive economies, it is almost impossible, after the first innocent inspiration. It is because her poems embody both a search for and a discovery of how precisely the job can be done, that Laura Riding's poetry has operated on other poets – as she very justifiably points out – as 'a new primer of poetic linguistics.'

Her pursuit is religious only in the sense that Wittgenstein's demands on and final despair with language can be called religious. She is not so alone as she claims in forcing poetry to 'the breaking point', but since her *Collected Poems* – which evidently convinced her that in poetry she had failed her notion of the truth – she has published no new verse. She now claims purer poetic conscience for her silence than for her poetry.

However she may feel she failed her notion of the truth, we can

From *The Unaccommodated Universe* (Santa Barbara, Black Sparrow Press, 1980).

say she did not fail poetry till she stopped writing. One senses a deep mistake in her sort of absolutism, an angelic sort of miserliness. Some abstract, suicidally-high demand for an ideal has got the upper hand of the creature sunk in the chattering fever of approximations and compromise which is the life of expressive speech. Nevertheless, it is the steady pressure of this demand through the poems which gives them their marvellously purposeful tension and inner moral coherence.

Perhaps her secret lies in this combination of a concentrated, ruthless drive towards things beyond language with a new-molten, supple, wild and free language. She has a 'religious' respect for the thing to be said, but no respect at all for the available means of saying it. 'The poetry does not matter.' But only a poet with an immense natural verbal gift can get away with that. The naïvely mathematical computerized ideal of language which one associates with the linguistic philosophy closest to her main theme is the opposite of her type of precision. Her language is truly primitive speech, a medicine bag of provisional magic and rough improvisation – childlike, playful, bizarre, in a perpetual restless state of dissolution and re-invention. It is a selfless language, created on the spur of the moment by her fierce, close, lucid, entranced, sensitive and wary pursuit of the actualities beyond them. Her nearly incredible precision is the precision not so much of the cold meaning of words as of expressiveness – in which many things beside a clear eye relentlessly on the object combine. Her weird music and patterning, her unfailing surprise – the greater poetic field that words begin to wield when they come fully alive – all that seems to have been incidental to her special state of attention, which was essentially contemptuous of words. Her priorities were right. To respect words more than the truths which are perpetually trying to find and correct words is the death of poetry. The reverse, of course, is also the death of poetry – but not before it has produced poetry.

As a 'new primer of poetic linguistics' her poems are as fresh and exemplary as ever they were. No doubt poets will go on being as grateful for them in the future as they have been in the past.

Crow on the Beach

Any reader who is unfamiliar with the Trickster Tales of early and primitive literatures, or who doesn't think those 'folk' productions have any place in the canon of serious literary forms, will probably try to relate Crow to something more familiar within the Western modern tradition. What usually comes up is Black Comedy of the sort that became fashionable for a while in post-war western Europe. But to make this relationship is misleading.

Black Comedy (as I understand it) and Trickster literature have superficial apparent resemblances, to be sure. But they are fundamentally so opposite that those seeming resemblances are in fact absolute opposites, as negative and positive are opposites.

Black Comedy is the end of a cultural process, Trickster literature is the beginning. Black Comedy draws its effects from the animal despair and suicidal nihilism that afflict a society or an individual when the supportive metaphysical beliefs disintegrate. Trickster literature draws its effects from the unkillable, biological optimism that supports a society or individual whose world is not yet fully created, and whose metaphysical beliefs are only just struggling out of the dream stage.

In Black Comedy the despair and nihilism are fundamental, and the attempts to live are provisional, clownish, meaningless, 'absurd'. In Trickster literature the optimism and creative joy are fundamental, and the attempts to live, and to enlarge and intensify life, however mismanaged, fill up at every point with self-sufficient meaning.

It is easy to confuse the two with each other, because historically they sometimes coexist, and psychologically they often do so – or at least they do so up to the point where the negative mood finally crushes out all possibility of hope, as often demonstrated in our own day, so that the biological processes of renewal and reproduction

From 45 Contemporary Poems: The Creative Process, edited by Alberta T. Turner (Harlow, Longman, 1985).

simply give up and cease. Black Comedy expresses the misery and disintegration of that, which is a reality, and so has its place in our attempts to diagnose what is happening to us. But Trickster literature expresses the vital factor compressed beneath the affliction at such times – the renewing, sacred spirit, searching its depths for new resources and directives, exploring towards new emergence and growth. And this is how the worst moment comes closest to the best opportunity. 'When the load of bricks is doubled, Moses comes', etc. From the point of view of someone trying to cope with external circumstances just as they are, Black Comedy can seem too narrow and cynical, in its selection of evidence, almost like the statement of a paranoia, but Trickster literature can seem irresponsible, in its refusal to be daunted by the opposition.

That is only a proverb of course. If the load of bricks is quadrupled, Moses too might be squashed flat. Trickster's appearances guarantee nothing. In fact, they might be ominous – coming disaster can be aphrodisiac.

Trickster and sexuality are connected by a hotline. In an individual's life, Black Comedy is like a metaphor of inescapable age and illness, as if it were founded on the chemical disillusionment and breakdown of the cells. But Trickster literature corresponds to the infantile, irresponsible naïvety of sexual love, as if it were founded on the immortal enterprise of the sperm.

It needs a sharp eye to separate the two. In Black Comedy, the lost, hopeful world of Trickster is mirrored coldly, with a negative accent. In Trickster literature, the doomed world of Black Comedy is mirrored hotly, with a positive accent. It is like the difference between two laughters: one bitter and destructive, the other defiant and creative, attending what seems to be the same calamity.

Maybe at bottom that is what Trickster is: the optimism of the sperm still battling zestfully along after 150 million years.

Cultures blossom round his head and fall to bits under his feet. Indifferent to the discouragements of time, learning a little, but not much, from every rebuff, in the evolutionary way, turning everything to his advantage, or trying to, he is nothing really but an all-out commitment to salvaging life against the odds. All the other qualities spin round that nucleus, on long ellipses, but his high spirits and trajectory are constant. The sperm is looking for the egg – to combine with every human thing that is not itself, and to create a new self, with multiplied genetic potential, in a renewed world.

In the literature, the playful-savage burlesque of Trickster's inadequacies and setbacks, which is a distinguishing feature of the genre, is an integral part of the intrinsic human realism. And it is this folk-note of playfulness, really of affection and fellow-feeling, which does not date, no matter how peculiar and extravagant the adventures.

The recurrent quest of trickster, as the spirit of the sperm, is like a master plan, a deep biological imprint, and one of our most useful pieces of kit. We use it all the time, spontaneously, like a tool, at every stage of psychological recovery or growth. It supplies a path to the God-seeker, whose spiritual ecstasy, or the ecstasy he works for, hasn't altogether lost the sexual *samadhi* of the sperm. A little lower, like the hand of his Fate, it guides the Hero through his Hero-Tale, embroils him, since he's mortal, in tragedy, but sustains him with tragic joy. Beneath the Hero-Tale, like the satyr behind the Tragedy, is the Trickster Saga, a series of Tragicomedies. It is a series, and never properly tragic, because Trickster, demon of phallic energy, bearing the spirit of the sperm, is repetitive and indestructible. No matter what fatal mistakes he makes, and what tragic flaws he indulges, he refuses to let sufferings or death detain him, but always circumvents them, and never despairs. Too full of opportunistic ideas for sexual *samadhi*, too unevolved for spiritual ecstasy, too deathless for tragic joy, he rattles along on biological glee.

Each of these figures casts the shadows of the others. The Trickster, the Hero, and the Saint on the Path meet in the Holy Fool. None of them operates within a closed society, but on the epic stage, in the draughty arena of 'everything possible'. And each of them, true to that little sperm, serpent at the centre of the whole Russian Doll complex, works to redeem us, to heal us, and even, in a sense, to resurrect us, in our bad times.

This particular view of the Trickster Saga was my guiding metaphor when I set out to make what I could of Crow.

In 'Crow on the Beach' Crow confronts what he thinks is the sea.
Yes, it is the sea. Simultaneously, at this moment, his eye is
overshadowed by a subconscious vision of the womb. The womb
that he has forgotten, the one that bore him, and the womb of his
Beloved – which he will find when he overcomes his own perversity,
and learns what he is looking for (and what is looking for him).

The hopeful sign is that he recognizes pain – or rather 'travail'. He
does not recognize it, so much as become conscious of it by
projecting it, because he too is in pain, though he doesn't know it.
Everything in himself that he refuses to acknowledge is in pain. And
pain calls to pain. Mystified, he detects this. He experiences the
whole exchange, yet observes it as a non-participant. In other words,
he is still infantile – he evades the reality in himself. Or, for some
reason or other, cannot yet recognize it, so does not take responsibility for it, and so remains infantile.

The language of this piece – as of most of the *Crow* pieces – is
really determined by the fact that it is a song-legend. As a legend the
archaic perspective requires simplicity of a particular kind. The
whole problem of composing a song-legend, in the thick of contemporary literatures, is the business of reaching the right kind of
simplicity – and then hanging on to it. So it seems to me. And one has
to have a taste for simplicity.

Complexity, as a fact of our consciousness, is highly attractive,
and tends to commandeer all the available blood, in any constructive
mental effort. There is a simplicity on the near side of it, which is a
matter of selecting and generalizing the teeming external effects.
There is another simplicity on the far side of it, which is a matter of
handling the nuclei. As styles of language, they provide opportunities for different kinds of penetration, but successful legend employs
the latter.

Considering 'Crow on the Beach' as a song among songs, the
dominance of melody (the kind of melody that will carry a legend),
in the voice of it, tends again to select for itself an elemental
vocabulary – one that has, like music itself, kinaesthetic or at least
physical roots. That seems to have happened, sure enough, but I
only offer it as an observation. I suppose a close analysis of the

vocabulary might come up with some account of the melody as a variant of a certain species, pinpoint its psychosomatic characteristics, etc. Whatever that may be, the melody controlled the selection of words – as a physical act summons just the right hormones. The special function of the melody is the only law to the language of Crow.

Perhaps it should be said that *Crow* grew out of an invitation by Leonard Baskin to make a book with him simply about crows. He wanted an occasion to add more crows to all the crows that flock through his sculptures, drawings, and engravings in their various transformations. As the protagonist of a book, a crow would become symbolic in any author's hands. And a symbolic crow lives a legendary life. That is how *Crow* took off.

Inner Music

There exists a recording of an interview with Walter de la Mare, made shortly before he died. Sitting in his room, he talks about this and that, feeding titbits to the tape recorder in a rather wary and cornered way. Eventually, he deflects attention to a tree, visible from his window. He then goes on to recall how one day during a thunderstorm he happened to be watching that tree just as a bolt of lightning struck it. The bang and flash were startling enough, but not as startling as what the tree did. The tree, he said, simply threw off all its bark. 'Like a girl throwing off her clothes.'

His description of this, the slow musing phrases of his old but wonderfully alert and living voice, the surprised and surprising cadences of it, as that marvellous, shocking, curious moment rises again before him, make up one of the most uncanny vocal evocations I know.

What seals the purity of it is that his anecdote is followed, almost immediately, by his recitation of one of his poems. The effect is of a sudden closing off. Not that he was a bad reader of his own verse. Rather the opposite. Listening to him there, you hear what you hope to hear from a poet's reading of his or her own verse: you hear the peculiar, inner music, the singing ensemble of psychological components, which determines the possibilities of the verse. And he does project the verse perfectly.

But you listen in vain for the de la Mare of the lightning-blasted tree. The delicate, searching, naked music with which he unearthed the memory of that vision, and in which you seemed to hear the inmost chords of his sensibility – that is absent. For any of us who recite verse or prose there is a lesson here.

Another odd experience showed me a different lesson. I had made an adaptation of Seneca's *Oedipus*, for Peter Brook. Working toward the simplest most direct release of the energies in that strange play, I had reduced the original to a skeletal oratorio, and a vocabulary of a bare few hundred words. At the same time, I had tried to maintain, overall and in detail, a sense of pattern: patterns of rhythms, patterns of weight and of mood, patterns of cadences, just as in a piece of music. And the actors were of a quality that could make the most of this: they included Irene Worth, Sir John Gielgud, Colin Blakely, Ronald Pickup, all virtuoso speakers of verse and shapers of scenes.

Two or three days before the opening night, Peter Brook lined up the entire cast on stage (thirty-six altogether) and asked them to declaim the play, from where they stood, without moving a limb, at double speed, and in very loud, flat, Dalek-like voices – i.e., without any expressive inflection whatsoever. The purpose of this exercise was to shake them out of any vocal mannerisms that might have become fixed, and mechanical, during the very long rehearsal. But the results were unexpected.

The actors set off, full tilt. And within minutes, I realized I was undergoing a new, extraordinary verbal experience. The play, in fact, had become utterly verbal, in an unfamiliar but overpowering way. Without the visual distraction of actors acting, and without the cerebral distraction of voices interpreting, but at a speed which demanded the utmost concentration of attention, the words began to happen in a depth where their meanings were liberated and magnified. We were all packed inside a hurtling rocket that had shed every material circumstance and was now travelling on in pure sound. It is difficult to describe or to know just what was going on, but everybody felt it. The field of electrical power became nearly unbearable. One of the actors fainted, and a stage hand sitting in the front row also fainted. When it was over Peter Brook and I looked at each other in astonishment.

It occurred to me then, were Shakespeare's plays performed in something approaching this style, this speed and inwardness, this explosive, express containment? Was this how those colossal structures got airborne? And in fact, the closest thing to it that I have heard was the Comédie-Française playing Racine and, indeed, *Richard III*.

I felt I had glimpsed a whole greater existence of drama, one which our English stage has forgotten. Maybe this was how the rigid, stilted, masked actors of the Greek amphitheatre performed their megaphone tragedies and sent members of their audience raving in iambics for days afterwards.

Those Greek plays were close to liturgy. The gods and the underworld were still listening, and it was intended they should hear. And not only in Ancient Greece, but all over the world, in all places, at all times, wherever men try to reach the ear of spirits, or of gods, or of God, they use incantatory speech. They abandon all workaday tones and inflections – without which we human beings can hardly understand each other – and resort to this more or less frenzied plainsong. As if those spirits etc. had somehow let it be known that they will listen to nothing else. And this is inborn. We all discover it the moment we need to pray.

We have strayed some way from Walter de la Mare and his tale of the tree. But not so far, maybe, from Yeats's reading of his poems, or from Eliot's.

Whether we approve or not, we have to accept that when we recite verse or shaped prose we invoke something. And what hears us, and approaches, is human spirit: closer and fuller human spirit. The question is: what is human spirit, is it a desirable thing? And do we want a little, or a medium amount, or a lot? How deep is it, where does it end, what powers swim up or fly down through it, are they frightful or benign? And we have to think of the reciter too. Is the reciter looking for amusement, or a thrill, or a scare? What is he looking for? And is he inside a magical, protective circle, or out of it?

In his lecture on the Duende, Lorca gives an account of what some people, at one time and in one place, expected of incantation. He describes the singing of the Andalusian flamenco singer Pastora Pavon, in a tavern in Cadiz:

She sang with her voice of shadow, with her voice of liquid metal, with her moss-covered voice, and with her voice tangled in her long hair. She would soak her voice in manzanilla, or lose it in dark and distant thickets. Yet she failed completely: it was all to no purpose. The audience remained silent . . . Only a little man . . . said sarcastically in a very low voice: 'Viva Paris!' as if to say: 'Here we do not care for ability, technique, or mastery. Here we care for something else.'

At that moment Pastora Pavon got up like a woman possessed, broken as a mediaeval mourner, drank without pause a large glass of cazalla, a fire-water brandy, and sat down to sing without voice, breathless, without subtlety, her throat burning, but – with Duende. She succeeded in getting rid of the scaffolding of the song, to make way for a furious and fiery Duende . . . that made those who were listening tear their clothes . . .

Something of the sort was described by Layard, in his memoir of the excavation of Nineveh. He tells there how an itinerant bard gave a performance, in the tent one night, to the tribesmen who were working on the dig, and how he, Layard, watched, in absolute incredulity, as the audience writhed on the carpets, cried out in anguish, ground their teeth – while the bard sang his epic.

Are these excesses? Incantatory dialogue with the Duende, or with its relatives, occupies the inner gulf, on the brink of which the London Academy of Music and Dramatic Art holds its examinations. Few of us have much inclination to go over that brink. Walter de la Mare had no inclination to go over. And there he is on the brink, quite safe, with his tree. Teaching his exemplary lesson.

Or is he? Maybe what makes his tale of the tree so haunting is precisely that – a breath of the Duende. It doesn't disturb his tea-time courtesy, but perhaps it lifts the voice in those strange eddies. I vividly remember my response when I first heard Michael Hordern speak Shakespeare. I had come to believe it was impossible for a modern English voice and temperament to cope with that language convincingly. But there he was, speaking quite calmly, exactly as he speaks with his friends: a voice supercharged with intimate modulations, conscience, concern. And it was perfect. Those long speeches of Ulysses, in *Troilus and Cressida*, rose up and searched through all their complexities, very much as Walter de la Mare's voice searched through his memory of the lightning-struck tree. And just as naturally. Words and cadences clasping each other gently, naked, seemingly artless, inevitable, saturated with unforced emotion, enclosed in a deep, still imagination of the business in hand. Was the Duende there? Not the blood-freezing Duende of Pastora Pavon, maybe, but something – an overshadowing awareness of it, a presence. Not the speech of the Duende, but a darkness, the gulf of the Duende, beneath the voice of the actor.

1988

Keats on the Difference between the Dreamer and the Poet

In the lines

> The poet and the dreamer are distinct,
> Diverse, antipodes, sheer opposites:
> The one pours out a balm upon the world,
> The other vexes it.

what I imagine he meant was that true poetry (he was very keen on the necessary discrimination), the stuff which mankind finally values, is a healing substance – the vital energy of it is a healing energy, as if it were produced, in a natural and spontaneous way, by the psychological component of the auto-immune system, the body's self-repair system. In contrast to this, the works produced by what he calls 'dreamers' would be composed of the stuff of the symptoms of the malady – the symptoms, that is, as distinct from the healing response (I know they are sometimes, in physical medicine, hard to distinguish). The energy in the works of these dreamers would be a katabolic energy, the imagery would be projected from the agitation and distress of the actual process of destruction, a dramatization of the excitements of the onslaught of the disease and the collapse of the organism.

Keats doesn't argue it, but I suppose it's self-evident, that these 'dreamers' are the voice of the first phase of the malady, and are just as necessary as they are inevitable, in that they express the first awareness of the disease (when these 'dreamers' aren't new, they are nothing). They are the voice of the malady making itself known, issuing its manifesto, declaring the full nature of its presence and directing its threats, and this voice is defined by the pattern of pain it makes in the 'dreamers'. The equivalent of all this in the writer's works (presumably he's responding to some particular social-political situation in which he's immersed – however he might have

Reply to a correspondent, c. 1986.

been attuned to that by a private hurt) would be subject matter palpably drawn from the specific political-social issues, with all emotions and concerns confined to them.

This first phase includes most writers, and what they write is immediately comprehensible because the whole vocabulary of its materials is shared by everybody immersed in the same epidemic plight. The second phase, if it arrives at all, has to draw its energies from quite a different source – not from a source generally distributed throughout prevailing circumstances, but from a source in the biological core of an individual. These energies, that Keats called 'balm', make the healing work out of themselves. We recognize them, eventually, because we find they do in fact heal us – or they make us feel as if we were being healed, we search them out like the sick animal searching out the specific healing herb. Finally, mankind values these works because it needs them. In the end, it doesn't treasure anything else. Apart from curiosities, these are the only relics of any people or age that we hang on to – and we do that because they still carry 'healing' power. Though maybe we only call it 'beauty'.

The odd thing about this healing quality in true art is its mysterious relationship to 'subject matter'. It issues most intensely through music, but what subject matter does music have? What's the effect on the real power, and the real beauty, of music, if we inject social and political concerns into it? Even in painting this 'healing' stuff seems capricious, in its attitude to 'subject matter'.

To cut all this short, maybe I should say that I do think there is a 'proper' and an 'improper' source – not materials but source – for poetry. The 'proper' source is the source of that healing energy. The 'improper' source is – anywhere else. The 'materials', by this definition, can be anything at all that the healing energy feels like using. But if those materials are not selected by the healing energy itself, if they are selected instead by the cerebrations of ego, or by any impulse from any other corner of us, then the proper power and beauty of the 'healing' substance will be that far vitiated.

Poetry and Violence

Two questions posed by Ekbert Faas

This is an attempt to give more informative answers to two questions posed in an interview by Ekbert Faas in the London Magazine, *January, 1971.*

FAAS: Critics have often described your poetry as 'The poetry of violence'. . . . How does such poetry relate to our customary social and humanitarian values and to what degree can it be considered a criticism of those values?

HUGHES: I'm aware of that phrase mainly through young students who write to me asking for more information about my 'poetry of violence', as they call it.

In relation to my verse the word 'violence' was originally used by Edwin Muir, in his review of my first collection, where he qualified it as 'admirable violence' – speaking about the poem titled 'Jaguar'. What is 'admirable violence'?

Isn't this a social question: how to define the word 'violence'? It depends on where you stand – in the invisible but supersensitive and overlapping fields of defensive behaviour.

In the 'Song of Songs', the beauty of the beloved is described as 'terrible as an army with banners'. 'Admirable violence' there, perhaps, even if it is feminine beauty.

When Saul fell on the road, as he is said to have done, and ceased to exist, while Paul the Father of the Church rose up in his place and in his skin, Saul could justifiably have called it 'homicidal violence' (since he was not merely displaced but annihilated), but Paul could properly have called it 'admirable violence', since it united him with Christ and his highest spiritual being. How do those kinds of 'violence' relate to 'our customary social and humanitarian values'?

My poem 'Thrushes', from my second collection, has sometimes been cited as 'poetry of violence'. The charge centres on a triple image: the thrush in the act of killing a worm, Mozart's brain in the act of composing, and the feeding shark in the reflex action of biting at a bleeding wound in its own body. Here is the whole poem:

Thrushes

Terrifying are the attent sleek thrushes on the lawn,
More coiled steel than living – a poised
Dark deadly eye, those delicate legs
Triggered to stirrings beyond sense – with a start, a bounce, a stab
Overtake the instant and drag out some writhing thing.
No indolent procrastinations and no yawning stares.
No sighs or head-scratchings. Nothing but bounce and stab
And a ravening second.

Is it their single-minded-sized skulls, or a trained
Body, or genius, or a nestful of brats
Gives their days this bullet and automatic
Purpose? Mozart's brain had it, and the shark's mouth
That hungers down the blood-smell even to a leak of its own
Side and devouring of itself: efficiency which
Strikes too streamlined for any doubt to pluck at it
Or obstruction deflect.

With a man it is otherwise. Heroisms on horseback,
Outstripping his desk-diary at a broad desk,
Carving at a tiny ivory ornament
For years: his act worships itself – while for him,
Though he bends to be blent in the prayer, how loud and above what
Furious spaces of fire do the distracting devils
Orgy and hosannah, under what wilderness
Of black silent waters weep.

Before I can answer your question, we ought to be clearer about what those critics might mean by 'violence'. Then maybe see how this poem defends itself in court. The critics seem to be using the word with negative implications. Yet Edwin Muir uses it with positive implications.

How do readers understand it, in that phrase 'poetry of violence'?

I would like to get this clear, because the poem quoted above is in fact a comment on a kind of violence – a very particular kind of violence, a particular mode, that needs to be distinguished and defined quite sharply, if the poem is to get a fair hearing with some chance of being understood.

When you arrange the common uses of the word in a pattern you can see just how the confusions about its meaning arise. First of all, the word obviously covers a great range of different degrees of seriousness. By seriousness I mean serious in the way of moral and spiritual consequences. The general image behind the word is always a vehement action that breaks through something, but the moral and spiritual consequences can be all-important and immense or they can be nil. One imagines the line of a graph of increasing seriousness, with the word recurring all the way along it, from weak, loose meaning with nil or trivial consequences at one end to strong, specific meaning with enormous consequences at the other. Yet at any point on the graph it is the same little bald word 'violence'. Simultaneously, wherever it sits on the graph, the word can have either positive implications or negative. Isolated on a page, the word can give no idea of how serious it is meant to be, or whether its implications are positive or negative. These crucial extras depend wholly on context. And when the word is used virtually without context, as in that phrase 'poetry of violence', it is not actually meaningless but it is a word still waiting to be defined. It still contains all the different degrees of seriousness, and every positive or negative implication: they are all writhing around inside it, waiting to be selected.

Or rather, they are laid out, on that graph of increasing seriousness, in a symmetrical pattern, like the chromosomes on the genetic nucleus of the word, waiting to be selected into some particular life.

At the weak, loose extreme, though the ethical implications are trivial or nil, the meaning can still be negative or positive. One can use the word 'violence' to describe a passion, a cavorting horse, or a dancer, and be perfectly well understood to mean something positive and exciting admiration. More usually, even at this weak, loose extreme, the word carries negative implications – as in the media phrase 'sex and violence'. Generally, in this case, it signifies forceful physical damage inflicted on the person or the property of another, but here too, when the 'violence' is contained within a tight, exemplary system of just retribution, the moral and spiritual consequences are considered to be slight and under control. If the physical damage begins to escape the system of controls, and larger negative moral, spiritual consequences begin to be felt – as can sometimes happen in the media – then the violence shifts along the graph. It begins to move towards a stronger, more specific degree of seriousness.

At the other end of the graph, at the strong, specific extreme, 'violence' is in another world. The real negative vigour of the word now comes to the fore in the idea of *violation*. The core of its meaning opens up, to reveal a rape of some kind, the destruction of a sacred trust, the breaking of a sacred law. Central to the general idea of the criminally lawless and the physically vehement is that particular horror of *sacrilege*. Meanwhile, the moral and the spiritual consequences have become all-important – contagious and far-reaching in their evil effects. This radical, negative, strong sense of the word 'violence' seems to be its primary one. That's the meaning we use when we call Hitler's gang 'men of violence'. All our vigilant apprehension is fixed on it with good reason. Behind that sense of the word lies everything we have learned about the explosive evil in human nature.

Nevertheless, at this extreme, too, the word can have positive implications. The meanings of the action are now inverted. We no longer have a murderous force which violates a sacred law. Instead we have a life-bringing assertion of sacred law which demolishes, in some abrupt way, a force that oppressed and *violated* it. The image I suggested for this strong, positive violence ('admirable violence') was the sudden spontaneous conversion of Saul to Paul. The moral and spiritual consequences are again all-important, contagious and far-reaching, but now considered entirely good.

What this suggests is that at both extremes, and all the way along the line of the graph, the 'positive' meanings of the word 'violence' are secondary, recessive. Throughout the range of the word's uses, the common assumption is that the implications of the word must be negative. Where the positive sense is intended only a very clear and carefully defined context can preclude the negative assumption. But that positive sense is obviously no less real and important, no less useful, for being secondary and requiring special treatment. In its way, the strong, positive mode of violence ought to concern us more than the strong negative, since behind it presses the revelation of all that enables human beings to experience – with mystical clarity and certainty – what we call truth, reality, beauty, redemption and the kind of fundamental love that is at least equal to the fundamental evil.

My poem 'Thrushes' is an attempt to bring one aspect of that strong, specific, positive violence into focus, an attempt to provide a carefully defining context for it and to make some comment on it. In aligning the Thrush and the Shark, the poem is trying in its way to isolate and reveal the Paul in the Saul. And then to make a comment on our human reaction to that kind of revelation.

But from the pattern of meanings that I have sketched out, it is easy to see how this poem first of all attracted the loose, weak, negative usage of the word 'violence', and how the charge then became more serious.

The presence of the Thrush and the Shark are responsible. A good many of us are upset by scenes – on television, perhaps – of animals killing and eating each other. And most of us will condemn such scenes, in some way, as 'violent' – violent in an aura of cruelty. Here we are using the word at the weak, loose extreme of the graph of seriousness: the behaviour of the animals in their societies cannot be said to have any spiritual or moral consequences for us in ours. Nevertheless, our feelings about those scenes are not feigned: the revulsion, the pains of compassion, can be acute.

When such viewers become readers, they automatically interpret the phrase 'poetry of violence' in that loose, weak, media sense, and so find it an appropriate label for a poem that brings into close-up a Thrush killing worms and a Shark turning on itself the killing procedure intended for others. The Critics, who are also viewers turned readers, make the same interpretation, and so feel the phrase is valid. But they are aware of the more serious meanings of 'violence'. And they are eager to plunge for dramatic commentary into the negative depths. So they drag the poem down there as far as they can. And down there, inevitably, the condemnations begin to sound more serious.

Even so, their remarks about the violence of the poem continue to revolve around the Thrush and the Shark, the predators killing to eat. In other words, these critics seem to be trying to impose on the weak, loose, media sense of 'violence' something of the moral and spiritual significance of a 'violence' close to the strong, negative extreme. And they are doing this to images that are, from my point of view, strongly positive: metaphors (as I said) of Paul being revealed in Saul. For an explanation of what these critics are doing, maybe one has to go back to their weak, loose, media reaction to the behaviour of predators killing and eating on a screen.

Our reaction to these filmed scenes is burdened by the fact that most of us continue to survive only by devouring parts of several different dead animals each week – and often enough each day. Moreover, these are animals that have been killed by methods and in circumstances that make any wild predator's kill seem by comparison merciful and blameless. For all who are horrified by this predation on the screen, our own internal involvement in the killing and eating of animals can only exist as an equally horrifying crime. And beneath it, but inseparable from it, moves our extraordinary readiness to exploit, oppress, torture and kill our own kind, refining on the way all the varieties of the lie and all the pleasures of watching others suffer, and violating in the process every law and sacred trust. Personally, each one of us likes to believe that we belong with the few, the abnormal, sometimes regarded as the saintly, who would never take part in these more depraved acts of violence. But we have to accept what controlled experiments have (if only on a small scale) demonstrated: that once given licence most people will dutifully, zealously, zestfully inflict ultimate pain on others. Likewise, we have to accept what history repeatedly demonstrates on the large scale: that the alternative to the rule of 'sacred law' is not universal brotherhood but anarchy, massacre, the ultimate negative violence.

However we accommodate ourselves to this strange tacit criminality of ours, in effect we either accept it into our view of reality or we refuse to accept it. Since it is a criminality that we feel has been thrust upon us and that we deplore, we are inclined to refuse to accept it. We tend to dissociate ourselves from it, and suppress any sense of our own implication in it. Hence the phenomenon of a vigorous human carnivore leaving the room sickened at the sight of lions killing and devouring a zebra, and announcing that a world in which such things go on is simply too horrible, without giving a thought to just how, say, the hamburger beef that we munch has been stunned by a bolt through the top of the skull, throat slashed while the heart still beats, body hoicked up by the heel, subjected to whirling knives, zapping power saws, ripping hands before – within eight minutes – a half-ton bullock hangs in clean dry swinging halves ready for the middlemen. Or how the roasted lamb that makes our mouths water had to be stunned/ electrocuted through clamps (like earphones) on the eyeballs (for better contact), before etc., etc.

The reaction that critics extend over my poem 'Thrushes', in their use of the word 'violence', is a muddle of all this hugger mugger bad feeling – a rejection touched into life by the focused image of a Thrush 'more coiled steel than living' killing a worm to feed its family. This is probably felt to be worse, even something of a 'violation', for being committed by Browning's and Hardy's beautiful and heroic singer. Some blame, I suppose, is smudged on to the perpetrator of such a libel against one of the darlings of our pastoral idyll. A little of this, maybe.

If the word 'violence', used in this phrase, brings that crying and screaming though concealed and unconfessed slaughterhouse with it, as I believe it does, then my superimposing of the Thrush (killing its worm) onto Mozart's brain (composing its music) makes things even worse. The sense of impropriety, if not vandalism, in the juxtaposition, and of near-blasphemy in the comparison, jangles even harsher alarm bells. As if a wanton act of 'violence' had been performed, this time, by the writer – perhaps with the express,

Dadaesque intent of violating the reader's sensibilities.

Their worst suspicions will be confirmed when such readers reach the Shark that in its feeding frenzy blindly snaps at its own wound. To have this image of a frenziedly self-devouring shark super-imposed retrospectively, as a likeness, on to the pulsing, rapturous play of Mozart's inspired brain, might seem to put the atrocity, the 'violence' of the whole operation, beyond doubt.

But any reader who hangs on to the plotted course and argument of the poem will surely find something different. Considering the three images – Thrush, Mozart's brain and Shark – as hieroglyphs, only one has a clear self-evident meaning. So that one is the key to the others. Mozart's composing brain – the lump of animal brain tissue producing Mozart's music – has a single plain meaning: divine activity in something fleshly. However else we interpret the image, our ideas revolve around this fixed, central axis of meaning.

The other two, Thrush killing a worm and Shark doing as described, have as I say uncertain and still-undefined meaning. Still to be defined, that is, in this context.

Neither Thrush nor Shark can properly be defined by the weak, loose negative meaning of 'violent'. There are several factors in each situation contradicting that sense. The Thrush is doing what it has evolved to do, and is feeding its young as well. The Shark is doing what it has evolved to do and what uniquely determines everything about it, but has been tricked, in innocence, to turn the activity against itself, unknowing. So other meanings open up in both images.

The question now becomes: among the varied meanings of these two images is there one, in each, that corresponds to the meaning of Mozart's brain: divine activity in something fleshly?

It is not unorthodox to see that there is a clear and strong sense in which both Thrush and Shark are obeying – in selfless, inspired (i.e. lucid) obedience, like Mozart's brain – the creator's law which shaped their being and their inborn activity. And they are obeying it with that effortless instantaneity which is a 'divine' characteristic, also, of Mozart's composition.

This is where what the critics called 'poetry of [negative] violence' begins to assert its credentials as poetry of positive violence, poetry about the working of divine law in created things.

The poem now becomes, logically, an attempt to wrench a universal reality – the characteristics of divine law as it operates in created things – away from the stereotype, sentimental, weak, loose, media misreading of it in Thrush and Shark (and in the natural world generally). By pushing through precisely those activities that provoke the blindest reflex of the stock response the poem tries to reach a clearer understanding beyond. The clearer understanding would be: recognition of the operation of divine law in the created things of the natural world. Mozart's composing brain is one pole of this activity, the Shark's behaviour the other, while the Thrush killing to feed its family is a combination of both.

Under this law these are not 'violent', in the negative sense that their physical vehemence incurs guilt and blame and unacceptably endangers the rule of law. On the contrary, they are innocent, obedient, and their energy reaffirms the divine law that created them as they are.

If this is so, if this can be admitted as a fair interpretation of the first two of those three stanzas, then I suppose the poem does begin to look like a 'critique' of a certain attitude. And this attitude, yes, is the one, I suppose, that recoils from the poem in what I've called a stereotype, sentimental fashion. The attitude that recoils from animals killing animals on the screen – with a disapproval that masks the speaker's implication in the process which among other things constructs the unspoken abattoir between the bullock in the field and the steak on his plate. The attitude that effectually denies its own guilt and openly condemns what it unconsciously colludes with and profits from. Whatever orthodox values re-enforce that attitude (whether we call them humanitarian or not) must be questionable.

The poem then goes on to identify the author with this attitude and with all who tend to react in this way. Obviously, it isn't a tirade from the dock, condemning all who condemn it. It may be in the pulpit, but as one of the sinners, haranguing itself, trying to bring itself to its senses – trying to repair its damaged sense of reality and the failure of its self-knowledge. Trying to break out of 'our customary social and humanitarian values' and push through to that clearer understanding.

The last verse makes this plain. The Thrush finding and killing its worm, Mozart's composing brain, and the Shark, at their incredible, superhuman speeds, are 'at rest in the law'. Their agile velocity is a kind of stillness. At peace with essential being. Only we humans – 'terrified' by what our debilitated sense of reality sees as negative 'violence' in the activity of the Thrush and the Shark, and renouncing any possibility of sharing Mozart's 'divine' facility – cannot attain that peace. We cannot attain it because we are divided within ourselves against such spontaneous allegiance to the 'divine' law. The cultivated split in human consciousness has exacted this price. As a result (and this is the gist of the last lines) that 'divine' faculty of spontaneous allegiance to the creator's law is trapped within us, and locked up. Deprived of access to life, it is therefore deprived of the possibility of any genuine adaptation to life. And so it is diabolized (in frustration) or invents a metaphysical bliss (in sublimation) or simply mourns (in despair and resignation). In other words, it has been 'violated' (and has suffered crippling 'violence') by our settling for too-easy substitutes that support our social contracts. It has been 'violated', that is, by 'our customary social and humanitarian values'.

That's the sermon. The problem is that even if the poem were to succeed in clearly distinguishing positive 'violence' from the negative 'violence' that threatens 'our customary social and humanitarian values' with anarchy, massacre etc., it would still be unwelcome. Positive 'violence' – as clearly illustrated again in that image of Paul emerging from Saul – also threatens our 'customary social and humanitarian values' with the pains of self-reappraisal and self-correction, the pains of a closer self-adjustment to the 'divine' laws outside and within. The pains that the three Magi in Eliot's poem describe as 'hard and bitter agony'. Our common rejection of those pangs of transformation is incorporated in that last verse of the poem. While the first two verses strive to elect that 'positive' violence into high definition, to make Thrush and Shark, like Mozart, heroes of that positive and 'divine' immanence in reality itself – the last verse is written by a reader who feels inadequate to the challenge. It is written from within the 'customary social and humanitarian values' which confirm and even make a virtue of this sense of inadequacy – which accept the outlook that 'cannot bear very much reality'. These values, the poem says finally, protect the familiar human condition, that is alienated from its spiritual being as it is from its animal integrity and from a lucid acceptance of the true nature of the activities by which it survives. This condition, and these moral values that console it, always have been regarded as highly questionable – since at best they tolerate and at worst collude with the evil consequences.

And so, to answer your question finally, yes I suppose you could say that in so far as it succeeds in stating its case as I've just outlined it, the poem does relate to those values and does make some kind of criticism of them.

Other pieces of mine also cited for 'poetry of violence' are part of the same effort.

A schoolteacher wrote asking various questions about my verse, among others: 'are "Hawk Roosting" and "Pike" simply exercises in empathy designed to reflect the violent and destructive power latent in nature?'

I answered that my first principle concerning the interpretation of any poem is to let it mean whatever it can – to any reader, since every head will find its own meaning in any shapely collection of images.*

---

* In general, I assume that the interpretation of a fable (or poem, or symbolic mystery of any kind) that is of most use to us is the one we make for ourselves. The whole point of using fables for mental and spiritual training, as in the Sufi schools, rests in the fact that if the search for meaning in such things is a self-search then our understanding is transformed from within, according to our own resources and possibilities. Any illumination that has not been paid for, in this way, from within, cannot really belong to us. It remains as mere external information that leaves our life, our understanding of ourselves, the development of our innate potentials, our grasp of life itself, unchanged and perhaps even obstructed. Perhaps even weakened. Essentially, it is worthless to us. A teacher can help us to our interpretation only by hints and examples that stimulate our self-search – by another story, perhaps, or a metaphor, or an example. One particular fable that illustrates this truth succinctly appears in a collection of Sufi teaching stories compiled by Idries Shah. When students write to me, as they often do, asking for the explanation of some poem of

But then I did tell him what my own interpretation of those pieces was, first pointing out that both Hawk and Pike (like the Bull) are motionless, or almost motionless. In a planned, straightforward way, I began them as a series in which they would be angels – hanging in the radiant glory around the creator's throne, composed of terrific, holy power (there's a line in 'Hawk Roosting' almost verbatim from Job), but either quite still, or moving only very slowly – at peace, and actually composed of the glowing substance of the law. Like Sons of God. Pike (*luce* = fish of 'light'*), Apis Bull† and Horus. I wanted to focus my natural world – these familiars of my boyhood – in a 'divine' dimension. I wanted to express my sense of that. Again, these creatures are 'at rest in the law' – obedient, law-abiding, and are as I say the law in creaturely form. If the Hawk and

---

mine encountered in their classwork, I sometimes answer with this fable, as follows: The Sufi teacher had just told his student a certain story – a story which, properly understood, would open their minds and hearts to the next phase of their training. A new student (or perhaps he was a stubborn, slightly Westernized student) was baffled by the story and asked what it meant. The teacher then asked the questioner: 'If you had selected an especially fine peach at a fruit-stall, and had paid for it, and if the fruit-seller then peeled your peach, and ate it, in front of your eyes, before handing you the skin and the stone, what would you think?' The student was baffled here too, and so asked again: 'But Master, I do not understand this story either. Please explain it.' Whereupon the teacher patiently repeated the story of the peach.

* Luce is another name for Pike. From the old name in Latin – Lucius. (Lux=light.)

† A schoolboy once sent me, as his classroom interpretation of this poem, 'The Bull Moses', almost exactly the fragment of myth that was in my mind when I wrote it. The Bull, in his interpretation, was indeed Moses, leading the sacred people out of their prison in African Egypt, like the souls out of the underworld, into their promised land of a spiritualized life. He got everything except the deeper background in which Moses (who in legend is 'horned') was the Son of Osiris, the God of the Dead. The Son of Osiris is Horus, who is Osiris reborn. Horus is the Falcon. But Osiris is the Bull. This Bull is therefore the other form of that Falcon, and both are forms of God. The Falcon retained his divine credentials as baby Horus became infant Christ – emerging with them into Hopkins's poem. The divine credentials of the Bull, which were drawn from the Bull cults of Africa, were strengthened in Egypt and passed, with genetically distinct continuity, into the bull cults of the Mediterranean and Ireland. The Bull Apis and Osiris became one in early dynastic times. And in the latest Ptolemaic period Osiris as the Bull Apis – Serapis – was the chief god. I was not trying to translate all this into my memory of a particular bull that I knew well. But as I say it was in my mind as I wrote. And the boy located it.

the Pike kill, they kill within the law and their killing is a sacrament in this sense. It is an act not of violence but of law.

In writing these verses, then, I was trying to express what had been with me from the beginning. And when they emerged into the world of readers and became known, in the late fifties, I was startled to hear how others interpreted them.

FAAS: Robert Conquest, though he included four of your poems in *New Lines* II, did so only after rejecting the poetry of violence in his introduction. Like 'Hawk Roosting', your two Jaguar poems are often interpreted as celebrations of violence.

HUGHES: Perhaps I've answered that. How do you suppose these pieces appear to readers of other nationalities? Perhaps this whole debate is a fieldful of old-fashioned English windmills. Doesn't the entire world feel much as I do, about these beasts? One of the most painful passions of my fifth or sixth year was the desire to possess a lead rhinoceros, about eight inches long, in the window of Tetlaw's at the end of the bridge in Mytholmroyd. As lead animals went it was quite large, more expensive than most, and I never got it. The loss tortured me for years. But I was merely a bit before my time. After the last war, the British Government slaughtered a vast number of rhinos in Kenya, I think 40,000, to make way for a monoculture scheme growing monkey nuts, and nobody batted an eyelid. They were regarded as horrid violent brutes in those days. But now – the whole world adores rhinos. Either to cherish the five or six thousand survivors, or to kill and possess or absorb some relic of this evidently holy beast. It is the same with tigers, jaguars – with all the creatures of the natural world.

This change, in everybody's – or almost everybody's – attitude to animals, is not a fad. It's part of a gigantic change in 'our customary social and humanitarian values'.

Maybe you could say the predators become suspect when they appear in art or iconography as symbols of some otherwise hidden psychic force in human beings. In general, such symbols are recognized and interpreted one way or another, and in retrospect they can often be linked to a psychological episode. Jung claimed to have detected in the dreams of Germans, between the wars, a rapidly increasing population of lions, panthers, big dangerous cats. Retrospectively, one interprets what that meant. In the sixties, the Yugoslav Serb poet Vasko Popa wrote a powerful cycle of poems about the Serbian national Saint: St Sava of the Wolves. The Serbs are St Sava's wolves. During the seventies he told me that whenever he gave a public reading in Yugoslavia, students would begin to shout out, demanding the wolf poems, and then when he read them would become wildly excited – so much so that he was alarmed and puzzled. I asked him what he thought it meant and he said: 'I don't know. But I fear – very bad things.'

Within his system, Blake's Tyger was like the animal form of his Los. And Los was his terrific embodiment of divine life-energy – his symbol, one has to suppose, of the vast upsurge of psychic energy that accompanied, all over Europe, the French Revolution, to which Blake was so susceptible. Even if Blake's Tyger could be connected in this way to the forces behind the French Revolution, one cannot imagine that if he had suppressed the poem any tiniest wisp of that psychic energy astir in the world would have gone back to sleep.

Yeats certainly connected the Rough Beast in his poem 'The Second Coming' to an upsurge of psychic energy that would, in his opinion, transform society. Yeats's symbol is politically more complicated than Blake's though in the end – as a spiritual symbol – amounting maybe to the same thing.* But in the case of this poem too, whether the Rough Beast truly was in a confined sense connected to Irish Nationalism, or in a wider sense to forces moving in Asia and

---

* This great cat had taken up residence in Yeats's mythos long before it roamed into Germany. In his 1889 volume *The Wanderings of Oisin and Other Poems* appears the following:

> On Mr Nettleship's Picture at the Royal Hibernian Academy
> Yonder the sickle of the moon sails on,
> But here the Lioness licks her soft cub
> Tender and fearless on her funeral pyre;
> Above, saliva dripping from his jaws,
> The Lion, the world's great solitary, bends
> Lowly the head of his magnificence

Europe, one can hardly suppose that if Yeats had suppressed the poem anything would have happened more quietly or kindly.

Even if one could want to unwish the French Revolution, and every international harmonic of it (which would include, presumably, Blake's Tyger), the fact remains that it happened. In the same way even if one could deplore Yeats's lifelong efforts to galvanize his countrymen, and even if one could prefer the 'customary social and humanitarian values' of England's stranglehold policy on Ireland to Yeats's own values which, being revolutionary, put him somewhat in tune with all revolutions, the fact remains that 'The Second Coming' is an image of events, not propaganda. If Yeats feared that some of his verses in the past might have sent out some young men to get shot, he was referring to passages that did have a propaganda-like explicit

—

> And roars, mad with the touch of the unknown,
> Not as he shakes the forest; but a cry
> Low, long and musical. A dew drop hung
> Bright on a grass-blade's underside, might hear,
> Nor tremble to its fall. The fire sweeps round
> Re-shining in his eyes. So ever moves
> The flaming circle of the outer Law,
> Nor heeds the old, dim protest and the cry
> The orb of the most inner living heart
> Gives forth. He, the Eternal, works His will.

Th   as actually entitled, interestingly enough: 'In the midst of the fire, and   hurt', the Lion family being gathered on 'a rocky eminence' surrou   ning forest, under a sky of smoke and flames. Beyond the fiery veil of the   glimpse of the new moon. The descriptive part of the poem, includii   musical roar of defiance' is taken from the descriptive paragraph in the   talogue. The Blakean association, which the Blake-saturated Yeats co   missed, was made literal in the painting by the antelope, also seeking r   e fire, crouching beside the Lioness. Yeats wrote this poem in 1886, wh   ly twenty-one. The question is, what drew him to that subject? Retrospec   and Robert Conquest might have pointed out that this was the year Glad   ntroduced a Home Rule Bill for Ireland, the year in which Yeats became an active Nationalist. But Jung might also point out that it was one year after he had become a Hermeticist – had become one officially, so to speak, by founding the Dublin Hermetic Society (he was Chairman). In other words, whatever crudely political interpretation the symbol might be given, it had its place right from the start in a larger 'sacred' mythos based largely on occultism and Eastern religious philosophy, a place similar in kind, that is, to that of Blake's Tyger in Blake's mythos.

political directive to their theme – verses that could conceivably be read as incitements to violence, poetry of an utterly different kind from 'The Second Coming'. I would agree with Conquest, some might have been better off without those words. But among those pieces of mine I cannot see anything remotely resembling such propaganda-like explicit, political or philosophical exhortations – or anything urging anybody in any direction whatsoever.

Blake saw his Tyger in a 'vision', and tried to make sense of it by controlling it, yoking it with the Lamb (Christ, its apparent antithesis) and the God of Job. This was Blake's way of accepting the inevitability, the reality: as Job accepted all acts and all consequences from his God. Yeats in a similar way controlled his Rough Beast by characterizing it as Christ (to be born in Bethlehem, but 'Christ the tiger'), coming as if to transform the Roman Empire. At the same time, this 'Christ' was the Messiah at his 'Second Coming' – which brings the end of the world, but also the Kingdom of God. On a third level, this Rough Beast is

A shape with lion body and the head of a man

'somewhere in sands of the desert', in other words – the Egyptian Sphynx. In Yeats's learned iconography, this beast incorporates the Egyptian lion form of the Great Goddess bringing, out of the desert, an era of devastation. But again, behind that calamity, having purged the land, according to her myth she renews it. This is Yeats's way of accepting the inevitability of something that may quite well be dreadful, but is in his view part of reality itself. And as in Blake's poem, and as in Job, the revelation of this reality must be finally good, as 'He, the Eternal, works his will'.

The point about these examples is: does it make any sense whatsoever to say that in these poems – Blake, Yeats, or Popa were 'celebrating violence'? Or does it make more sense to say: 'these sacred animals emerged into the field of vision of these poets, charged with special glamour, 'terrible beauty' and force, and the poets simply felt compelled to make an image of what they saw – at the same time trying to impose some form of ethical control on it'. In this sense, such poems simply bear witness. And I would have thought, any culture that would prefer to be without poetry of this kind – one would prefer to be without.

Since the late fifties, when that phrase 'poetry of violence' was first used, like many others I have watched with some amazement a particular development – a historical development – which can now be called a 'movement' in the broadest sense. When my first collection was published, the literature on which I had spent most time was elusive, rare, or expensive and for the most part to be found only in one or two specialist shops or the big libraries. Since then, all sacred texts, all mythological compilations and studies, all repositories of folklore, all commentaries and histories of religions and occult movements, all biographies of saints, sages, prophets, holy men, with a huge volume of new, related material dug out from previously inaccessible manuscripts or other languages, have become near-popular publications in a mass market. During the same period, books and more recently television programmes about wildlife and natural history have become virtually a craze, throughout much of the world. Along with this, maybe more visible in the US, countless changes have slowly but surely returned the Paleolithic world, the Pagan or natural world, to 'sacred' status, bringing with it, in the most curious fashion, the natural world's first and foremost representative – woman. All these things are clearly interconnected. It is the massive resurgence of something as archaic and yet as up to date – as timeless, and as global – as the 'sacred' biology of woman. Many other things, some more acceptable than others, have emerged riding the same wave. And the universal movement in which all these different currents make one tide is the movement to save the earth by a reformed good sense and sensitivity – to correct the régime of our 'customary social and humanitarian values', as it advertises itself, and rescue not only mankind from it, but all other living things: to rescue 'life' itself.

In retrospect, if my creatures are floating on the banner of any specific, historical tendency, as Robert Conquest and others have implied that they are, I hope it will turn out to have been this one.

1992

The Poetic Self:
A Centenary Tribute to T. S. Eliot

At a hundredth birthday I hope I can say that I am still youngish. But old enough, even so, to have grown accustomed to the tectonic shifts and readjustments in the literary and academic continents, as each new generation adapts itself to the Eliot vision and voice – to his continually growing presence. Those efforts of accommodation and understanding are part of a natural, historic process. But even where their public worth is slight, they can still be grateful, personal offerings. I would like to add to them with a small observation of my own.

A toast may be enough like a sermon to require a text. The text I have chosen is a very ancient one: the voice of Poetry as the voice of Eros.

I know T. S. Eliot distinguished at least three voices of Poetry. Without questioning what he had to say about those, I would like to float a tentative hypothesis, a sort of unified field theory, and ask how far it can be applied to his own poetry.

First of all, I need to recruit the traditional idea of the poetic Self – that other voice which in the earliest times came to the poet as a god, took possession of him, delivered the poem, then left him. Or it came as the Muse, after the poet's prayers for her favour. Shakespeare only half mocked it as 'that affable familiar ghost' which nightly gulled his rival with intelligence. For Blake, it was the 'authors in eternity'. For the young Yeats, 'a clear articulation in the air'.

This familiar concept is worth a closer look. The qualifications of the poetic Self (apart from its inspiration) were: that it lived its own life separate from and for the most part hidden from the poet's ordinary personality; that it was not under his control, either in when it came and went or in what it said; and that it was supernatural. The most significant of these peculiarities was that it was supernatural. In ways that were sometimes less explicit than

Written in 1988 and published in *A Dancer to God: Tributes to T. S. Eliot* (London: Faber and Faber, 1992).

others, it emerged from and was merged with a metaphysical Universe centred on God. And it did this happily throughout history, right up to the beginning of this century.

I want to draw attention to what happened when this poetic Self mutated, as it so notoriously did. Imagine if Eliot, like Yeats, had heard that 'clear articulation in the air'. He might have been very glad of the lines, but he would have found no difficulty in recognizing the voice as an audial hallucination, in attributing it to a source located in his own subconscious mind, and in describing it as such to others.

Between the two men, born only twenty-three years apart, the shadow had fallen. It was human consciousness, we now see, and not simply the poetic Self, that had mutated. The undertow of Eliot's early tortured self-examination was the knowledge that this had irreversibly happened, that religious institutions and rituals had ceased to be real in the old sense, and that they continued to exist only as forms of 'make-believe', ways of behaviour rather than of belief. A new kind of reality had supplanted them. In the twinkling of an eye, as Nostradamus would say, the whole metaphysical universe centred on God had vanished from its place. It had evaporated, with all its meanings.

This emptiness was Eliot's starting-point. What seems curious was the suddenness of it. The historical convulsions leading up to it could be and were read as either death-struggles or birth-throes, and obviously they were both. But in spite of all those clear prophecies and ominous preparations, the actual birth, the final switchover from amniotic ocean of buoyant soul to free-fall gulf of elemental oxygen, came as a stupefying shock, and with anything but a whimper, when the First World War left the truth bare. It was as if only now, at this moment, mankind was finally born. For the first time in his delusive history he had lost the supernatural world. He had lost the special terrors and cruelties of it, but also the infinite consolation, and the infinite inner riches. In its place he had found merely a new terror: the meaningless.

We see now that Eliot was the poet who brought the full implication of that moment into consciousness. It formed the features of his genius. It determined the novelty and scope and import of his greatness. And it decided his unique position in the history of poetry. That desacralized landscape had never been seen before. Or if it had been glimpsed, it had never before been real. Eliot found it, explored it, revealed it, gave it a name and a human voice. And almost immediately, everybody recognized it as their own.

It is natural to ask: what was it about him that so fitted him for the part? Because it is strange that, though so many other poets shared something of his awareness, no other actually embodied the vision and lived it, and articulated what that meant, as if the inescapable truths of it were inborn, as he did.

Perhaps it casts some preliminary light on Eliot to deflect the question slightly, and ask how this overwhelming desacralization of the Western World affected Yeats. Looking at him obliquely, and surveying only the bolder contours of his life and work, most readers would say that the distinguishing peculiarity of Yeats, among poets, lay in his preoccupation with the supernatural. Even to his earliest contemporaries this seemed already anachronistic, and as time passed it began to look even sillier: at best a wilful indulgence, at worst a little bit crazy, and, by any light, evidence of his fundamental lack of seriousness. To this day, when it is no longer done to doubt his seriousness, his appetite for the occult, for spirits, fairies and the ancient demi-gods, seems to many of his admirers incomprehensible, an eccentric, mistaken search for a system that might have been better supplied by something that all others understand or share, as indeed it did to Eliot. From Yeats's point of view, obviously, it was anything but eccentric. He never really abandoned his early resolution, to make the work of poetry his first concern, the world of magic his second. And by magic as we know he did mean the real thing: arduous negotiation with spirits; regular, systematic, ritual dealings with the supernatural and supersensible realms. For him, the methodical work of magic had the kind of importance that accurate nuclear physics had for the makers of the Bomb: it was the path, as he saw it, towards the effective, practical fulfilment of his purpose – a life-work which he dedicated, quite consciously, to the service of his idea of Ireland.

One might well ask what instinct drew him to the supernatural in the first place. But the questions amplify hugely when one observes how every step and circumstance of his embattled life seems to have fed his spiritual energy and reinforced his spiritual priorities. And when one observes, too, just how effective and positive and many were the parts that this occult energy enabled him to play. It is certainly too simple to say what must have been partly true, that his powers increased in proportion to the determination with which he opposed, magician's sword in hand, the ungovernable tides of secular materialism, especially the tide from England, as if that daily labour served as some kind of gymnasium for a freakish one-man religious system.

Part of Yeats's pattern comes a little clearer, perhaps, when we set him in an anthropological context. It is fairly easy then to recognize him as a shamanic type. The classic moment for the advent of the messianic shaman, the Saviour, arrives, as history repeatedly shows, where the material hopes and resources of a people truly do fail, and the desperate appeal to the miracle of spirit is incarnated, to a greater or lesser degree, in some abnormal individual. The sense of tribal disaster that animated Yeats was certainly compounded by shock waves from Nietzsche, Darwin and other epicentres, but the decisive event, imprinted on the face and voice of his every fellow-countryman as in the Irish landscape itself, would be that prolonged, genocidal humiliation where the Great Famine and the mass emigrations that resulted from it, falling across the childhood of his parents, were subjectively experienced by all who felt themselves to be Irish as the ultimate defeat, the bitter culmination of seven centuries of British policy in Ireland.

Yeats's calling came to him, in a sudden awakening, as three simultaneous obsessions. Irish nationalist politics and the supernatural possessed his intellectual life, while Irish myth, legend and folklore took hold of his poetry. He donned his spiritual breastplate of hermetic disciplines and within a very short time had formulated his life mission on the grandest scale: to restore the energy and defiance of the ancestral heroes and lost gods to the prostrated soul of Ireland. This was pure shamanic thinking of the most primitive brand. It was closer to the visions of the Sioux Shaman Black Elk than to anything in the political or even poetic traditions of Western Europe. Throughout his labours as a political activist, Yeats's inspiration remained shamanic: to remake 'the ring of the people', to restore heroic, spiritual unity to his nation. His outspoken political statements all glow at some point into a shamanic flame, a sort of St Elmo's fire: where the enemy seemed about to triumph, eternity would put forth flaming fingers and bring their work to nothing; the moment before Ireland's destiny foundered on the rocks, a flaming hand would be laid upon the tiller. No matter how he was battered, as he was, by sharp-cornered modern realities, through all the tossings of his combative existence he swerved from his 'boyish plan', as he proclaimed exultantly, 'in nought'. He emerged into every new phase with his militant spirituality more joyful and tougher than ever. His political effectuality has been ridiculed by those who ridiculed the mysteries of spirit in which he put such faith, but after his lifelong campaign, fought stubbornly and exclusively from the nimble vantage of a first-century battle-chariot, Yeats thought it no accident when his own image of his poetic self, the warrior-saviour Cuchulain, materialized in bronze inside the O'Connell Street Post Office.

Surveyed in the same context, in the same broad way, and in comparison with Yeats, Eliot too looks not a little shamanic. In nervous temperament, and in the known psychological events of his late adolescence and early manhood, he is an even more extreme and characteristic example of the type than Yeats. But in him, the process of becoming aware of his calling was somehow more problematic. It was more agonized and finally more awesome. For one thing, through the whole, first, most vulnerable phase of it, he lacked any formal, or – as Yeats would have put it – magical defence. He survived and went forward on pure, naked character. The tribal disaster, in his case, was presumably just that convulsive desacralization of the spirit of the West. His tribe, perhaps, included all Western man, or perhaps, even, simply spiritual man. His homeland, in this sense, was that 'infinitely gentle, infinitely suffering' thing's hold on the nature of reality, and on the nature of consciousness, in a universe that had, in primitive fashion, lost its soul. But his response to the calamity was, maybe by the very nature of the calamity, which isolated the victims, more individualized than Yeats's, more remorselessly focused within the wounds and exigencies of his own secret being. So it can seem to be a more crucial, a more surgically precise, more urgently human endeavour, being more privately personal at the one extreme and more universally public at the other. This appears in the difference between Yeats's heroic but untranslatably Irish Cuchulain and the universal, almost biological entity that emerged from the gulf to perform Eliot's inner drama.

Eliot's first consciousness of his task evolved from his attempts to deal with his sense of inner devastation, his perception of just how this general spiritual catastrophe had maimed and paralysed him, and of how this injury emptied life and the world of meaning. It is enlightening to watch his precocious intellectual skill bringing him to dead end after dead end, as he struggled to understand this condition in the very terms of the secular intelligence that had created it. And when his poetry opened a way, very briefly, during his impulsive experiment in Paris, where he put together 'The Love Song of J. Alfred Prufrock', he did not know how to take it. Perhaps he felt the time too soon and his hands too weak. He recoiled to the other extreme, into his determined attempt to adapt himself to a career in academic philosophy. At this point the summons to his real work rose before him in a significant form. At the time, he did not recognize it as a serious call. He acknowledged it as a disturbing, recurrent fascination, even an obsession. From this distance we can see that it was the old-fashioned thing: a religious vision. A half-primitive, nightmarish figure: the image of St Sebastian, a naked holy man, bound to a stake and pierced by many arrows. Outwardly, at least, it seemed to be St Sebastian. But Eliot himself wasn't so sure.

Who was it? What was it? Among other things it was proof, perhaps, that Eliot was able to contain within himself, more fully than any of his contemporaries, none of whom invented anything like it in inclusive complexity, depth and power, the spiritual tragedy of his epoch – of which this was an image, as it was in a more specific way of his own immediate psychological plight. Within this icon, that ascendant spirit of totalitarian, secular control – sceptical, scientific, steeled, flexible, rational, critical – displays its victim, the most profoundly aware and electrified plasm of the martyred psychosoma.

We see now more clearly the annunciation that stood behind Prufrock. However disparagingly Eliot tinkered with the various forms he tried to give it, this enigmatic vision effectively stopped him in his tracks. Even in his first explorations, it drew him out of his intellectual ego, out of his world of space and time, away from the academic temptation and into its own peculiar agony.

We have no problem nowadays in seeing that the God-centred metaphysical universe of the religions suffered not so much an evaporation as a translocation. It was interiorized. And translated. We live in the translation, where what had been religious and centred on God is psychological and centred on an idea of the self – albeit a self that remains a measureless if not infinite question mark.

Before the translation became a near-universal mythology, there was a draughty interim. It seemed as though the poetic enterprise might be over. Even in the 1940s and 1950s it was common to hear poets lamenting the futility, the irrelevance and above all the obsolescence of their art in the modern world. It is perhaps not so much an irony as a piece of evolution's natural economy that the little mechanism of free-association, which Freud picked up indirectly from Schiller, who used it to unblock his creative flow, should have been the means of dismantling the old-style mystery of poetic inspiration and the poetic self – or rather, of translating them.

In the end, of course, nothing disrupted the basic arrangements. The translation was first class. An ordinary ego still has to sleep and wake with some other more or less articulate personality hidden inside it, or behind it or beneath it, who carries on, just as before, living its own outlandish life, and who turns out, in fact, to be very like the old poetic self: secularized, privatized, maybe only rarely poetic, but recognizably the same autonomous, mostly incommunicado, keeper of the dreams. Psychoanalysis simply re-drafted the cotenancy contract in the new language. But in the process it did slightly change some things. By shifting the emphasis of certain clauses, it confirmed this other self, this new-style possibly poetic self, in powers that had previously often been challenged. It ensured, for instance, that this *doppelgänger*, though it might remain much of the time incognito, will always be dominant, with its hands, one way or another, on the controls; it will always possess superior knowledge about what is happening and will happen to the creature in which it dwells; and, more important, and reintroducing with a bang the heady higher gyroscope of a sacred creation, it may represent and may even contain, in its vital and so to speak genetic nucleus, the true self, the self at the source, that inmost core of the individual, which the Upanishads call the divine self, the most inaccessible thing of all.

But more important still, psychoanalysis re-established, as its first principle, the ancient and formerly divine first law of psychodynamics, which states: any communion with that other personality, especially when it does incorporate some form of the true self, is healing, and redeems the suffering of life, and releases joy. In this respect, at least, the new and desacralized world has ended up very close to the most archaic and spiritualized, where poetry from the true source was acknowledged to be divine because it heals, and redeems the sufferings of life, and releases joy. As if it secreted, in some drug-like essence, the ungainsayable reassurance of the Creator himself.

There is one further well-worked law, fundamental to psychoanalysis and to the modern secular outlook. This concerns the inevitability with which the true self, once it is awakened, and no matter how deeply and silently buried in the bones it may be, will always try to become the conscious centre of the whole being.

If we specify a poet in whom the poetic self is indeed, in this way, the true self, then the translation from old-style poetic self to new-style has left virtually everything intact, except the climate of expectation and possibility in which his readers live. And this very rough identification holds good, I believe, for Eliot. He is, in fact, an exemplary case. In his poetry all the characteristics of the new-style poetic self are apparent, present in the fullest possible strength, without obscuration or dilution, and my comments tonight really concern only him.

The translation has changed one or two things for the poet. It has also sharpened our awareness of what is actually going on in his work. It has changed things for the poet by removing his susceptibility to the trance condition, the mood in which the poetic self could overpower the whole mind in a more unhindered fashion. That this susceptibility has gone is a fact. There are some obvious psychological reasons for its demise, all connected with the loss of instinctive self-subjection to the greater authority of spirit. As Goethe remarked, the necessary trance is the most fragile piece of the poet's equipment. The mere presence of another person in the same house was enough to destroy his. But the pervasiveness of secular scepticism operates generally. Even Balinese dancers, trained from childhood to enter the trance in which their movements can happen, utterly lose the ability after quite a short dip into western attitudes. For any poet, this loss means acute distress. It means, in effect, that the poetic self's bid to convert the ordinary personality to its own terms, or to supplant it, or to dissolve it within itself, will be more successfully resisted. And this in turn means depression – the unproductive poet's melancholia. Or it may take the form of violent psychological or even physical breakdown, or religious crisis. A stealthier osmosis, in modern times, requires exceptional disciplines of monastic self-surrender – evidently. Again, Eliot is almost the only example among modern poets to suggest that this might be one possible way to complete the inner process.

He underwent both the depression and the violent collapse of ego. The ordeal of parturition, from which *The Waste Land* emerged, marks at least one occasion where his ordinary personality had to be forcibly displaced, before that other speech and that other life, his true speech and life, could be spoken and lived even temporarily. He underwent the religious crisis, in circumstances that seem to have been only less openly painful. And as I hope to show, he submitted himself, in his private meditation and poetic work ('humility is endless') to the slow, gradual change, according to that pattern where the true self remakes the ego in its own image, till the individual is wholly transformed, and the true self takes over, as openly as may be, the activities and satisfactions of life in the world.

The details support these generalities. Because in each case the make-up of the poetic self is so unique, its idiosyncrasies have consequences that are as peculiar as they are fateful. The new translation has sharpened our eyes to observe this. The poet's each successive creation can be read as the poetic self's effort to make itself known, to further its takeover. This effort embodies itself in a complete visionary symbol of the poetic self and its separated predicament. The distinguishing features of this kind of image are just these – that it is visionary, that it is irreducibly symbolic, and that it is dramatically complete.

The successive visions evolve in time according to the way the poetic self evolves in its hidden life. But in the series which make up the poet's opus, the earliest are often the most revealing, either because the interfering ego is weakest then, or because these creative visions are very like conventional serial dreams, in that the first successful representation is likely to be a compact index of everything to follow. The final poetic object is inevitably a mongrel, a record of the conflict of selves, partly what the limited, vigilant, personal ego has made of an ultimately unfathomable vision, partly what the vision has made of the inadequate ego, and partly the result of the contractual labours of a go-between or mediator, that third entity who argues both sides, or curses both sides, or despairs between them, or is torn apart by them, or successfully makes – on some terms or other – peace. But the ego might have good cause to resist. When the true self, for all its supremacy, happens to be deadlocked with some fatal disease or psychic death-sentence, and the conclusion is forgone, the knowledge will be there in the emerging image of the self's declaration.

The image that Keats found was of this sort: 'Endymion', 'La Belle Dame Sans Merci', 'The Pot of Basil', 'Lamia', are complete images of the poetic self locked in a death-struggle, and predict the fate that took Keats with it. Coleridge's vision of 'The Ancient Mariner' is another, also ominous, though with a saving difference, in that it prophesied a metaphysical death to the poetic self – but to the ordinary ego a long posthumous life telling the metaphysical tale. This illustrates what I mean by the 'fateful' quality of this kind of image. It can be just as surely so where the prognosis, as in Eliot's case, is harrowing – but ultimately good.

All this is a great simplification, besides being well known, but I have taken a detour through it because it clarifies my main point, and assembles the precedents, the relevant ones, for an answer to the question with which I began, where I asked, to change the wording slightly, what link is there between Eliot's poetry and that seminal deity of the ancient world – Eros, the god of love?

Nowadays Eros is a fluid term, coursing through all the familiar biological effects. Formerly, too, he had many names, faces, biographies. I want to define him more narrowly.

But my first step, not at all a digression, is another question: what is the real name of that quasi-divine figure who appears in Eliot's unforgettable early poem, 'The Death of Saint Narcissus'? Here is the whole poem:

The Death of Saint Narcissus

Come under the shadow of this gray rock –
Come in under the shadow of this gray rock,
And I will show you something different from either
Your shadow sprawling over the sand at daybreak, or
Your shadow leaping behind the fire against the red rock:
I will show you his bloody cloth and limbs
And the gray shadow on his lips.

He walked once between the sea and the high cliffs
When the wind made him aware of his limbs smoothly passing each
    other
And of his arms crossed over his breast.
When he walked over the meadows
He was stifled and soothed by his own rhythm.
By the river

His eyes were aware of the pointed corners of his eyes
And his hands aware of the pointed tips of his fingers.

Struck down by such knowledge
He could not live men's ways, but became a dancer before God.
If he walked in city streets
He seemed to tread on faces, convulsive thighs and knees.
So he came out under the rock.

First he was sure that he had been a tree,
Twisting its branches among each other
And tangling its roots among each other.

Then he knew that he had been a fish
With slippery white belly held tight in his own fingers,
Writhing in his own clutch, his ancient beauty
Caught fast in the pink tips of his new beauty.

Then he had been a young girl
Caught in the woods by a drunken old man
Knowing at the end the taste of his own whiteness
The horror of his own smoothness,
And he felt drunken and old.

So he became a dancer to God.
Because his flesh was in love with the burning arrows
He danced on the hot sand
Until the arrows came.
As he embraced them his white skin surrendered itself to the redness
    of blood, and satisfied him.
Now he is green, dry and stained
With the shadow in his mouth.

If we grant this mysterious being respectable status, and call him one
of Eliot's earliest and most strikingly successful 'objective correla-
tives', and one moreover of compelling visionary impact, we can
then ask, still using his own terms, what 'dark embryo' does it
deliver to the light?

Before we try to answer we might just check that the poem does stand very oddly alone, in an odd position, at the threshold of the *Collected Poems* yet not within. Outside the mature work, there is nothing remotely like it – except the fantasia of 'St Sebastian', which serves, rather, like an aborted twin, to intensify the survivor's uniqueness. Yet within the *Collected Poems* almost every poem, certainly every major poem, seems related to it in some uterine fashion.

Eliot seems to have liked it. He evidently considered letting Pound publish it, and though he thought better of that he did acknowledge the poem's membership of the family when he implanted key lines from it into *The Waste Land* – where again they became key lines. In retrospect, *The Waste Land* can look like the full-term accouchement where this 'Death of Saint Narcissus' would be a surgical colour slide of an early stage of the foetus. In a similar way, the major poems which follow it as if they had grown out of it, persuade us to accept this work – for all its germinal, raw tenderness – as the first portrait, perhaps the only full-face portrait, of Eliot's genius.

The next conjectural step, in consolidation of that last remark, is quite a large one. Does this poem present an image of Eliot's poetic self? I think it does exactly this. I ask you to believe that the poem records the moment when, looking into the pool beneath his ordinary personality, Eliot's poetic self caught a moment of tranced stillness, and became very precisely aware of its own peculiar nature, inheritance and fate, and found for itself this image.

Can a single early poem carry so much responsibility, even when we allow for what we know of Eliot's obsessive interest in the theme? Among his published early poems one other piece presents a very recognizable Eliot persona which might be thought just as likely a candidate for the role of the poetic Self's image. This is 'Humouresque', Eliot's lament for his dead marionette.

Humouresque

(after J. Laforgue)

One of my marionettes is dead,
Though not yet tired of the game –

But weak in body as in head,
(A jumping-jack has such a frame).

But this deceaséd marionette
I rather liked: a common face,
(The kind of face that we forget)
Pinched in a comic, dull grimace;

Half bullying, half imploring air,
Mouth twisted to the latest tune;
His who-the-devil-are-you stare;
Translated, maybe, to the moon

With Limbo's other useless things
Haranguing spectres, set him there;
'The snappiest fashion since last spring's,
'The newest style, on Earth, I swear.

'Why don't you people get some class?
(Feebly contemptuous of nose),
'Your damned thin moonlight, worse than gas –
'Now in New York' – and so it goes.

Logic a marionette's, all wrong
Of premises; yet in some star
A hero! – Where would he belong?
But, even at that, what mask *bizarre*!

The two poems complement each other. The marionette is
another form of the early Eliot's familiar Laforgue dandy of wittily
rhyming, ironic self-deprecation. He is a failed larval variant of the
rueful Prufrockian self-parody who feels himself inadequate not
only to the appeals of love and life, but to a whole flashing cloudful
of higher demands. He is no St Narcissus. Yet there is something of
St Narcissus about him: he shares that curious neurasthenic self-
awareness of himself as a thing, a puppet on strings. But while St
Narcissus consecrates in a dance his horror of his own beauty, this
marionette burlesques the pathetic ugliness of his own emptiness.
He is Eliot's parody of the ego who longs to be that other, even

[281]

as he excuses himself from the unmanageable confrontation; the self who is, one way and another, no more than a shadow of what he dissociates himself from so regretfully. He is the fatally-drained obverse of St Narcissus, striving to construct and maintain a brittly correct face for the outer world, while the entire life of his organism has been sucked up into that burning, sacred but far-removed and fugitive existence of the poetic self, that self-abandoned, anachronistic 'dancer to God', St Narcissus, who lives in a language as unlike that of Laforgue as possible, a language saturated with that of Holy Scripture, as he suffers and bleeds his way into the ultimate life of a death in God.

So even 'Humouresque' redirects us to St Narcissus as the accurate, real, sensitive portrait of the original poetic self, just as surely as the later poems point back to these two figures to confirm their contrapuntal roles.

However we look at it, 'The Death of Saint Narcissus' is far from slight. The actuality of this dancing aboriginal is weirdly disturbing. And the visionary definition, the deep-focus radiance of the scene, is uncanny. His balletic, orgiastic sanctity suggests the presence of the true self in an unveiled form, and something more too, something like Blake's 'fury of a spiritual existence'. Remembering Coleridge's Mariner and Keats's La Belle Dame, and thinking ahead through Eliot's future, we look again at this protagonist. We wonder what the implications might be.

The name St Narcissus is pointedly compounded and odd. It stirs up a welter of premonitory signals – the drowned self, the female, disembodied, crying voice – from the fable of Narcissus, but at the same time fixes primarily that aspect of the image as a mirrored reflection. While the poem opens the holy figure to a tangle of origins that are simultaneous primeval, far back in organic life, primitive and classical, the name pins him to a martyred Christian future. Though it sets him historically in the second century, as a former Bishop of Jerusalem, it makes an emblem of him and embeds him in the mythic, hieratic light of the mystery religions, where the earliest, ecstatic mystai in the caves and the last Gnostic frenzies in the desert dance the one dance.

In this last role he reveals an even more specific history.

Painted on a tomb wall, he would have to be identified as some form of Eros/Dionysus, the androgynous, protean daemon of biological existence and the reproductive cycle. He remembers his other lives: as a young girl, a fish, a tree. He has lived (and still lives) the sexual life of both female and male; he is the god who was (and is) a fish; he is the god in the tree. He is the god who 'could not live man's ways' and who, as the elemental and timeless incarnation of all the dying gods of the birth, copulation and death mythos – Thammuz, Attis, Osiris and the rest – was one way or another torn to pieces, mourned for and reborn: the god who was finally assumed as the tragic, sacrificed form of Eros, simply the god of love. In this way, the poem openly reclaims the sanctity of biological and primitive feeling, and fuses it with a covert, Loyolan variant of the life and death of Christ.

Having said that, what gives a reader pause is maybe what prompted Eliot to withdraw the poem from publication. Whether it is too gauche or too bold in its intimate self-revelation, almost its self-exposure, is difficult to say. The physical details and the subjective feeling attached to them are experienced with such first-hand intensity they reduce the mythic/historic context to nothing more than a theatre backdrop, while this dance in the foreground is suffered through like a biological transformation, so nakedly that it is shocking – holy but shocking, in the way that an axolotl held writhing in the fingers, or a squirming, bared foetus might be said to be holy but shocking. As the image moves it transmits a high-voltage *frisson*, a sort of alternating current of voluptuous horror and mystical rapture: a supercharge, one might say, of the richest erotic feeling going through a very bizarre transmutation.

If this is an 'objective correlative' for Eliot's poetic Self, what are the implications, the consequences, for him? Setting aside the Ancient Mariner and La Belle Dame, and giving only a steadying glance towards the more startling but maybe more comparable example of Nietzsche's vision encounter with Wotan, we could fix our attention, first of all, on the fact that the mirror image of Eliot's poetic Self is a god, and not only a god but (albeit in disguise) the supreme autochthonous god of the natural cycle and of the cultures of the West.

On the negative side, this suggests that the poet's ordinary life will be pre-empted, that sacred responsibilities will be imposed, whether he accepts them or not, and that some heavy personal cost will be exacted.

Up to this point, Eliot's Eros bodes no better than Nietzsche's Wotan. The similarity ends there. Wotan enforced his programme on Nietzsche, and maybe that was the human cost, exacted at the end, through those last years. But Eros exacted his cost at the beginning. Everything about Eliot's early life suggests that in some obscure part of himself he had foresuffered the sacrificial death of that deity even before he began to write under compulsion. This event, which was so much of his theme, and which lies so visibly among the roots of his poetry, can be seen as the spontaneous occurrence, in extraordinarily vivid and literal form, within him of that universal phenomenon, the traditional shaman's crucial initiatory experience of visionary dismemberment. And just as only after that 'death' (and after being reassembled by divine beings) the conventional shaman can begin to turn his abnormal powers and susceptibilities to account and launch out on his poetic, dramatic, visionary, healing-trance enterprise for the benefit of his people, so Eliot's case suggests how closely the creative, redemptive activity of poetry (of art in general) conforms to this thaumaturgical, natural process: where the shaman is possessed by the daemon of his own excess of natural healing power, as if artistic creation were the psychological component of the galvanized auto-immune system. After the sacrificial death, for Eliot, came the years of mourning. But before the end came rebirth.

Stopping short of the suggestion that the form of Eros alive and dead in Eliot's vision is also the daemon of the auto-immune system, we can see that for him the 'fateful' consequences wait within this particular deity's potential for suffering, for spiritual and moral recovery and growth, for universality, and for the most intimately human historical significance.

In other words, the 'bloody cloth and limbs' of St Narcissus lie at the root of the family tree of Western cultures. This doomed, epicene, immortal exquisite, dancing his archaic Aphrodisian/ Dionysian role in the tree of nerves, anticipates, as Eliot depicts him, the greater part of Western spiritual developments till they coalesce, ultimately, into the person of Christ, and ramify through all the Christian values of our civilization. The whole achievement is innate in the secret, naked god. At the same time, even in so early a poem, Eliot holds all possible relationships carefully open, and certain attitudes of this shape-changer more than suggest a kinship with the blue-faced Hindu Krishna who performs, one way and another, the epiphany at the core of Buddhism, cognate with the divine self, 'that person in the heart, no bigger than a thumb, maker of past and future', the child in the lotus who 'beyond suffering suffers from life to life'. In this perspective, the holy manikin, so spookily alive in Eliot's poem, appears as a skeleton key to the spirituality of the East as well as the West.

I keep well in mind that I am talking about Eliot's concealed (and for the most part incomprehensible to him, too) inner life. No discussion of this can get much beyond hints followed by guesses. Even to the most flexible hypothesis St Narcissus can never be more than a symbol, a composite cryptogram, for what was actually living there in Eliot's hidden being; and the word 'divine', with its relatives, can never be more than a convenient finger-post pointing towards those orders of experience which mankind goes on stumbling into, in terror and awe, even while he argues about them in terms of brain rhythms and brain chemistry. But however we approach it, we have to accept that what was actually there, behind the symbol he found for it, was decisive. And this is the sense in which that early vision determined, at each crossroads, the unique route of his poetic adventure, the unusual kind of greatness he was able to achieve, and the altogether unprecedented, universal and near-papal authority in which his greatness finally came to rest. Even that epithet 'papal', used so often jokingly, chimes aptly back through all I have been saying.

This link between the form that Eros takes in his early poem, and what Eliot was able to accomplish in his poetic career, holds the kernel of my argument. As a hieroglyphic device, a genetic code, 'The Death of Saint Narcissus' is true to the event, but it cannot explain some things. It cannot explain Eliot's single-minded intensity, the tenacity with which he explored all that opened within and beyond that inner confrontation, nor the quality of the intellectual/ moral gifts which enabled him to turn that inner exposure and opportunity to such prodigious account. It only tells us why, once the sufferings of Eros had emerged and constellated as the drama of his life, that direction of his inner evolution became inevitable. The theoretical alternative of inwardly disconnecting from the painful process and escaping into some kind of anaesthesia was as impossible for him as if by the failure of his self-protective nerve-chemistry. Where 'the ordinary wakeful life of the ego' was cut off from the spirit's search, he seems to have experienced it as a damnation, a bestial and mechanical horror, 'meaning Death'. Indeed, it was *The Waste Land*, the nightmare vision of the desacralized world, where the chosen Son of Man, opposing God, cursed by the prophets, stared from the protozoic slime, in a circle of meaningless reflexes.

As all observers agree, he was a bafflingly elusive and complicated being. His work and personality together present a maze of riddles. But the view I have proposed, which is no more than a tendered appraisal of the double existence forced on to him by his strangely masterful other self, makes it possible to see several features of his life and work in a fairly coherent pattern.

It throws some light, of a kind, on what one might call the biology of certain extreme attitudes evident in his personality and his prose. It illuminates, for instance, what he meant by the word 'impersonality', and by his insistence on the clean division between the poetry and the man, and why, for him, such precautions were so fundamental. And perhaps that special urgency, the psychological acuteness and depth of his critical intelligence, drew more than a little of its curious authority from the inner disciplines which were, in his case, survival techniques, by which he simultaneously protected his inner world of precarious gestations and sacred events, and yet maintained a sceptical, vigilant distance from what were by ordinary standards its impossible, supernatural demands, while at the same

[286]

time he negotiated with it in a perpetual 'summit' crisis effort to make meaningful sense of it and to come to terms with it.

Consideration of this life of double-exposure helps, too, in any understanding of what was, maybe, almost an occult ingredient in the maelstrom disturbances that beset him. But most concretely of all, it throws into relief a pattern of completeness and inevitability behind the poems.

The quality that we feel to be his 'greatness' is there in each passage of the verse, and usually in each line. But even in these minutiae of verbal tone, cadence and texture, it is 'greatness' of a densely characteristic and consistently blended sort. The notable distinction of it is that it stands slightly outside, a reader sets it automatically slightly outside, what we think of as the 'literary'. To compare it in this respect with the work of any other poet in English throws this peculiarity into relief. In all his poems up to the end of *Ash-Wednesday* the poetry lacks that provisional air of 'licence', a sense of liberties taken, such as pervades even the most solemn moments of any other major poet. Usually this licence, of word, metaphor or whatever, is the very wings of their flight, the improvisatory genius that lifts them over gulfs. Contingent struggle, expedient means, exuberant freedom from all sacred control, the fluidity of extempore solutions, for almost all poets these are the stuff of invention. Eliot eschews them utterly. His near-uniqueness in this particular appears even more sharply in the relationship between his poetry and certain passages of the King James Bible. Even such a comparatively profane book as *The Song of Songs*, in that translation, gives no sense of 'provisional licence'. If Shakespeare, Milton, Blake, Wordsworth, others, were to replace any chapter of that with a piece of their own characteristic verse, though each might produce a masterpiece, we can see that the most important thing would be lost. The sacred inevitability, that radiant, incantatory wholeness and finality, which is the glory of the King James translation, is a language inspired by profound, unbroken mythical/religious feeling, untainted by literary motive or secular fantasy, and presented as an offering to God, if within hearing of man. One can feel behind the wording of each verse the impersonal seriousness of a holy purpose deepened and accumulated through centuries. In this sense, the translators were not composing a literary work, and the results remain outside 'literature'. Eliot strove to reconnect his feeling and, on the evidence of it, his motivation too, to those of the King James translators, so we might expect the ghost of their solidarity to lift his words a little outside 'literature', as indeed it did, more and more noticeably as his faith consolidated itself. But these efforts were merely part of his deliberate attempt to open himself to that other ghost, the god within St Narcissus, that consanguineous voice which had spoken to him at his beginning.

The Song of Songs could be (we are told it well might have been) a text from some part of a ritual oratorio concerning an Eros/ Thammuz or similar deity. And so the pierced god, the incantatory flight, the sensual/mystical exaltation, those integral components of Eliot's affliction, brought him closer, in a secret, proprietorial sense, to *The Song of Songs*, than any translator. Maybe this was his umbilical link to biblical poetry in general, as to the language and authority of a prophet of the sacred values. If the two main currents of power in *The Song of Songs* are erotic feeling and mystical adoration, a sustained ground bass of overwhelming erotic feeling mingling with what might be called a higher harmonic of mystical, self-sacrificial adoration, it is exactly this combination which oscillates from one pole to the other in 'The Death of Saint Narcissus', and which rises to those moments in 'La Figlia Che Piange', in the hyacinth girl passage in *The Waste Land*, and in parts of *Ash-Wednesday*, providing the surge for those highest peaks in the love poetry of the language. We feel the same amalgam throughout his poetry – it is the musical body of the voice; but apart from these almost pure moments we hear it everywhere suffering, embroiled with the anguished complexities of that severe puritan ego, in swarming variation of pain and sublimation, the mutilated sacrament which the god's tragedy is in any world but particularly here in this modern one, and which stamps the substance of each line. Or if not of absolutely every line, certainly of every juxtaposed pair of lines. The electrical charge and transmission of that drama at the centre delivers its coded signal at every point in the whole magnetic field. But it is in Eliot's successful, artistic projection of this whole drama that his full greatness reveals itself.

Considered as a drama, with a beginning, middle and end, his poems recapitulate the historical evolution of the deity from the earliest primal form of Eros to the incarnation worshipped by a modern mystical Anglo-Catholic. At the same time, and in the same terms, they recapitulate the psychological process which moves from the death (in whatever circumstances) of primitive Eros in the psychosomatic order, through the alchemy of mourning, to the rebirth of Love as a Christ figure in the spiritual order. Phylogony and ontogeny of the entire metamorphosis cohere, in the richest and densest way, in the organic development of the *Collected Poems*.

The unfolding of the action can be followed poem by poem. The advent of the divinity, the Love-god, passes (after Prufrock, the diffident John the Baptist, who deplores his own incapacity to acknowledge let alone evangelize for the god whose death he has already in some way foresuffered) through the sacrificial dismemberment and scattering of the parts. This death is the psychic devastation behind the limbo of *The Waste Land*. The dark night of the fragments scattered and crying lies behind *The Hollow Men*. In a harrowing rebirth, out of the nadir, the Christ soul emerges, surrounded by 'Journey of the Magi', 'Animula', 'Marina', 'A Song for Simeon', each of which stands in an emergency relationship to its nativity. This new soul is a resurrection of all the energies of Eros, but now refocused, within the Christian ethos, in adoration of the supernatural woman of *Ash-Wednesday*, who brings him to submission before God the Father. The final drama of his decision to reject the world publicly and become a dancer to God (completing the life-plan laid down in 'The Death of Saint Narcissus') rises through the parable of *Murder in the Cathedral* to the rose-window, many-petalled choreography of the dance before God in an English chapel, which is the pattern of the *Four Quartets*.

At that point the poetic Self and the ordinary personality, the Rose and the Fire, became one. In religious terms, the sufferings of the god and the sufferings of the ego were, as near as may be, united in a pattern of redemption. In poetic terms, his heroic, sacred drama was triumphantly completed. From dismemberment in the meaningless, he had rescued a spiritual wholeness, and reconstructed a new ground of rejoicing. And as he performed this feat he created, in his poetry, a ritual dramatic form which established that process as a real possibility for others. What had begun as a shamanic crisis-call to regeneration, in the depths of the adolescent, matriarchal psyche, a dark place of savage drumming which he referred to often enough but never tried to disown, drew him through those flames of the tragedy of Eros into an *imitatio Christi* and the paternal authority of a high priest in a world religion.

That Eliot undertook this task on such a large scale, and accomplished it in such terms, goes some way towards suggesting the true measure of his greatness. This is how his poetry comes to stand, as it seems to do, at the centre of revelation in this age, and, as poetry, to stand there alone.

My opening text was: the voice of poetry as the voice of Eros. If poetry is the voice of Eros, or, perhaps, the text of some fragment of the loves and sufferings of Eros, it might be argued, from what I have proposed, that Eliot is the purest of all poets, the most authentic of all poets. What other poet's work concerns itself so exclusively with, and presents so profoundly and passionately and completely, in all its human implication, the life and death in the flesh and the resurrection into spirit of that god? It is one more peculiarity about Eliot: he wrote virtually no occasional verse, or only so little as to remind us of its virtual absence, no discursive verse of the secular ego – which makes up, after all, approximately 100 per cent of what the rest of the world writes. Where the sacred drama found no release, or could beam no refracted light, he simply wrote the very different language of his prose. And when the drama was completed – as no other poet in English ever did complete it – he was released from the labours. He had achieved a genuine happiness, symbolized and realized in his late marriage, united to his true self and to the world.

As I said at the beginning, I offer these remarks as a tentative unified field theory. I fancy the substance of the theory can be seen – like a fish lying beneath a turbulent, swift but clear current – from a certain angle, at a certain slant of light. I have suspended scholarly disbelief, and adopted the attitude of an interpretative, performing musician. As he reads the score, the musician imagines he finds the living spirit of the music, the inmost vital being of a stranger, reproduced spontaneously, inside himself. And so he describes his performance in the style of programme notes, as an exploratory X-ray of processes within the dark embryo, though he knows perfectly well that even the most rigorous scholarship hardly hopes to get beyond its own space-flights of subjective phantasmagoria.

It would take an iron nerve to be more than tentative in this field. Each year Eliot's presence reasserts itself at a deeper level, to an audience that is surprised to find itself more chastened, more astonished, more humble, where the whole task of understanding can seem more and more like King Lear endlessly trying to fathom the unspeaking mystery of Cordelia.

Perhaps it has not been easy for our century to accept that Eliot is not merely a great poet, but a poet who stands in English with maybe only one other name; a poet, as I have tried to describe, of an utterly new species, who produced pages that prompt a reader to ask where their equals are to be found.

It is certain that I am not the only person to wonder what two or three pages exist, in world poetry, to set beside 'Gerontion', or the second part of *Ash-Wednesday*. And as Pound said, where are the nineteen pages to stand beside *The Waste Land*? Or the thirty pages to stand with the *Four Quartets*? Even when we produce challengers, can we ever be certain about the judgement?

Note

The centenary dinner for T. S. Eliot was given by Mrs Eliot at his favourite restaurant, L'Écu de France in Jermyn Street, and coincided with the publication of the first volume of her edition of his letters.

This address seemed to me too compacted in its burrowing and perhaps at some points arcane argument, and also too long, to be delivered as a toast, in the form printed here. On the occasion, I delivered a shortened, simpler version.

Now even the original seems far too simple and impressionistic. Only a much fuller treatment, I think, could begin to substantiate my basic suggestion, in which I propose that Eliot the poet completed, with almost unique high definition and brilliance, the sacral, inner transformation of a certain type of sensibility, and that his poems are dramatic formulations of the distinctive phases through which this transformation must pass. It seems to me that only one other poet in the canon of English poetry is really comparable to him in this respect: the 'god' who confronted Eliot in his early days, disguised here as St Sebastian, and dramatized there in his 'juvenile' poem 'The Death of Saint Narcissus', was the same 'god' who appeared before Shakespeare when, at the age of twenty-eight or so, he summoned for the first time a purely poetic theme – and found himself dealing with the death of Adonis. And the subsequent fate of this 'god' in Eliot provides the hidden psychic drama, as I describe, for each of his mature poems, just as the subsequent fate of Adonis, in Shakespeare, provides the hidden psychic drama for each of his mature plays. At least, that is my suggestion in this address, though as I say only a much lengthier work could begin to validate it.

Shakespeare and Occult Neoplatonism

Occult Neoplatonism, as a movement, began in Italy in the early sixteenth century. It was a response, consciously devised and directed, to the deepening schism of the Reformation. At that time a strange collection of ancient writings was translated, attributed to Hermes Trismegistus, who was thought to have been an Egyptian sage from the period of Moses;* and whose visionary ideas seemed to anticipate both Plato and Christ. The possibility that this work seemed to offer, of returning to the fount and origin of all spiritual revelations, and of finding the genetic common denominator, so to speak, of them all, in some grand universal synthesis centred on a Christ figure, created immense excitement. Somehow this book of wisdom made available everything in man's psychological history that Catholic orthodoxy and Protestant militancy excluded. The new synthesis, therefore, was open on principle to the religious, spiritual and philosophical systems of the earlier world, and of the world outside Christianity. Wherever appropriated, these were reduced to a single system of symbolic correspondences. All known mythologies, that is, were reduced to a single but inexhaustibly rich and compendious language of metaphorical terms, or images – the vast thesaurus of a new language of signs, precisely defined by their histories, in which the new cosmology could be expressed. What remained was to give this cosmology a structure and to find a means of integrating it with an active spiritual life.

Rather than presume to convey the breadth and sweep of Hermetic Occult Neoplatonism† through the sixteenth century (which it barely survived), I will pick out the salient features of the

---

* Actually a compilation of treatises, partly Gnostic, from the first and second centuries AD.
† The series of books by Frances Yates, published by Routledge, covers the subject exhaustively.

movement as it came within the orbit of Shakespeare's known social and literary world, and as it can be seen to relate to his imaginative life, his treatment of the themes of the Reformation, and his relationship, in particular, to Prospero. But a general idea of the scope of the movement as a whole emerges from this account by Mircea Eliade:

A most surprising result of contemporary scholarship was the discovery of the important role magic and Hermetic esotericism played, not only in the Italian Renaissance, but also in the triumph of Copernicus' new astronomy, i.e., the heliocentric theory of the solar system. In a recent book, *Giordano Bruno and the Hermetic Tradition*, Frances A. Yates has brilliantly analysed the deep implications of the passionate interest in Hermeticism in this period. This interest discloses the Renaissance man's longing for a 'primordial' revelation which could include not only Moses and Plato but also *Magia and Cabbala* and, first and foremost, the mysterious religions of Egypt and Persia. It reveals also a profound dissatisfaction with medieval theology and the medieval conception of man and the universe, a reaction against what we call 'provincial', that is, purely *Western* civilization, and a longing for a universalistic, transhistorical, 'mythical' religion. For almost two centuries Egypt and Hermeticism, that is, Egyptian magic and esotericism, obsessed innumerable theologians and philosophers – believers as well as sceptics and crypto-atheists.*

In effect, the Hermetic Occult Neoplatonist vision of the universe and of man was given a structure, and was psychologically activated, by a combination of memory systems and Cabbala. Memory systems were already naturalized in classical and theological tradition. Basically these were mental maps, fixed in imagination, on which the whole summa of knowledge and speculation could be arranged, with each item anchored to its place on the map by a mnemonic visual image. Usually the map took the form of a stairway from the lower Hell, through the intermediate worlds, to the Divine Source. St Thomas Aquinas had authorized devices of this kind, partly through the prodigious example of his own colossal memory, and partly through his dispensation (later annulled by the Puritans): 'Man cannot understand without images.' He was

* Mircea Eliade, in 'The Occult and the Modern World', *Occultism, Witchcraft and Cultural Fashions* (University of Chicago Press, 1976).

regarded as the patron saint of memory maps of the Catholic spiritual cosmology, and Frances Yates suggests that Dante's *Commedia* is virtually a memory map of the *Inferno, Purgatorio* and *Paradiso*, furnished with a sequence of charged images, historically defined figures and self-evident, graphic episodes which become the mnemonic symbols, and the lexicon, of the poet's vision, encompassing his entire intellectual and spiritual universe. The whole work serves as a complete Catholic meditation, formulated like a liturgy, raising Dante (or the reader) from a commonplace, profane condition (the worldly fear of the call) to ecstatic contemplation of the Divine Source.

Cabbala was introduced to Occult Neoplatonism by its founding father, Pico della Mirandola. The Cabbalist's Tree of Life is a pattern of ten ascending stations (Sephiroth – Angelic Powers) positioned on and between the pillars of Justice and Mercy, mounting from the lowest Hells to the Divine Source. These ten stations form a graded system of symbolic correspondences, each station being like a file in a filing cabinet, or like one of the chakras in the body of a yogi, the ganglion of a whole realm of being, from the lowest in the tenth to the highest in the first. The ten stations encompass all the possibilities of existence. Everything in the universe, attached to its symbol, can be given its proper place on the Tree, according to its spiritual quality and significance. So the Tree becomes a model of the nested hierarchies of the universe, a contrivance for imagining the ordered universe – in other words, a means of organizing the psyche by internalizing the knowable universe as a stairway of God. Climbing in meditation through the stations, on the path of the Serpent of Wisdom, the practitioner endeavours to raise his consciousness, step by step, towards union with the Divine Source.

Because the language of Cabbala is Hebrew, the language of biblical God and the angels, and because the structural imagery of the Tree of Life is biblical and Talmudic, and because this strange apparatus for contemplation of the Divine Creation was thought to be the very Temple that Christ would build again in three days, and because it was, coincidentally, the most formidably established and sophisticated, the most awesome in occult reputation, of all memory maps, and because it was operated by techniques of meditation that at the very lowest were like devout prayer while at the highest they resembled communion with supernatural beings, if not with the Divine Emanation itself, it provided Pico della Mirandola with what appeared to be the natural framework, syntax and psychic discipline for his new system of symbolic correspondences, by which he hoped to renovate and refashion the disintegrating Christian spirituality of Western man. All that was required was for him to lift Cabbala out of Judaism, and recentre it on Christ, which he did. In this way he created the Christian Cabbala that became the nervous system (or the prototypical model for it) of all variations of Hermetic Occult Neoplatonism.

Attempts have been made to trace the presence of Cabbala in Shakespeare's plays, particularly in *The Merchant of Venice*. But there is much about Cabbala that a dramatist could use without him being a serious occultist. On the other hand, the assiduous practice of Cabbala, for some period of his life at least, could help to explain (as it does with Yeats) several aspects of Shakespeare's imaginative development, quite apart from his apparent attitude to religion and his handling of myths.

The main currents of Occult Neoplatonism converged, in one sense even came to a climax, in England, during the last two decades of the sixteenth century. The great, formative figures of this final phase of the movement were Giordano Bruno and John Dee, then both at the height of their powers.

Dee was Queen Elizabeth's mathematician, consultant to navigators and the builders of the navy, and the most celebrated English philosopher of the day: a man of prestige and influence. His Occult Neoplatonism was imperialist, messianic, Christian Cabbalist, moving towards a deepening preoccupation with the conjuration of spirits and angels that eventually almost swallowed him up. He had been tutor to Sir Philip Sidney, the admired luminary of the intellectual, literary circle from which the Elizabethan poetic renaissance sprang, and which was inherited, after his early death, by the Earl of Essex, patron to Sir Francis Bacon and the closest friend of

Shakespeare's patron, the Earl of Southampton. Dee had also been tutor to Fulke Greville, the Warwickshire nobleman who so famously declared himself 'friend to Sir Philip Sidney' and in the same paragraph, for some reason not so famously, 'master to William Shakespeare'. So it seems likely that Shakespeare knew plenty about Dee and his Christian Cabbala.

Bruno came to England in 1583. This Italian, impassioned, combative evangelist of the new vision made an impact. His brand of Occult Neoplatonism was a combination of Ancient Egyptian religion, a Copernican universe that was also a gigantic image of the spiritual creation, and a phenomenal cultivation of memory systems. All these systems of his were based on principles similar to the Cabbalist's Tree of Life; in other words each was based on some form of a ladder of symbolic correspondences, every correspondence fixed with its mnemonic image, ascending from the lowest orders of existence, through the angelic powers of the planets (which functioned as Sephiroth), to the Divine Source which, in Bruno's system (as in Dee's) was Divine Love. The practitioner operated any of these systems like the Cabbalist, mounting the ladder, locking his meditation into overdrive (the *furor* of Love) by various procedures of ritual magic (that would now be called techniques of self-hypnosis). On the way, like the Cabbalist, Bruno strove to open 'the black diamond doors' of the psyche, releasing visions, revelations of divine understanding, and even supernatural intelligences and powers. This 'magically animated imagination', as he described it, was the key to his teachings. He called his mnemonic images 'seals', meaning 'sigils', a sigil being the signature of a daemonic being. These entities of Bruno's, like Dee's angels, did not exist as scholastic abstractions, crowding on to the point of a needle. Just as for the Cabbalist, they had personality and were open to human negotiation, accessible to the attuned mind of the magically trained adept, susceptible to his manipulative will, and were able, properly handled, to raise him to near god-like awareness and being. So it was claimed. Bruno stayed in England for three years, writing several books, lecturing and disputing on his system. He published his major work on memory maps, *Seals*, in England in 1583, and dedicated two other works, during his stay, to Sir Philip Sidney. With all religions and all mythologies conscripted into his giant synthesis, this 'awakener of sleeping souls' (his own term for himself) looked down on the savage conflicts of the Reformation as on the 'squabbling of children', and created a cyclone of controversy (at one point he had to take refuge in the Italian Embassy) in the superheated atmosphere of this small society that secreted Shakespeare just coming of age and Sir Francis Bacon in his mid-twenties.

Bruno's ideas had their effect, presumably, within the already established magnetic field of Dee's, but the extent of Bruno's influence in particular can be judged, maybe, by the degree to which certain prominent features in his version of Occult Neoplatonism now seem, in retrospect, characteristically Elizabethan, not to say Shakespearean. Shakespeare's mystical deification of love has been linked to Bruno's *eroici furori*, and Berowne's great rhapsody about the divine power of love, in *Love's Labour's Lost* (IV. iii. 324–45), is a direct response, it has been suggested, to Bruno's teachings – and almost a direct expression of them. One of the most famous speeches in the plays, Ulysses's great exposition of cosmic, social and psychological order in *Troilus and Cressida* (I. iii. 85–124), could be drawn directly from Bruno's vision of a Copernican cosmos physically, morally and spiritually centred on the sun. Bruno's universe, as I have indicated, is simultaneously an assemblage of spiritual powers; everything in it is an image, or *umbra*, or *sigil*, or *hieroglyph*, of a spiritual entity. In his inner theatre of meditation these images, taking on daemonic autonomy (the vitality of powers from beyond them), revealed a universe of which, on occasion, he might conceivably have said:

> These our actors,
> As I foretold you, were all spirits and
> Are melted into air, into thin air:
> And, like the baseless fabric of this vision,
> The cloud-capp'd towers, the gorgeous palaces,
> The solemn temples, the great globe itself,

Yea, all which it inherit, shall dissolve
And, like this insubstantial pageant faded,
Leave not a rack behind. We are such stuff
As dreams are made on, and our little life
Is rounded with a sleep.

The Tempest, iv.i.148–58

This agglomeration of forces, adaptable to every human mask, essentially innocent and amoral until embroiled in the moralizing, distorting passions of human limitation and polarity, unfathomable in existential being, at bottom simply the *prima materia* of creation and inseparable from it, is for Bruno, and, as I shall argue, for Shakespeare too, Divine Love – the ectoplasmic or magnetic, vital substance of the Goddess of Complete Being herself.

Bruno first and foremost propounded his system (and sought royal sponsorship for it throughout Europe) as a solution to the political and spiritual dilemma of the Reformation. In some quarters, on that level it penetrated deeply (Shakespeare's ethical design can be seen, as I shall attempt to illustrate, partly as an Occult Neoplatonist and perhaps even a Bruno-esque solution to that dilemma). But Bruno's most potent and immediate influence, like the most potent influence of Dee, radiated from his magical 'technology' – the methods developed for gaining access to and control over the spiritual powers. It is not difficult to see why Hermetic Occult Neoplatonism exerted such fascination, offering, as it did, psychic release from the claustrophobic cells of Catholicism and Protestantism, and seeming to promise limitless computer power of thought and knowledge. But early in the development of the movement that heady openness to all spiritual paths took a sinister turn. The example of Cabbala, and the authorization of magical practices given by Hermes Trismegistus himself, prompted Cornelius Agrippa to revive the whole ancient corpus of ceremonial magic, sorcery and necromancy, and to incorporate it into the system. This cast a terrific spell on a certain susceptibility in the spirit of the times, in England. Agrippa became a revered authority on occult operations (as Marlowe's Faust acknowledges, when he determines to be

as cunning as Agrippa was
Whose shadow made all Europe honour him).
Doctor Faustus, 1.i.144–5

After this (although the holy discipline of Jewish Cabbala, and the strenuously Christian ethical controls of Christian Cabbalists, protected the movement for a while), as far as his many and powerful enemies were concerned, the Hermetic Occult Neoplatonist trafficked with the devil. In particular, he trod a knife edge between the increasingly turbulent, buffeting opposition of Catholic and Protestant. In some way the outlawed, imperilled idealism of such practitioners, and the violence of the reaction against them, became terms of the greater religious conflict. This is powerfully illustrated by two notable results, two of the most luminous acts by which that explosive epoch declares its inner nature to our own: Marlowe's *Doctor Faustus* and Shakespeare's *The Tempest*.

In the 1580s and even in the 1590s, evidently, in some circles (for instance, the group for whom Shakespeare wrote *Love's Labour's Lost*) Bruno was regarded as a realist. One of the most significant elements in his teaching (and the same could be said of Dee's) was that he presented himself not as the high priest of a new religion, nor even as a philosophical theologian, but as an empirical investigator – as if he were exploring the real anatomy of the divine universe for the first time (albeit finding himself spiritually transfigured in the process). His theme is still the nature of the soul, and the unified spirituality of creation, but everything now happens in a laboratory which is also a mental gymnasium, and the entire operation is pervaded by a new pragmatic spirit – the scientific spirit.

One might recognize this spirit in Shakespeare too, in his analysis – so extraordinarily objective and methodically thorough – of human subjectivity. And it is certainly possible to recognize it in the group which included, on the one hand, Chapman, whose works are saturated with the occultist's magical outlook, and on the other hand the hard-headed sceptic Ralegh and the mathematician Hariot, whose combined enterprise opened North America to English settlement. It also touched Sir Francis Bacon, whose own shrewdly covert and rationalized Occult Neoplatonism found belated expression (posthumously published in 1627) in his *The New Atlantis*, which, though later claimed as one of the holy books of Rosicrucianism (with Bacon himself claimed as one of the founding fathers), was the acknowledged inspiration (almost the first draft of their constitution) for the Royal Society eventually formed in 1660, which in turn founded the English tradition of practical science and pragmatic philosophy.

Bacon reveals a familiarity with the Hermetic, alchemical and Rosicrucian texts, as well as with the work of Bruno and Dee. Several curious questions in the Shakespeare/Bacon debate would become simpler, perhaps, if one could accept that Shakespeare and Bacon might well have been as close as Bacon and Ben Jonson undoubtedly were. And there is abundant evidence that Bacon was the intimate confidant and adviser of his noble patron, the Earl of Essex, and was also close to Essex's constant companion and Shakespeare's patron, Henry Wriothesley, the 3rd Earl of Southampton. In other words, Bacon was a likely member of the group for which *Love's Labour's Lost* was written. This would help to explain the fact, pointed out by Jean Overton Fuller in her book about Sir Francis Bacon,* that the names of that play's three principal Lords, attendants to the King of Navarre, and of the Lord attendant on the Princess of France, are all but identical to the names on the passports of Anthony Bacon (Sir Francis's brother) and his entourage during their visit to Navarre some years earlier: namely, Biron (which becomes in the play Berowne), Dumain (which becomes Dumaine), Longaville (unchanged) and Boyesse (becoming Boyet). The anecdote would be regarded as an in-joke of the group. *Love's Labour's Lost*, apart from its generalized Bruno-esque Neoplatonism, contains more particular indications of what become, eventually, specifically Rosicrucian features. Its plot is less likely to have been the result of one man's influence and special

---

* *Sir Francis Bacon: a biography* (London and The Hague: East-West Publications, 1981).

interests – whether Bacon's or Shakespeare's – than a situation projected from the shared preoccupation of the whole group: an excited and perhaps argumentative preoccupation with different kinds (Dee's versus Bruno's, perhaps) of Occult Neoplatonism, tending towards a deliberate plan of common study, in a retreat, withdrawn from society, with the beginnings of a manifesto and rules of conduct. This immediate, social background makes the whole drama a highly topical and meaningfully instructive joke that is also serious (but that is inevitably rather obscure, forced, irrelevant, to anyone not in on the peculiar situation). The opening speech of the play, by the King of Navarre to his three Lords, plants this situation dead centre:

> Let fame, that all hunt after in their lives,
> Live register'd upon our brazen tombs,
> And then grace us in the disgrace of death;
> When, spite of cormorant devouring Time,
> The endeavour of this present breath may buy
> That honour which shall bate his scythe's keen edge,
> And make us heirs of all eternity . . .
> Navarre shall be the wonder of the world;
> Our court shall be a little academe,
> Still and contemplative in living art.
> You three, Berowne, Dumaine, and Longaville,
> Have sworn for three years' term to live with me,
> My fellow-scholars, and to keep these statutes
> That are recorded in this schedule here . . .
>
> *Love's Labour's Lost*, I.i.1–18

Longaville instantly vows obedience, with a line:

> The mind shall banquet, though the body pine

I.i.25

that Shakespeare took more seriously in Sonnet 146:

> Poor soul . . .
> Why so large cost, having so short a lease,

> Dost thou upon thy fading mansion spend?
> Shall worms, inheritors of this excess,
> Eat up thy charge? Is this thy body's end?
> Then, soul, live thou upon thy servant's loss,
> And let that pine to aggravate thy store;
> Buy terms divine in selling hours of dross;
> Within be fed, without be rich no more . . .

But this proposal, in the drama, as Berowne points out with dismay, excludes woman and the love of women. The plot that follows is the machinery by which this wrong-headed project is corrected – to include the love of women. Where the Puritan mode of Occult Neoplatonism, in which magical studies were adapted to investigate creation, in Baconian resolutely objective style, excluding the subjective love-creation of the Goddess, was forcibly corrected by the Goddess herself. The Princess of the great kingdom of France, and her three aspects, her three Ladies, impose on the King of the petty realm of Navarre and his three Lords a new mode of Occult Neoplatonism, one that not only includes her but is centred on her and her love. This correction is the occasion for Berowne's passionate conversion to the divinity of love, when he delivers his long, Bruno-esque rhapsody to love's power.

> Other slow arts entirely keep the brain,
> And therefore, finding barren practisers,
> Scarce show a harvest of their heavy toil;
> But love, first learned in a lady's eyes,
> Lives not alone immured in the brain,
> But, with the motion of all elements,
> Courses as swift as thought in every power,
> And gives to every power a double power,
> Above their functions and their offices.
> It adds a precious seeing to the eye;
> A lover's eyes will gaze an eagle blind;
> A lover's ear will hear the lowest sound,
> When the suspicious head of theft is stopp'd:
> Love's feeling is more soft and sensible

Than are the tender horns of cockled snails:
Love's tongue proves dainty Bacchus gross in taste.
For valour, is not Love an Hercules,
Still climbing trees in the Hesperides?
Subtle as Sphinx; as sweet and musical
As bright Apollo's lute, strung with his hair;
And when Love speaks, the voice of all the gods
Makes heaven drowsy with the harmony.

Love's Labour's Lost, IV.iii.324–45

The rest are converted with him. But this does not mean that their grand, ambitious plan for a prolonged course of self-transformation, in some retreat, withdrawn from society, is abandoned. On the contrary, the Goddess and her three selves present the convertites with a reformed plan, which includes the Hermetic Rosicrucian discipline of austerity:

[In] some forlorn and naked hermitage,
Remote from all the pleasures of the world;

v.ii.803–4

and of visiting the sick:

A twelvemonth shall you spend, and never rest,
But seek the weary beds of people sick

v.ii.829–30

and again, specifically for Berowne, the Shakespearean Bruno of this ritual instruction by the Diotima-like female:

to win me, if you please,
Without the which I am not to be won,
You shall this twelvemonth term, from day to day,
Visit the speechless sick, and still converse
With groaning wretches; and your task shall be
With all the fierce endeavour of your wit
To enforce the pained impotent to smile.

v.ii.856–62

She continues:

then, if sickly ears
Deaf'd with the clamours of their own dear groans,
Will hear your idle scorns, continue them,
And I will have you, and that fault withal;
But if they will not, throw away that spirit,
And I shall find you empty of that fault,
Right joyful of your reformation.

v.ii.871–7

In these early lines, the Rosicrucian *dulia* of helping the sick with active love, selflessly, in the crowded busyness of life, while at the same time cultivating the ambitious soul in solitude, prefigures that 'pity, like a naked new-born babe', which becomes incarnate in the reborn saintly self of the tragic hero, at the ultimate point of self-transformation that still, for Shakespeare, lies ahead. In this way, *Love's Labour's Lost* is an image of the Occult Neoplatonist's ethos in its Shakespearean mode – which also, at this point, turns out to be a Rosicrucian mode. It maps out Shakespeare's own self-directing future course, sketched in Sonnet 146, ritually undergone in *As You Like It* and *All's Well that Ends Well*, and realized in full through the complete development of the Tragic Equation. But at this point, in terms which later became, as I say, historically, Rosicrucian.

It can be seen here, maybe, why Bruno's 'technology' fitted so helpfully into the English conflict in its early Shakespearean phase – in what might be called its *Venus and Adonis* phase. By Newton's day (whose secret alchemy and astrology persisted like a vestigial reflex), which was the aged Milton's day (whose Christian Cabbalism died between the pillars of the Temple), the conception of 'Truth' had radically purged itself of any taint of human subjectivity, emerging like a new, brassy sun as stern cosmic dualism, a supernal *conjunctio* of atomic materialism and mathematical law. The Goddess, in other words, had been violently and finally defeated, Marduk-style, and converted, Tiamat-style, into the inert, material domain of her conqueror, while her 'magical' and 'divine' creative powers had been expropriated, aboriginal-style, as his 'science'.

[305]

Long before this moment, however, in England Occult Neo-platonism's dealings with the supernatural had proved suicidal. Since the movement aspired so openly to dissolve both Catholicism and Protestantism in its own greater synthesis, they combined effectively to liquidate it. The magical theory and practice, so easily seen as diabolism, was the exposed underbelly. For Catholicism this 'most imaginative idea of the Renaissance' became devil worship and heresy (Bruno was burned at the stake in Rome in 1600). For Protestantism it became plain devil worship (John Dee was discredited, and died rejected and destitute in 1608). For Puritanism it was devil worship and idolatry (hence the pictographic imagery of memory systems – and the divine faculty of the Occult Neoplatonist, imagination itself – became anathema, even as an educational technique, in the Puritan society). For materialist, rational philosophy it was a superstition. For science, an absurdity. It disappeared from the intellectually respectable range of ideas and was pushed so deep into Hell (with the witches) that sensible men soon feared to be associated with it. In the works of Shakespeare, or anywhere else, it ceased to be visible (and much of Shakespeare, accordingly, ceased to be visible). In later centuries it stirred occasionally, where revolution cracked the crust of suppression, and reached up an arm to embrace Goethe – who was wondered at. And Blake – who was deplored. And Yeats – who was ridiculed.

While Shakespeare was still alive, it had retreated into various more or less secret societies and brotherhoods, modelled on Islamic Dervish orders, and strongly coloured by Sufi influences, as with the Masons and Rosicrucians.*

Frances Yates refers to contemporary suggestions that English

---

* Shakespeare's mysterious lifeline link of affinity with the Sufism of Islam may be partly explained by these Hermetic Occult Neoplatonist secret societies. Idries Shah (in *The Sufis*, London: W. H. Allen, 1964) has explained the term 'Rosicrucian' – a Christian-seeming image of the Rose at the centre of the Cross – as a 'translation' of a composite term in Arabic meaning 'a particular (Dervish) discipline – to extract the marrow (of spiritual meaning)', and used by Sufis as a general term for their spiritual exercises. The Occult Neoplatonist societies took over the mistranslation as a name (as they also took over the name 'Masons') – as they certainly took over other symbolism, procedures and doctrine from the dervish orders.

acting groups were involved in the Rosicrucian movement. She surveys the Catholic Ben Jonson's familiarity with German Rosicrucian writings (he had served as amanuensis to Sir Francis Bacon), and with their alchemical interpretation of 'the fables of the poets, Jason's Fleece, the Garden of the Hesperides

> Thousands more
> All abstract riddles of our stone.'

She interprets *The Alchemist* (1611) as Jonson's Catholic, derisive 'counterblast' to *The Tempest* (1611),* where Prospero is so thoroughly an Occult Neoplatonist magus that he is commonly regarded as a portrait of John Dee (when he is not regarded as a portrait of Shakespeare himself). Dee's writings are known to have had a decisive influence on the Rosicrucian movement, but it is a curious fact that the main sacred book of European Rosicrucianism, *The Chemical Wedding of Christian Rosenkreutz* was composed (published 1616) by the German author, Andreae, who had devised plays 'in imitation of the English dramatists' (his own words) and who in *The Chemical Wedding* seems to be sleepwalking through a phantasmagoric reminiscence of Shakespeare's last dramas.

One of the most peculiar memory systems to influence Bruno was associated with theatre. This was Camillo's Memory Theatre, an actual theatre-like structure, which seems to have resembled a gigantic filing cabinet of token images. Again, after Bruno's death, the most famous was the Memory Theatre of the Occult Neoplatonist Robert Fludd, a self-proclaimed Rosicrucian and Hermetic philosopher, active in the first decades of the seventeenth century. Frances Yates argues that this Memory Theatre (described and illustrated in Fludd's works in detail), another gigantic, systematically interlinked hierarchy of images, uniting Heaven and Earth, with an operational ladder of ascent and somehow incorporating the Cabbalist's Tree of Life, was based on Shakespeare's actual Globe

---

* Since *The Alchemist* was registered in October 1610, the 'counterblast' could have blown in the opposite direction.

Theatre. The metaphor of a theatre for the structured image system and 'magically animated imagination' of the Occult Neoplatonist, where surprising entities emerge from 'the black diamond doors' to make revelatory pronouncements, is apt. But the Tree of Life type of memory map, as a thesaurus of symbolic correspondences, an organized compendium of 'hieroglyphs', each with its family of fixed yet evolving connotations, has obvious implications for an organically unified cycle of symbolic dramas, and also for a unified poetic imagination. Bruno's version of Hermetic Occult Neoplatonism was founded on his notion of the Ancient Egyptian religion (and I hope to show how uncannily familiar with this particular mythology Shakespeare himself was, too), and his use of internally structured emblems, his 'seals', owed a good deal to his idea of Egyptian hieroglyphs. He understood the poetic possibilities of this type of image (as did Aquinas) and adapted them to specifically poetic use, with deliberate method, as an illustration of these possibilities, in the sonnet sequence that he dedicated to Sir Philip Sidney, rather as Pound made the attempt to naturalize the principle behind the internally structured ideograms of Chinese characters to English poetry three hundred years later.

Without assuming that Shakespeare was a devout Occult Neoplatonist, or was more than amused by the ingenuities, curious about the claims, and intrigued by some of the concepts, one can suppose that out of this vast complex of archaic, magical, religious ideas and methods, the following items caught his attention:

The idea of an inclusive system, a grand spiritual synthesis, reconciling Protestant and Catholic extremes in an integrated vision of union with the Divine Love.

The idea of a syncretic mythology, in which all archaic mythological figures and events are available as a thesaurus of glyphs or token symbols – the personal language of the new metaphysical system.

The idea of this concordance of mythological (and historical) figures simply as a Memory System, a tabulated chart of all that can be known, of history, of the other world, and of the inner worlds, and in particular of spiritual conditions and moral types.

The idea of this system as a theatre.

The idea of these images as internally structured poetic images – the idea of the single image as a package of precisely folded, multiple meanings, consistent with the meanings of a unified system.

The idea of as-if-actual visualization as the first practical essential for effective meditation (as in St Ignatius Loyola's *Spiritual Disciplines*, as well as in Cabbala).

The idea of meditation as a conjuring, by ritual magic, of hallucinatory figures – with whom conversations can be held, and who communicate intuitive, imaginative vision and clairvoyance.

The idea of drama as a ritual for the manipulations of the soul.

It might or it might not be too much to add to this list the four ethical aims fundamental to Cabbala. They could just as easily be cited as the four fundamental aims (and achievements) of Shakespeare's cycle of dramas, becoming more refined and pronounced with each successive work.

The first is to achieve harmony between the fixed and the free, between the severe formal powers of Judgement and the flowing spontaneous powers of Mercy; the second is to achieve the sacred marriage, the conjunction of masculine and feminine; the third is to redeem the Shekina from the abyss of the demons, where the Shekina is the Divine Spirit (originally the soul of Israel (Ariel), imagined as female, the soul as God's bride) immersed in material existence; and the fourth is to attain mastery over – or defence against – the demonic powers of the abyss. These four principles are also the cornerstones of the Gnostic myth of Sophia which rises so forcibly into the substructure of the 'romances'.

In spite of his polyglot fluency in that international current of metaphysical systems, within the plays Shakespeare's own radical myth remained true to itself, almost with the integrity of an organism, as it evolved.

Myths, Metres, Rhythms

Mythologies are dodgy things. By 'mythologies', here, I mean nothing more than the picture languages that we invent to embody and make accessible to casual reference the deeper shared understandings which keep us intact as a group – so far as we are intact as a group.

In an intact group the pool of shared understandings is like a shared bank account of the group wealth. Each member has instant access to the whole deposit. Since it is spiritual or psychological wealth, it does not diminish by being spent. Rather, the more lavishly it is circulated, the greater inner wealth and 'security' each single member feels to have. Intercommunication of those deeper shared understandings, through the tokens of the mythology that represents them, strengthens the unified inner life of the group. One of the mythologies of gazelle herds is a flicking of the tail. One gazelle flicks its tail – and the tail-flick goes from gazelle to gazelle right through the herd, while they all keep their heads down nonchalantly feeding. To the individual gazelle it must feel like a communal brief prayer, meaning: while we all exist as one gazelle, I exist as full strength gazelle, immortal gazelle. The mythology of ants is coded into a stroking of feelers over feelers and a tapping at each other's bodies. Whenever two ants of the same colony meet they sing this tribal mythical song presumably in sweet harmony, skilfully incorporating any news. What the performance means to each ant, perhaps, is: we, a mighty people, are all one: I am a mighty people. The benefits are self-evident.

When the shared group understanding of all members is complete then a mere touching of the tokens of their mythology is enough for complete communication. Each verbal signal illuminates – with the voltage of the whole group's awareness and energy – those members of the group who exchange it. Anything approaching that, perhaps, can be utilized by few modern writers. Perhaps in primitive groups,

Bilingual.

or in small nations that are still little more than tribal assemblies of ancient, inter-related families, where the blood-link can still be felt, the conditions for it are more likely. In those circumstances, language can be said to be full of meaning. Hence the answer of the old Hopi woman to the Anthropologist who asked why Hopi songs are so short. 'Our songs are short' she said, 'because we know so much.' Meaning, because we all know so thoroughly the mythology of our system of shared understandings, which is the life of our people, nothing needs to be explained. She might have added: and because we have no quarrel with it.

If that sounds like cultural stasis, cultural stasis might feel like a perfect state to those who enjoy it, where the culture is psychologically rich – as the cultures of old groups generally are. But a system of deeper understandings together with a perfect knowledge of the mythology that keeps the system conscious, shared by the whole group, does not necessarily mean cultural stasis. It can supply the foundation strength for the most effective outer activity. As in Athens, during the great century. As in Jewishness throughout the last two thousand years. And as in Japan since the last war.

In our modern multi-cultural societies, obviously things tend to be different. Here, many groups and their mythologies, their systems of shared understandings, are jumbled together and forced to get on with each other. Inevitably a multi-cultural society develops, or tries to develop, a lingua franca. In the simplest form of this situation, each citizen – of the sub-group in which they grew up, on the one side, and of the federation of sub-groups into which they graduate, on the other – has to be bilingual. The first language, limited to the shared understandings embodied in the mythology of the sub-group, is a barrier to communication with any other sub-group. The second language must by definition exclude the idiosyncratic shared understandings and mythologies of any of the federation's incorporated sub-groups, since it tolerates only what all can share. From the point of view of the lingua franca, the solidarity system and mythology of any sub-group tends to appear parochial, old-fashioned, limited and limiting – to be indulged, if at all, only as local colour, as entertainment for a kind of armchair culture tourism. From the exclusive point of view of any sub-group, the lingua franca appears shallow, arbitrary, empty, degraded and degrading, even destructive, if not altogether meaningless. Setting aside just how any writer resolves or fails to resolve this dilemma, the fact remains that each modern literary work has to take its place on a continuum between some sub-group's (the author's) system of shared understandings (and its mythology) and the most inclusive, ideally global wavelength of a multicultural lingua franca. Whether the writer intends it or not, is even conscious of it or not, by the very act of bringing the work to linguistic focus they fix it at some point on that continuum. Just where that point is becomes clear only after publication, which is the act of presenting the work to readers from every other subgroup and from every inter-cultural mixing pool of the lingua franca.

At that moment, very naturally, the author becomes aware of any failure in the work's ability to communicate. The authorial thought then pops up: is this some reader from a confined and isolated subgroup, berating me for not belonging to the same? Or is it some internationalist of the latest polyglot vortex of the lingua franca who finds me untranslatable into newest pidgin terms (for by definition lingua franca, in a whirling melting pot of a world, is a mercurial thing, a dancer of many veils, swayed by every fleeting fashion and above all dominated by a passion for the new, for the not-old)? They are pointless questions, of course. While that new global multiculture writhes like a sandstorm out of every television, the writer can only grope along, transmitting what are intended to be meaningful signals, the most meaningful possible – in the hope of seeing somewhere a flick of tail in response or of meeting antennae lifted and vibrating in joy.

Two small examples of failures in communication, from my own experience, illustrate what gulfs of emptiness can open behind very slight frowns of bafflement. Because of chance circumstances in my own sub-group upbringing, one 'mythology' that I found ready to hand was the natural world – all the various creatures of the world, and their doings, in their places or out of them. As a mythology, it had the advantage, too, one might think, of being universal and timeless. A hare now behaves in much the same way and is dreamed about by human beings all over the earth in much the same terms as it was thousands of years ago when it first appeared in human iconography, or hundreds of thousands of years ago when man first began to hunt and think about it, and as it will behave hundreds of thousands or even millions of years hence, probably long after it has left the human race behind. So it should be a reliable, durable piece of mythological picture language for the kinds of understanding that are embodied in cave-drawings, Japanese Netsukes, Inuit figurines – which certainly do pierce the barrier between groups and sub-groups: a range of understanding and feelings that seem universal, fundamental, simple. And the same with all creatures.

I realized the error of this idea when I heard a US urban poet exclaiming in utter incomprehension about some verses I had written dramatizing a wren. He had absolutely no idea what the poem was about. It was not my literary style that baffled him: other pieces of mine he could respond to perfectly well. It suddenly struck me: here was someone who had never seen a wren, and who had grown up right outside the culture in which wrens have a rich, ancient, mythic, popular history. Someone, perhaps, who had no feeling for birds. In Hebrew, I'm told, pretty well all birds are lumped together in one word: bird. In any case, the wren was certainly no part of his mythos. My poem makes that demand: the wren must be part of the reader's mythos. As a fox for a Japanese, a coyote for a Navajo. It is not Mickey Mouse's doings that make him fascinating: it is the fact that he is our old friend Mickey Mouse. I was reminded of the difficulties I have often encountered in some verse that assumes in the reader familiarity with a picture language mythology that I simply do not share. For my urban critic, my dramatization of the wren was empty of meaning. Most poems are mixed and generalized enough to provide something for most, and in fact a deliberate confusion of effects will usually elicit a response, since it challenges the interpreter in us, who soon imports an interesting meaning. But the picture language based on a single species of bird is too precise to attract the interpreter, and too exclusively specific to admit the person who knows nothing about it.

Just as there are many other picture languages similarly precise and specific. My wren, perhaps, was an example of this commonest kind of non-transmitting symbol of the psychological life, within certain kinds of verse.

The average reader knows far more about Hamlet than about the wren. One could easily write about Hamlet sitting in a chair, so preoccupied, melancholy and inert that he lets a garden spider spin a large web between his leg and the leg of his chair – and one could be sure that, though it might not have suited Tolstoy much, at least literate audiences right round the world would not be baffled by the image. One could be pretty sure that most such readers would set it within a satisfactory idea of Hamlet's whole situation, and would see that it belonged – in other words, would not find it ridiculous, or out of character, or arbitrary.

But if one wrote about a wren singing itself into convulsions, most if not all of the same audience would find the image obscure, arbitrary, forced: their memory archive would be quite empty of any context in which any bird would naturally behave like that. Some might respond to a surreal notion of the possibility, as of a fox hypnotized by a flashlight going into a trance and levitating slowly, chanting a Buddhist sutra as it ascends into the darkness. But if one dramatized that idea of the wren singing itself into convulsions, and went on to give it the role of a forest recluse, a sort of Celtic Saint, liable to ecstatic frenzies whenever he glorifies his Creator, to the bigger part of any audience it would sound daft – pointless, whimsical. Why a wren? Why not a missel-thrush? Why not a nightingale – far better known as a singer maddened by love? But to write of even these heroic singers as 'singing themselves into convulsions' would sound perverse, over the top. Keats and Hardy described the raptures of these birds without going so far as 'convulsions'.

In other words, unless one establishes the full, naturalistic context of such a peculiar idiosyncrasy, and supplies the credentials for the reality within which wrens actually do behave like that, it is impossible to use this bird's inclination to 'sing itself into con-vulsions' as the accepted feature of a well-understood symbol in a 'shared' mythology. It is impossible to do so simply because you cannot trust your audience to supply the missing 'reality context' of first-hand direct experience and affectionate familiarity: the context of shared understanding of the natural world. It is impossible, that is, as things stand, to use the wren as a 'symbolic figure' – even in a mythic world that might be no more 'serious' than a cartoon parable.

If one wants to go beyond the most generalized and traditional idea of the Wren, any new information has to be supplied *as information*, as in:

> . . . the poor wren,
> The most diminutive of birds, will fight –
> Her young ones in the nest – against the owl . . .

In these lines Shakespeare takes no chances. He makes sure that his audience knows exactly what he's talking about. He not only reminds – or informs – them that the wren is the smallest of the birds, he also makes sure that they know it is a bird. Quite a lot of people are not absolutely sure that a wren is a bird. And quite a few more are in doubt about its size. Having set his wren in the natural history of the birds, as the least of them, he then introduces his surprising piece of specialist data – as a further fact of natural history, an item of scientific observation. The audience has been carefully informed, as if Shakespeare assumed them to be totally ignorant. The listener who thought a wren might be a pixie in the shape of a goitre or a bird the size of a duck now knows better, and understands Shakespeare's image into the bargain.

Addressing a similar audience, and wanting to make an image of the wren's convulsive singing, and thereafter to draw some further meaning out of it, one would have to begin: 'The brown wren, the smallest of the birds and one of the most secretive, living a hidden life in brambles and dense hedge-banks etc.' – and only after establishing all that could one go on to: 'When the wren sings it puts itself into the most unexpected posture, crouching low, half-spreading its wings and shivering itself into what seems to be a hysterical vibration of its whole body, somewhat like a fledgeling abasing itself to its mother for food (that would have to be explained) but in a fashion more stylized and extreme, the nape of its head pressed back and down between its shoulder blades, the gape very wide and singing straight upwards etc., and for the duration of the song the bird seems to be in some sort of contorted seizure, almost an epileptic convulsion etc.'. Even then, only the potential bird-lover, the one having a natural affinity with birds, would be able to make the intuitive leap and programme that new information into the stereotype of the wren. This idea of a wren's singing frenzy is far less translatable into human terms than the idea of a wren defending its young against a gargoylish predator. Once one begins to realize what should be obvious, that the shared, familiar, primitive knowledge of the wren's singing behaviour, as of its behaviour and life in general, simply does not exist – except in a very few widely-scattered individuals – one remembers the Hopi woman. At the opposite pole, among our atomized sub-groups we share so little, on most levels, that our lingua franca is virtually empty of real meaning and every reference has to carry its own essential context, spelt out and specified, if it is to be more than jargon babble for most readers even on the most naturalistic level. But that kind of sharp focus on the contextual particularities, the natural history, in objective terms, is precisely what precludes any casting of the chosen bird in a mythic role within a pattern of deeper shared human understandings relating to group life. This is how the atomization of shared 'mythologies', which reflects the atomization of the deeper shared understandings, makes symbolic works less and less likely, and the old ones less and less comprehensible – except as scholarly reconstructions.

Recently I received a courteous and yet baffled letter asking me to give some clue about what was going on in a poem I wrote about a Grasshopper. I had composed this to go with a painting by Leonard Baskin, in a book for young people about flowers and insects. As with the piece about the wren, I wanted my verses to belong – in their very different way – to a tradition that has always given me the keenest literary pleasure. This tradition is typified by the Yoruba Hunter's poems (translated by Ulli Beier) that are included in Faber's anthology *The Rattle Bag*. The Yoruba poems depend on a shared, total, realistic, direct experience of the creatures that are their subjects. They are confident that the most vivid feeling of realism can be touched alive by hyperbolic irony, burlesque dramatizations, comic surreal associations. They are in fact a kind of joke – an affectionate joke – as primitive folktales about animals tend to be.

As a mythic symbol, the Grasshopper has, or had, a traditional character and role, with familiar generalized meanings. At the same time, for those who ever stepped into any grassy place in England before Agrochemicals imposed their final solution, Grasshoppers were not that long ago as common as grass. And the large airy web of intimate pleasures that was inseparable from the thought of English country summer was also inseparable from the miniaturized, grotesque mechanism and ubiquitous, startling behaviour of the Grasshopper – as if he might have been the little electric battery that kept switching the whole thing on and off. So when I came to write about him (knowing that the watercolour was going to supply all the reminders for identification), I did not feel to be writing in an archaic or necessarily obscure mode when I composed this:

In the Likeness of a Grasshopper

A trap
Waits on the field path.

A wicker contraption, with working parts,
Its spring tensed and set.

So flimsily made, out of grass
(Out of the stems, the joints, the raspy-dry flags).

Baited with a fur-soft caterpillar,
A belly of amorous life, pulsing signals.

Along comes a love-sick, perfume-footed
Music of the wild earth.

The trap, touched by a breath,
Jars into action, its parts blur –

And music cries out.

A sinewy violin
Has caught its violinist.

Cloud-fingered summer, the beautiful trapper,
Picks up the singing cage

And takes out the Song, adds it to the Songs
With which she robes herself, which are her wealth,

Sets her trap again, a yard further on.

Now my correspondent made me conscious of what I knew, that as
far as an English audience is concerned these verses draw obliquely
on a mythology (the Grasshopper's summer world) that has all but
vanished from England, and the mode seems, well, obscure at the
least. Except in one small patch (a few yards square), it is several and
I could nearly say many years since I saw a Grasshopper in the wild
in England. So I have to accept that for a big part of the population
(maybe for all that part which is still 'discovering poetry'), the first-
hand mother's-milk and childhood sort of knowledge of the Grasshopper's world, the 'mythology' in which my verses find their
meaning (which is also the human world), simply isn't there. It could
well be, I saw now, that my correspondent had never seen one, let
alone held one. And perhaps TV Natural History programmes don't
supply the right kind of direct experience for these creatures to enter
the mind's 'mythos'. I wrote back to my questioner as follows:

The 'trap', waiting in the field-path, is the Grasshopper itself. In other
words, the Grasshopper is a trap made of struts, springs – as you might
imagine a tiny insect-trap made out of dry grasses etc.

The 'caterpillar', which I describe as the 'bait', is the Grasshopper's own
'belly of amorous life' – which does look and feel like a little caterpillar,
among the brittle stalky, raspy, dry-grassy parts of the rest of its body. It
throbs and twitches, eager for a mate.

This 'trap' – part beautifully engineered contraption, part sexual 'bait' –
has been set to catch a 'Song', one of the 'love-sick, perfume-footed Musics
of the wild earth' which are wandering like ecstatic spirits about the woods
and fields. These 'Songs' are very difficult to catch – being one of God's most
elusive and precious creations.

[318]

Soon, a Song (silent, still uncaught) comes along, searching for the sexual life – on which it lives (Song being nourished by love).

Touched by a breath of this hungry Song (perhaps as it sniffs at the bait) the trap leaps into action – that is, it is sprung. (If you've ever held a grasshopper in your closed hand, and felt its kick, you'll have the idea of a tensed trap being sprung.) In fact, it blurs into action by seizing the Song – with its legs, as you know. It seems to us poor humans that the grasshopper itself is singing, or at least making music.

The trap has caught a Song – 'Music cries out'.

As if a violin (the Grasshopper) should, like a trap, trap the sexual spirit of music in the soul of the violinist who plays it (who has been lured to it, to find in it the soul-partner – the physical voice of music – that he craves for). As I say, as if a violin should trap its violinist. As the violinist, while he pounces on the violin, to draw the sexual vitality (the music) out of it, is trapped by and battles with his instrument – which seems to draw the song out of him.

A tricky both-ways business.

This 'trap' (the Grasshopper) has been set by the Summer – I imagine her as a Paleolithic Goddess-Huntress. She made the trap, with magical, delicate skill, so that she could catch those Songs, as if each Song were the rich, beautiful pelt of an animal – 'With which she robes herself', as if she were only visible-audible because of this robe of 'Musics of the wild earth'. Having taken out the Song, she then sets the trap again, in a slightly different place. To us, it seems that the Grasshopper leap-flies a yard or so, and sits motionless again – tensed and set – waiting for another Song.

So the poem is a little story – quite simple when you identify the characters, and the situation.

However this may clarify the 'plot' of the poem, it can never supply all on its own the living memory of the total world within which this little action takes place, and on which it still depends for its meanings. It can only be 'a sort of translation' of one world and its mythology into the terms of another world and mythology – my correspondent's, where perhaps it now sits with no more real life than verses (with notes) about Quetzalcoatl. The only hope for this particular piece, maybe, is that, unlike Quetzalcoatl, Grasshoppers might conceivably make a comeback in England and be once again vivid figures in the familiar, shared mythology of children.

Two Musical Traditions

Orthodox Metre

The 'mythologies' that give meaning to language are one thing. The rhythms that give musical expressiveness to it are another. In my first collection of poems, one piece, describing motionless horses in the early morning under the edge of the high moor, ends with a couplet:

> Between the streams and the red clouds, hearing curlews,
> Hearing the horizons endure.

When Roy Fuller reviewed the book, which he did in a serious, considerate sort of way, he seized on that last line and pointed out, confidently, that it was 'unsayable'.

Roy Fuller's experience of the many different musics of verse is not small. I find his verse musically satisfying in its own mode but never – and obviously he would not want it – musical in the same way as that line of mine. My point is that whether that line has or has not anything to recommend it, it was composed in a particular musical mode, different from Roy Fuller's, and I left it in that form because it caught just the musical effect that I wanted. Roy Fuller would say: what effect? In other words, he could not accept the line as verse because he was deaf to the musical mode.

It struck me then, and even more strongly later on when I heard him and others reciting their own verses, that there are at least two quite different musical traditions in English verse – traditions revealed not only in the way verse is composed, but perhaps even more evidently in the way it is recited (and therefore the way it is read).

Almost all the verse that we commonly think of as being 'traditional' and almost all the verse now being written in English, is metrically simple. That is to say, each line moves from beginning to end under a single metrical law, using each syllable's 'natural quantity' (the emphasis and time-value given to it in natural, conversational speech) in such a way that the metrical law is self-evident and cannot be mistaken. Whether this kind of verse is arranged in regular, formalized rhymed stanzas, regular, pentameter blank verse, or is more or less free, without any discernible metrical pattern except the one it happens to create as it trots along – as does any sentence in prose – it is scored, so to speak, for the casual, conversational voice, and anybody can sight-read it straight off, without difficulty. It is musically accessible to every kind of reader, even those with the least cultivated ear. The majority of readers read all verse, no matter what its tradition, as if it were of this kind.

A classic example is this passage from Addison's 'Letter From Italy, to the Rt Honourable Charles Lord Halifax, 1701':

> While you, my lord, the rural shades admire
> And from Britannia's public posts retire,
> Nor longer, her ungrateful sons to please,
> For their advantage sacrifice your ease,
> Me into foreign realms my fate conveys
> Through nations fruitful of immortal lays,
> Where the soft season and inviting clime
> Conspire to trouble your repose with rhyme . . .

Samuel Johnson said of this verse that it had 'always been praised, but never beyond its merits, being more correct with less appearance of labour and more elegant with less appearance of ornament than any of his other poems'. The significant word here is 'correct'. The matching of the metrical pattern (chosen by Addison) to the natural 'quantities' of the syllables in his chosen words is so correct that the reader cannot mistake it. The reversed first iambic foot in line five, and again in line seven, fall naturally. In that sense, the only possible metrical flaw, it might be thought, is in the last line quoted, where a modern ear, reading only 'natural quantities', inclines, because of the quick dive out of sight of the second syallable of 'trouble', to skip the strong beat on 'your' and to read:

> Conspíre tŏ tróublĕ yŏur rĕpóse wĭth rhyme

which trips the voice to stumble over the last iambic foot. The result (since the required number of stresses in the line has been so firmly established in the previous lines) is annoyance at a slight hiccup in the metronome. In fact, the line can be read without this deformity only if the voice imposes, forcibly, a *musical interpretation* on the possibilities. By introducing a slight pause after 'trouble', and letting a slight drawl of emphasis settle onto 'your', the line is restored to its full pentameter value, but at the risk of insinuating an arbitrary, extraneous and unwanted implication: 'your' has become 'yours, my lord, as distinct from mine or theirs'. To a modern ear, therefore, the line is not absolutely 'correct', though if that special emphasis on 'your' were intended by the writer, then the slight irregularity could be seen as a demonstration of some skill, subtly dramatic, providing opportunity to an actor or reader to 'fetch out' (Hopkins's phrase) the meaning.

Robert Graves's poem, 'The Revenant', is another example of using only the 'natural quantities' of words, but in verse that eschews any discernible, regular metrical pattern beyond a general observance that the lines be short (though one line, late in the poem, places five iambic feet in a perfect pentameter) and five to each stanza. This versification, too, is 'correct', without any show of 'labour' (it is markedly casual, in its clipped way). And as this first verse shows, it is likewise elegant without 'appearance of ornament' – being in fact plain to the point of meanness:

> To bring the dead to life
> Is no great magic.
> Few are wholly dead:
> Blow on a dead man's embers
> And a live flame will start.

Graves had a good deal to say, on different occasions, about letting each poem find its own unique and unpredictable musical form. But he can be seen here reaching a steadying hand to the bannister:

> To bring the dead to life is no great magic

is a strong pentameter line.

> Is no great magic. Few are wholly dead

is again a strong pentameter line that echoes and strengthens the antithetical structure of the first, more so by sharing one of its phrases. But however these lines are read, whether as three 'free', short phrases or as telescoped pentameters in disguise (the rest of the poem tends to evade that hidden pentameter more resolutely), the words can be given only the one metrical pattern. The result is Graves's own style of ordinary speech in free verse, apparently utterly different from the strong, inescapable, formal metre of the Addison rhymed couplet and yet like it in one respect – that it uses words according to their 'natural quantity' and any reader, speaking in the most casual, conversational style, can sight-read it straight off.

One more example. This translation of part of a poem ('Suffering') by the well-known Czech poet Miroslav Holub was made by the English-speaking Czech George Theiner, whose inner ear was as free as a literate mind can be of English musical clichés, but whose English was nevertheless very pure (he spent his early years in England) and revealed a sure sense of the 'natural quantities' of English words.

Ugly creatures, ugly grunting creatures
Completely concealed under the point of a needle behind
    the curve of the Research Task Graph,
Disgusting creatures with foam at their mouths, with
    bristles on their bottoms,
        One after the other
        They close their pink mouths
        They open their pink mouths

        They grow pale
        Flutter their legs
            as if they were running a very
            long distance

They close ugly blue eyes
They open ugly blue eyes
   and
   they're
   dead.

But I ask no questions.
Noone asks any questions.

Again, though there is no ghost of a regular metric to be heard, whatever casual-seeming metre these lines do have can be musically interpreted in only the one way – which corresponds to the 'natural quantities' of the words. Anyone can sight-read them straight off.

As with the Graves, it would obviously be a mistake to think that because these lines obey no formal, metrical pattern, as the Addison does, they lack music. The whole point of Graves's phrasing is to enforce, as by distinct directions in a musical score, the pitch, pacing and timing of each phrase. Most poets (with surprising exceptions) are keenly aware of this sort of thing. Graves breaks

> To bring the dead to life is no great magic

into

> To bring the dead to life
> Is no great magic

to produce a check, a slight change of key, a new focus, even a new thoughtfulness, which has dramatic effect – musically dramatic effect. For every half-sensitive reader, that typographical break is a visible signal of that musical effect and serves to induce it. Any reader who ignores it and simply reads through the enjambement without modulation is to that degree misreading Graves's meaning, destroying his music, and missing one of poetry's keener pleasures. The single pentameter line into which I reshaped those two phrases contains no such visible signal. In that case, the effect has to be imported by the reader. The reader's voice, scanning the whole line ahead, as a performing musician would, for maximum expressiveness according to the meaning, introduces the effect as it were

[324]

wilfully, in the way of 'musical interpretation'. But even so, this effect concerns only the pacing and pitch of the phrases. The 'natural quantities' of the words remain as they were, automatically dominant and dictating the simple metre, as in casual speech.

In the case of the Holub translation, exactly the same rules operate. The 'English' is pleasing, first, in so far as the words are so placed that the metrical sequence of their 'natural quantities' is musically, dramatically, apt and effective, as in:

> They grow pale
> Flutter their legs
> > as if they were running a very
> > long distance.

And as far as the metrical aspect is concerned, this is the only law: that each phrase be musically, dramatically apt and natural to say. The larger music, which builds the poetry into effective passages, is codified by the typographical placing of the lines on the page. The brief, isolated phrase:

> They grow pale

mimes the event: all the paling faces grow still and come into close-up in a long 'freeze', which is created by the kinetic ushering movement of 'grow' pushing into the naturally emphasized, held still-shot of 'pale', while the isolation of the line converts this distinct single event to a mini-climax. Then

> Flutter their legs

startles by contrast – an ictus of panic that transforms the transfixed 'pale' of horrified realization and biological change into a sudden desperate attempt to escape. The effect is filmic, as 'pale' is scrambled to 'fl' and starts scrabbling hopelessly to be out and away ('utter'), flailing its legs like wings in airlessness, which reduces those finite little legs to pathetic futility.

The two single phrases, brought into conceptual collision in this way by a musical break (the line end) and by the contrasts within the tight juxtaposition (which makes a couplet) create a physiological crisis of hopelessness and helplessness. This is amplified into a long, held, swelling and finally fading note by:

> as if they were running a very
> long distance

where all hope scampers away and fades into a flat, empty non-event – that 'long distance' – like the souls fleeing from the doomed bodies that in all their flailing cannot move a step. Going through the poem in this way it is clear – and the voice intuitively follows all the implications – that the typographical notation conducts the poetic music-drama of the phrasing. This is where translation becomes original poetry. But – this is my point – that typographical notation is at every juncture nothing more than a formalization, and thereby a heightening, of the natural pacing, placing and emphasis of the voice in natural speech. As a result, here too the reader is never at a loss. Such lines might seem boring, or bad in all kinds of ways, or the reader's musical interpretation might be insensitive and their feeling for the dramatic spirit of words defective, but at least all the lines are for every reader easily sayable, when spoken in a natural, conversational way.

Unorthodox Metre

A complication enters, it might be thought, with Hopkins's 'sprung rhythm'. Hopkins's prosodic innovations – beginning in 1876 with 'The Wreck of the Deutschland' – seemed to his contemporaries (with only one or two bemused exceptions) metrically grotesque, musically incomprehensible, unsayable.

Yet according to Hopkins, 'sprung rhythm' was nothing very new. He described it as something quite straightforward:

Sprung rhythm is the most natural of things. For (1) It is the rhythm of common speech and of written prose when rhythm is perceived in them. (2) It is the rhythm of all but the most monotonously regular music, so that in the words of choruses and refrains and in songs written closely to music, it arises. (3) It is found in nursery rhymes, weather saws, and so on; because, however these things may have once been made in running rhythm [Hopkins's term for regular English metres], the terminations having dropped off by the change of language, the stresses come together and so the rhythm is sprung . . . but nevertheless, in spite of all this and though Greek and Latin lyric verse, which is well known, and the old English verse seen in Pierce Ploughman are in sprung rhythm, it has in fact ceased to be used since the Elizabethan age, Greene being the last writer who can be said to have recognized it. For perhaps there was not, down to our days, a single, even short, poem in English in which sprung rhythm is employed – not for single effects or in fixed places – but as the governing principle of the scansion. I say this, because the contrary has been asserted . . .

He never mentions Smart or Blake, whose long poems are 'sprung rhythm' throughout. Some of Blake's shorter pieces, too, avoid fixed, strict metre successfully enough to qualify as 'sprung rhythm' of a kind. But it is more surprising that he overlooks Coleridge.

Two poems in particular, in the *Collected Poems* of Coleridge, should have interested Hopkins. If he had acknowledged these two pieces above all others as the immediate clue to his own metrical theory and practice, or to the simplest form of it, that would have seemed understandable. One of them, 'Christabel' Part I, has turned out to be one of the most – some might argue the most – seminally potent English poems of the nineteenth century, not just musically but in several ways.

The musical or metrical aspect of the innovation is more purely isolated, maybe, in the other poem, the shorter of the two – eleven lines that he titled 'The Knight's Tomb':

> Where is the grave of Sir Arthur O'Kellyn?
> Where may the grave of that good man be?
> By the side of a spring, on the breast of Helvellyn,
> Under the twigs of a young birch tree!
> The oak that in summer was sweet to hear,
> And rustled its leaves in the fall of the year,
> And whistled and roared in the winter alone
> Is gone, – and the birch in its stead has grown. –
> The Knight's bones are dust,
> And his good sword rust; –
> His soul is with the saints, I trust.

In the *Collected Poems*, published the year of his death (1834) this piece was called 'an experiment for a metre'. He had never let it be printed before, but he had recited it, and it had travelled orally – making a great impact on Scott. Rather as, very much later, though before Hopkins wrote the sentence in which he failed to notice it as a precursor or to use it as his perfect example, it would make its mark on young Yeats.* But why was he reluctant to publish it in his lifetime? In metre and atmosphere it seems very close to 'Christabel'. The autobiography coded into the simple Coleridgean symbols suggests that it was composed some time after 7 October 1800, when he walked from Wordsworth's cottage perhaps back over Helvellyn – his usual route – carrying the confirmed knowledge that his poetic genius had somehow died. But from that same date, he had qualms about publishing 'Christabel'.

He kept 'Christabel' back for sixteen years. And then, when he did finally publish it, he prefaced it with a curious apologia. To any modern reader, the most obvious thing about this poem is the weird unspecified sexual act on which it revolves. At that time too, in 1816, the first reviewers pounced on the same thing. Hazlitt recoiled from 'something disgusting at the bottom of the subject', and spread the rumour that Geraldine was actually a man. Another called it 'the most obscene poem in the language'. Neither the Wordsworths nor Coleridge recorded what William had said of the poem when he rejected it from the second edition of the *Lyrical Ballads* – but one can imagine prudery must have spoken as firmly as prudence. During the sixteen year interim, when manuscript copies of the poem were circulating and Coleridge often recited it, others presumably felt and said the same. As one of the most active men of letters of his day, he had every reason to be aware of their sensitivities, pelted as he was by their criticisms. Yet in this preface he makes no attempt to excuse his subject (as he does elsewhere with, for

---

* Yeats's poem 'The Falling of the Leaves'

> Autumn is over the long leaves that love us
>   And over the mice in the barley sheaves;
> Yellow the leaves of the rowan above us,
>   And yellow the wet wild-strawberry leaves . . .

in particular, but also throughout Part I of 'The Wanderings of Oisin', both published in 1889.

instance, 'The Three Graves' or 'The Wanderings of Cain' or 'Kubla Khan'). The only thing that seems to worry him here – apart from his concern to preclude the charge of his having plagiarized works by others that were in fact offspring of this very poem – was what readers would make of his *metre*. What he actually wrote was:

. . . the metre of 'Christabel' is not properly speaking, irregular, though it may seem so from being founded on a new principle: namely, that of counting in each line the accents, not the syllables. Though the latter may vary from seven to twelve, yet in each line the accents will be found to be only four. Nevertheless, this occasional variation in number of syllables is not produced wantonly, or for the mere sake of convenience, but in correspondence with some transition in the nature of the imagery or passion.

The only other poet in the canon who expresses this kind of anxiety about the audience's incomprehension of his metre is Hopkins. And in these sentences Coleridge anticipates the essentials of what Hopkins will say, seventy years later, in his drafted preface to his poems and in his letters, explaining his 'new rhythm'. Coleridge presents his innovation as an experimental 'new principle' – exactly as Hopkins will. In fact Coleridge gives a technical analysis of the basic law, his 'new principle', which turns out to be the very same thing as Hopkins's 'sprung rhythm', described by Hopkins, almost in Coleridge's very words, as 'scanning by accents or stresses alone without any account of the number of syllables, so that a foot may be one strong syllable, or it may be many light and one strong.'

In Coleridge's case it surely seems a lot of fuss about very little. Could there really have been such cultural opposition to such a slight metrical novelty? Evidently there could. Sir Walter Scott had tried to swallow 'Christabel' and 'The Knight's Tomb' whole – but his published imitations of the metre had already drawn a barrage of fire that Coleridge could now expect for himself. It might seem to us unbelievable that sophisticated readers should be unable to supply the musical interpretation to sort out:

> The one red leaf, the last of its clan,
> That dances as often as dance it can,

Hanging so light, and hanging so high,
On the topmost twig that looks up at the sky.

But Coleridge, like Hopkins, knew his public, and this was waiting
for 'Christabel' in 1816:

We have long since condemned in Mr Scott . . . the practice of arbitrary
pronunciation, assumed as a principle for regulating the length or rhythm of a
verse; and we hereby proclaim to all whom it may concern, that they are guilty
of neither more nor less than bombastic *prose*, and not even conscious of
bombastic *verse*, who rest their hopes in the acquiescence of their readers to
their own 'arbitrary pronunciation' . . . When Virgil [writes verse in his way]
. . . when Homer [writes verse in his way] . . . ; when Shakespeare [writes
verse in his way] . . . they are all equally above that imitative harmony, that
affected adaptation of sound to sense, which nothing but German music and
German poetry could ever have attempted. They would have started with
horror and astonishment from such an effort as that which Mr Coleridge is
constantly making; namely, . . . to versify the flattest prose, and to teach the
human ear a new and discordant system of harmony . . . we think that the
time is fast approaching when all minds will be agreed on it . . . any versifier,
who widely differs from the established standard of our nobler authors, will
be directed into that Limbo of vanity from which he most certainly emerged.

We may laugh at this *fiat* from a Civil Servant of the Ministry of
Orthodoxy, based as it is on an official prohibition of natural speech
rhythms as well as on a comical disregard for just how Virgil, Homer
and Shakespeare achieved their more celebrated effects, but in
England it has been regularly updated, with undiminished scorn,
complacency and confidence, on some notable occasion or other,
right up to the present day.

Coleridge's 'new principle': Its Origins in Song

When Coleridge and Wordsworth were preparing the first edition of
Lyrical Ballads, in the first flush of their friendship, they interpreted
what they wanted to achieve as a response to some almighty
pressure of the new. But Coleridge divined this pressure – obsessi-
vely – as a new music, a new rhythm, something that haunted his
ear, exactly as 'sprung rhythm' would haunt Hopkins's.

A surprisingly large proportion of his *Collected Poems* are 'metrical experiments'. Many are straightforward adaptations of classical metres. But he tried to break out beyond that. Experimental combinations of scansion symbols are scattered through his note-books. It is clear from these that he tended to regard rhythm and cadence as the primary poetic impulse. One can believe that all his verse other than the blank verse began as a drummed-out tattoo, a sketched choreography of line lengths, rhythms and rhymes – before he looked for the words. Even his blank verse, maybe, was affected by the habit of this priority. Regretting that his old friend had not written a greater bulk of poetry, Wordsworth blamed the amount of time he spent on 'experiments for metres'. But anyone who listens closely to the two of them must wonder, now and again, just where Wordsworth's great signature tune itself came from. Rather like Sidney before him, Coleridge was constantly digging through to a sea of music that he could hear but not reach. Like somebody imprisoned in a tossing galleon – his only release was into that music. And the three visionary poems, 'Kubla Khan', 'The Ancient Mariner' and 'Christabel' are the story of how the music burst in on him and took him by surprise.

When the two poets gravitated towards the Ballad form for certain things they wanted to do, they were aware that each wanted something quite different from it. For both, Ballad was the appropriate vehicle for their revolutionary radicalism. It came to them through two routes, with unmistakable credentials. Direct from old British tradition, where it was the poetry of 'the common people'. And indirect, via German Romanticism, which was a dominant element in the cultural shock wave that accompanied the French Revolution. In its original form, the ballad is by definition the most objective, most impersonal, most anonymous poetic genre. Passing through the hands of Goethe and his successors, it had become an imaginative form of *lyric* – the most subjective, most personal, most individualized poetic genre. Either way, to promote the Ballad as a poetic form, in embattled England, at that time, was a political act. In its old role, it declared solidarity with 'the common people'. In its new role, it declared allegiance to the revolutionary 'new' continental sensibility and outlook. In the first, it reached objectively outward to share the archaic strengths of 'the people'. In the second, it opened a subjective way inwards – to the Sphynx. With a divinatory sense of what they wanted to do, Coleridge and Wordsworth titled their joint enterprise *Lyrical Ballads*.

Even within the native British tradition, the ballad has a double nature. On the one hand, it is the indigenous form of narrative song, emerging from pure melody as no other poetic form does, and tending, in the most intense and admired specimens, to archetypal themes opening backwards into religious myth. On the other hand, it is the indigenous popular humdrum form of poetic narration, simply a way of telling ordinary though striking tales. Common to both extremes is a uniquely tempered style of plain and direct language. In the first mode this can rise (as was developed in Germany) to fantastic and even surreal song. In the second it is content with common happenings and common speech.

The two poets divided these two realms of possibility quite consciously between themselves. Wordsworth by mutual agreement took the common happenings and common speech. Coleridge chose what they called the 'preternatural' – which turned out to be the demonic element of song. Or rather, in 'Kubla Khan', whether he liked it or not (and he did not, finally) demonic song had already chosen him. That is the subject of the poem: the demon of song emerges and claims the singer.

Most commentators set 'Kubla Khan' in the autumn of 1797 – as the first of the aforementioned visionary three. Whatever date this piece floated into Coleridge's opium trance at Ash Farm, it seems to precede the other two psychologically. Internally, it is connected to them very tightly. It stands as an operatic Overture and very brief Act I to the Act II of 'The Ancient Mariner' and the Act III of 'Christabel' Part I, while the fragmentary 'Wanderings of Cain' serves as musical interlude and mini-overture to 'The Ancient Mariner', and 'The Ballad of the Dark Ladie' does the same for 'Christabel' Part I. That is to say, the three visionary poems constitute a single tragic drama, in which the tragic hero is Coleridge himself, and in which the tragic heroine is the demon of song (see 'The Snake in the Oak', page 373). Though he renounced her, he was left with the 'score' of her song, in 'Christabel' Part i. His renunciation was so violent (so complete that it destroyed his life from that date), he was unable to take the musical novelty of her 'score' any further. And in fact, as we have seen, he felt compelled to dissociate himself even from this – calling it an experiment and at most, a 'new principle'. Nor was anybody else able to take it further. Several adopted it without adapting it. Christina Rossetti in particular produced one or two masterpieces – but within the laws of the 'new principle'. Seventy years had to pass before Hopkins came along and joining the dance of Coleridge's 'last red leaf' began also to adapt it:

> Degged with dew, dappled with dew
> Are the groins of the braes that the brook treads through,
> Wiry heathpacks, flitches of fern
> And the beadbonny ash that sits over the burn.

The metre is still Coleridge's 'new principle', but already metamorphosed, by the virtuoso touch, into Hopkins's own 'sprung rhythm' which, as he defines it (harking back to Coleridge's and Wordsworth's first revolutionary idea) is 'a rhythm of common speech'. In this quatrain from 'Inversnaid', the brilliant kinaesthetic dance and immediacy, the energetic abundance of living voice, work directly through their familiarity (in the reader's ear) as natural speech rhythms. Every phrase is a different, vivacious rhythm, a spontaneous-seeming, surprising, fresh response to one thing after another. At the same time, obviously, each unit of response, each compound or simple 'rhythm of natural speech', is locked into that four stress pattern, just as in 'Christabel'.

In practice, then, Hopkins modifies his definition of 'sprung rhythm' as 'the most natural of things' by combining it with the most 'unnatural of things' – a basic, repetitive rhythmic pattern in which the number of accents is fixed.

All this may seem rudimentary, and is so. But the question that I touched on before seems to remain. When Coleridge felt that his combination of speech rhythms and a simple recurrent pattern of fixed stresses would be too much for his more orthodox readers, it turned out that he was right – and that even his careful explanations could not penetrate the contemptuously dismissive arrogance of a cultural ascendancy that was simply deaf to what he was talking about, as well as opposed to it on principle. Hopkins's development of this kind of 'combination' took off into far greater complexities than Coleridge ever did, but even here, in the simplest basic form of 'Inversnaid', where his adaptation stays well within Coleridge's 'new principle', he too felt it needed explaining – as when he gives an example to his most sympathetic listener, Canon Dixon:

> Ding Dong Bell
> Pussy's in the well

and elucidates it painstakingly, in the plainest ABC terms: '. . . if each line has three stresses or three feet it follows that some of the feet are of one syllable only'. Like Coleridge, Hopkins was only too aware, evidently, that even at this level he was making what still was, in 1878, an unacceptable musical demand on his orthodox reader.

The Demands of Musical Interpretation

If we attempt to understand this demand, we have to leave technicalities, and test things on ourselves. The most obvious novelty of demand, in both Coleridge and Hopkins, is the demand on the reader's voice, for what might be called a new kind of psychosomatic co-operation with the vitality of the statement. Or, to go back to a phrase I used earlier, it is the demand for a new kind of 'musical interpretation'. The voice has to make a shift, from the speaking mode to what – for want of the right word – one might call the 'performing' mode. That is, it is a demand for creative musical input, from the reader. The couplets

> Hanging so light, and hanging so high
> On the topmost twig that looks up at the sky
> 'Christabel'

or:

> Wiry heathpacks, flitches of fern
> And the beadbonny ash that sits over the burn
> > 'Inversnaid'

compel the reader to co-operate physically. Each line is like a dancer who, if you are going to read the line at all, forces you to be a partner and dance. Or is like a singer whose voice you can join only by singing the same melody. You can pronounce the line as silently as you like, but that launching of the inner self into full kinaesthetic participation is, so to speak, compulsory. Otherwise, you can't read the line. You have to back off, stay a wallflower, and call it 'unsayable'. As everybody knows, between the sitting or standing person and that same person dancing there gapes an immense biological gulf. The same between a casually talking or silently listening person and that same person suddenly bursting into song. The gulf is so great that many people need special conditions before they can get across it. Some can never cross it at all. It is easy to underestimate this. In fact, what is required is that the familiar person becomes, in a flash, an entirely different animal with entirely different body chemistry, brain rhythms and physiological aware-ness. And there is more to it than fear of the biological leap.

And yet, obviously, it is a natural enough thing, in the right circumstances, to leap that gulf. And almost as a rule it produces the most intense pleasure for the one who does. In some cases, there is no problem because the impulse of the leap arrives involuntarily, as when the first casual remark: 'Hello, what's this?' becomes, in a flash, 'What the bloody hell!' – not without intense pleasure. In dance and song, and in poetry, for some reason, as Coleridge and Hopkins understood, it is more of a problem. Even so, 'Christabel' and 'Inversnaid' are child's play compared to Hopkins's more ingenious obstacle courses. Here, the gulf can open very wide.

Intimations of this second, greater gulf are felt wherever 'natural quantities' do not exactly coincide with the required number of stresses in the line. A very slight suggestion of this can be felt in that crucial line from 'Christabel':

> Which is lord of thy utterance, Christabel.

Supposing this phrase were being used to address Christabel in conversation, most people would follow 'natural quantities' and say:

Which is lord of thy útterance, Chrístabel.

But in the poem, where the pattern of stresses has been established, the voice that inclines to lag in 'natural quantities' is whipped forcibly into the dance step by the law of the beat. In other words, the voice has to summon further 'musical interpretation' and pronounce 'Christábĕl' slightly against 'natural quantities', as a ritualized 'Chrístabél'. And so this line, encountered in isolation, could not necessarily be sight-read off by anybody – as the Addison, Graves and Holub quoted earlier could. It is not following a simple, single metrical law. It lives within a tension between two laws: the law of 'natural quantities' and the law of the 'hidden' pattern of stresses. This again is nothing very new. It is commonplace throughout Chaucer. And this case is, as I say, very slight. If the 'musical interpretation' required by most of 'Christabel' and 'Inversnaid' is of the first degree, then this is barely edging into a more complicated second degree. In context, it would hardly be noticed as anything different by any modern sight-reader. Yet there is that difference. And this second degree of metrical complexity, as I have termed it here for convenience, exists as a distinct tradition.

In this second degree of metrical complexity the line does not move obediently from beginning to end, or even for some part of its length, under a single simple law of 'natural quantities' that coincide correctly with a fixed metrical pattern. Instead, it explores its way through a field of flexing, contrapuntal tensions, between two simultaneous but opposed laws – that is to say, between a law of 'natural quantities' set in opposition to the law of a fixed, basic metric pattern. Most poets dip in and out of this occasionally, for 'special effects' or accidentally. But Hopkins developed it systematically with at least one very curious result.

In sending his poems to Robert Bridges, Hopkins had found a reader who combined the most sophisticated ear for verse with the most orthodox temperament. Among other pieces, he sent him

The Windhover:

To Christ our Lord

I caught this morning morning's minion, king-
 dom of daylight's dauphin, dapple-dawn-drawn Falcon, in
   his riding
Of the rolling level underneath him steady air, and striding
High there, how he rung upon the rein of a wimpling wing
In his ecstasy! then off, off forth on swing,
 As a skate's heel sweeps smooth on a bow-bend: the hurl and
   gliding
 Rebuffed the big wind. My heart in hiding
Stirred for a bird, – the achieve of, the mastery of the thing!

Brute beauty and valour and act, oh, air, pride, plume, here
 Buckle! AND the fire that breaks from thee then, a billion
Times told lovelier, more dangerous, O my chevalier!

 No wonder of it: sheer plod makes plough down sillion
Shine, and blue-bleak embers, ah my dear,
 Fall, gall themselves, and gash gold-vermilion.

If Bridges had read 'The Windhover' for the first time without
Hopkins's scansion marks one wonders what he would have made
of, say, that sixth line:

 As a skate's heel sweeps smooth on a bow-bend: the hurl and
   gliding

Looking for the metrical law, he would probably have tried to match
'natural quantitites' with something remotely approximating a
Latin hexameter. And he would have come up with

 As a skáte's héel sweeps smóoth on a bów-bénd: the húrl and
   gliding

which is how the line works out when read in the usual way, under a
simple, single, metrical law, following natural quantities. It is easy to
find plausible beauties in this seven stress interpretation, and even to

argue that it enhances the syncopated whirlwind of the countergust
that comes in on the next line:

> Rebuffed the big wind.

From which the still small voice of:

> My heart in hiding

emerges with thrilling effect.

Bridges would then probably have dwelt thoughtfully on the
novel structure of the first part of the line:

> As a skáte's héel sweeps smóoth on a bów-bénd

He would have recognized this as a particularly effective 'staggered'
pentameter, and asked himself, perhaps, why Hopkins hadn't rested
content with that. As if it might be a line to rhyme with another
striking pentameter from another Hopkins poem, 'The Sea and the
Skylark':

> Frequenting there while moon shall wear and wend

which he had been perfectly happy to leave as it was. After all, that
'skate's heel' phrase does have a peculiar felicity. It exactly mimes
the long, powerful, almost slow-motion sweep of the skater kneeling
under his momentum into that bend. Bridges would appreciate,
perhaps, the metrical ingenuity that can make 'sweeps' the most
important word in the line, receiving an apparently pivotal stress,
while at the same time letting the voice lift over it (as if it might be, in
fact, no more than a mere 'is') and letting 'skate's heel' ride lightly
through it, holding something of the true stress that fell on 'heel'
while leaning more and increasingly more into the true stress now
descending onto 'smooth'.

Bridges might have wondered if this particular phenomenon, where
an apparently heavy beat surrenders its metrical precedence to other
syllables elsewhere, might be what Hopkins called 'a stress of sense,
independent of the natural stress of the verse'. Or whether it was what
he called a 'secondary stress', or even an 'outride' – though usually his
'outrides' seemed to be more lightly stressed intercalary syllables.

This bustle of approximate yet technical-seeming terms, in which

Hopkins tried to satisfy his own scholarly conscience with a formalized code of scansion, while at the same time inventing a practical aid for the baffled orthodox readers of his more wayward compositions, indicates just how inadequate any terminology of notation must be, to render the subtleties of musical modulation within lines that have abandoned strict, regular metre. He usually resorted to broader, more impressionistic gestures, and spoke of the voice 'treading and dwelling', or 'the voice passing flyingly over all the foot *in some manner* [my italics] distributing among them all the stresses of the one beat'. Or (less confidently) 'the meaning is "fetched out" by the stressing; and the stressing is indicated partly by the normal word accent and syllabic strength, partly by contextual suggestion, and partly by alliteration and assonance.' Or (retreating further) 'which syllables however are strong and which light is better told by the ear than by any instruction that could be in short space given' – or (beginning to dither) 'though sometimes the line may be scanned either way'. Or (finally giving up) 'but with *the degree of stress* [my italics] so perpetually varying, no marking is satisfactory. Do you think all had best be left to the reader?'

On the other hand, Hopkins knew that it could not be left to even his most musically-imaginative readers. And however Bridges may have admired

As a skáte's héel sweeps smóoth on a bów-bénd

as a mimetic pentameter, Hopkins's own instructions indicated that it was nothing of the sort. This phrase, far from being allowed five gulps of accentual oxygen, somehow had to get by on only three. As far as accents go, the whole sonnet is orthodox, with only five to each line. Hopkins sets this rule in the opening line: a surprising but metrically 'correct' (in Johnson's sense) pentameter:

I caúght this mórning mórning's mínion, kíng-

(though even here he cannot resist a grace note on '-ion' of 'minion' to bring that final clang onto 'king-'). Within this pattern, reaffirmed here and there throughout the poem, the 'skate's heel' has to lift its weight off the ice and take to the air:

As a skáte's heel sweeps smóoth on a bów-bend: the húrl and
  glíding

Whatever Bridges made of that, to a modern ear the line now
springs into life in a new way. It becomes a marvellously suggestive,
intricate, clear sequence of actions that mimes, very precisely, a
particular sequence in the bird's flight. That 'skate's heel' phrase,
formerly heavy with the G force of the skater's momentum kneeling
into the long bend, is now light, electrified, aloft. It reproduces the
forceful, slicing parabola of the small falcon's body, tensed and
compacted by the pressure of the wind against it, wings half-closed,
half-open, and braced. This physically intimate sense of a taut,
bladed, hurtling missile steered at unnatural speed by a crouching
pilot, on a veering balletic arc, against and through and over a hard,
invisible resistance, is jammed into the reader's effort of suppressing
and forcibly over-riding the bumping turbulence of heavy beats that
the words of the whole line, by natural quantity and by stubborn,
refractory shape, try to assert against the internal, metrical assertion
of only five accents. This same, slightly off-balance, brilliantly
constantly-corrected balance produces those flickering, stabbing
touches of the wings, trimming the ailerons, that carry the bird
across and up off the page like a hallucination.

Once the reader is faced with performing this flight, there is no
way to get out of it. The natural quantities of the words used and the
five stress law of the hidden pattern are braced against each other in
a wind-tunnel of counterpointed tensions so extreme that the voice
is snatched beyond kinaesthetic co-operation into something more
like anaerobic emergency. The reader has to get airborne – has to
levitate into song. Or into whatever kind of 'utterance' it is that
makes this line 'sayable'.

This leaping of the gulf, from speech into song, breaks a sound-
barrier. The breakthrough, from a mundane mode into a sacred
mode is the crux of Hopkins's theme, in this poem in particular. But
it has a more general application, throughout his work. The physical
keel of the falcon's breastbone – so like a 'skate's heel' in fact – is
scored across an impossibility – till he bursts, head down, through a

metaphysical barrier, into spirit. This physical, tunnel collision and sudden burst through into spirit freedom beyond is dramatized, in this very line, by the placing of the colon. The falcon hits it, head on, full tilt, and is instantly on the other side of it, in the loose, freed, fling-out beyond it, like the sprinter on his anaerobic eight second dash bursting out beyond the tape, on his own momentum, arms flung up, legs loosely swinging. Just so:

> the hurl and gliding

seems to go up and over and

> Rebuffed the big wind

wonderfully miming that arms up, tossed up, mounting arc of a surf-ride across the wind at the end of a falcon's long swoop – lifting him to his next high station as a trembling crucifix.

In the end, though this line is well into that second degree of metrical complexity, braced under extreme tension between the law of 'natural quantities' and the hidden law of the five stress line, in practice it presents no great difficulty. The five stress basic pattern is known, Hopkins is acknowledged as a special case, and most readers are prepared to give him the benefit of every doubt. If there is a difficulty – more prominent elsewhere than in this line – it lies in actually enunciating all the lighter syllables 'flyingly' and with natural ease.

Unorthodox Metre, Reversed Rhythm

A slightly more testing form of this second degree complexity emerges sometimes with lines written in what Hopkins called 'reversed rhythm'. Here, as everywhere in this business, defining terms seem inadequate. Hopkins begins: 'By a reversed foot I mean putting the stress where, to judge by the rest of the measure, the slack should be, and the slack where the stress, and this is done freely at the beginning of a line and, in the course of a line, after a pause.' He then goes on: 'The reversal of the first foot and of some middlefoot after a strong pause is a thing so natural that our poets have generally done it, from Chaucer down, without remark and it commonly passes unnoticed and cannot be said to amount to a formal change of rhythm, but rather is that irregularity which all natural growth and motion shows.' That is straightforward enough. But he then adds: 'If, however, the reversal is repeated in two feet running, especially so as to include the sensitive second foot, it must be due either to a great want of ear or else is a calculated effect.' So this, perhaps, is where the orthodox reader will call a halt and stand on principle.

Hopkins calls his 'reversed rhythm' also 'counterpointed rhythm', quoting, as illustration of 'counterpoint', the line: 'Bút to vánquish by wísdom héllish wíles', from Milton's *Paradise Regained*. To avoid confusion with the un-reversed kind of counterpointing typical of such lines as that from 'The Windhover', quoted above, I will stick to 'reversed' as the descriptive term.

Hopkins must have been aware of a particularly brilliant specimen of 'reversed rhythm' – the only full line in that mode (to my knowledge) between Hopkins and Milton. It occurs in Keats's 'Endymion'. Though Keats's sentences (more freely in this than in any other of his poems) swim with unhindered variety among the fixed rhymes and iambic pentameters of his couplets, his experiments in 'sprung rhythm' are comparatively rare, and he certainly never used it as a 'governing principle', though he was fond of that reversed first foot. In the attractive single stanza 'Written on May-day', which must have materialized within days of 'Ode to a Nightingale', five of the ten pentameter lines, and perhaps six, carry a reversed first foot. Yet he knew how to reverse a foot midline to telling effect already in 'Endymion':

> To the swift, treble pipe and humming string.

Here, by converting the first two iambic feet to one anapaest (xx/) and a single stress, he throws the reversed stress of 'swift' against the natural stress of 'treble' to produce a syncopated flourish, a musical emphasis like the swirl and stamp in a dance-step – which is counterpointed against the iambic expectation. It is a touch of natural genius, an inspired and effortless miming of the event described. But it is nothing to what he has already done in the line that precedes it. Here, no less than four of the five iambic feet are reversed, producing a violently syncopated line of wonderful beauty and kinaesthetic power – a line, maybe, that could have begotten much of Yeats:

> Young companies nimbly began dancing

Keats launched into this line with a slightly unorthodox but not unusual opening: 'Young companies'. This could have been regularized, in a perfectly conventional way, as:

> Young companies were dancing in a ring.

Here the 'Young' yearns for a stress, but it controls itself modestly in the common interest of the two-stress 'cómpaniés', to which it belongs as a partner, and the dance measure of the whole pentameter line to which it is thereby committed. Or seems to be committed. In fact, that opening phrase 'Young companies' is suddenly overtaken and swept away by the maenadic 'nimbly began dancing'. This produces the first option of musical interpretation, where the slightly stately (stately because it is suppressing irregular impulses) 'Young companies' are caught up into the whirling fling of this phrase out of the blue: a somewhat solemn dance-step suddenly breaks, mid-measure, into a weightless wild cavorting:

> Yoŭng cómpănies nímblў bĕgán dáncĭng

where that rhythm /xx//x is mounted irresistibly on and against the iambic formal metre. Possibly this is how Keats continued to read it, since in this binary form, where the first half remains stately while the second half goes wild, a lingering stress of emphasis, like the last note of a song, does try to settle onto that '-ing', which is also about to beg the stress of rhyming with 'string'. This gives the whole line that aforementioned hovering style of counterpointing common (to modern ears) in Chaucer – which is no doubt where Keats had picked up the possibility. But to a modern ear with musical intuition, liberated by the new, modern wave of the accentual tradition, by awareness of Yeats as well as of Hopkins, and by a consequent retrospective revaluation of the earlier music of the old alliterative tradition, another option of musical interpretation suddenly snaps into life. The second part of the line reaches back and snatches the first part into the new dance, lifts it into the vortex, releasing the formerly suppressed impulse in 'Young' and sweeping that stress on '-ies' off its feet, producing:

Young companies nimbly began dancing

This new rhythm is mounted against the metrical expectation of the whole line – the expectation laid down by the 312 preceding lines of the poem so far. It would be hard to find in Hopkins a more perfect or more perfectly used, more hauntingly used, reversed rhythm.

'Reversed rhythm' would seem to be distinguished from 'sprung rhythm' in requiring a basic time-scheme not merely of a fixed number of accents but of strictly regulated metrical feet. The line discussed above, from 'The Windhover', which could be called a virtuoso development of the metric mode of 'Inversnaid', or for that matter of 'Christabel', gained its effect from mounting its 'natural quantities' to produce the required five strong beats with five naturally stressed syllables – but without any regard for where they came in the line, as long as they came naturally and paced out the line's full length; and without any regard for how many lighter syllables there might be, as long as they ran naturally in the team of the strong five. But the lines from Milton and Keats gain their effects only by complying with Hopkins's definition of 'reversed rhythm' – 'putting the stress where, *to judge by the rest of the measure*, the slack should be, and the slack where the stress'. In other words they mount their 'natural quantities' against the mechanical demand of a strictly metrical basis – against a strict iambic pentameter line, in fact. One can see why Hopkins described this 'reversed rhythm' as counterpointed. And one can see that it is so in a far more pronounced and articulated fashion than occurs in that line from 'The Windhover'. The two metrical laws – the rhythm of 'natural quantities' and the basic measure – are not merely in tension, they are combatively out of synchrony, producing explosive yet tightly-controlled effects of syncopation in every foot. On the other hand, the distinction between 'reversed' lines and lines of more abundant 'sprung rhythm' is fluid. As the number of light syllables in the sprung five-stress line sinks towards and below the basic pentameter's natural five, effects of 'reversed rhythm' begin to crop out: for example, in the line:

> Rebuffed the big wind. My heart in hiding . . .

which abruptly follows the superabundance of:

> As a skate's heel sweeps smooth on a bow-bend: the hurl and
>   gliding

I am attempting to trace the simplest possible path through a jungle that can be massively mined with technical complexities. My three steps so far are: first, lines obeying a single, metrical law; second, lines moving through a field of tension between two metrical laws; and third, lines moving through a field of tension between one law not merely braced against the other law but 'reversed' metrically against it.

In spite of Coleridge's and Hopkins's apprehensions, the modern orthodox reader can usually cope without too much difficulty with the first two of these. And given a clear knowledge of the basic metre, lines like those quoted from Milton and Keats are not incomprehensible, or 'unsayable'. But the challenge to the orthodox ear becomes, more problematic where rather than extra syllables crowding in, as in Coleridge and the longer lines of Hopkins, they begin, as I have described, to drop out altogether.

In the line from *King Lear* (1.iv.299):

> Hear, Nature, hear! Dear Goddess hear!

the law of 'natural quantities' might seem to insist on six beats – which in practice fall into a time unit of five. If six full beats were imposed here, by wilful 'musical interpretation', it would be an almost unique alexandrine: six feet with only six words and only eight syllables:

Héar, Náture, héar! Déar Goddéss, héar!

where the stress could fall on either 'God-' or '-dess' or be distributed 'in some manner' over both. Perhaps some actors do beat that out, a solemn drum. But obedience to the play's pentameter norm lifts the full stress off 'Dear', leaving that word as a 'stress of sense', and puts clean stress onto 'God-'. This produces a five stress line with two dipthongs that (like the cartoonist's *Kersplatt!*) coil up the power and release it where Shakespeare wanted it:

'-tuře héar!

and:

-děss hear!

and though breathed in an undertone the result involves the speaker in a prayer of total kinaesthetic participation only a dial-degree or two away from incandescent, devotional fury.

But if that basic pentametric pattern had not been firmly established, which is to say if the reader of that line had no awareness of the five required beats, as if it were some prayer whispered in a novel, then the reader would look for 'natural quantities' and might well find:

Héar, Nǎtǔre, héar! Děar Góddéss, héar.

Or, if the reader knew that this was indeed a line of verse written to a definite metrical pattern but was uncertain just which one, then the scanning research for the likely metre might well come up with:

Hěar, Náturě, héar! Děar Gódděss, héar!

as if it might be followed with the line:

Stretch forth thine hand, and feel no fear

from 'Christabel'.

The outstanding oeuvre in which this stripped down or truncated metric is employed as a regular option throughout the repertoire, and sometimes, in the lines of five accents, almost as a governing principle, is that of Wyatt. The problems caused for his orthodox readers by this unorthodox music of his throw a strong light into the historical relationship between the two musical traditions.

Wyatt died, at thirty-nine, in 1542, but within fifteen years his prosody had become incomprehensible. For his first editor, Tottel, in his *Miscellany* of 1557, it was already unacceptable. In Wyatt's most famous poem, 'They fle from me', Tottel corrected the metre of fourteen of the twenty-one lines, virtually rewriting many of them.* In retrospect, one can see that his publication announced the final triumph of a process that had visibly begun with Chaucer, who first introduced those continental models of metre and versification. For a hundred and fifty years, the outcome had seemed uncertain. But now, quite suddenly, in those fifteen years between Wyatt's death and Tottel's correcting of his metres, the powers of the new orthodoxy had become absolute. Presumably this was connected, in some obscure way, with Henry VIII's momentous break from Rome in 1533. That Tottel's demands reflected not only the tyranny of a particular pedant, or of a fashion, but a genuine and profound change in taste, affecting all English poets, is evident in the verse written thereafter and in the popularity of Tottel's collection, which went through nine editions in the next thirty years.

Tottel's ideal was Petrarch. His verse specimens, in the *Miscellany*, were meant to provide models of metrically correct prosody for the courtly versifiers of the new high culture, and a standard for 'the stateliness of the stile removed from the rude skill of common ears.' This anticipated what Dryden would so notoriously have to say, a hundred years later, concerning the style of verse proper for a gentleman of education and breeding. Both Tottel and Dryden are making the essential point: the metrically correct mode is the socially correct or as we might say now the politically correct mode. Whatever fails to achieve this social correctness must be by definition not only vulgar and incompetent, but impermissible. Tottel did not reject Wyatt's 'irregularity' because he preferred a different art. He rejected it because he could hear nothing in it but cacophony,

---

* 'Tottel' for convenience: some other could have done the correction.

vulgarity and above all – incompetence, plain, crude failure to qualify through simple lack of skill. Even more ominously, according to this new orthodoxy Wyatt and the old poetry were hopelessly crippled by 'the bondage of speech', while correct metres were gracefully free of any such base limitation. Already, that is, the strictly metrical tradition's hostility to the 'rhythms of common speech' had asserted itself, as a law of the land.

In modified form, this is what Coleridge met in 1816 and what Hopkins met in the late 1870s. But Wyatt, who in essential ways can be a subtler musician than either of them, remains the test case. Tottel's corrected version of 'They fle from me' has gone on being preferred in anthologies right up to the present day. In 1928 Rollins, commenting on Tottel's *Miscellany*, described Wyatt as a 'pioneer who fumbled in the linguistic difficulties that beset him and prepared the way for Surrey's smoother lines and more pleasing accentuation.' Rollins was reaffirming quite automatically the cultural values that Tottel had so successfully helped to impose in 1557, that Dryden had effectively made law in the 1660s, that Coleridge's critic (quoted earlier) had so confidently (and successfully, in so far as it was part of what discouraged Coleridge) reasserted in 1816, and that almost every English literary critic between Tottel and Rollins has accepted, more or less unquestioningly, as the distinguishing credentials of English Poetry *per se*, without which verse is 'neither more nor less than ("bombastic" or "the flattest") prose'.

But how would those authorities have sounded to Wyatt? Much as they sounded to Coleridge (when he tried to promote his 'new principle') and to Hopkins (when he tried to explain his 'sprung rhythm' and find one understanding reader). From Wyatt's point of view, this four hundred year deafness to his musical achievement, and to that whole tradition in which he was a conscious supreme master, can only have seemed like a poetic Dark Age. He might have used harder terms. After all, Tottel (with the approval of his followers) did not simply ignore Wyatt, he attempted to destroy and remake his masterpieces, and only the accidental survival of a few manuscripts saved them. And in the case of the judgement delivered by that critic of 'Christabel', one can't help imagining what such official zeal would have become if given the 'Power and Will' of, say, the Writer's Union of the Stalin era.

The solidarity against Wyatt's music began to break down in the twenties and thirties. The developing appreciation of Hopkins possibly had something to do with it. (Hopkins's poems were first published in 1918, in an edition of 750 that took ten years to sell out.) Appreciation of Hopkins derived in turn, perhaps, from the new recognition of the art and purpose behind the reversed, counterpointed metres of John Donne. And this particular sophistication (as a superior artistic excellence and refinement in English Poetry) had become audible, largely through such American readers as Eliot and Pound – ears from right outside the historically closed cognitive system of the English orthodoxy.*

* Wyatt's first reappearance at the threshold of recognition is interesting. In Tottel's versions, he had sunk into the shadow of Surrey, then all but disappeared for the next two and a half centuries, emerging, if at all, only to be pushed back under Surrey's feet. In the first full edition of Wyatt's own versions, in 1816, the editor, Nott, noted 'a certain earnestness of expression, and a dignified simplicity of thought, which distinguish Wyatt's amatory effusions from Surrey's, and I might add from every other writer in the language.' The sudden lift in that last phrase warms the heart. It explains why Nott took the trouble. But he failed to restore Wyatt's metres to general comprehension. At the end of the century Courthope was also responding to Wyatt's passionate strength and originality – still without identifying any particular metrical means. In the next full edition of the original texts, in 1913, the editor Foxwell found great virtue in Wyatt but again failed to locate any of it in the metre.

One of the first to suspect perhaps some deliberation and skill in Wyatt's unorthodox metrical art was Tillyard – the year after Rollins had dismissed it and reaffirmed Tottel's superior taste and ear. Tillyard arrives at his perception through Donne. The strenuously counterpointed 'tough' prosody of Donne was then coming into high, modern fashion, and Tillyard could confidently say that the 'roughness of Donne' is not 'barbaric' but 'cultured' and 'the very stamp of his passion'. Before one can altogether believe that Tillyard means what he says, here, or even understand quite what he means, one would like to hear how he scanned some of Donne's satires, or better still how he read them. Perhaps I am doing him an injustice. And in the case of Wyatt he is confronting 372 years of more or less unshaken orthodox opinion. Even so, while his remarks demonstrate some nagging recognition that Wyatt's 'rough' metres often carry some peculiar, unique beauty and quality, he refuses to believe, in the absence of orthodox metre, that anything but accident can have enabled Wyatt to bring it off. Or rather, if some fine wild 'intention' or deliberate unorthodoxy of Wyatt's chanced to produce a moving line or two, it was just a lucky chance, as a man might jump over the table and the remains of the feast far more

Here is Tottel's version of 'They flee from me', as printed in a well-known anthology re-issued in 1991. The Editor has gone one better than Tottel, and corrected the first line of the second stanza, where Tottel had struck to Wyatt's original.

———

impressively than he might walk round it with the others, though the impulse was just as likely, more likely in fact, to result in something too 'hopelessly rough'.

Tillyard felt that in Wyatt both extremes of 'roughness' occur – the plainly 'barbaric' in some places but 'cultured' (like Donne's) in others. The social implications of Tillyard's vocabulary are Tottel's, updated and correspondingly seasoned. He perceives a 'transition from gross to refined irregularity'. He is hedging his bets. He modified 'cultured' and 'refined' when he came down to specific instances, and described the following as 'expressive but intentional irregularity of metre':

> Sighs are my food, drink are my tears
> (Clinking of fetters such music would crave);
> Stink and close air away my life wears;
> Innocency is all the hope I have . . .

But on the whole he felt (the orthodox metrical regularity firmer beneath his feet) that Wyatt's strength lay in the shorter lines of his lyrics. Using Tottel's courtly dismissive, he finds that 'some of those [poems] written in the heavier metres [pentameter seven or eight line verses, or sonnets] are uncouth'. (Tottel had gone the whole hog with 'swinelike grossenesse'.)

Since Tillyard cannot detect any metrical systematic basis for 'musical interpretation' in what he finds 'expressive and intentional', it is hard to see how he can be so confident that there is no 'intentional' subtlety escaping him in what he finds 'hopelessly rough'. Obviously he can't; he is shrugging his shoulders and modulating his voice. The only 'chance' in the matter is whether Wyatt's deliberate metrical intention, in each line of these short, highly wrought pieces, happens to coincide with a sayable cadence somewhere in Tillyard's orthodox ear. In the way that

> That now are wild and do not remember

unmistakably hits a bull's eye however you say it.

Tillyard exposes his uncertainty amiably enough. He definitely does hear something special. But he has Walter de la Mare to thank, perhaps, rather than Donne. He recognizes 'They flee from me' as a poem full of 'deliberate irregularity of rhythm.' He particularly admires the strong unorthodox beauty of the line:

> It was no dream: I lay broad waking

and sees no difficulty at all in setting the three heavy stresses on 'I láy bróad wáking'. Then again, finding his way to the musical peculiarity of 'strange' in that line

> Into a strange fashion of forsaking

through a far less strikingly counterpointed line of Donne's, he notes that Wyatt can do the same sort of thing, and 'succeeds in getting the stress on "strange" well

They flee from me, that sometime did me seek,
With naked foot stalking within my chamber;
Once have I seen them gentle, tame, and meek,
That now are wild, and do not once remember,
That sometime they have put themselves in danger
To take bread at my hand; and now they range
Busily seeking in continual change.

—

enough.' If this seems a bit mealy-mouthed, he then reveals why. Having offered us this glimpse of Wyatt's musical mastery (which must have sent de la Mare, one imagines, into a trance of joy), Tillyard promptly withdraws it, in his note to this poem, with: 'On the other hand, it might be thought that the substitution by Tottel of "bitter" for "strange" has its merits'. In other words, whatever 'expressive and intentional' successes Wyatt's genius may rise to, Tillyard, in his heart of hearts, might prefer to see them corrected by the regimental bandmaster. He then goes on, overcome by nostalgia, to praise Tottel's replacement of Wyatt's miraculous last line with that 'indignant repetition of "How like you this?"' as – according to him – 'more telling'. After this, one wonders what he can have meant by his phrase 'the transition from a gross to a refined irregularity'.

Then again, though he does not venture to mark stresses, from his description of how it is to be read one could almost imagine that he scans

That now are wild and do not remember

with the correct musical interpretation of a five beat line. In his words, it 'gives the feeling, by the heavy pause we are forced to make on the word "wild" and the consequent effort of continuing, of slow fitful thought.' But from there he turns immediately to welcome the effects (moving 'more freely', as he says, and 'gaining speed . . . by a smoother rhythm') of what he calls the 'shortened line':

Therewith all sweetly did me kiss

so converting one of the most physically-actual, delicately-placed, voluptuously-felt, provocative kisses in our entire literature

Thérewitháll swétely did me kýsse

to something like an accidental thump on the ear in a College mock-madrigal song and dance act:

Therewith all swéetly dĭd me kiss

The interest of Tillyard's edition is in Tillyard's own position on the cusp between the two traditions. His delighted response to some of Wyatt's unorthodox metrical effects is real and spontaneous. It is enlightening to watch his tentative perception in the actual process of being corrected and censored by his own far stronger allegiance to metrical orthodoxy and all that it represents.

Thanks be to Fortune, it hath been otherwise
Twenty times better; but once especial,
In thin array, after a pleasant guise,
When her loose gown did from her shoulders fall,
And she me caught in her arms long and small,
And therewithal so sweetly did me kiss,
And softly said, "Dear heart, how like you this?"

It was no dream; for I lay broad awaking:
But all is turned now through my gentleness
Into a bitter fashion of forsaking,
And I have leave to go of her goodness,
And she also to use new-fangledness.
But since that I unkindly so am served:
"How like you this," what hath she now deserved?

But what Wyatt actually wrote (the original copy is in his own hand) was quite different. Here is his first verse:

They fle from me that sometyme did me seke
    With naked fote stalking in my chambre.
I have sene theim gentill tame and meke
    That nowe are wyld and do not remembre
    That sometyme they put theimself in daunger
To take bred at my hand; and nowe they raunge
Besily seking with a continuell chaunge.

As can be seen, Tottel's ear was offended by every line of this except the first and the sixth. He was particularly irritated by lines two, four and five. According to the correction he made of these three, he either assumed that Wyatt had been trying, with pathetic clumsiness, to rhyme '-ambre' with '-embre', following that up with a slovenly makeshift '-aunger' as a gesture towards the third rhyme required by the scheme; or else, realizing that Wyatt was in fact trying to get away with rhyming on the '-er' sound in each line, he refused to let that pass as anything but rank ineptitude in the art, sheer ignorance of how to behave. In either case, like an impatient schoolmaster, he had to show Wyatt the correct deportment of the iambic pentameter, and at the same time protect his readers from contamination.

A modern poet would have little difficulty in accepting those three rhymes on '-er'. This same modern poet could likewise accept the apparent irregularity of the number of stresses in each line, and of the number of syllables – the apparent freedom of the lines, in fact, from any fixed form. The verse would be read just like speech, loosely controlled within an overall harness of rhymes – three of them touched only lightly. If this were a modern poem, and if this modern poet were asked: 'But how many stresses are there in those three lines, the ones that rhyme on '-er', how many accents does each one carry?' he or she would probably then say: 'But that's not the point. Stresses don't matter. Each line is just a natural cadence, like speech. If you insist, I suppose the first

> With náked fóte stálking in my chámbre

has four, like that. The next

> That nówe are wýlde and dó not remémbre

also has four, slightly differently placed, like that. And the third

> That sómetýme they pút theimsélf in daúnger

well, that seems to have five, spaced like that. But that's not the point. This poem isn't written in 'metre'. It is internally free of any particular metre. Though I think those lines sound good – natural and good. In fact, I think they're rather wonderful.

> With náked fóte stálking in my chámbre

gives me the shivers. And

> That nówe are wýld and dó not remémbre

sounds like a phrase in some wild sort of Italian song.'

This modern liberty of approach was beyond Tottel, as it was beyond anybody in Tottel's world. As it was beyond Wyatt. Wyatt was not of course writing 'free verse' within a loosely containing rhyme scheme. He was writing with every syllable under metric control *of a kind*: he was listening keenly to stresses, and to what the stressed syllables did to the unstressed, and he wanted to get them exactly as he wanted them. Tottel also was listening to stressed and unstressed syllables – but in his new different metrical tradition that was deaf and hostile to the tradition in which Wyatt wrote as a master.

If this first verse had been the whole poem, Tottel might have paused. Wyatt was known to have written many poems to sing to his own lute, and in general he displayed an acquisitive, magpie delight in new possibilities of stanza form (he is said to have introduced the Sonnet to English). Knowing that songs set to music frequently follow an eccentric metrical pattern when read without the music, and knowing of Wyatt's near-perverse experimentalism in verse form, Tottel could easily have assumed that those three lines in question had indeed been warped to fit a particular music, and were four stress lines anyway – Wyatt's little technical surprises within the conventional *rhyme royal* pentametric stanza. He might then have tolerated, grudgingly, the irregular syllabic length of the lines – even the last one that manages to cram in twelve.

But the second and third stanzas restored Tottel's confidence in his suspicion that though Wyatt could write impressive poems he was metrically incompetent. These stanzas establish beyond any doubt that Wyatt is indeed basing his poem on *rhyme royal*, one of Chaucer's favourite forms, with seven pentameters to each verse. In Wyatt's words:

> Thancked be fortune, it hath ben othrewise
> 　Twenty times better; but ons in speciall,
> In thyn array after a pleasaunt gyse,
> 　When her lose gowne from her shoulders did fall,
> 　And she me caught in her armes long and small;
> Therewithall swetely did me kysse,
> And softely saide, dere hert, howe like you this?
>
> It was no dreme: I lay brode waking.
> 　But all is torned thorough my gentilnes
> Into a straunge fasshion of forsaking;

> And I have leve to goo of her goodenes,
> and she also to use new fangilnes.
> But syns that I so kyndely ame served,
> I would fain knowe what she hath deserved.

In these two stanzas the lines corresponding to the second and fourth in that first stanza each contain a clearly sounded five beats. Meanwhile, as can be seen, other lines, such as the sixth of stanza two, and the first, third and sixth of the last stanza, according to the measure throughout the poem, ought to do the same but seem not to. That is to say:

> With naked fote stalking in my chambre

> That nowe are wyld and do not remembre

> Therewithall swetely did me kysse

> It was no dreme: I lay brode waking

> Into a straunge fasshion of forsaking

and

> But syns that I so kindely ame served

all have to carry five strong stresses each. Meanwhile, several other lines that carry the five required stresses comply neither with a ten-syllable syllabic rule nor with a five-iambic metrical rule, but are each unruly in their own way.

It was enough for Tottel. As an officer of the new laws, he set about bringing the poem to civilized order.

The suddenness and completeness with which this new orthodoxy took control of English metre is not more extraordinary than the unanimity with which everything else, within English tradition, was rejected. Surrey is usually cited as the first poet of stature to make an example of conformity. But the serious influence came a little later – from Spenser. Though Spenser's delicacy of ear and musical genius, through much of the register, were equal to any in that age, he subjected them to the new regime with a convertite's enthusiasm that was positively militant. 'The Accente' he wrote, which sometimes gapeth, and as it were yawneth ill-favouredly, coming short of that it should, and sometime exceeding the measure of the number . . . [is] . . . like a lame gosling that draweth one leg after her . . . and . . . like a lame dogge that holds up one legge. But it is so to be wonne with custome, and rough words must be subdued with use.

Spenser could well have been thinking of those verses of Wyatt's here, as he lines up his own syllables on the parade-ground and drills them to march in iambics. The natural tendency of words to do anything else, no matter what, is now thought boorish, barbarous, deplorable – a coarse result of 'the rude skill of common ears'. But it seems to have been more than a question of manners or 'education'. Sensibility itself had been culturally maimed. Among Spenser's courtly audience, the art of bracing 'natural quantities' *against* the basic formal metre, for intensified and subtler musical expressiveness, and for a more intimate immediacy of voice, could no longer be distinguished from clumsiness or plain lack of skill. The problem that Wyatt's apparently crippled lines presented to Tottel (and to all his like-minded successors, right up to 1929) is closely paralleled by the problem that the alliterative lines of *Gawain and the Green Knight* have presented to scholars up to this moment. Wyatt, like Chaucer, was clearly able to hear – and appreciate – the music of *Gawain*'s lines (or of the verse in that tradition). Both could still use what they wanted of it – Wyatt wanting a little more than Chaucer.

In fact, Wyatt's hand-wrought, gnarled, burr-oak texture owes more than a little to the alliterative tradition. The long-unpublished collection of poems by Wyatt and his circle, known as the *Blage Manuscript* (edited by Muir in 1960), contains several in which Wyatt's courtly but temperamental pentameters can almost be seen emerging from the knotty alliterative technique. One first line

Dryvyn to Desyre, a drad also to Dare

which is straight old English stock, showing courtly corruption, is followed immediately by

Bitwene two stoles my tayle goith to the ground

which could easily be Wyatt. The next line, which combines the alliterative line's consonant pattern with a ruffling early Elizabethan dramatic pentameter:

> Dred and Desire the reson doth confound

is followed after two or three lines with one that, while still deep in the alliterative oaken bole, nevertheless half struggles out of it to flourish, again, a typical Wyattian bitter-sweet paradox:

> Desirous and Dredfull, at Lybertye I go bound

Though Wyatt filters this inheritance through Chaucer's delicate mesh, it is hard to escape the impression, reading the Blage collection, that Wyatt's talent did emerge from the alliterative work as from a matrix. These are the first half-breeds of Chaucer's mass-insemination. Perhaps it was this very strain in Wyatt that narrowed Tottel's officious ethnically cleansing eye. Wyatt's lines retain only a twang of the Shibboleth and a certain unpredictability, but it was obviously enough. His music had to undergo the operation. It was there – somewhere between Wyatt and Tottel (only a generation) – that all understanding of that alliterative tradition, as an evolved and sophisticated form of verbal music, seems to have been finally lost. At least, as far as the high culture and the new orthodoxy were concerned, it was lost.*

In the half-century that followed Tottel's *Miscellany*, theorizing about the possibilities, variations and ideals of English prosody became intense. But as Spenser's remarks witness, with the exception of Donne and certain dramatists, and the setting of words to a particular music, the work of the avant-garde became largely a matter of perfecting the English equivalent of the French and particularly the Italian models. When native poets jibbed at the constraints, and felt the need to search experimentally for a more varied music, they tended to search higher in the high culture, and tinkered with classical metres, as did Sidney and his circle, and Campion. In all that time, it seems, nobody made any attempt to re-

---

* *Piers Plowman* had its champions, mainly among the clergy. A new edition in 1550 was reprinted twice that year and again in 1561.

introduce or adapt or make anything new of the old metre of the *Gawain* tradition. As if every memory trace of it had gone.

It has never been recovered. When the sole surviving text of *Gawain* re-emerged into public life (about a hundred years ago, from a famous Elizabethan library) the scholars who set about divining its basic metre were – as their disagreements proved – baffled by it.

They were baffled, as I say, just as Tottel had been by Wyatt. But unlike Tottel, they had no strong, single preconception, no inflexible rule, which the old poem could be assumed to have violated here and there, through the poet's ignorance or incompetence, or through bad copying, and into which it could now be corrected. Or rather, they had only a couple of rough guidelines – one in the metric of such older poems as *Beowulf*, which seems to carry four stresses, and another in the metric of such poems as *Piers Plowman* (contemporary with Chaucer, slightly after *Gawain*) which was generally thought to carry seven. Accordingly, the scholars split into two camps, one reading *Gawain* with seven beats to the line, the other reading it with four.

The team for four seems gradually to have won. But detailed analysis of the problems (there is an admirable survey by Marie Boroff, Yale, 1962) suggests how tentative the whole business is. Because the traditional mode of recitation, the 'live' music, has been so utterly lost, and because *Gawain*'s lines carry no self-evident indication of just what the basic metre might be, it has to be tentative. We would find the same problem with:

> That nowe are wyld and do not remembre

if that were the sole, quoted fragment of a lost poem. Or even if we had only the first stanza. Wyatt's metrical intention, his own mode of recitation, would be impossible to guess. Since we have the other stanzas, giving the metric norm, we can reconstruct Wyatt's music in this line, by 'musical interpretation'. But in the case of *Gawain*'s lines, obviously the problem can never be resolved.

It is doubtful, for instance, whether Hopkins would cast his vote with the team for four beats. Or for that matter with the team for seven. As a striking line from *Gawain* (spelling modernized) the following would be metrically typical:

Christ's lily and beast of the waste wood.

But where ought the accents to go? In Hopkins's 'Wreck of the Deutschland', where this line actually occurs (verse twenty, line six), it carries not four accents, as *Gawain*'s lines are said to do, and not seven either, but five. One can be certain of this because, first of all, the structure in each of the stanzas is the same, as far as stresses go, and observing his own rule strictly throughout the poem he gives this sixth line five beats. Any reader accustomed to Hopkins's 'reversed counterpoint' reads this nine-syllable specimen easily as:

Christ's líly and béast of the wáste woód

Exactly the same, according to his own practice, Hopkins himself would have scanned the following, automatically, as:

Eách híll had a hát a míst-hackle húge

which is line 2081 in *Gawain*. Here the first five words precisely match the cropped reversed rhythm of the first four words in Hopkins's line above. Hopkins would have had as little difficulty, one imagines, with most other lines in *Gawain*, always following his regular practice of bracing the rhythm against five beats. He would have scanned:

Of hóar oáks full húge a húndred togéther (*Gawain*, 744)

very much as he scanned his own:

And, eýes, heárt, what loóks, what líps yet gáve you a
                      ('Hurrahing in Harvest', line 7)

and:

Hít him úp to the hílt that his heart súndered (*Gawain*, 1595)

exactly (except for the last light spillover syllable) as he scanned his own:

Dúrance deál with that steép or deep. Here! creép
               (Sonnet beginning 'No worst, . . .', line 12)

and:

> Of hárd hewn stónes úp to the táblez (battlements)
> > (*Gawain*, 789)

exactly as he would have scanned his own:

> The heárt réars wíngs bóld and bólder
> > ('Hurrahing in Harvest', line 13)

but for the extra syllable in 'to the', where 'the' is anyway so negligible that many old English dialects would elide and swallow it in a single glottle stop preceding the noun. The way Hopkins chops and distorts syntax to achieve rhythmical effects that can be matched so closely in *Gawain* (as in that bizarre line seven from 'Hurrahing In Harvest' above) could almost make one suspect that he must have seen an early transcript of the old poem (perhaps published in some journal) and collected a few startling rhythms, as he admits to collecting the counterpointed rhythms in Milton.

This speculative and provisional reconstruction of the music of *Gawain*'s unknown metre through Hopkins's known practice not only suggests how the music of Wyatt's short lines can be reconstructed from their known basic stress pattern as established by the whole poem, it also identifies just which tradition of 'musical interpretation' the results belong to. In one way, it is the prosodic tradition anathematized and banished by Tottel and by the orthodoxy thereafter. But in another way, it is the tradition inherent in the natural sprung rhythms of English speech. If Hopkins never saw a line of *Gawain*, which seems likely enough, his resuscitation of *Gawain*'s rhythms, after 400 years in oblivion, would still not be astonishing. A few hints from other old alliterative poems, which he did see,* and the natural life of English, could account for everything except the genius of Hopkins.

Just as Hopkins does in 'The Windhover', Wyatt states the basic

---

* According to his own practice, he would have read most of the lines in *Piers Plowman* with five beats each, as a matter of course.

metrical pattern, on which he will make his melodic variations, simply and clearly in the first perfect pentameter line:

> They fle from me that sometyme did me seke

Immediately he sets in contrast against that Italian mannequin his first pure English surprise:

> With naked fote stalking in my chambre

If that were a line in Chaucer (as it well could be), one would assume that the 'e' on 'fote' were being sounded, to produce a full iambic pentameter with feminine ending:

> Wĭth nákĕd fótĕ stálkĭng ín mў chámbrĕ

A delicate and beautiful line. But even in that version one can feel the libidinous dramatic life of 'stalking in my chambre' pressing for a different release. Anyway, Wyatt's other poems indicate that this final 'e' has become mute.

What he has done here then, is to let a syllable drop out of the orthodox iambic line. Once that syllable goes, three things happen together. First, the line is reduced, as if counted out precisely on the finger-tips, to ten syllables. This has the effect – after killing off the iambic pentameter with a feminine ending – of raising the strong spectre of an iambic pentameter with a masculine ending: as if the light '-re' of 'Chambre' were now being forced to take on a counterpointed strong beat against its own natural quantity, and a metrically free syllabic line of ten syllables were being conscripted into strict iambic metre.

In fact the heavy natural stress of 'stalk-', now brought so hard against the heavy stress of 'fote', has the effect of reversing the rhythm of that whole last phrase – counterpointing it against the ghostly iambic undervoice. This produces:

> Wĭth nákĕd fóte stálkĭng ín mý chámbrĕ

These five stresses, though they are technically present, are in practice sabotaged by the natural quantities of 'stalking in my chamber', that insist on going past quickly. The voice tries to lift over the word 'in', unless – and this is the third clinching step of the process – *those three stresses, required by the pentameter basic pattern, are enforced by wilful musical interpretation*. In other words, this last phrase, trying to hurry, is forced to slow down. i.e. the sinister stealth of 'stalk' is allowed to surge powerfully but gently and smoothly on through '-ing in my chambre', with the effect of yoking three strong beats (that begin with 'stalk-') into the phrase (in Hopkins's words 'distributing them in some manner').

With nákéd fóte stálking in my chámbre

The key to the line is that especially heavy and prolonged stress on 'stalk-'. One imagines Wyatt's lute and singing voice conducting it all without difficulty.

The creature owning that 'naked fote' has been identified as one or several of various species. The greater drama emerges if it is assumed to be the woman introduced more openly in the second stanza. This moment then becomes one of the erotic high points of the poem – miming her ghostly, slow, naked-footed, illicit, searching approach across the dark bedchamber. Beautiful as the four-stress interpretation of the line is, the two stresses thereby pitched onto the second group of words whisk the bare-foot lover across the room too briskly. But the five stress interpretation, as sustained by Wyatt's voice and now inaudible lute, holds his lost, helplessly-infatuated woman there like a ghost, in a stabbing vision from which the whole poem then expands like the slow realization and full arrival of the pain.

In a similar way, Wyatt's lute and the reader's musical interpretation launch into:

That nówe are wýld and do not remémbre

Here again, Wyatt has so to speak dropped a syllable from the middle of the line. The consequences, one imagines, were again easily controlled by the lute. As before, the result is to *reverse* and counterpoint the second half of the line. Because natural quantities here insist so strongly on

and dó nŏt rĕmémbrĕ

'musical interpretation' has to brace the required three heavy stresses 'in some manner' against it, and once again forcibly slow the whole phrase down. It does this by letting that 'wyld' – which is the peak in the power graph of the whole line – requisition the 'and' as a carrier of its own long and heavy stress. In effect, the complaint and lament of 'wyld' is drawn on through 'and', which is not allowed to drop out of the sostenuto scheme of emphasis. This leaves the last phrase

and do not remembre

as a floating, slowed cry, *sotto voce* perhaps but a cry nonetheless. The gain in penetration – as with a lengthened arrow – is a real one. And the whole thing depends on the 'musical interpretation' of 'wyld' and the modulation of that 'and'.

Similar handling 'fetches out' the musical beauty and truth of feeling, the nakedness of feeling, in each of Wyatt's so-called 'irregularities'. No poet ever cut deeper into the nerve than he did in these lines. But as can be seen, at each point he is simply drawing on the repertoire of possibilities that Tottel, and the orthodoxy after him, banished.

In examples of this kind, the terms 'sprung rhythm', 'counter-pointed' or 'reversed' rhythm, are no more than conductor's batons lying on the music stand. What counts is the 'musical interpretation' that can make those uncertain sequences of syllables (which made Tottel in 1557 and Rollins in 1929 shake their heads so pityingly) draw blood.

Verse written within this tradition, or drawing on this tradition, runs two risks of being musically inaccessible to the orthodox reader. The first occurs when the visible pattern is set at such a remove from the hidden pattern, against which the writer braced it, that the hidden pattern is concealed and lost to the reader. As in *Gawain*. And as

With naked fote stalking in my chambre

Or as

The heart rears wings bold and bolder

[363]

would be if found in isolation. Possibly Wyatt's friends would not have been at a loss, with their lutes to hand. And obviously Hopkins was not at a loss. But a modern reader who, as I remarked at the outset, is accustomed to reading almost all verse in casual, conversational style, as if it were metrically simple – following that single, simple metrical law – will often be at a loss, even if the line occurs among fairly regular pentameters. Or rather, they will not be at a loss, they will simply speak the line, or attempt to, as if it were a metrically simple statement, in other words as if it were a line of 'free verse'. If the metrically simple version chances to coincide with an attractive rhythm, as in

That now are wyld and do not remembre

it is accepted as a deliberate albeit licentious felicity. But if the metrically simple version introduces an ugly, off-balance rhythm, or a tongue-twister, the reader might well complain, as Tottel did, that the line is technically incompetent, or, as Roy Fuller did with that quoted line of mine, that it is 'unsayable'.

However, even when the reader has been unseated by this failure to observe the hidden metrical law, all is not lost. There is still a hope that once the reader has been instructed in just what the hidden law is, they will then – *jump the gulf*. They will take that leap from the speech of simple metrical structure in the orthodox tradition to the song of complex metrical structure in the unorthodox tradition. If the reader is willing, all is well. But if the reader jibs at the brink, and flatly refuses – then the line has to remain, for that reader, 'unsayable'. *

To return to my simple starting point, the line of mine that gave Roy Fuller the difficulty occurs at the end of a poem composed in lines of varying lengths – though in general the 'governing principle' is a line of five accents. The preceding line, for instance:

Between the streams and the red clouds, hearing curlews

---

* Wittgenstein's astonished discovery of how he could jump this gulf *deliberately*, and of how this transformed his understanding and appreciation of verse (Klopstock's) in which up to that point he had been unable to see or feel anything, must be *the* most dramatic illustration of just how the two poles are charged and what happens when the spark jumps. Narrated in Ray Monk's life of Wittgenstein.

can hardly be anything but a five stress line. On the two or three occasions that I have heard others recite it, they always scanned it:

Betwéen the stréams and the réd clouds, héaring cúrlews

When I first heard this it came as a shock. In my own head I had never heard the line as anything but: ╱

Bĕtwĕen thĕ streams (╱) ănd thĕ red clouds, héariñg cúrlĕws

where the prolonged rising introductory phrase lifts the whole line to a physical height and launches it as a 'melody' (as distinct from a statement) in which the 'red clouds' and the 'curlews' can be suspended, against the backdrop of unending sky. After that, the final line comes as a condensation of a similar rhythmical movement. Again, scansion marks seem inadequate to score the shape of the phrase as I hear it. It oscillates somewhere between interpretations that look slightly different – but only as two parts of a harmony. For another reader I would scan it (pronouncing 'horizons' with stress on -'riz'-) ╱

Héaring the horízons endúre

The first stress falls on 'Hear-'. The second is 'distributed in some manner' over both the '-ing' and the pause between that and the next word (and is therefore a stress of sense that falls partly in silence). The third stress falls on -'riz'-. The fourth falls mainly on -'ons' but, after slowing that syllable down and keeping its profile up extends itself over 'en-', 'distributing itself in some manner' over both. The fifth stress then falls on '-ure'. But to my ear, spellbound as it is by the unorthodox tradition, the most natural thing is to hear it slightly more plastically shaped, almost (but not quite) as:

Héariñg thĕ hŏrízoñs éndúre

where 'Hearing' has the value of a single stress, with a slight pause for after-echoes to fade from the '-ing', and the final four stresses heap up one from behind the other, all prolonged and all at different levels, until the last one, '-ure', is held into the blue distance, like the recession of horizons behind horizons on the Pennine moorland being described.

Postscript

In English, Hopkins traced 'sprung rhythm' back to 'the Old English verse found in *Pierce Ploughman* (sic)'. The technical form of this poetry was brought into Britain by that pre-Conquest mingling of warrior peoples originating in Germany and Scandinavia. Their two-part, alliterative accentual line served as a spinal column for the poetic organism that evolved among those interbreeding strains, finally emerging into the Middle English of Langland's *Piers Plowman* and *Gawain and the Green Knight*. The political aspect of this well-known genealogy has a bearing on the social/cultural problem confronted both by Coleridge, in his introductory note to 'Christabel', and by Hopkins.

By the time *Piers Plowman* and *Gawain* were composed, in the fourteenth century, this tradition had become the poetry of the people – variously imprinted by the dialects of the provinces. At that moment, with a single body of work, Chaucer (Langland's contemporary) revealed that it was not the poetry of the Court.

The King's Court, with its baronial aristocracy, held a peculiar position in England. Even after three hundred years, it still regarded itself, to some degree, as an army of occupation, racially distinct, centred on its defensive castles, still claiming rights to its ancestral possessions in France, still maintaining a primary allegiance to French and Continental culture, and still, most important of all, speaking the language of superior status, the vocal code of the social and political ascendancy.

It is tempting to speculate about the effects, on England's poetic culture, of that vocal code of superior status. Presumably French lasted so long as the Court language (into the sixteenth century, for some uses) at least partly because it provided such a convenient form of this code, instantly brandished in every confrontation – the voice of the Conqueror's occupying army.

When the Court began to speak English, we can be sure that the one thing they hung on to, the one 'trick of the voice' they made sure was not lost in the shift from Court French to Court English, was that code of superior status. The mode of speaking the new Court

English had to announce, somehow, as ringingly as the French had done, that the speaker was not one of those defeated and subject tribal villeins who spoke their own strange Babel of English (Germanic) dialects. It had to announce, without any possibility of a mistake, that this was the 'King's English'. If this happened, then the new, masterfully asserted 'King's English' was the one dialect of English that had to display, as its most pronounced and obvious characteristic, that it did not derive from any corner of Englishness. And something of the sort must have happened. It is unimaginable that any human group, in the same situation of power, at such a precarious moment of rapprochement, would not have done the same.

Chaucer was the sensitive underside of these courtiers. He divined the human richness of this new double world coming to consciousness in a single language – probably because he belonged to both sides. His innovation was to naturalize in an English poetry the up-to-this-point alien culture of the Court class. He did it by transposing those French and Italian verse forms together with the wealth of Renaissance and Romance culture on which they drew, into the Court's simplified new English, for the Courtiers among whom he lived. Immediately they recognized their own authentic poetry. And recognized that it was as distinct from native English poetry, in temper, music, and spirit, as their new 'King's English' was from old native English speech.

At a single stroke, Chaucer had ejected the 'rum, ram, ruff' of the native alliterative ('sprung rhythm') tradition from the high culture. His voluminous, popular, utterly new work had established, in its place, the rule of Italian/French strictly metrical, iambic, rhymed verse as the poetic tradition of the new 'King's English'.

He would not be the miracle of Chaucer if he had succeeded in reproducing the smooth, metrical regularity of his continental models. But since subsequent history confirmed Chaucer's cultural *coup*, and since the victors write history as their own, it is not surprising that this moment is celebrated as 'the dawn of English poetry'. It was perhaps something of a red dawn. If there is a Civil War within English poetry, perhaps it opened here, where Chaucer's

[367]

marvellous oeuvre laid down the front line of battle along which the metrical, disciplined squares of the 'King's English' would ever after – sometimes successfully, sometimes not – defend it against the resurgent 'sprung rhythms' of the tribes. And maybe the confusions of this sporadic war have been compounded by that other civil conflict, referred to above, which opened along roughly the same lines at the same time, within English ways of speaking English. One has to suppose there must have been some such very definite historical genesis for such a War, if only because it is still being waged so vigorously, and still under such distinct banners, in Scotland, Wales, and Northern Ireland as well as in England, devastating the British like no other nation.

To see the full irony of this Battle of the Metrical Forms and this intertangled Battle of the Modes of Speech, in Britain, you have to be Welsh, Scots or Irish. You have to be one of those, that is, who failed, in successive defeats, to stop the Anglo-Saxon, the Scandinavian and finally the Norman invaders stealing the country from beneath them. Just as Chaucer's rhymed iambics displaced the Germanic alliterative sprung rhythm, so that long clangorous line had in turn displaced the verse forms of the indigenous Celtic peoples, who held in common one of the most evolved and sophisticated poetic traditions in world history.

Perhaps the chronic war between the new Chaucerian and the Old English tradition was able to continue, with occasional flare-ups, through the following centuries, for a simple reason. On the one hand, the class which inherited and constantly reasserted the Military Occupation's governing role, and with it that speech code of superior status, also constantly re-enforced the rule of strict metrical forms, which went on consolidating itself as a poetic tradition founded in the court-centred 'high' culture. On the other hand, though the Old English poetic tradition degenerated to stunted popular rhymes, the innate music of its 'sprung rhythm' survived and multiplied, underground, like a nationalist army of guerrillas, in the regional dialects of common speech. Yet in some ways, the older Celtic traditions survived more intact and resilient than either. For one thing, the actual nations survived, separate but attached, concentrated in isolation, like powerfully active glands, secreting the genetic remnants of a poetic caste selectively bred perhaps through millennia. The different languages also survived, with the relics of their unique poetic traditions still sacred.* When we speak of Chaucer as the 'fountain undefiled' of English poetry's delicacy, or of Beowulf as the buried reservoir of English poetry's strength, we are probably glossing over the fact that these two have spent so much of their time, to change the metaphor, like male and female spiders, trying to avoid or paralyse each other, and that the good moments have come only where they have managed an electrified, always precarious coupling. But we are certainly overlooking the fact that without the enveloping, nurturing Celtic matrix, English poetry would be unrecognizably different and vastly deprived.

The fluctuating relationship between the two foreground contenders follows the graph of English poetry throughout its history quite closely. For various reasons, the Celtic presence is usually to be found supporting the old English, and as time passes becomes less and less separable from it. The fortunes of the relationship, in fact, make a curious cartoonish scenario, if it can be viewed as a marriage, in which the old or unorthodox tradition is the bride and the new, metrically strict orthodox tradition the groom.

The honeymoon, where each is conceding tenderly to the other in great love, though the groom is in adored control, would be Chaucer. With Wyatt come the first difficulties: the first spats – aphrodisiac but spats – where she begins to demand her way (wants to run off with the king himself) while he wrestles to control her. His sudden severity, forcing her to obey, with a hard Reformation face, would be Surrey, alias Tottel. His remorse, fearing that he might have crushed her spirit, remembering her voluptuous passion, wooing her afresh, trying every device, pleading in vain, would be Sidney. Then she erupts, love-mad, imperious, dazzling, tempestuous, alarming, while he fights to subdue her, in Marlowe and early Shakespeare. The marriage becomes uncontrollable: his more and

* The notoriously arduous poetic colleges of the old Celtic world were still active well into the seventeenth century. The last fully-trained Gaelic *fili* died as recently as the 1720s, one on South Uist, another on the Isle of Skye.

more desperate attempts to regain control are simply shattered by her astonished rage, or her vengeful fury, as she overwhelms him, drags him by the hair, storms through the house smashing things at every interruption, remembering every tiniest slight a million times magnified – till he fears for his sanity: middle Shakespeare. While he dotes in second childhood fondness on their daughter, she becomes a Sycorax, joins a coven, sleeps in her coffin to terrorize him etc.: late Shakespeare and Webster. Next, the lugubrious phase, they live in the same house but separated: this is Milton. From his bedroom resounds the martial-domestic organ-toned doctrine and discipline of puritan wedlock, drowning out the last lamentings that emerge from hers (in which he has walled her up).

What followed then was a historical accident, but it completed, with a kind of inevitability, the seemingly final collapse of this marriage. At his Restoration (1660), returning from his fourteen years of exile at the French Court, the half-French, French-educated Boileau-smitten Charles II established in England a Court culture that became instantly the only culture and that was in all respects, except for its actual language, French: values, manners, taste, ideals, forms, all French, and the more exclusively so by Charles's understandable revulsion from the English tradition (specifically from the Anglo-Saxon tradition, as idealized and politicized by Milton) that had abolished Monarchy and beheaded his father. This new Court culture, which became overnight the politically correct culture, enforced, like a divorce decree, the use of the Boileau-style rhymed couplet as the ultimate poetic form of 'the King's English'. On that date, the old tradition, the now wretched and demoralized wife, was divorced, deprived of all access to the property that had once been wholly hers, and kicked out of polite literature. She fell into the gutter and survived in a fashion, thereafter, as Hopkins noted, only among Broadsheet Ballads, folk-rhymes and the like. Her pleas, her very voice, had become inaudible to the orthodoxy behind the high windows. Dryden, Pope, Swift, Johnson, sought her out in dark alleys and on back stairs, stroked her hair and gave her money and told nobody.

A slight disturbance occurred with Smart, who broke out of his madhouse fetters – the couplet again – picked her out of the street and worshipped her as the mother of God. After that, the couplet, in its court livery, policed the highways, though her confidence was returning and she was giving the glad eye openly here and there, and even ran off with young Chatterton. Suddenly the shock wave of the French Revolution threw her simultaneously into the arms of Blake, Wordsworth and Coleridge. Unwithered by age, rejuvenated by excitement, she mustered a terrific effort to remind her estranged husband of everything. Staring at her through his three faces, he thought for a wild moment that yes he could make it work. Blake even re-invented a form of her old pre-Conquest verse, like the million gold threads of a gigantic, nostalgic love nest – though in fact he approached her in there with some terror. Coleridge, in the bridal chamber, giddy after a night of bliss and horror, hallucinated a cloven hoof on her blue-veined foot and hid his head in the Black Forest. Wordsworth begot a child on her then shut himself into a glass mountain. Burns alone rose to the occasion and accepted her terms, though the strain killed him. Shelley begot a Frankenstein android on her and drowned himself in delirium. Byron found her weeping at his door but could not take her seriously. The moment had passed. Iambics restored public calm. Keats trying to follow her back into mourning failed to return. Only Clare survived, wandering the countryside, calling her name, trudging the roads like Wordsworth's rejected, certified, lost youth, till the shades of the Northampton General Lunatic Asylum closed about him. Tennyson became the official mourner, over his nightly port. The orthodoxy resumed control of the highways so completely that when Hopkins heard:

> She is not dead:
> There lives the dearest freshness deep down things

and made a new attempt and even followed her, as he thought, through Wales into Ireland (as if his Catholicism itself were a lonely, forlorn, backtracking effort to locate the divorced, unheard-of or thought-to-be-defunct woman of the well-spring), his letters to her were as if written in invisible ink – or, if spelled out even to such a meticulous ear as Bridges's, unsayable. She could only get to him by candle-light, as a midnight, North-North-West mad nun, her finger to her lips.

1993

The Snake in the Oak

The Mythos of Coleridge's 'new principle' of Metre

Tho' Christianity is my *Passion*, it is too much my intellectual Passion:
& therefore will do me little good in the hour of temptation and calamity.
Coleridge, *Letters*

The Tree of Knowledge, from a fifteenth-century Swiss manuscript

Introductory Note

In the Essay 'Myths, Metres, Rhythms', I set Coleridge's 'new principle' of metre within an 'unorthodox' tradition of English prosody, where it conformed to a particular, well-established set of laws (unorthodox, but laws) for manipulating stressed and unstressed syllables throughout the verse line. In that sense, his 'new principle' was far from new, and he was neither introducing a novelty, as he supposed, nor indulging himself in Germanic and wilful caprice, of which he was accused. He was merely reviving, after a 150 year gap, a native mode of verse rhythm, characterized by distinct, objective features, easily identifiable whether in a nursery rhyme or in Shakespeare.

At the same time he was obviously aware, with an intensity that blinded him to the precedents in earlier verse, that his 'new principle' had emerged from a subjective compulsion to search out, within himself, a *new* rhythm – as if the release of what he had to give depended absolutely on his finding that inner 'fountain'* of his own music.

I mentioned that behind the designation 'unorthodoxy', in all the poets who belong to that tradition, there lurks an insistent, peculiar subjective factor – an instinctive attempt to include the experience that orthodoxy excludes, a spontaneous effort to find direct expression for balanced wholeness of being (within which orthodoxy is merely one role among the interplay of many). As I suggested, the contingency of England's political and social history has divided and apportioned the poetic bent of the soul in just that way, between the orthodox and unorthodox traditions of metrical forms. As far as poetry goes, I simplified the division in a rough

---

* Claiming his 'new principle' of metre as his own invention, and anticipating the charge that he must have copied it from somewhere, in particular from Walter Scott and Byron (who had in fact copied it from him), he wrote, in the 1816 Preface to 'Christabel': 'For there is amongst us a set of critics, who seem to hold, that every possible thought and image is traditional; who have no notion that there are such things as fountains in the world, small as well as great; and who would therefore charitably derive every rill they behold flowing from a perforation made in some other man's tank.'

metaphor about a difficult marriage, where the 'unorthodox' finds itself cast, inevitably, as the turbulent woman.

Even in the most literal sense, this woman does tend to appear, as such, in the works of the distinctive authors of the 'unorthodox' tradition. She is presented either as a real woman, central to the author's life; or in some larger symbolic role; or as a blend of both. In Wyatt, one can find her as a real woman with a very particular personality. In Donne, the undefined women of his love poems are foreground to his deeper struggle with the Great Female – his early Catholicism.*

In Shakespeare, the particular woman of the *Sonnets* is the foreground to the Great Female Catholicism, who is again foreground to the Greater Female of Paganism resurgent.

What the English church could call Paganism resurgent (rejected or pursued – i.e. prohibited or passionately courted and if possible embraced) has been the dominant theme of European poetry ever since. A curious twin, perhaps, to what the Church calls Godless Science.

In that lineage, Coleridge obviously holds a special place.

This following piece grew out of a remark (in that essay on 'Myths, Metres, Rhythms', cf. page 332) about the unity of Coleridge's three visionary poems. Here I go a little deeper and argue that the three poems together make a single myth, which is also, as a poet's myths always are, (among other things) a projected symbolic self-portrait of the poet's own deepest psychological make-up. Coleridge formulates his myth with extraordinary clarity, coherence, consistency, and with such simplicity that it delivers the full, massive immediacy of the psychobiological event.

It is the myth of what made him a poet. In that sense, it is specifically the 'creation myth' of his unique music – of the use to which he puts his 'new principle', in fact. It is the myth, likewise, of what destroyed him.

At the same time, given his mind, his curiosity and his reading, it

* Donne's Lament for her 'death' – the Virgin Mary's death – can be read (as Ben Jonson half-divined) into the two extraordinary Anniversary Elegies on the death of the 'virgin' Elizabeth Drury.

crystallized out of traditional materials and so became the representative myth of a conflict between certain traditions – religious and
intellectual – in which Coleridge was a casualty, and perhaps a
martyr.

The point I wish to make in this preamble is that though I call the
three poems in question a three act tragic opera, with overture and
interludes, Coleridge presents them as one map. In other words, the
symbolic world of the three poems has a pictorial simultaneity. The
whole thing is there from the first moment, in 'Kubla Khan' – even in
the opening five lines of 'Kubla Khan'. The three poems resemble a
triple exposure photograph of the same person, the second shot
made after zooming in much closer, and the third much closer again.

To describe this gradual poem by poem development of the
symbolic map would be straightforward. Once Coleridge's main
symbols have been identified, and their place and function in his
double nature grasped, everything unfolds like the plot of a play,
with the various characters (the symbols and symbolic figures)
coming and going, interacting, changing, revealing more of their
true nature, as they work out Coleridge's fate. To present that
simultaneity of the three exposures, however, is slightly more
complicated – or rather, it must make some extra demand on the
patience of the reader. But if it does, the initial demand is no more
than we expect from the opening scenes of a play, where the
characters are fully present but still mysterious, moving in all their
vigour and yet divulging little of what their significance will be in the
play's completed action. The presence of a great reptile, for example,
in the first scene, would only be explained bit by bit through the
whole play. Our testy demand for instant, full explanation – of every
point as it appears – has to be suspended. The following exploration
of Coleridge's visionary map requires a similar approach.

1 Two Selves

Coleridge was two people. From childhood, throughout life, he had
the occasional feeling that he was a 'hive of selves'. But mainly he
was aware of being two. 'Who that thus lives with a continually-

divided Being can remain healthy?' he cried, in a Notebook entry of 1805. Twenty years later, he identified the two selves precisely:

Ah, but even in boyhood there was a cold hollow spot, an aching in the heart, when I said my prayers – that prevented my entire union with God – that I could not give up, or that would not give me up – as if a snake had wreathed around my heart, & at this one spot its mouth touched at & inbreathed a weak incapability of willing it away . . . that spot in my heart [is] even my remaining and unleavened *Self* – all else the Love of Christ in and thro' Christ's love of me.

The Christian Self was the one he wanted to be – from the time he was the youngest child of the Vicar (and Headmaster) of Ottery St Mary, to the time he was the ferociously eloquent and informed eight-year-old prodigy, to the time he all but accepted the salaried post of Unitarian preacher in Shrewsbury (in the middle of writing 'The Ancient Mariner'), to the times he increasingly filled his published writing, Notebooks and letters with his Christian pre-occupations: increasingly and intensifyingly Christian-Philosophical up to the day of his death. One Christian Self.

On the other hand – that 'unleavened *Self*'. What happened to him? Lying there, immune to Christ's love under the kiss of the serpent – refusing to pray or take any part in the Christian Coleridge's efforts to speak, as Wordsworth did (or as Wordsworth almost did), with 'the language of the whole man'. There in the pious boy. Still there in the fifty-three-year-old Christian ruins of a man.

What was he up to all those years?

'The unleavened *Self*', refusing to have anything to do with Christianity or its moralizing intelligence, wrapped with a great snake, who constantly kissed him.

Two selves.

11 Susceptible Coleridge

Coleridge was besotted with woman. At the same time, few can have so specialized in such terrifying nightmares about such terrifying women. He said he had been his mother's darling. Perhaps he had. The baby of the family – the last of ten. Somehow, very early, he made the connection: woman is the source of all bliss, all love, all consolation. Then everything went wrong. Fighting for mother's exclusive love against seven brothers, he lost. He curled up in the window seat, behind his books, like Eliot's *animula*, and became what also fascinated him, a terrible *Upas Tree* – a logomanic moralist withering every other leaf and sprout within reach.

Very likely, most likely, for a while he truly had been his mother's baby darling. But soon, and from the evidence quite soon, she had to defend his brothers against his intellectual weaponry. In that battle for her exclusive love, which he could not possibly win, he found her repeatedly on their side. One can imagine the schizogenic plot, that he had to live through, on their crowded little rectory stage.

When his beloved father died, STC being only ten, his mother sent him off to the monastic garrison of Christ's Hospital – from which, it seems, he was allowed to return to her bosom only three or four times in the rest of his school days. During this period he shifted his passionate dependence onto his sister, Anne – who then died, after a long illness, just before he left school for university. Later on, to one half-affectionate woman or another, he would say his mother never gave him any feeling of what it was to have a mother. When she died, he neither attended her funeral nor even wrote home (where his eldest brother George had succeeded their father as Vicar).

In his early twenties, the pattern recurred. He lost his first love Mary who seems, at least in his anguished retrospect, to have supplied all his supercharged emotional and erotic needs. But then he let Southey force him (that is how Coleridge himself felt about it, later) into marrying a girl of religious family – his first Sarah. He came to regard his betrothal to her as the worst 'crime' of his life – against her and against himself. Euphoric self-deception, one of his greatest natural gifts, got him through the first two years. But who knows what he was like as a husband? When William and Dorothy Wordsworth rented a house close by, simply to be near him, his marriage began to chafe and suffer. While Sarah nursed baby Hartley, STC was off day and night with his new soul-mate, returning to rhapsodize to her about his new soul-mate's 'exquisite sister' – the new soul-mate he shared with his new soul-mate.

Coleridge does not seem to have blamed himself for Sarah's resentment, painful as he found it. But as a gallant and above all honourable fellow, a Christian of enthusiastic, sincere idealism, he kept renewing his efforts of happiness and affection with her. But what did they actually amount to? Opium, too, had entered his life.

And while Sarah waited sourly in the Nether Stowey cottage, what was the submarine and subterranean effect of Wordsworth's sister on her husband – out there under the moons of their mid-twenties, on the high downs over the deep romantic chasms of the Samuel Palmerish, magical, North Somerset Paradise, gazing across the Western Sea? Coleridge already worshipped Wordsworth, calling him the greatest man he had ever met and the greatest living poet. And here was the brilliant, untamed, woodland spirit, with her ethereal nerves, the 'nymph' of the source of Wordsworth's great river, the rapturous sybil of the oracle, the deeply disturbed and disturbing Dorothy.

His mother had sunk into the underground sea. His first love and any other sirens had slid away down the icy caves. This incandescent, twenty-six-year-old spinster – described as 'wild' and 'gypsy' – a moon doomed to the wane, love-sick for everything, for Pan in fact, must have been herself something of a drug, for Coleridge, at that time. She certainly had her effect, probably more by what she evoked than by what she could ever fulfil in person. He dutifully preached on Sundays, but every night of the weekday, according to the poems he was writing, he dreamed a very different life – as if he had subconsciously emigrated following his great plan, and had indeed set up his Pantisocratic Paradise (but internally) in the American wilderness, with the aboriginal tribes, on some such half-Goddess of a river as the Susquehanna (he had picked that river purely for the name), among the bellowing of rutting alligators which he had read about in Purchas's account of his travels in the Carolinas (and had duly noted at some length). Somewhere in his imagination, the long-pondered Constitution of Pantisocracy, the ideal society of philosophers, had fallen to pieces, but like a rich humus – i.e. the wild life under it, the 'slimy things with legs' lashed into new vigour, new wild hope in the dark. Apparently, briefly.

III A Glimpse of the Oak

Wherever he went, Coleridge's overpowering eloquence, what he himself described as the 'velocity' and 'music' of his thought, the voluminous sweep of his torrential ideas, the sheer energy of his mind, became a legend.

At the same time, in his sense of himself he was acutely aware of what he repeatedly referred to as '*an absence of Strength*'. He formulated this idea in all kinds of ways:

My strength is so small in proportion to my Power – I believe, that I first from internal feeling made or gave light and impulse to this important distinction, between Strength & Power – the Oak, and the tropic Annual or Biennial, which grows nearly as high & spreads as large, as the Oak – but the wood, the heart of *Oak*, is wanting – the *vital* works vehemently but the Immortal is not with it. (Notebook)

Just as obsessive as the idea was that image he had found for *Strength* – the Oak Tree.

The Oak Tree, he felt, was missing.

This notion of missing strength was tightly connected to another. What his audience saw as a spectacular aerobatic display of mental activity and language Coleridge himself saw, from the inside, as a fearful escape from something. Again, this notion obsessed him. It came to be part of the constant supervision he kept over all his mental processes – a woeful almost incessant commentary on his exalted facility of intellectual analysis and verbal expression.

. . . my eloquence was most commonly excited by the desire of running away & hiding myself from my personal and inward feelings, and not for the expression of them, while doubtless this very effort gave a passion and glow to my thoughts. (Notebook)

His perpetual dismay and, often, distress over this particular failing was a permanent emergency, lucid and minutely watchful. He simply accepted that the intellectual self, in his case, had evolved as an escape capsule of some kind, forever scrambling clear of the perilous gulf of his feelings, and soaring somewhere above. Nobody could have studied the escapology of this reflex as fascinatedly as he did. After the first great collapse of his hopes (about 1800, coinciding with Wordsworth's rejection of 'Christabel' from the second edition of *Lyrical Ballads*) he began to detect it in every cerebral flicker:

why do I always turn away from any interesting Thought to do something uninteresting? . . . is it a cowardice of all deep Feeling, even though pleasurable? (Notebook)

One could collect a small anthology of his comments about just this. They exhale from his constant sense of the misery of it – the encroaching devastations of it.

Yet it is this escape capsule that he lives in, writes all his journalism from, talks to friends, guests and strangers from, sends up his pyrotechnic monologues from, lectures and preaches from, moralizes from and prays in – that he identifies himself with publicly, privately, spontaneously, completely. This fleeing self. And it is this self that lacks *Strength*.

That lacks, in his words, the Oak.

Hence his constant efforts to attach himself to some substitute for this missing Oak Tree: 'My nature needs another nature for its support'. In all his relationships, he was aware of this secret motive and need.

Yet he never seems to have entertained the thought (which nowadays would occur to such a person automatically) that the Oak could be growing well, and the Strength could be deeply rooted, in that very part of himself which he feared so much. And that he lacked it only because it was precisely what he fled from. Perhaps the burning fiery furnace of evermore anguished feeling, which he hadn't the courage (as he admitted) to enter (his 'cowardice of all deep feeling') – perhaps that was the Oak itself in torment. This never seems to have struck him as a possibility. Yet this is evidently what it was. For a very short period, just the one period in his whole life, through the first months of his friendship with Dorothy and William, from the autumn of 1797 to early summer 1798, he was able to confront those feelings and deal with them in their own terms. The result was the three visionary poems. His visionary poetry, as it turned out, was simply this: the language and concentrated, easy courage of mind that could explore, analyse and express the world of his Unleavened Self, of the Snake, of those feelings difficult to face. In that case, if the symbolism of his Unleavened Self were consistent, one could expect to find this visionary poetry centred, something like the cosmology of Norse myth (and something like the inner world common to many Shamanic traditions)* on that great tree – specifically the Oak. And also, on the Snake.

Through what follows I hope to demonstrate how completely this expectation is fulfilled – in covert form in 'Kubla Khan', openly in the two great narratives, 'The Rime of the Ancient Mariner' and 'Christabel'.

Perhaps one could say, what he had fled from in his earliest days was the tortured tree of feelings that his fixation on his mother had become. As if he had internalized her as the original dragonish Oak. His Strength, grown from her first love, had become his Terror. One can imagine, if she could have assured him of her exclusive,

---

* The great axis of the nine worlds of Norse cosmology was *Yggdrasill*, usually described as a cosmic Ash Tree. In almost all shamanic traditions, the tree is somehow central – as the spine common to both this world and the other, or to an upper world, a middle world and a lower world. The concept survives in major religions. Odin, the Norse Allfather, hangs on Yggdrasill for nine nights, a spear through his side, in shamanic communication with the Giver of Spiritual Gifts, according to his own song:

> I hung in the windshaken tree
> Nine long nights I hung there
> Pierced with a spear
> An offering to Odin
> Myself to myself –

which made Christ a familiar figure to the Norsemen. A rich account of the Tree in shamanism can be found in Eliade's *Shamanism* (details on p. 58). The tight relationship between the Tree and the Serpent (and the Woman) is basic to the old symbolic representations of Goddess Religion in Pre-Christian tradition: a general account can be found in Joseph Campbell's *Masks of God* volumes (Secker & Warburg).

unreserved love, the Oak itself would have seemed to lift him, fearless, into its arms and supportive strength. To re-enter the world of the Oak, and re-unite himself with it, he needed the Oak's Strength. In other words, what he required in his adult life, and what he knew he required above all else, was not merely 'another nature' for the support of his own, but a substitute for her assured love. The assured love of friends, but most of all the assured love of a loved woman. This love would be like the Oak transformed. In one place he actually writes:

Why is love like an Oak-tree? 1. The myriad roots with the one tap-root deep down as branches high / Earth & Heaven – the present growth still consolidating into the entire trunk – the Nest – the shelter – the leaves pushed off only by the new growth. (Notebook)

And for those few months, that mutual infatuation between himself and his revered Wordsworth and the beloved yet untouchable Dorothy somehow supplied his need. Like spiritual parents (Wordsworth automatically took the paternal role, eldest of five orphan brothers and originally intended for the Church), this brother and sister somehow recreated, for Coleridge, in a precarious yet effective way, the primal, unfallen bliss – the 'Nest' in the Oak, where infinite creative courage and acceptance of every truth about himself right back to the womb became child's play.

But the moment passed quickly. The signs are that this 'Nest' was falling to pieces by early summer of 1798. Coleridge records that he and Wordsworth are beginning to find their 'data dissimilar'. As the lease on the Wordsworth's rented house approached its end, inevitably new plans formed. The first edition of *Lyrical Ballads* was completed and off to the printer. With its publication ahead, new adventures opened like a vista. A tour into Germany, the study of German philosophy, beckoned like the next expansive phase of their brilliant, combined advance. As if the seclusion of the last year had been mere preparation. But the circle was obviously broken. Their love-feast of what Dorothy called 'three bodies with one soul' seemed hardly begun, and several years of their now habitual mutual dependence (with passionate episodes) were still to come. But as far as Coleridge's real needs were concerned, in retrospect one can see it was over. Subtle but radical incompatibilities between the two poets, that had been smothered up to now, were waiting only for the public reaction to *Lyrical Ballads*. Then they would be exposed as treacherous reefs. Also, by the time the three of them next came together, in Cumberland, hoping to renew their magic power-circle, Coleridge would be struggling with a new passion. The great love of his life, the second Sara, the sister of Wordsworth's future wife, would be on the scene. And though Coleridge would entertain, for a while, ecstatic dreams of a new 'Nest' in the Oak with this new Sara, there was no practical way in which it could ever happen. Very soon those new hopes would be converted to new, unprecedented agonies, pouring into the awakened terrors of his 'personal and inward feelings' like burning pitch.

Meanwhile that provisional Somersetshire Oak, which had so flourished under the love and husbandry of William and Dorothy, and had given him the nerve to seize the visionary poems, had painfully 'gone'. The actual felling of this particular Oak, the Oak of his inspired months, occurred in 1800 when Wordsworth rejected the completed 'Christabel', and in a note to the second edition of *Lyrical Ballads* dissociated himself from 'The Ancient Mariner' with words that demolished Coleridge's poetic ambitions as well as the poem. After that, Coleridge hesitated to think of himself as capable of writing poetry. 'The poet is dead in me', he wrote a little later, and he meant it. That alternative world of his visionary poetry, which he had penetrated with such difficulty (and so flukishly), had closed again. Or rather, had once again become too terrible to face. When that substitute Oak was felled by Wordsworth's decision and remorseless words, it too toppled into the old internal conflagration, a Burning Oak tossed into a Burning Oak, with such an explosion that Coleridge simply fled. He soared into stratospheric safety (this time for good):

Poetry is out of the question. The attempt would only hurry me into that sphere of acute feeling from which abstruse research, the mother of self-oblivion, presents an asylum.

From this time onwards, for the next few years, extreme images settle onto the pages of his notebooks, here and there, in smouldering isolation, like sparks from those very flames. Either as a poetic idea:

Devil at the icy end of Hell warming himself at the reflection of the fires on the ice.

Or as a sudden, exclamatory cry:

Were I Achilles, I would have cut my leg off to get rid of my vulnerable heel.

Or (perhaps even more startling) as a mad paradox (unwittingly just as self-revealing):

To be sure, some good may be imagined in any evil, – as he whose house is on fire on a dark night, his Loss gives him light to run away –

Or plain self description:

To lie in ease yet dull anxiety for hours, afraid to think a thought, lest some thought of anguish should shoot a pain athwart my body, afraid even to turn my body, lest the very bodily motion should induce a train of painful thoughts –

The madness of all that mutilated feeling was the Medusa writhing of the incendiary Oak – the terrifying Hydra of the Oak. It pursued him as a gargoylish woman, a metamorphic dragonish hag into those extraordinary nightmares that made his sleep, quite regularly, nights of screams. These screaming nights of his were also legendary, among his acquaintances. A jotted Note for a poem gives a glimpse of what his poetic visionary mythos had become by 1806: 'Death first of all – eats of the Tree of Life / & becomes immortal describe the frightful Metamorphosis / weds the Hamadryad of the Tree / their progeny – in the manner of Dante / –'. But the strength to face and write it was long past.

Much later in his life, towards the end, when the erotic uproar was almost entirely sublimated into his Christian obsessional preoccupation – then once again that divine missing *Strength*, the missing love of his Creatress, of the creative power itself, hovered before him, still inaccessible:

Elohim = Robora, the Strengths, connected with the image and notion of the TRUNK of an Oak.

Elohim means the earliest Jehovah – Jehovah as the 'Lord of Hosts' and Creator of the Universe. The Jehovah of Job as distinct from the later Jehovah of Mercy and Forgiveness. In other words, the term signifies the Jehovah who took over the nature and attributes (in all but sex) of the Great Goddess.* Biblical descriptions of some of His acts reproduce almost verbatim earlier descriptions of the same acts performed by the Great Goddess – Anatha (cf. page 429). The word *Elohim* specifically incorporates, therefore, the Powers of the Great Goddess as suppressed under the name of Jehovah – as in the combination *Yahweh Elohim*. To a degree, then, *Elohim* is 'that other God' who is 'greater than Jehovah' (cf. page 419), and who turns out to be, in Coleridge's visionary poetic mythos, 'the great, nameless Female' (cf. page 415), who just as she did in Pre-Jehovan Israel inhabits, like a Hamadryad,† the Tree.

The Oak.

This is how it continued to appear to Coleridge's rootless, wind-carried, torrent-hurried, self-anaesthetized bubble of an intellectual, Christian, fugitive Self. In his own words.

IV The Tragic Opera

The three visionary poems, which came in a hurried sequence, can be read as a single work, a grand opera. 'Kubla Khan' is like the Overture and a brief Act I.

---

* This Great Goddess incorporates fish and serpent. Moses's magical power (as in his staff) was serpent power. His brazen serpent (*Numbers* 21: 8–9), that healed any bitten by a snake who looked at it, and was worshipped with burnt offerings, hung in the Temple up to Hezekiah's reformation in the seventh century BC. Jehovah was depicted with snake legs (on amulets) up to the second century BC.

† '(1) *Mythological*: A wood-nymph fabled to live and die in the tree she inhabited. (2a): *Zoological*: A large, very venomous hooded serpent of India . . . allied to the Cobra. (2b): A large baboon of Abyssinia.' *OED*. The Hamadryad was to the tree what the more familiar Naiad was to the stream: a tutelary spirit – i.e. a supernatural attendant protector.

The Snake in the Oak

Kubla Khan

In Xanadu did Kubla Khan
A stately pleasure-dome decree:
Where Alph, the sacred river, ran
Through caverns measureless to man
   Down to a sunless sea.
So twice five miles of fertile ground
With walls and towers were girdled round:
And there were gardens bright with sinuous rills,
Where blossomed many an incense-bearing tree;
And here were forests ancient as the hills,
Enfolding sunny spots of greenery.

But oh! that deep romantic chasm which slanted
Down the green hill athwart a cedarn cover!
A savage place! as holy and enchanted
As e'er beneath a waning moon was haunted
By woman wailing for her demon-lover!
And from this chasm, with ceaseless turmoil seething,
As if this earth in fast thick pants were breathing,
A mighty fountain momently was forced:
Amid whose swift half-intermitted burst
Huge fragments vaulted like rebounding hail,
Or chaffy grain beneath the thresher's flail:
And 'mid these dancing rocks at once and ever
It flung up momently the sacred river.
Five miles meandering with a mazy motion
Through wood and dale the sacred river ran,
Then reached the caverns measureless to man,
And sank in tumult to a lifeless ocean:
And 'mid this tumult Kubla heard from far
Ancestral voices prophesying war!

   The shadow of the dome of pleasure
   Floated midway on the waves;

Where was heard the mingled measure
From the fountain and the caves.
It was a miracle of rare device,
A sunny pleasure-dome with caves of ice!

A damsel with a dulcimer
In a vision once I saw:
It was an Abyssinian maid,
And on her dulcimer she played,
Singing of Mount Abora.
Could I revive within me
Her symphony and song,
To such a deep delight 'twould win me,
That with music loud and long,
I would build that dome in air,
That sunny dome! those caves of ice!
And all who heard should see them there,
And all should cry, Beware! Beware!
His flashing eyes, his floating hair!
Weave a circle round him thrice,
And close your eyes with holy dread,
For he on honey-dew hath fed,
And drunk the milk of Paradise.

The Overture states the situation and the themes, in simplified symbolic form, ending with the line:

A sunny pleasure-dome with caves of ice!

The rest of the poem, from the line:

A damsel with a dulcimer

to the end, constitutes Act I. 'The Ancient Mariner' then follows as Act II. 'Christabel' Part I brings the drama to an end as Act III. Two other poems are germane to the single plot of these three works. One is 'The Wanderings of Cain', which functions both as an Invocation to the whole Opera and a mini-overture to Act II. The other is 'The

Ballad of the Dark Ladie', which functions as a mini-overture to Act III and as a bridging passage between Acts II and III.

In the context of this drama the Overture presents a tentative resolution – a truce proposed in trance – of the deadly conflict between Coleridge's two selves. I say 'deadly', considering what the real outcome for Coleridge was to be – which he will describe as 'cutting my own throat', and which he will endure for a lifetime thereafter as an increasingly 'Christian puritan' deadness to the life of the body, of the Oak, and of poetry.

But in Kubla's Paradise, as in a Mandala, the antagonisms are suspended in a pattern of co-existence. This symmetry of polarities within the poem has received plenty of comment. Perhaps the most important one is invisible – as will appear later.

The intellectual aspect of Coleridge's usually dominant Self is manifest in the imperial magnificence of Kubla's pleasure gardens, where everything flourishes, both the perfectly ordered and the utterly wild, under his benign and delighting contemplative super-vision – as if this might be a microcosm of his realm. Within this enchanted (as in an opium-trance) consciousness, even the Unleavened Self is permitted to live out its true nature, gratifying its elemental needs. Or at least, it looks as if that is what is going to be permitted. The poem is like the stage ready for action, all but empty of dramatis personae. The sole human presence, as the curtain rises on the gorgeous scenery, is the woman wailing for her demon lover. But her actuality is conjectural, ambiguous: syntactically she is both there and not there. And in any case the lover for whom she wails has not yet arrived.

Nevertheless, her 'savage place', her love-tryst 'deep romantic chasm', is the spectacular centre-piece of Kubla's paradise gardens, as if he might stroll out along the high terraces with his courtly guests, so that all might be thrilled, in the moonlight, by his preternatural menagerie – this woman's tigerish love-making with a demon in the abyss of the thunderous geyser, while the whole paradise resounds to music produced by natural riverine instruments.

As I say, the Overture presents all this as a joy proposed. It offers the possibility which throughout Acts I, II and III Coleridge will explore, in his doomed attempt to integrate, in some scheme of co-existence, his Christian and Unleavened Selves.

In this Overture the possibility seems to be real (albeit envisioned in trance). But as this first section comes to a close, with rumblings of the action about to begin, the reality intrudes, like thunder in the offing. The ominous lines:

> Kubla heard from far
> Ancestral voices prophesying war!

awaken this dream to the voices of a quarrel that insists on being real and refuses to be resolved or appeased. In the context of the three poems and of this crisis in Coleridge's life, the 'ancestral voices' opposed in war (both historically and psychologically) are those arising from Protestant Christian belief on the one side and those arising from the chthonic and biological energies of Pagan vision on the other. They are the voices of his two selves, now drawing up for the decisive last battle, or rather for the last three engagements of the last battle, which the three poems will enact.

The three Acts are also variations on a single theme: the Female's 'call' to the Unleavened Self and the Christian Self's attempt to reject it. But the intensification, and progressive magnification into close-up, from poem to poem, amounts to a linear dramatic development from beginning to end. The drama is not over, the tragedy not complete, until Coleridge abandons the struggle to undo his Unleavened Self's willing surrender to the 'call' and physically flees – into Germany where the hyperactivated aura of his Christian/intellectual self can protect him, abandoning the Oak, leaving it to burn or smoulder away in agony for the rest of his life.

In the introductory note to these speculations about the unity of the three poems, I suggested that in fact they make a single myth – the myth dramatized in the Three Act Tragic Opera. I further suggested that this myth could be called the Creation Myth of Coleridge's 'new principle' of metre – of the 'music' that he finally delivered in 'Christabel'. Looking broadly at the three poems in which, step by step, this music emerges, a common feature sticks

out. Once the poet's two selves have been distinguished and roughly
identified, it is clear that each poem revolves around the otherworld
female. This semi-supernatural figure modulates from the love-sick
mesmeric bringer of ecstatic joys in the Overture and First Act, to the
deathly triumphant evil in the Second Act, to the sexually irresistible
demon in the Third Act. Or at least these are the faces she seems to
present. In each poem this woman is directly, not to say violently,
opposed to the Christian values of the Intellectual Self.

But she is further complicated (or simplified, maybe) by one
consistent attribute. In her first manifestation, in 'Kubla Khan', she
is *the giver of the gift of divine and magical song* that can create an
Emperor's paradise in air. In her second manifestation, in 'The
Ancient Mariner', she is the giver of a terrifying/beautiful vision that
is simultaneously *the strange power of (hypnotic) speech* in which it
can be told. And in her third, she is the mesmeric *Lord of Utterance*.

In other words, whatever else she may be, this woman is the spirit
of the poet's own *incantatory language*. And Coleridge's Tragic
Opera — tragic for him and tragic for her — is at one level (not the
least important level) a dramatization of the naked mythos of this
'preternatural' figure. In this way, as I said earlier, it is the 'creation
myth' of his 'new principle' of metre (which was the primitive form
of Hopkins's 'sprung rhythm').

v To Paint Kubla Khan's Paradise

Looking at the paradise depicted in what I called the Overture, one
gets the impression of a great sphere, or perhaps an ovoid, broader
at the bottom.

The 'sunny pleasure dome', with its gardens, woods, and river
valley, is at the top. A little below, tucked in somewhat under the
dome, beneath a forested overhang, removed from the direct
sunlight that falls on the dome but mysteriously open to the moon, a
deep fold encloses the source of the river. These are the upward,
outward features, like the hair and splendid brow, with the spiritual
eyes, and beneath it the sensuous perhaps rather crude mouth, of an
exotic humpty dumpty.

At the bottom, and within the egg, the 'sunless sea' lies puddled and horribly cold.

From the underside of the dome-capped Paradise at the top, a mass of shaggy, long honeycombs of ice hangs downwards, inside the egg. The drainage system of the River Alph, filtering down through these ice-caves, lengthening them downwards, like icicles in a waterfall, pours into the deathly cold that radiates upwards from the freezing sea beneath. As if Kubla might descend through the basement of his pleasure dome into these caves, with the right tackle, and peer down through the ice-walls, or directly down through the flues, into the 'measureless' gulf.

A hydraulic system magically syphons renovated fluid up through certain of the caves from the infernal sea, geysers it violently out from the chasm beneath the pleasure dome, then lets it wander by gravity five miles down the river valley before it dives again through the ice-caves back into the interior and the lifeless ocean below.

With more details, this could be the Indian Miniature painting of the physical appearance of the whole system.

The interest of the place, obviously, lies in the fact that there is more to it. It is a cartoon of Coleridge's psyche. And the river is the Alph. What is so special about the Alph?

Coleridge was a Devonshire boy (and never lost his Devonshire accent, any more than Wordsworth ever lost his Cumberland accent or Burns his Scots). If his grandfather's clan had marched on Exeter, from their high homelands immediately to the West, they would have come down the valley of a stream called the Alphin Brook. But he cannot have meant that.

The Alph is a 'sacred river'. In what way 'sacred'? And how is the 'savage' chasm, from which the Alph erupts so explosively, both 'holy' and 'enchanted'?

And who would that woman be anyway, down there in the dark – wailing for a 'demon lover'? From which pantheon would this 'demon' emerge? One assumes, in Kubla's garden he would not be a sulphurous, Christian, witch's sort of Sabbat Satan. He would be more Oriental, more of a 'god' in mortal disguise, an avatar of Shiva, or at least an unpredictable nocturnal deity, like Psyche's incognito visitant:* a *daemon*, like Socrates's Eros, rather than a *demon*.

Or a dionysiac, possessed man, perhaps. This was the line –

. . . Woman wailing for her demon lover –

that bowled Byron over, who then persuaded Coleridge (as if against his better judgement, according to Coleridge) to publish the poem (after keeping it unpublished for nineteen years).

Also, there is a mystery about the 'mingled measure' – which can only be music – which comes both from the caves (the ice-cave drainage system) and from the 'fountain' (that erupts 'half-intermitted' and makes rocks dance in air). How do they make music? What sort of music?

One thing is certain: any 'mingled measure' that accompanies the pleasures to be had under Kubla's dome must be equally delightful.

So what is this music? Or indeed, what sort of fountain and what sort of caves *make music*?

VI The Nightingale and the Nocturnal Dinosaur

In *The Road to Xanadu*, John Livingston Lowes dug back through Coleridge's Notebooks and known reading, excavating levels buried in the imagination behind 'Kubla Khan' and 'The Ancient Mariner'.

Poems of this kind can obviously never be explained. They are total symbols of psychic life. But they can be interpreted – a total symbol is above all a vessel for interpretations: the reader fills it and

---

* In Psyche's story, the 'latest born and loveliest vision far' on which Keats based his Ode, Psyche's jealous sisters persuade her that her lover, who visits only in the pitch dark and whom she has therefore never seen, is in fact a monstrous snake – rather as Coleridge himself was persuaded, about his visionary inspiration, by his orthodox contemporaries. (And as Lycius, in Keats' *Lamia*, was persuaded, about Lamia herself, by his friend the philosopher Apollonius.) When Psyche lit an oil lamp, to get a peek at her lover as he slept, she saw not a serpent but the great god Eros himself. A hot drop of oil from the lamp of critically sceptical examination fell on his shoulder, whereupon he awoke and instantly abandoned her. As the Muse abandoned Coleridge.

drinks. According to that, what I have to say here may be of use only to me. The only value of these remarks to some other reader may be – to prompt them to fill the vessel up for themselves, from their own sources. Like the variety of potential readers, the variety of potential interpretation is infinite. Lowes's discoveries, then, explain nothing. But they do give interpretation a nudge.

Sticking to the few questions that I asked, one can follow Lowes some way – but then go further, or pick up what he ignored.

Behind the Alph he finds, among other fascinating curios, the Nile – which is 'sacred' per se. But is that enough for 'an interpretation'? Then he finds various tributaries for 'holy' and 'enchanted', linked to the river, but trickling also from various mountain paradises. Again, do I want more?

For the 'demon lover' he does not find much that leads anywhere. Nor for the 'wailing woman' – referring only to Coleridge's note about 'wild poem on a maniac', who may or may not have been a woman, and to his other note about a 'maniac in the woods', who certainly was a woman.

His richest findings open beneath the 'mighty fountain'. Direct physical precedents include: springs that explode upwards from a bottomless source, or from an underground sea, having burrowed from some other land, tending to converge again at the source of the Nile.

The fountain's primaeval violence and sound combined have other sources – of which Coleridge took careful note. The most impressive concern the 'alligator hole' in the American wilderness:

the alligators' terrible roar, like heavy distant thunder, not only shaking the air and waters, but causing the earth to tremble – & when hundreds and thousands are roaring at the same time, you can scarcely be persuaded but that the whole globe is dangerously agitated . . . (Notebook)

That is striking enough. But then Coleridge adds a description of the alligator in rut – an incredible account of convulsive display, thunderous bellowing, belched-out vapours, churning the lagoon – 'all to gain the attention of the favourite female'.

So here is a shattering commotion in a water-hole, a large,

erotomanic reptile and the most tremendous of all primordial love-
songs – the mating call of a kind of dinosaur, no less.

Lowes merely notes the metaphorical association – as if a poetic
metaphor might be nothing but a poetic metaphor. And a reader
might well have let it pass easily by: there are no reptiles in the
'savage place' where the woman wails and the Alph erupts. Or are
there?

In his Notebook, while he was focused on alligators, Coleridge
noted the alligator's eye – 'small and sunk'. A Coleridgean goes
direct – as if alerted by a burglar alarm – to Geraldine's eyes in
'Christabel'. On the other hand, 'Christabel' is not 'Kubla Khan'.
(Or at least, not yet).

Keeping those alligators pinned to their place in Purchas, with a
small cleft snake-stick (a bit too light for them) Lowes notes (from
the Notebooks – immediately following the entry about 'A maniac
in the woods' (female) being 'scourged by rebunding (*sic*) boughs')
the lines about a nightingale:

> 'Tis the merry nightingale
> That crowds, and hurries, and precipitates
> With fast thick warble his delicious notes,
> As he were fearful that an April night
> Would be too short for him to utter forth
> His love-chant, and disburthen his full soul
> Of all its music! –

which eventually went into Coleridge's poem 'The Nightingale'.
Lowes passes lightly. But here, in the exhalations of the underworld
from which 'Kubla Khan' rises, the Nightingale's 'fast thick warble',
'that crowds, and hurries, and precipitates', can be heard through
the Alph's

> ceaseless turmoil seething,
> As if this earth in fast thick pants were breathing,

and through the wailing of the woman in the dark chasm, uttering
her 'love-chant' and striving 'to disburthen her full soul' for her
demon lover, and no less clearly through the bellowing of the

alligator whose convulsions, by now, are rising more insistently into the boil of the 'mighty fountain'.*

Perhaps one resists that association between the wailing woman in the dark chasm and the alligator roaring in the Carolinas, even though the treacherous mind has been so quick to spot the link, like a strand of moonlit mucus, between that same alligator's eyes and the eyes of Geraldine. As for the 'slimy things that crawl with legs' in the rotting slime of the Nightmare-Life-In-Death – (the Puritans were right, poetic metaphor is shamelessly promiscuous).

Still, one begins to feel that somewhere between the nightingale's

---

* According to several Notebook entries from his time in Malta (1804), Coleridge responded to reptiles as to no other animal. His descriptions of two or three encounters with lizards have a drama, a precision and close-up, riveted, joyous fascination every bit as alive as Lawrence's. He even wants to tame one, and keep it as a pet. But he relishes just as much the hints and rumours of their deadliness. Notice where and how the reptiles enter, in the following Note, during his visit to Sicily:

'. . . wound down a road of huge pits, *dimples*, & stairs of Limestone, and came to the view of the arch over the Torrent. Wound down to the Torrent, the River leading our horses thro' such a steep narrow gutter of solid rock / O what a place for Horses / on the Banks 2 High Stones on each side the path, each as large as Bowder Stone / in the Torrent Women & Boys at least 50 washing i.e. thumping & rubbing their cloathes against the Stones in the Torrent. O this savage and unforgettable scene! Huge Stones & huge Trees, & small & large Trees and stones & the HIGH HIGH great wall & all one long chamber! & the savage women in the Torrent, hairy *men*like legs – Oleander! Ivy! Myrtle / and all the Pot herbs – lovely Lizards
  The Paradise / . . .'

If any other, later writer had made this diary entry – if Ruskin or Tennyson had written it – one could suspect them of plagiarizing consciously or unconsciously the 'savage place' in Coleridge's 'Kubla Khan', where his poem had showed them how to feel and rhapsodize about such a combination of effects. But since it is Coleridge himself writing this, it is not so much self-plagiarism as a more fully explicated gloss on the feelings of that passage in the poem. In other words, it is more explicit about the 'savage women', right there in the water, and introduces the 'lovely lizards' right where, at the peak of his ecstatic response to the whole scene, the reptile ought to appear in the poem but is suppressed. The alligator, and his/her saurian associates, suspended as a hidden presence in the poem's 'mighty fountain' are allowed, in the diary version, to come into the open as 'lovely lizards' – immediately producing the cry of consummation, 'The Paradise'. What I am implying here is that exactly the same primal event enthralled him in the Sicilian gorge, recorded in the diary, as had produced the vision in the poem. The diary is merely more literal about the actual components.

'fast thick warble', the alligator's volcanic oestrus, the Alph's 'fast thick pants' that shake the earth like the breast of a woman wailing for her demon lover, and the woman wailing under the moon for her demon lover – a song of some kind is twisting into existence, a 'mingled measure' like the braids of current in the Alph itself.

VII A Viking Romance

Once all the stops of this particular flute of Marsyas* are brought into play, the fountain of Alph certainly can be said to make music – or to sing. But what about the 'caves of ice'?

Lowes brings a fascinating mechanism of association up behind these caves, again out of Coleridge's reading.

Their music might resound more clearly, though, if they were fitted into the acoustics of the whole Temple – in so far as this egg-shaped Paradise of Kubla's can be called a single Temple-like structure of 'preternatural' 'symphony and song'.

And other answers rise to meet the various questions that I asked, if one resorts to another aid – conveniently close, provided by Coleridge.

For some time before the arrival of 'Kubla Khan' (for my purpose, I assume those commentators (the majority) are right, who date it late October 1797), Coleridge had been toying with the idea of a long poem about 'The excursion of Thor' – 'in the manner of Dante'. Whatever this meant, it meant an activated familiarity with Norse myth. By activated I mean grasped, pondered, ransacked for the workable, set simmering in the creative oven – i.e. the imagination with some purposeful plan for a work to be produced.

One doesn't normally associate Coleridge with the gods of Asgard. On the other hand, through the late 1790s he was

---

* An allusion to the basic, primitive musical instrument of a kind of Pan, which Marsyas was. I refer to Marsyas rather than to Pan because, just as Coleridge's visionary music challenged the Orthodoxy and was defeated, so Marsyas challenged Apollo to a musical contest and was defeated. Marsyas was then skinned alive by Apollo – as one might metaphorically say Coleridge was flayed by the official committee of the Orthodoxy.

preoccupied, if not fascinated, by all things Germanic. Hence Thor – among his very meagre list of planned works (Milton had a list of over ninety).

In any case, even if they were no part of his proposed plot, two stories in particular must have risen from their depths to lie close under it. One – the myth about Thor's fishing for the Midgard Serpent, the giant sea-snake who encircles the Earth at the bottom of the sea and is the sibling of Hel, Queen of the Underworld and Death. The other – the myth about (usually) Hermod's or Odin's descent into Hel's underworld to bring back the dead Baldur – an attempt that was frustrated by Evil herself, the great Mother of the diabolical Loki (who was in turn the father of Hel and the Midgard Serpent).

One can see this steely net of association hanging close to Coleridge's other planned big work – one that he discussed a good deal: *The Origin of Evil*. The ideas might seem more relevant to 'The Ancient Mariner' than to 'Kubla Khan', but once an imaginative idea is on the boil, the steam and flavours leak out at every available orifice. And creative imagination, like evolutionary biology, has a kind of unscrupulous economy about its emergency adaptations. The world plan of Norse Myth is also somewhat egg-shaped, with a lifeless, sunless ocean inside at the bottom. Matched to that sketch of Kubla's world-egg, it amplifies again some of the poem's strongest suggestions and most prominent ideas. Moreover, it shifts the whole complex deeper towards a more radical meaning of 'sacred', and a more universal 'total symbol' of life.

Matching the two as I suggest superimposes the mighty fountain of the Alph onto the 'roaring cauldron', Hvergelmir, which is located at the frozen end of Hel's underworld and is the home of the dragon Nidhogg, the eater of corpses, who gnaws also at the roots of the great tree that holds the worlds together. The cauldron in the under-world boils – and Alph's fountain throws its lid off. This cauldron water belches out from under the roots of the great tree, supplying the waters of the nine worlds, pouring back into sunless and lifeless Hel, and so into Hvergelmir once more, to repeat the cycle.

Two other fountains spring from under the great tree: the waters of Fate, tended by the three Norns, and the waters of Wisdom, from the Orpheus-like or Bran-like severed oracular head of Mimir.*

These 'preternatural' attributes pour into Coleridge's Alph and will emerge in the two poems that follow.

In particular, they strengthen the conflation of Alph's waters with the waters of a Hell that is half frozen, with the waters of Universal life, with a Queen of the dead and the underworld, who lives with Death (and who is the grand-daughter of Evil), with a corpse-eating giant reptile and by extension with a sea-serpent that fills the sea with its coils. At the same time, they enrich its current with powerful ideas of Fate and oracular speech, knitting the whole tangle inextricably into a great tree which is the backbone and spinal cord of the Universe. The great tree, usually identified in Norse myth as an ash-tree (though not always) would try to become, in Coleridge's imagination, the Oak Tree. Especially in a poem about his chosen hero – Thor, God of the Oak.

Thor did not go on any excursion for Coleridge. The Mariner went on the excursion. Was he a god or tutelary spirit of the Oak?

VIII Mingled Measures

The 'mighty fountain' that bursts from the 'savage place' is already massively vocal. But the first mention of the music comes almost at the end of this opening Overture, in that phrase

> mingled measure
> From the fountain and the caves

These 'caves of ice' also contribute to the pleasures of this Paradise. If anything, the caves are a more marvellous component of the 'miracle of rare device' than the fountain. They are apostrophized, twice, with the same rapture as the 'sunny dome'. Clearly, their part in the 'mingled measure' is important.

These caves seem to function as flutes of some sort, perhaps a

---

* The severed head of the poet Orpheus continued to sing, and became an oracle in the shrine of Dionysus, on Lesbos. The severed head of the Crow-god Bran continued to sing and became an oracle of Britain, eventually buried in a shrine on Tower Hill.

gigantic natural organ. And the Alph makes new, other music, a measure to mingle with that of the fountain, as it pours through them, out of the Paradise into the underworld. Coleridge was fascinated by musical instruments of this kind – harps and flutes played on by natural forces.

The concert of water-music begins to come together. The lust-mad giant reptile of the Alph's source (which in the creative cauldron with Coleridge's earlier poetic plans has to share genes with the Norse Nidhogg and the Midgard Serpent i.e. with the reptile of the underworld's dead waters and with the sea-snake of sea-snakes) will return transmogrified later. But here, in 'Kubla Khan', its roarings are mingled and muffled through the woman's love-sick wails (albeit for a demon) that have been strained through the throat of a heart-bursting Nightingale and, all the time gaining in beauty without losing in volume, are further transmuted, by the technology of the caves, to the measures that accompany the delights of the sunny dome.

In Coleridge's imagination, therefore, the Alph exists, coming and going and at every point of its cycle, as a river of 'holy', 'enchanted', 'demonic', 'oracular', 'fateful', 'elemental', 'love-mad' music and song that emerges from the other world and returns into it.

The presence of the Norse cosmology, in Kubla's Paradise, might be no more than an echo-chamber of harmonies, a scoring for contrabasso, or a shifting gloomy fluorescence in a tapestry that was already rich enough, if it were not for Coleridge's well-established interest in Thor as the protagonist of a long poem 'in the manner of Dante'. That being so, one can reasonably suppose that the hovering co-substantiality of Norse myth, in the whole poem, actually amounts to a structural influence, integral to the dynamic workings of the symbols and to the central meanings of the poetry. This influence becomes much more palpable and evident in 'The Ancient Mariner'.

But this very cosmology points simultaneously to an even more significant model of a divine Paradise – one that must have pressed on Coleridge, in the circumstances, with painful immediacy. In this greater model, every element – but especially the river – is unquestionably sacred. It is the river of absolute sanctity. And though it is not described as a song it is above all the river of ultimate love and of the ultimate Word.

IX Divining the Spring on Mount Abora

Within this same poem, 'Kubla Khan', the drama now opens with a second, quite separate vision, which constitutes as I said a brief Act I of the action proper, beginning with: 'A damsel with a dulcimer'.

All readers recognize the abrupt change of focus and scene at this point. In effect, Coleridge has wakened up. It is as if his Unleavened Self, in the role of the Demon Lover, had arrived too late – just as the Paradise evaporates together with the woman who was wailing for him. Simultaneously, as happens when dreamers wake up, the vision of the paradise, that had seemed actual, is translated into a quite different *memory* which is yet the same. He 'saw and heard' the woman wailing for him in the savage cleft of Kubla's Paradise, but now he remembers her – in a fading image – as 'A damsel with a dulcimer'.

In a desperate attempt to hang on to her, his visionary lens closes in on this woman – apparently to the exclusion of everything else. She fills the foreground. But in this seemingly simplified image all the elements of the first vision are still there, disguised. The woman wailing for her demon lover has modified her style. Her sexual ferocity is now secreted in the irresistible siren-serenade of the black Abyssinian damsel, playing on a dulcimer and singing of Mount Abora. The sunny dome and paradise gardens, with everything contained thereunder, have reappeared as Mount Abora. The river erupting from the chasm has not vanished. It too has been secreted: its source into Mount Abora, its flowing body into the Abyssinian damsel herself, its sound into her song. Lowes has unravelled enough mythic and legendary geography uniting Mount Abora with the Alph, and both with the sources of the Nile, to supply plenty of active if latent meaning clustering around the multiple, interchangeable natures of the river and the woman. Here again are the serpents, the giant slimy things that crawl with legs, bottomless springs, underworld seas, eruptive fountains etc. – flowing into a river who is also a woman with a musical instrument in one hand and snakes in her crown (as in Apuleius's vision of Egyptian Isis).

The word 'Abora' is as much a key to the code of this second section as 'Alph' (deciphered later) is to the code of the first. And the details go further than Lowes takes them. Coleridge was an addicted punster and manipulator of letters in names. In Abora, whether consciously or not, he unites A + B (= Alphabet) + ora, where 'ora' is the imperative of the Latin 'orare', which means primarily 'to pronounce a sacred formula' or simply 'to pray', producing *oracle*, *adoration* etc. (or as habitually used by Coleridge in this very form: *ora pro nobis* – 'pray for us'). The root word is the Latin *os* – mouth. The whole hieroglyph, or cryptophone, 'Mount Abora', would be automatically deciphered as a rich pun by, say, Coleridge's close friend and fanatic co-punster Charles Lamb* who, according to Coleridge (Notebook), 'addeth to the Orphic epithetical polynomy of the Natura Naturans the title of the Diva Diapanta Punifica or the Divine All-puntress, and deemeth the Natura Naturata one great complex *Pun*, or Pun of Puns.' In fact neither of them, in each other's company, could have let the opportunity go by. Lamb, if not Coleridge, would read off Mount Abora as 'Mount Alphabeta Oracular Mouth', or 'O Mountain of Alphabet, pray for us!' As if to say 'O Mountain of the Word, pray for us!' Just as we do now.

So Mount Abora becomes the sacred mountain of the divinity within utterance itself. The setting then dramatizes its attributes, just as the setting of the Overture dramatized those of the River Alph. And the shared identity of that river and this mountain becomes even more definite. While the Alph is both the voice of a love-sick woman and a fountain of sacred utterance that issues in a 'mingled measure' of song and music, Abora is a mountain of sacred utterance, the source of a sacred river, that issues through a bewitchingly seductive damsel in 'symphony and song'. And this second woman, this damsel, converts the listener, Coleridge's Unleavened Self, into the demon that the first woman wailed for in her chasm under her waning (nearly dark) moon.

---

* I assume it was Lamb, but it could equally well have been Southey.

There is another link, one that must have pressed on Coleridge, in this confrontation, with the sharpness of steel-wire bonds. Among Lowes's findings in Coleridge's immediately relevant much-plundered reading, Mount Abora is associated with a prophesied war that will free all Abyssinia (i.e. all the catchment of the Nile's headwaters) and extend its empire 'as far as Jerusalem'.

In 'Kubla Khan' Coleridge's imagination knew exactly what it was doing. Maybe the ur-form of the two great narratives that follow was what fled when the person from Porlock knocked on the door. Everything in those two poems, as he eventually dug them out, is anticipated here in the Overture – everything essential, as if they were indeed conceived as a single work in parts, like Eliot's *Waste Land*. (Closely related, in fact, to that poem.) Coleridge is somehow aware, in the first five lines of 'Kubla Khan', just what a revelatory event this irruption of the Alph will turn out to be. He recognizes the Alph as the 'birth' of 'demonic' love becoming song. This is the 'nativity', in the sacred epic of his Unleavened Self's adventure as *an inspired incantatory language*. The 'nativity' (in the sacred drama of his own life and fate) of his poetic 'Word'.

Accordingly, this river is aptly identified by the first sound of the Alphabet. But a quite different river is already thundering to be heard through the same letters. This other river appears in the last chapter of 'The Revelations of St John', the most famous (and the most familiar in particular to Coleridge) of all Christendom's visions of a heaven on earth. There God speaks through an angel to John saying: 'I am Alpha and Omega'. At this point in the chapter God is speaking in the person of His Son, The Lamb, where 'Alpha and Omega' is the beginning and the end of the life of the Word – of Christ's life. 'Alpha' therefore corresponds to the Nativity of Divine Love. And St John, in his non-opiate trance, hears these words only a few verses after being shown Divine Love not as a God-man being born but as a *river*, pouring out into the world: 'a river of water of life, clear as crystal, proceeding out of the throne of God and of the Lamb.'

In Coleridge's poem, either the river of 'holy' demonic love and the poetic word, which springs from beneath Kubla's pleasure dome

and is called *Alph*, has displaced the river of Divine Love and of The
Divine Word, which springs from beneath the throne of God and
The Lamb and is called 'Alpha and Omega' – or both Paradises are
somehow here together and the two rivers are one and the same
river. As if there existed perhaps only the one Paradise and river of
love and sacred utterance – but reflected differently in each of
Coleridge's two selves. In his Unleavened Self it is reflected as it
appears in 'Kubla Khan'. But it is reflected (as I said earlier, *invisibly*)
in the opposite Christian Self as he knew it in Revelations.

In Revelations St John is surrendering to the 'call' of God. In
'Kubla Khan' Coleridge is all but surrendering to the 'call' of that
female. St John is rapt, and Coleridge is likewise rapt. St John is
possessed by his Christian Self and is sanctified. Coleridge is
possessed by his Unleavened Self and is demonized.

Or rather, not quite. In this first Act, Coleridge has heard the
'call', has had the opportunity, but has let it slip. All he knows is that
if only he could 'revive within' himself the damsel's 'symphony and
song', he could seize the opportunity and surrender to her 'call'
absolutely. He would then be inspired by such a miraculous power
of music 'loud and long' that he would be able to recreate

> that dome in air,
> That sunny dome! those caves of ice!

exactly as St John had beheld, just before being shown the river, the
Holy City of Jerusalem coming down out of heaven from God –
hanging in air like a vast candelabra of precious stones that take ten
packed verses to particularize. Then he, Coleridge, would be caught
up not into that 'river of the water of life', pouring from beneath the
throne of God and The Lamb, but into that pythian gusher of erotic
song from the oracular cleft of an African sybil, a voluptuous houri
whose voice dements the listener. And this listener, Coleridge
himself, understands that he would have drunk his intoxication, his
'milk of paradise' and his 'honey-dew', not from the river and tree of
Eden, but from the nectar flow of her song. The whole paradoxical
image, in which a demonic woman wails and sings against the
invisible Holy City, is a total symbol of the climactic spiritual

psychological crisis within the Unitarian Minister Coleridge – where he is longing to submit to the song.

In other words, in this Act I he responds to the 'call' with a will, but then at the last moment he recoils. Or rather, while his Unleavened Self rises into the ecstasy of:

> . . . with music loud and long,
> I would build that dome in air,
> That sunny dome! those caves of ice!
> And all who heard should see them there

his Christian Self reels back in horror, crying:

> Beware! Beware!
> His flashing eyes, his floating hair!
> Weave a circle round him thrice,
> And close your eyes with holy dread.

And the shift demonstrates clearly that Coleridge leaps, in these very lines, from his Unleavened Self to his Christian Self – where he finds himself calling for his Unleavened Self to be exorcized, or at least neutralized like an imp from hell. Coleridge obeys his Christian Self's injunction, the 'call' is rejected, and the poem comes to an end. This is the first of the three circles that he will weave around that strange woman's attempt to emerge and claim him. It is the first skirmish of the aforementioned prophesied war, and with this first victory, the first statement of his tragic choice.

The character-change from the woman of the sacred river to the river-woman of the sacred mountain is curious. Perhaps in the Overture he makes an image of his own destiny, with its 'sunless sea', in tragic foreboding. But in this brief Act I, maybe he interpreted his own case conjecturally, as it might be if he could only fuse his genius somehow with Wordsworth's. Though Wordsworth's indomitable, granitic massif loomed so large eventually over Coleridge's fall, it obviously provided exactly what Coleridge needed, during this first year of their friendship, to buttress his self-confrontation. Just as Dorothy's whisper in his ear lifted his courage. Together, as I have said, those two made a timely Oak Tree. Or instead of an Oak with a Serpent, 'the same only different' – a mountain with a wild nymph. For the time he was composing 'Kubla Khan', 'The Ancient Mariner' and 'Christabel' Part I, his genius really did have the form that it took on here in Act One: a high Mount Abora, a Mountain of the Moon peak of exalted confidence, love and far-seeing clarity, from which the torrent of inspiration poured.

x Learning to Fly: First Lesson

The powers that were repulsed in the First Act, by that Christian voice crying 'Beware! Beware!', come back with a vengeance in the Second. Here in 'The Ancient Mariner' they declare war in earnest.

Or the 'call' – from the woman in the 'savage place' and from the Abyssinian maid – rejected in 'Kubla Khan', is presented to Coleridge again. And this time he has no choice. It is no longer a 'call'. It is now a *fait accompli*.

But he has to be dragged out to where he can hear it. His Unleavened Self is whirled helplessly to the battlefield – where his Christian Self will lose. The 'call' takes that form: the announcement of the Christian Self's defeat.

But the whole visionary event, in which he is whirled to the confrontation, had been prepared for in at least three distinct stages. The first, in his early life. The second, in his first attempt to write a large scale, sustained, mature poem. The third, in his first collaboration with Wordsworth.

The first stage involved his mother and brothers at home in Ottery St Mary. When he came along, his mother already belonged to his seven older brothers. Their rivalry with him – for her loving attention – was concentrated in the one closest to him in age. This brother, said STC later, 'had a violent love of beating me'. Everything came to a head, as he later described it, when this brother destroyed a special cheese treat that their mother was preparing for STC, who now knocked his tormentor down. In the fight that followed, young STC grabbed a knife to settle things – and was disarmed by his mother. He then fled in guilt, remorse, rage against both brother and mother intense enough to keep him out hiding and sleeping by the River Otter, through a 'dreadful stormy night', till he was finally frozen and too weak to move, by which as he claimed later: 'I was certainly injured – For I was weakly, & subject to the ague for many years after.' He recalled this incident throughout his life, remembering it mainly as an attempt to make his mother miserable, a last resort bid to become her lost but found and now therefore best-loved lamb. Whether or not this was one of those small childhood happenings that affect the whole adult character, it certainly epitomized in extreme form his relationship to his brothers, to his mother, and to the wilderness of stormy nature.

To begin with, it gave him a dramatically staged, sensationally intensified image of the chronic torture of his childhood: the source of human love first reassuring him, then violently rejecting him and replacing him with his rival. According to his own analysis, as his Notebooks witness, he habitually fled from the love-anguish of his 'personal and inward feelings' into his intellectual, moral self, his Christian Self, his aloof and invulnerable sanctuary in the window-seat. But on this momentous occasion he fled in precisely the opposite direction. In retrospect, the path he took is familiar. He plunged not into 'abstruse research, the mother of self-oblivion', but into the elemental wilderness of storm and darkness, to find the two things impossible to find in his family and in his ordinary life: first, the superior substitute comforter and strength, who will have to emerge from Nature itself – like God; and second, the mother he has just lost, who must now come searching for him on a deeper level, where brothers do not exist and her love belongs to him alone.

This composite, substitute comforter who will be God, Nature and Mother combined will appear – compelled by his extreme sufferings – and will right every wrong, restore every bliss, supply the perfect love of the very source that created him. She will emerge from the wild Creation itself, out of the storminess of the elements, out of the Otter in spate, wailing for him to return. She will find him, sing him a lullaby that will recreate Paradise, and she will give him her breast of milk and honey dew. She will speak words that will mesmerize him with bliss as she wraps him in her arms.

His ordeal out there – like a little cub Shaman – freezing to death, will force her to manifest herself and give him all this.

Later on, this strategy cropped up again almost as a fundamental idea, in situations of crisis. At the most superficial level of daydreaming, maudlin self-pity and loneliness, something like it recurred to him now and again, recorded in his Notebooks. On the philosophical level, one could say it was mightily dignified as his Pantisocratic Socialist Utopia – a flight into freedom from competition ('all property in common') and from human malice and strife ('all motive for evil removed') in the American wilderness, where thunder set the alligators bellowing, and the love-mad alligators bellowed like thunder, and the fountain boiled up in a paradise.

On the poetic man-of-letters level it rehearsed itself and brought him relief, so long as he was physically able, in his driven, scrambling flights – more flights than walks – over the Cumbrian or Scottish Mountains. On those occasions he grasped and embraced the beauties of the natural world as if only these could console him – though it was never more than invitation and promise, the real thing was always absent. His hectic, headlong abandon was like that of a man searching in despair. And he says it often enough in his Notebooks quite clearly, the more intense the natural beauty the more agonizing is his awareness – the woman who should be here, and part of this, is missing.

But on the poetic visionary level, it lifted him into a paradise in air, where the woman wailed for him, then beckoned and sang to him; it whirled him to the other side of the storm-blast; and it sent him out roaming motherless to pray in the midnight oak forest. Three visionary adventures.

But before these three real flights, it took him somewhere else. It brought him to what I called the second stage of preparation. In this stage, the basic sequence – flight into the wilderness, encounter with the Mother/God/Nature entity, and return to the rectory – was crucially modified.

XI Saying Goodbye to Wordsworth

When Coleridge and Wordsworth met they were both Pantheists of a kind. Letting their enthusiasms fly loosely over their basic religious values, both regarded everything as spiritual and tried to believe it inhabited by spirits. Stopping well short of animism, they found themselves entertaining this outlook as a mode, perhaps, of keeping their senses and apprehensions at full stretch. The spirits of Nature were not more individualized or motivated than the spiritual aspect of nature's elements and features. And all were functionaries of the all-inclusive Universal Spirit, that both poets called God.

They were that aspect of Nature which could be shared by a spiritual human being. Whoever internalized these spirits became to that degree Nature-like. Wordsworth based his religious philosophy on just this. Since he regarded Nature as the natural, the real and the true, it followed that whoever internalized the spirit of Nature partook thereby of the natural, the real and the true – in its Universal spiritualized aspect. Hence:

> One impulse from a vernal wood
> > May teach you more of man,
> Of moral evil and of good,
> > Than all the sages can.

And the rest of it.

Coleridge saw more in Nature than this (and was eventually not sure that he liked what he saw), but in the early days he believed something like the same. Nevertheless, he was not satisfied with it. Wordsworth's approach seemed to him limited. He sensed in it a certain antagonism to the phantasmagoric, to the inner world of symbolism, of dream, of psychic mysteries projected. He criticized it – or Wordsworth's stolid loyalty to it – for its 'meanness'.

Coleridge's idea of 'spirits' included that whole other dimension – the inner world, perhaps even the fringes of a supernatural world, projected by imaginative vision. The inner world not as a climate of feelings that saturated outer events and objects of sense, as with Wordsworth, but as a realm of autonomous dramas, of peculiar states of being, of unfathomable sub- or supernatural personalities, related to the outer world in no simple fashion. This was where he and Wordsworth began to find their 'data dissimilar'.

While Wordsworth was still unknown, and feeling his way, he agreed to call this speciality of Coleridge's the 'preternatural' – as distinct from his own speciality, the 'natural'. He was even willing to indulge Coleridge as far as to sit down and collaborate with him in writing 'The Wanderings of Cain'. Or at least, to make the attempt. And when his invention refused to co-operate, he tried again – much more successfully – with 'The Ancient Mariner'.

But what Coleridge's 'preternatural' world turned out to be was the demonic world of the psyche. And of an extraordinary psyche at that – its spirit-like forces controlled not by the moral will but first and foremost by sexuality, its strange terrors and demands, its dionysiac, elemental music, and the archaic pantheon of energies that emerges with it.

The public reaction to 'Ancient Mariner', which stood as the introductory poem in the first edition of the *Lyrical Ballads*, helped to wake Wordsworth up to what was happening. By the time Coleridge had finished 'Christabel' Part II, for the second edition, two years later, Wordsworth was fully alerted. And alarmed and repelled. He began to withdraw from both Coleridge and his poems – as Coleridge sensed immediately.

But this occult disposition, from which Wordsworth now stepped back, was already there in the Miltonic poem that Coleridge toiled at for some years before he met Wordsworth – 'The Destiny of Nations – A Vision'.

XII A Dummy Run on the Astral Plane

'The Destiny of Nations' opens with an address to 'The Word, the Life, – the Living God', then presents the Creation as a great machine operated by spirits – where even the bad spirits are good for man because they make him think in spiritual terms and so 'train up to God'.

Where Wordsworth had his mountains for what Keats (with a not dissimilar but less pious idea) called 'mental weight-lifting', Coleridge had already been attracted to the spirit-infested Polar Regions. He describes how the bracing exercise of imagining – internalizing – these supernatural forces exalts the Laplander:

> For Fancy is the power
> That first unsensualises the dark mind,
> Giving it new delights; and bids it swell
> With wild activity; and peopling air,
> By obscure fears of Beings invisible,
> Emancipates it from the grosser thrall
> Of the present impulse, teaching Self-control,
> Till Superstition with unconscious hand
> Seat Reason on her throne.

Coleridge goes on to say how the more frightening the imaginings are, the better they are for the soul, which is sensitized and hurried that much quicker to an acceptance of the 'victorious goodness of high God'. Is this like 'Fear of the Lord is the beginning of wisdom'? What is more revealing is the 'frightening' example that he chooses for illustration to his argument:

> Wherefore not vain,
> Nor yet without permitted power impressed,
> I deem those legends terrible, with which
> The polar ancient thrills his uncouth throng:

(awakening them towards God and Reason)

> Whether of pitying spirits that make their moan
> O'er slaughtered infants, or that Giant Bird
> Vuokho, of whose rushing wings the noise
> Is Tempest, when the unutterable Shape
> Speeds from the mother of Death, and utters once
> That shriek, which never murderer heard, and lived.

This *doppelgänger* of the Albatross simply sails up. With foreknowledge of what is to come, one might pause to note that this Giant Bird is an emissary of 'the mother of Death'. In Norse myth, the

Triple Grandmother of Hel, Queen of Death, was Evil herself. But this is not Norse myth. And this 'mother of Death', whoever she is, punishes homicides. So Vuokho is the bird form of a kind of Nemesis – a guardian of Divine Law. The bird form of the Goddess of Life and Death dealing out Judgement on homicides. A good spirit or a bad? Coleridge flits away from it lightly. He speeds directly to a passage often noticed in relation to 'The Ancient Mariner':

> the Greenland Wizard in strange trance
> Pierces the untravelled realms of Ocean's bed
> Over the abysm, even to that uttermost cave
> By mis-shaped prodigies beleagured, such
> As Earth ne'er bred, nor Air, nor the upper Sea:
> Where dwells the Fury Form, whose unheard name
> With eager eye, pale cheek, suspended breath,
> And lips half-opening with the dread of sound,
> Unsleeping Silence guards, worn out with fear
> Lest haply 'scaping on some treacherous blast
> The fateful words let slip the Elements
> And frenzy Nature.

A wizard, in a trance, pierces the abyssal sea, to confront a Fury Form. A burlesque rehearsal for the Ancient Mariner's voyage, clear enough. It must have been pointed out, but it seems worth making the point again here: this is a straight transcription of an early ethnological account of the Shaman's flight. From the epic of Gilgamesh onwards, literature is full of mythicized and poetically adapted forms of such flights. But so far as I'm aware Coleridge is the first poet in English to refer to the Shaman's flight as technically such, and to make use of it, even if only in such a straightforward descriptive way, in verse. There is no doubt, in other words, that Coleridge has not merely followed instinct to that general type of experience – as Keats did in 'Endymion', 'Lamia' and 'La Belle Dame Sans Merci' (much influenced by Coleridge's example) – but has lit upon the thing itself, in its real context.

He then goes straight on, and comes to that part of the story which holds – as if he knew it – his own Destiny:

> Yet the wizard her,
> Arm'd with Tongarsuck's power, the Spirit of Good,
> Forces to unchain the foodful progeny
> Of the Ocean stream; – thence thro' the realm of Souls,
> Where live the Innocent, as far from cares
> As from the storms and overwhelming waves
> That tumble on the surface of the Deep,
> Returns with far-heard pant, hotly pursued
> By the fierce Warders of the Sea, once more,
> Ere by the frost foreclosed, to repossess
> His fleshly mansion, that had staid the while
> In the dark tent within a cowering group
> Untenanted. – Wild phantasies! yet wise
> On the victorious goodness of high God
> Teaching reliance . . .

This completes the early travellers' report of the shamanic flight and return. Coleridge wanted a 'terrible' legend, a terrific image, but this is the only one in a poem-full of 'terrific images' that is not allegorical. That is to say, it is the only authentic 'preternatural' event in what he regarded, over several years, as his most ambitious poetic work.

His anxious (as if obligatory) attempt to redeem his fascinated plunge into the 'wild fantasy' of his 'terrible legend', by surfacing into a sermon about God's goodness, with assurances that 'heavenly Truth' is 'winning her difficult way', by gradual missionary steps, to convert this wizard, is the first rehearsal of the reflex that will cost him so dearly.

In this passage, the tragic 'double' theology of his two selves comes clear for the first time. The Shaman's flight and return is under the protective power of a good spirit – Tongarsuck, and at the end of the episode Coleridge officially assimilates this good spirit to the coming Jehovah. Meanwhile he characterizes that Fury Form as evil. The creature in the sea's abyss, whom the wizard visited and 'by his enchantments' forced to 'unchain the foodful progeny' – i.e. the sea animals, seals, whales etc. that normally feed the people – is such a horrible being, such a Queen of Chaos, that her very name, if uttered, would 'frenzy Nature'.

The polarity is conventional. The God who protects the wizard's coming and going and belongs to the upper world is good. The Female Spirit who lives at the bottom of the sea and reigns in the lower world, with power over the sea creatures, is evil. This would resemble the Christian-Manichean division of the cosmos between God and Satan but for that evil Female's anomalous control of the source of food. In every other mythology, this Mother of animals and food is also the Mother of Life, in some form. She is not the opposite of the good God. She actually reigns in his place and antedates him: she *is* the good God, or rather she is the deity of Life and Death, like Job's Jehovah, beyond good and evil.

Coleridge can blame his informant. He gives his source (a history of Greenland), and adds a note:

They call the Good Spirit, Tongarsuck. The other great but malignant spirit a nameless female; she dwells under the sea in a great house, where she can detain in captivity all the animals of the ocean by her magic power. When a dearth befalls the Greenlanders, an Angekok or magician must undertake a journey thither. He passes through the kingdom of souls, over an horrible abyss into the Palace of this Phantom, and by his enchantment causes the captive creatures to ascend directly to the surface of the ocean.

In fact, this is a simplified account of one of the most celebrated of Eskimo flight scenarios, recorded in Coleridge's source by a missionary or other Christian witness who had misinterpreted it. The woman at the bottom of the sea is Arnaquagssak also known as Nuliayuk or Sedna. She truly is the Goddess at the source of things, at the source of the weather and fortunes of the Eskimo hunter's world, and virtually therefore the Goddess of food.* She is a Goddess who – like the Great Bird Vuokho's mother of Death – deals judgement. And here she is dealing judgement. She witholds the animals from the hunters only when some human being has breached a tabu. The Shaman's business is to undo the violation, and secure her forgiveness. She is regarded with terror and awe, but

---

* Further west, in Alaska, she becomes *Niggivik* – literally 'place of food'.

as Job regards Jehovah: and in that sense she can only be 'good' and never 'malignant'.

In spite of this initial misunderstanding, Coleridge has flown unerringly to the deity he needed to find. This account, already as I say central in his work, is enough to authenticate the shamanic flight-path of the Mariner's journey, when Coleridge's point-blank poetic honesty will see through his Christian interpretations and identify that female for what she is.

But then he will scramble out of his visionary moment of poetic honesty as fast as he can. And he will look back towards her, from his Christian sanctuary, as if he had never understood anything, and yet with his scarred retina retaining something, when he remarks in his Notebook (in 1802)

Alas! Alas! that Nature is a wary wily long-breathed old witch, tough-lived as a turtle, & divisible as the polyp repullulative in a thousand snips and cuttings, integra et in toto. She is sure to get the better of Lady Mind in the long run & to take her revenge too . . .

'The Destiny of Nations' prepared in this way for the third stage, where Tongarsuck and the Great Malignant Nameless Spirit, confronting each other in bigger and also more familiar roles, brought Coleridge directly to 'The Ancient Mariner'.

XIII The Symbolic Life

Apart from 'Kubla Khan', between 'The Destiny of Nations' and 'The Ancient Mariner' one more work had to be got through. This provided the third and final stage of preparation for the Mariner's journey.

In October 1797, in the first enchanted surge of his friendship with Wordsworth and Dorothy, Coleridge suddenly felt ready to write his long-pondered 'The Wanderings of Cain.' Very few men have attacked their brother with a knife in a fit of jealous rage, but since he had, the open connection between that and this fragmentary prose poem makes itself.

At the same time, in obvious ways, the strange work is like the

ruinous shipyard from which 'The Ancient Mariner' was launched –
or rather from which it launched itself.

Coleridge's other much-pondered epic, 'The Origin of Evil',
together with his Dantesque 'Excursion of Thor', and that curious
project, a long poem about Christian of *The Bounty* ('Captain Bligh!
. . . I am in Hell!') all gave way suddenly to a convulsive effort to
write out (in a single night!) this titanic fantasia about Cain's murder
of Abel and his sufferings afterwards.

Coleridge lived a symbolic life if anybody did – the kind of life in
which every event, even the slightest, seems to have the structural
rightness and resonance of an image in a deeply organized poem. But
nothing in it can have been more vibrantly symbolic than the bizarre
situation that he stage-managed on this night, when he persuaded
his adored new friend Wordsworth to collaborate in the hand-to-
hand re-creation of the primal fratricidal combat between the two
sons of Adam – the 'pious' and the 'unleavened'.

It could not have been more pointed if he had chosen the exact
anniversary of his earlier attempted fratricide and flight into the
night of storm beside the River Otter.

But the external situation, the archetypal psychodrama that he
had contrived, was merely apparatus. What Coleridge needed was
what it enabled him to bring about: i.e. his first, compulsive step
towards what he could no longer avoid – the showdown with *the
other*.

Wordsworth was to write Abel's murder, as Canto One.
Coleridge had to deal with Cain's guilt in Canto Two. Whoever
finished first was to start on the final Canto Three. At top speed,
Coleridge produced a prose poem unlike anything else he ever did.
Then he discovered that the bemused or unbemused Wordsworth
was still staring at blank paper – so the poem was abandoned 'in a
laugh'. But it was evidently enough. The necessary step had been
taken.

In spite of the Gothic genre operatics, which Coleridge inflated,
his figure of Cain emerges with some of the actuality of real vision –
hypnagogic and disturbing:

. . . and when Cain, his father, emerged from the darkness, the child was affrighted. For the mighty limbs of Cain were wasted as by fire; his hair was as the matted curls on the Bison's forehead, and so glared his fierce and sullen eye beneath: and the black abundant locks on either side, a rank and tangled mass, were stained and scorched, as if the grasp of a burning iron hand had striven to rend them; and his countenance told in strange and terrible language of agonies that had been, and were, and were still to continue to be.

The whole piece is as close to 'A Memorable Fancy' by Blake as it well could be without actually being by Blake. But more tightly articulated – with a palpably more painful relevance to the emergency of the author's life.

Inevitably Coleridge casting himself as Cain brought into play various aspects of the mutually fascinated but still untested rivalry between himself and Wordsworth, where Dorothy is in the foreground and Sarah with her small son in the background. Divination and prophecy are astir.

Coleridge could hardly, consciously, have supposed that Wordsworth was about to become all older brothers, soon to eject him pitilessly from every kind of love and blessing that he could hope for. But reading the piece now, one can fancy that Coleridge's wishful thinking is in control, and has succeeded, with Wordsworth, in fantasy, where he failed with his brother in reality – killed him for his usurpation.

But then worse pain dawns – as he divines, maybe, that Wordsworth has in truth somehow in some dimension already killed him. At this point, where Coleridge realizes that he is murdered Abel as well as guilty Cain, he drops through into the poem's deeper level – the visionary level, where Cain the 'unleavened' Coleridge has killed the Christian Coleridge, Abel.

Now the narrative becomes peculiar. In the brief Canto that Coleridge composed that night, Cain, persecuted by God, wanders through a forest in torments, until his little son, leading him to where he had found water in a desert, brings him to confront what appears to be the spirit of his slain brother Abel, who is also in torment. Abel then makes the strange statement: 'The Lord is God of the living only, the dead have another God.' And he adds that all who sacrifice to the God of the dead while living shall be wretched, but after death 'their toil ceaseth'.

Wanting only freedom from his torments, Cain now starts searching for this 'God of the dead'. Echoes come back, out of the future, from Nietzsche's *Zarathustra*. He appeals to the spirit who seems to be Abel to lead him to this other God. 'Who is this God of the dead? where doth he make his dwelling? what sacrifices are acceptable unto him? for I have offered, but have not been received; I have prayed, and have not been heard . . .' The spirit then leads him – towards the 'God of the dead'.

The cosmology here, clearly enough, has some resemblance to the Greenland Wizard's, in the division of realms between the two Gods – the God of the upper world being good, the God of the underworld (called a God, not a Devil) still to be assessed. Though Coleridge's note to the passage about the Wizard described that 'other God' as a 'malignant' and 'nameless female', in fact, as I showed she is the salvation of the people – their only hope. Just so here, the one whom Cain now seeks in agony and despair (much as little Coleridge ran off into the night of 'dreadful storm') is simply 'the other God' who can release him from his torments.

That would be enough to suggest how desperately Coleridge's Unleavened Self, the Cain in him, is now bent on finding the equivalent of what the Greenland Angekok found at the bottom of the sea.

There exists a rough sketchy continuation of this story, presumably an outline of the projected Canto Three. In this version, rather as 'The Ancient Mariner' will tell his tale to the Wedding-Guest, Cain tells his tale to his wife. He describes how he found in the desert a Juniper Tree, how he encountered the spirit of Abel, and how he then heard from Abel of 'another being who had power after this life, *greater than Jehovah*.' (my italics), and of what followed.

Abel is on his way to offer sacrifices to this other 'greater' God, and Cain allows himself and his son to be led. They come to 'an immense gulf filled with water, whither they descend followed by alligators etc.'. Having gone down through this 'alligator hole', they stand in a vast meadow where Abel offers a sacrifice of blood from his arm. He then persuades Cain to offer up the same, from his son's arm.

Cain is about to obey when a second spirit of Abel – this time the true one – descends from heaven attended by the Archangel Michael, and warns Cain not to offer up his innocent child. The first spirit of Abel now throws off his disguise, revealing himself as an evil demon, and flees pursued by Michael.

The sacrifice has not been made, the other God puts in no appearance – the aborted scenario disintegrates in a jangle of discords. Though it is clearly understood that if Cain had only shed blood from his son's arm, then the 'greater than Jehovah' would have claimed at least Cain's son – Cain's surrogate self. (For the 'child' here one can read simply Coleridge himself who, as he complained, felt always to be 'a boy' – on which he blamed much that went so bitterly wrong with his life.)

The whole work leaves a reader looking expectantly into the distance, across the vast meadow, wondering just what other God that might be, who requires blood from the arm and who is 'greater than Jehovah'. In this context, at least, it could not be the Fury Form or the blessed Arnaquagssak, not quite.

As Coleridge told the story of that night's collaboration in later years, he made it clear that he interpreted Wordsworth's inability to contribute as the great poet's tacit disapproval of the 'exceeding ridiculousness' of the scheme – a spontaneous moral judgement of such crushing authority that Coleridge instantly lost all confidence in this uppermost, most urgent theme of his secret life, and promptly disowned it. When he looked at it through Wordsworth's eyes, it simply shrivelled up, as he says, 'in a laugh' – a laugh which now really did smother the death-cry of Abel.

However, the myth of his destiny, the dilemma that he was going to have to live and die by, did not just leak away into the earth and evaporate under Wordsworth's baleful smile. Not just yet, anyway. It would take a few months. Meanwhile, Coleridge's account of the abandoned attempt concludes jauntily: '. . . and 'The Ancient Mariner' was written instead.'

No longer a collaboration, but now with a truly inspired nudge or two from Wordsworth. So, sad as ever but also wiser, Cain re-emerged.

XIV A Leaden Knock and a Golden Echo

'The Wanderings of Cain' is like Coleridge's first determined effort to confront his Sphynx. Re-enforced by Wordsworth's tremendous electrical field of concentration, and under Dorothy's eyes, he batters at the wall of intellectual ego – to break out and through to the 'other God', using second-hand (obsolete) methods and materials. He fails to get through or even to catch a glimpse of what light there might be beyond.

But as Coleridge seemed to know, the moment was ripe. And this effort, this apparent readiness to sacrifice something, this resounding need, woke something up on the other side. In an unguarded moment, 'Kubla Khan' then floats up out of the abyss (up through that 'immense watery gulf' of the alligators) as an answer, an invitation, even 'a call', from the Sphynx. Redefining the situation in highly original – and uniquely Coleridgean – terms. Presenting the same grisly internecine combat, but as an idealized reconciliation – in a paradisal Mandala, as I described it, beyond the opposites. Or with the opposites only just snarling in at the edges of the picture, like goblins of the *sangsara* on a Tibetan *tanka*, muttering about war.

At the same time, the Christian/Manichean conception of the 'other God' as *evil* – is corrected. This 'other God' now turns out to be a nymph (avatar of a Goddess, lover of a 'demon') of love-madness and of vision-building inspirational song.

Also, as an incidental detail, this 'call' reveals the other nature of the 'alligator hole', no longer a sink-hole of deathly waters, the entrance to the land of the dead, but now the teeming source of biological life, love, song and intoxicating beauty.

According to scholars' favoured dates, 'Kubla Khan' could well have followed 'The Wanderings of Cain', quite closely, in this way. Then 'The Ancient Mariner' began to emerge in early November.

xv Tongarsuck meets Arnaquagssak

Using the cave-drawing topographical map that he had already reconnoitred in 'The Wanderings of Cain', and combining it with the rough-old guesswork shamanic flight-path that he had appropriated in 'The Destiny of Nations', Coleridge took off – following his nose.

Anybody can trace the Ancient Mariner's route, station for station, in those two guides – remembering that they were very clear in Coleridge's memory, as he proceeded.

Matching his progress, in this way, it is easy to see that where Cain's nerve failed the Mariner's did not. The Mariner's role model was the Greenland Angekok – perhaps, as spirits go, he was that very Angekok now reincarnated; by great subjective need. But many other shamanic flights – from the poetic record – go with him, like consultants. As soon as he gets well out to sea, the sea takes control. He is whirled by the 'STORM-BLAST' (as prophets are snatched up into heavenly vision) to the encounter with the 'greater than Jehovah'.

The Mariner's vessel enters the ice, which closes around it as a crush of ice cliffs. Scylla and Charybdis, multiplied into a whole seascape. Instead of sailing around the outside of the globe, he has sailed into the inside of Kubla's ovoid cosmos, and here he is in the 'sunless sea', at the bottom of the egg. For continuity's sake (and imaginative economy) huge chunks of the ice that hung under Kubla's paradise and piped Alph's water down to the sunless sea, where it cooled and deepened again, have been torn loose by the torrent and are here floating.

They have not entirely lost their voice, these crags of cave. They are still water of Alph, if transposed – otherworld song frozen and now infernalized. They

> . . . cracked and growled, and roared and howled,
> Like noises in a swound

The 'mingled measure' regressing, maybe, to the original alligator uproar of the fountain source – the subterranean Hvergelmir, at the frozen end of Hel's underworld, towards which they are now drifting. But the terrible ogress of Coleridge's own regular bellowing 'swound' is maybe not wholly absent.

Some commentators have followed the Mariner's errant course as an example of what could happen to the Western World's maritime expansion when blown off course – a maze of doldrums and reversals, highly interesting, as it was too to Coleridge. But the poem is hospitable to every point of view, in the manner of good symbols.

Just so, as a logged account of a spirit adventure – the spontaneous quest undertaken by every soul in dire need, asleep or awake – the Mariner's course is a straight line to the goal. A bee-line to the honey dew and the crucial revelation. Certainly a dire need for Coleridge.

Since this is one of the few great symbolic poems, not an adventure yarn, we shouldn't be surprised if all the elements and natural features now become hieroglyphs – a picture-language engineering a change of worlds. The ice is the barrier: the perimeter crust of the other world. The presiding symbols in this scene-changing are the sun and the moon.

At this threshold the first world, the sun's world, lies behind, in mist, through which the sun moves hidden. The other world, the moon's world, lies ahead, in 'fog-smoke white' through which 'Glimmered the white moonshine.'

Since the sun's world, from which the Mariner brings his glare-goggles of conscience and expectation, and into which he will return, is Protestant Christian, this other world ahead will appear first of all as a Hell (as in 'The Wanderings of Cain').

Every feature of the Mariner's discoveries will be distorted, for the Mariner, in this same warp, by those orthodox goggles (and orthodox readers throughout the poem's history have had a similar problem) – till at one of the high points of the poem, the goggles drop off of their own accord.

And at the same point, as the Unitarian Preacher who has to make his poem acceptable to his congregation and to such unpredictably testy friends and opinion-makers as the minister manqué Southey, Coleridge himself will begin to have problems.

The Albatross is a complicated piece of work. Setting his higher controls aside for a moment, one can say that his role in the shamanic flight – the primitive, biological dream dimension of this excursion – is to serve as Keeper of The Threshold.* He is in his way, a simple form of the whole vision to come – an ABC form, for the Mariner, the new boy. In that role the bird is like Vuokho – emissary of the Nightmare Life-In-Death: of the putrescent death sea and of the teemingly radiant birth sea. That is his simplest function. So he lets the Mariner through the clashing gates, with a fair breeze, into the otherworld, where the revelation waits. And at this point the Mariner kills him: as if that were the necessary turning of the key.

The ship now emerges from one universe into another (occupying the same space and using the same matter – an idea that interested Coleridge). This is the place 'measureless to man', and the breakthrough is perfectly suggested in the couplet:

> We were the first that ever burst
> Into that silent sea.

Just which Universe this new one is appears now in the sun. It is no longer the worldly sun but – wonderfully startling in its context –

> like God's own head.

That is to say, the earthly and everyday Universe has been displaced

---

* Wherever the quest Hero or Heroine crosses into the other world, or takes the critical step into a forbidden mystery, The Keeper of The Threshold usually appears – most often in the form of a bird, animal or fish, sometimes benign and magically helpful, sometimes terrible and threatening destruction. Either way, directly or indirectly, this creature gives place (by immolation, by self-sacrifice, by transformation, by acting as guide or instructor etc.) eventually to the prize – as if it were some aspect of that prize, the only aspect of that prize visible to the untransformed adventurer in the opening phase.

by the *sacred* Universe, which is actually a kind of Heaven – a rather horrible heaven at this point, but God is there as if in person, nakedly confronting the Mariner.

It is the sun which is *too dreadfully* like God – as if God glared down into the upstaring face of the transgressor. A kind of guilt, in other words, has projected that alarming extra naked glory onto the sun, like a last warning. And in fact, the sun is already changing into something else. Its dreadful likeness to God's own head is a last admonitory flare-up of its God's-own-headlessness. It no longer belongs to this new Universe – which though it is the sacred Universe is not Jehovah's. This new Universe is ruled, as the poem now goes on to make clear, by a 'greater than Jehovah.' In contrast to the other Universe, which was hidden from its deity by many veils, this new Universe is naked before its deity – too naked, terrifyingly naked.

That extra conflagration in the sun has nothing to do with the killing of the Albatross. Countless folktales follow the same shamanic route that the Mariner follows here. In a great many of them, the animal on the threshold is a standard dramatis persona – as if an animal symbol of the wall of the ovum should confront the sperm. In the typical story of that kind, in this role, the Albatross would have said to the Mariner: 'If you want to go further, and find what you need (the infinitely good thing, the sacred bride, rebirth), you must first kill me.'

No such instructions are forthcoming, in the poem, nor does the Mariner betray any motive for killing the bird. He simply kills it – as if not knowing why. As if, in truth, it had asked him – and he had acted, almost, against his will. Nevertheless, though unaware of the archaic rules, the Mariner has obeyed them, and will be rewarded.

Meanwhile, the sun is changing.

XVI The Lunar Sun

Kubla Khan's paradise is still undergoing the infernal translation. As in classic hells, this too is half fire, half ice. The 'caves of ice' became a whole Antarctic of 'sunless sea', at the bottom of the world. And the 'sunny pleasure dome' has become 'a hot and copper sky' with a 'bloody sun at noon' stuck in the middle of it, dead overhead. The Mariner's goggles, one might say, (as in 'close your eyes with holy dread') have inverted all values.

But this sun which was, for a moment there, 'like God's own head', is now not only bloody but 'no bigger than the Moon'.

Within the literal meaning of the very few words used by Coleridge, the glorious briefly-Jehovan-seeming sun has become a different kind of sun-god: a blood-sacrifice god – which is at the same time a terror and a sinister moon.

Looking ahead, you see that within not many verses, having sunk, in an episode of pure nightmare, this hellish moon-like sun has been altogether replaced by the moon – a waning moon already familiar.

Regarding the three visionary works again as one drama, this large transformation of the Mariner's world has obvious parallels in the two other poems. In 'Kubla Khan' the imperial order of the 'sunny dome' yields the foreground and action to the savage chasm where the awesome fountain erupts and the woman wails for her demon lover under the waning moon. In 'Christabel', the moon which is full nevertheless looks 'both small and dull' – as the moaning Geraldine emerges from under the Oak Tree. In other words the moon is full, brilliant and yet, like the eye of the alligator, that Coleridge had so curiously noted, 'small and sunk'. This in turn anticipated the shift from the 'fair, large' and 'glittering', 'bright' eyes of Geraldine to eyes that were

> shrunk in her head
> Each shrunk up to a serpent's eye

on which the whole uncanny power of that poem turns and slithers into horror.

XVII The Other God: First Impressions

Through Coleridge's Protestant (sharpening to Puritan) goggles, the Mariner now sees that the 'silent sea' is actually a 'lifeless ocean' – is in fact rotting and burning with death-fires, like a deliquescent grave, reminiscent of Hel's putrid underworld.

Or reminiscent of that 'immense gulf filled with water' into which Cain descended 'followed by alligators etc.'.

Sure enough, there are the 'slimy things with legs' crawling on the 'slimy sea'.

This is the nadir of Coleridge's visionary journey – the point at which Cain had to let blood from his son's arm if he wanted to make contact with the 'greater than Jehovah'. The point at which the Greenland Angekok met that 'great but malignant and nameless Female', alias the Mother of food and of all life, and persuaded her to forgive mankind and permit the life-bringing animals to 'ascend directly to the surface of the ocean'.

On cue, out of the setting sun emerges a woman.

Not wailing for her demon lover, though she is in a savage enough place. And not singing, to a dulcimer, a song that transforms the listener to a demon of ecstatic but forbidden utterance. But the main difference, perhaps, between this woman and those earlier two is in the nature of her 'call'. It is no longer negotiable.

At first, she seems reluctant to reveal herself fully. 'A speck, a mist, a shape' – her ship plunges and veers uncannily in the dead calm. But the moment the Mariner does what Cain dared not do – bites his arm and lets the blood flow – she starts her approach.

The fact that he actually drinks the blood is clearly a sacrament of some kind. In the context – communion with a supernatural being – the blood is the God. That woman coming out of the moony sun that was 'bloody' is the deity of the blood-stream, the river of life.

At the same time he is sacrificing himself to her as an offering – in the sense that Cain's son would have been a sacrificial offering of the child self. And she comes to lap at the blood and to take him.

She emerges from the sun – that was formerly like God's own head, then like the bloody moon, and that is now setting. And this setting sun from which she emerges is seen, and vividly described by the Mariner, as if behind dungeon bars. These bars are formed by the bare bones of the ship that brings her. The image is simultaneously positive and negative. In so far as that ball of bloody fire is her home, it is outlawed and locked up (like Coleridge's Oak), and she comes as if out of its prison, as if freed and at large. In so far as it is still the sun that was like God's own head, it is sinking (giving place to 'the dark'), and is shut away by her emergence, by her taking possession of the Universe that seemed to be his.

She emerges, that is, as the women described in Coleridge's nightmares emerged, and at this point, the Mariner's attitude to her is much the same as the sleeping, sometimes screaming, Coleridge's was to them. She seems wholly negative, utterly horrifying. As in:

. . . a most frightful dream of a Woman whose features were blended with darkness catching hold of my right eye & attempting to pull it out – I caught hold of her arm fast – a horrid feel – Wordsworth cried aloud to me hearing my scream – heard his cry and thought it cruel he did not come / but did not wake till his cry was repeated a 3rd time – the Woman's name Ebon Ebon Thalud . . .

And several others that he recorded.

XVIII The Other God's Name

At first, the woman seems to be alone in a skeletal hulk that sails briskly through the dead stillness like the charred coffin ship of a Viking hero in the underworld of Hel.

All at once, it appears that she is accompanied by 'a Death'. Then again both figures seem to coalesce in the one person – a woman of erotic allure whose

> . . . lips were red, her looks were free,
> Her locks were yellow and gold

but who is also, at the same time, in some manner 'a Death' – 'white as leprosy'. The narrator, the Mariner, the inspired poet confronting the very spirit of his inspiration now identifies her, point blank, and with horror, as:

> The Nightmare Life-In-Death was she
> Who thicks man's blood with cold.

So this is the very creature, perhaps, the very snake whose mouth touched the 'cold hollow spot' on young Coleridge's praying heart, and would still be there to touch it on the old Coleridge's praying heart, too. But she also comes straight from 'Kubla Khan'.

Towards the end of this same year, 1798, Coleridge began to make a German vocabulary for himself, in his Notebooks. He subtitles *Part The First* 'names of Spirits, Men, Birds, etc', and the first and only entry under A is

Alpe: the Nightmairs

Possibly he already knew this word and enters it here as an old favourite. A good part of Coleridge's life seems to have been passed in spectacular nightmares about terrifying usually grotesque women, of the sort I quoted above.* But before he met the German

---

* A modern therapist might interpret the dream I quoted above as a desperate attempt, by some supercharged autonomous centre of split-off consciousness in the right hemisphere of the brain to remove by physical violence – by terrorist violence – the over-policing, over-discoursive, censorious vigilance of the left hemisphere of the brain, that was denying it access to life. According to the theory, this would manifest itself (in dream) as a terrible woman attacking the right side of the body – but particularly that capsule of the left brain's vigilant intelligence, the right eyeball. This is how comic cartoon inner scenarios, accompanied by metaphysical terror, and actual physical breakdown, correct the errors of ego – again according to the theory. Debunkers of the theory would say that Coleridge found his right eyelid swollen, when he woke, not as a result of the dream but as the obvious cause of it.

Even so, that woman's name is interesting: *Ebon Ebon Thalud*. Doubtless the hidden associations go deep – deeper than Coleridge himself could have followed them. But right at the surface lie:

Ebon = Black

Blackness = (Arabic) sacred wisdom

Ebon = (via Latin) 'from good' or 'out of goodness'

As an addicted etymologist, Coleridge, too, would find the following lying right at the surface of *Thalud*:

   Tha is the common stem of Thalassa = (Greek) sea

                Thanatos = (Greek) death

                    Anathema Maranatha = (Aramaic) the most religiously accursed thing. Used in Corinthians (1 xvi:22): 'If any man love not the Lord Jesus Christ, let him be Anathema Maranatha.' In a verse diatribe against titled patrons, improvised into his Notebook two or three years before the nightmare, Coleridge had used the phrase:

> However proudly nicknamed, he shall be
> Anathema Maranatha, to me.

Maranatha means: 'Our Lord is come', yet is used as a doubly intensified curse in which the missing word *Anathema* is to be understood – remaining unspoken only because it is so unspeakably unclean. *Anathema* was originally a thing devoted to divine use. Specifically, it was a thing devoted to the Goddess Anatha, in the preterm *Alpe*, which unites his nightmare women with both a white mountain, like Abora, and his sacred river Alph, he was as familiar with the Greek root *Alph* meaning 'whiteness' (as with the Latin root *Alb*).

Likewise, he was familiar with *Alphos* – meaning 'leprosy'. And with *Alphitos* – the form of the Greek white-faced Goddess who became a nursery bogey but who *healed* leprosy. He had read all the authors. And he had probably seen the connection made between Alphito and Albina – the Goddess of death and poetic inspiration who gave her name to Albion.

The river Alph who was also the waning moon woman, wailing in the holy chasm, who was the black Abyssinian maid singing of the Moon mountain source and the sacred waters of inspiration, recovers her name here more fully qualified as the Nightmare Life-In-Death, white as leprosy.

Who is also the 'great and malignant Female' who ought to be Arnaquagssak or Nuliayuk or Sedna, mother of the sea-creatures, spirit of the sea, Goddess of Life and Death.

Jehovan Temple at Jerusalem. More specifically, it was the fee of the temple prostitutes, given to the Goddess Anatha. The two words together, therefore, resemble a compacted verbal hieroglyph of the religious conflict dramatized in the visionary drama of Coleridge's three poems. The coded reference to that particular Goddess, via that particular paradoxical phrase of blessings inverted into a curse, in the name of this particular nightmare ogress, could hardly be more comprehensively precise.

Lud = The Celtic British God Lludd (the eponymous God-King of London, who was also known as Llyr, the original of Lear).

The compound of these particles, 'Ebon Ebon Thalud', is therefore virtually the Nightmare Life-In-Death as the High Goddess of Britain in her Black phase. It is certainly the 'preternatural' female of the visionary poems in her rejected (vengeful) phase. The nightmare occurred in Wordsworth's house, about a month after Wordsworth had rejected 'Christabel', and had effectively ejected Coleridge (so Coleridge himself understood it) from any further creative partnership in *Lyrical Ballads*. It preceded by only days Coleridge's first renunciation (in a letter) of his claims to poetic talent, in the terms (handing over all laurels to Wordsworth, demoting himself to nothing more than 'some kind of metaphysician') that were to harden through the rest of his life.

XIX The Ancient Mariner becomes one of the Other God's Creatures

The Mariner's blood-sacrifice, biting his arm and drinking the blood, is followed immediately by the coffin-ship coming alongside and the beautiful woman, throwing dice with death, crying 'I've won'.

What is dramatized here is something that happened long ago. Coleridge's Unleavened Self, as he tells us, always did belong to the coldly kissing reptile enfolding his heart. That sacrifice had been made before birth, when he sipped the milk and honey-dew of the womb. This new biting of the arm etc. is simply the ritualized reaffirmation of what had occurred in the dreamtime.

She always was the winner, the owner. There was never a time when she lost. She had embraced her prize, kissing it with her strange, blood-red mouth, from the beginning. Her casting dice and crying 'I've won' is again simply reaffirmation of what happened long ago, in the dreamtime.

What is new, and always changing, and always forcing her to drag Coleridge into a new observance of the ritual, a new performance of the *agon*, is the encroachment of the Christian Self – the Christian Self's constantly strengthening opposition to her claim, his constantly renewed and more Godly efforts to wrest the Unleavened Self from her coils, to christen it and to exorcise her.

The Mariner's tale began by her summoning the Unleavened Self, the Mariner, in her STORM-BLAST, from the sphere of the Christian self's influence. Events up to this 'I've won' are a progressive stripping away of the Unleavened Self's Christian accretions.

But now her cry 'I've won' plunges the Mariner totally into her Universe:

> The Sun's rim dips; the stars rush out:
> At one stride comes the dark

And the waning moon rises,

. . . with one bright star
Within the nether tip.

which is the Female with her beloved in her embrace, Coleridge's
heart within the curve of the serpent. At the same time the sails begin
to drip – as the trees in Paradise might drip with honey-dew. But far
from being revived by this magical drench, the two hundred sailors,
under the power of that moon, with astonishing suddenness, drop
dead.

Which is to say that the Mariner's Christian humanity – the active
spirits of his Christian Self's influence – cannot exist in the lunar
atmosphere of the Female.

Nevertheless, the Mariner still holds back from total acceptance
of her omnipotence. As if the Albatross were still doing the work of a
crucifix around his neck. As if its corpse were also the Christ-
Crossbow with which he had killed what – when it was alive – was
the emissary of the Female. Accordingly, the Mariner undergoes for
a while the horror of being a Christian conscience alive in the world
of the Goddess. Everything that was Christian is dead around him.
But those goggles still on his eyes, insisting on their Christian
perspective, will not let anything come alive in the world where they
cannot recognize life. Though he has given his blood, i.e. his heart,
to that Female, he still cannot surrender a certain dead-at-its-post
Christian intellectual militancy, with its Albatross Crossbow Crucifix like a mounted weapon.

When he prays, it is as he describes: he prays to Jehovah. But
somehow his Unleavened Self now has such power over his speech
that he cannot pray. Nothing comes but a 'wicked whisper', like the
'far-heard whisper' with which the Nightmare Life-In-Death's
'spectre-bark' vanished over the sea. Or like her secret kiss, perhaps.

It is now, as he recognizes the utter emptiness of his prayer to
Jehovah, the dry-as-dust dishonesty of it, that his Unleavened Self
suddenly takes over. The goggles drop off, as if ashamed. Instantly
he recognizes her in the sea-reptiles and watersnakes and finds
himself blessing these creatures – blessing the very things that were
formerly deathly and loathsome. Without doing more than, as it

were, opening his eyes, he is suddenly wholly in her world, overwhelmed by the divine beauty of it.

The albatross drops from his neck into the sea. In other words, it ceases to be a killed god pinned on a crucifix, and returns to her – perhaps as her newly living child. Instantly, the Mariner falls into a blissful sleep of drinking, like an unborn babe, while the ship, under the control of the spirit of the sea, carries him home.

At this point the Mariner has managed to rid himself absolutely of every Christian vestige, and to give himself wholly to that female, who now turns out to be the Mother of all life, reigning in a vision of beauty and bliss.

But one has to ask, does Coleridge himself know quite what has happened, as he struggles to rig the end of the poem, and negotiate the stages of the Mariner's return to the everyday world? Does he think something wonderful has happened to the Mariner, or something terrible – unspeakable? As the Greenland Angekok of a vessel flies back homeward, towards the old and good God Jehovah/ Tongarsuck, Coleridge's own Christian conscience revives belatedly – not the Mariner's but Coleridge's. The Christian Self in him hurriedly takes up the pen.

He now strives to get the boat under the control of good Jehovan or Tongarsuck-like spirits. But they are redundant. Other more profound forces are at work. And something, that the now fully awake Christian Self feels is like a 'frightful fiend', follows close behind, though it is what it always was, that 'wily, long-breathed old witch, tough-lived as a turtle, and divisible as the polyp', the mother of the rainbow sea-reptiles. This Nymph of the waters of Alph, of the ocean of Alph, content to have reaffirmed her claim, now overtakes like a submarine earthquake and sinks the ship, with its corpses of obsolete Christian automata.

xx The Tongue that Cannot Lie

One prototype Scots Ballad behind 'The Ancient Mariner' is 'Thomas Rymer'. In this straight account of a shamanic flight, a renowned Scots Wizard – whose legends still hang around the great startling breasts of the Eilden Hills above the River Tweed – was forcibly carried off, on horseback, by a Nightmare Life-In-Death Fairy Queen, and held for seven years in the underworld. When he returned, his speech – like the Mariner's – had been changed.

In that ballad – one of the greatest, with an especially sinister and unearthly melody – Thomas had been given, against all his protests, the very thing he did not want, and that he knew mankind would not accept: – 'the tongue that can never lie'.

The drama of the end of 'The Ancient Mariner' is created by the effect of the Mariner's 'strange power of speech' on those who hear him. The moment he moves his lips, before he could have told anything of his tale, the Pilot of the boat that rescues him falls in a fit. The Pilot's boy goes crazy. The Holy Hermit, much as advised at the close of 'Kubla Khan', raises his eyes 'in holy dread' and prays, and when he gets ashore he can hardly stand.

Most serious of all is his effect on the Wedding-Guest – who is perhaps Coleridge himself.

It is not merely the difficulty of fitting this vision of the triumph of the Pagan Great Goddess into a Christian conscience and way of life that sends Coleridge on his way 'like one that hath been stunned'. It is the fact that she triumphed. The tongue that can tell only the truth has told him that his Christian life, and the limited cognitive system that goes with it, is a lie.

The pious end of the poem is his hollow refusal of a 'call' he is too late to refuse. He refuses the fact – that his Unleavened Self and his 'Strength' belong to what he sees once more, now that he is back on dry land, as 'the great, malignant and nameless Female'. But refusing a fact is no good. And as instructed at the end of 'Kubla Khan', Coleridge can weave this second circle around his possessed Unleavened Self (though the 'flashing eye' has already become a 'glittering eye' and the 'floating hair' a greying beard and the demonic singer, who took up the song of Mount Abora, a loon), but it is quite useless.

The Mariner insists on being heard. The 'sunny dome' and the 'caves of ice' go on being rebuilt – but in Coleridge's infernalized perspective, where the female emerges as a Terror.

And what 'the tongue that can never lie' tells him, and will now go on telling him, about himself, destroys his life.

XXI Her Symphony and Song

Except for the very brief 'The Knight's Tomb' and a few lines in 'Lewti', Coleridge's unique music is confined to the three visionary poems. These are his true songs – appropriately, since they constitute the drama of his relationship with his Muse.

'Possessed' by this Muse of Song, he found his pure voice in the ballad form. But not in any old ballad. Only in *her* story. And within the two visionary narratives he developed it into a music so new that he had to apologize for its strangeness and explain it (in that brief introductory note to 'Christabel').

His inspired handling of the old four-line ballad verse – a line of four iambics followed by three, in two pairs, basically rhyming on the short lines – has hardly lacked recognition. The 'strange power of speech', that the Mariner claims has been bestowed on him for the telling of his story, actually is there, in marvellously compelling form.

At intervals, Coleridge introduces an extra four-stress line making an octosyllabic couplet (in all but one case) in the second half of the verse. The musical intensification, and the surge of strangeness, that come with this slight innovation, are easily felt.

It brings an effect of melodic liberation, a sudden surprising wildness, bursting from the tight form.

Again, here and there he introduces an extra syllable or two into the four or three iambics. This is not unknown in traditional ballads.* Still, whenever it occurs here, in 'The Ancient Mariner', it

---

* What is breaking through into Coleridge's poetry here, as pagan vision and a particular music, has a link with my argument in the essay 'Myths, Metres, Rhythms'. The following, from Robert Burns's 'Scrap Book' is to the point:

There is a great irregularity in the old Scotch songs, a redundancy of syllables with respect to that exactness of accent and measure that the English poet requires, but which glides in, most melodiously, with the respective tunes to which they are set. For instance, the fine old song of 'The Mill, Mill, O!' to give it a plain prosaic reading it halts prodigiously out of measure; on the other hand, the song set to the same tune in

produces what has to be called again a sense of sudden musical liberation, together with an intensification of the uniquely Coleridgean effect. This effect is partly musical, but mainly a characteristic style of simple but hypnagogic imaginative encapsulation, not easy to describe but instantly recognizable:

> And a thousand, thousand slimy things

or:

> And the rain poured down from one black cloud

or:

> And the bay was white with silent light.

When both couplet and extra syllable occur together, the Coleridgean effect is intensified yet again:

> Like waters shot from some high crag,
> The lightning fell with never a jag

or:

> For the sky and the sea, and the sea and the sky
> Lay like a load on my weary eye

or:

> When the ivy tod is heavy with snow,
> And the owlet whoops to the wolf below.

———

Bremner's collection of Scotch songs, which begins 'To Fanny fair could I impart', etc., it is most exact measure, and yet, let them both be sung before a real critic, one above the biases of prejudice, but a thorough judge of nature, – how flat and spiritless will the last appear, how trite, and lamely methodical, compared with the wild-warbling cadence, the heart-moving melody of the first. This is particularly the case with all those airs which end with a hypermetrical syllable. There is a degree of wild irregularity in many of the compositions and fragments which are daily sung to them by my compeers, the common people – a certain happy arrangement of old Scotch syllables, and yet, very frequently, nothing, not even *like* rhyme, or sameness of jingle, at the ends of the lines. This has made me sometimes imagine that, perhaps it might be possible for a Scotch poet, with a nice judicious ear, to set compositions to many of our most favourite airs, particularly that class of them mentioned above, independent of rhyme altgether.

Coleridge noticed this. When he started 'Christabel' Part I (before he had completely finished 'The Ancient Mariner') maybe he intended it to be another ballad in ballad form, but in the first verse the new music took over:

> 'Tis the middle of night by the castle clock,
> And the owls have awakened the crowing cock;
> Tu-whit! – Tu-whoo!
> And hark, again! the crowing cock,
> How drowsily it crew.

Then he burst out of the ballad stanza completely – but not out of the ballad mode.

XXII The Lady Out of the Oak

The action of 'Christabel' Part I, is simple and single. Geraldine casts a hypnotic spell over Christabel, seduces and sexually violates her – the poem ending with the seduced folded in the arms of the seducer.

The poem begins where Christabel, going out at midnight to pray under the old Oak Tree for her far-away lover, hears a moaning and finds Geraldine:

> The lady sprang up suddenly,
> The lovely lady, Christabel!
> It moaned so near, as near can be,
> But what it is, she cannot tell. –
> On the other side it seemed to be,
> Of the huge, broad-breasted, old oak tree.
>
> The night is chill; the forest bare;
> Is it the wind that moaneth bleak?
> There is not wind enough in the air
> To move away the ringlet curl
> From the lovely lady's cheek –
> There is not wind enough to twirl
> The one red leaf, the last of its clan,
> That dances as often as dance it can,

Hanging so light, and hanging so high,
On the topmost twig that looks up at the sky.
Hush, beating heart of Christabel!
Jesu, Maria, shield her well!

The mesmeric passes of these lines prepare the reader for the strange climax of the poem, in which Geraldine reveals the uncanny nature of her power over Christabel. I mentioned earlier that the preternatural woman in each of the three visionary poems is the spirit of a particular kind of utterance. I called her the spirit of Coleridge's *incantatory language*. She was Alph, the river of erotic and sacred song. She was the Abyssinian maid whose song demonized the listener. She was the Nightmare Life-In-Death alias Heaven's Mother alias Arnaquagssak who freed the Mariner from dumbness only when he sacrificed to her his own blood (drinking her in his own blood as it might be communion wine). And she is now the reptilian woman (Coleridge takes pains to let his reader know that) out of Oak, whose words mesmerize the Christian Self – or mesmerize the 'soul' of the Christian Self in the person of Christabel. In each case, this woman's utterance attempts to overpower, or does overpower, the Christian Self. In 'Kubla Khan' the Christian Self has to weave a circle around the effects of her song, and so exorcize her. In 'The Ancient Mariner' she overpowered the Christian Self completely: the Mariner is whisked back to the world of Christian values as the mad relic of her conquest. And in 'Christabel' likewise she has overpowered the Christian Self completely.

Again, in each case her power is exerted specifically over 'utterance'. The singing of the Abyssinian maid not only demonizes her listener it inspires him to magical, paradise-building song. Freeing the Mariner from his dumbness, she frees his tongue only to tell the truth of her tale with 'strange power of speech' – which repeatedly takes possession of him, whether he likes it or not. Finally, her hypnotic, preternatural power controls Christabel's speech so utterly that the victim is like an otherwise dumb puppet of her will.

Geraldine is the ultimate incarnation of this power. And the whole action of 'Christabel' Part I, it could be said, is shaped to display the

[437]

power in its moment of perfect triumph. Moreover, the power is convincingly authentic.* Geraldine declares the omnipotence of her lordship over Christabel's utterance in what is both the climax of this poem (and therefore the climax of the entire Three Act Tragic Opera) and one of the most mesmeric incantations in English poetry:

> In the touch of this bosom there worketh a spell
> Which is lord of thy utterance, Christabel!
> Thou knowest tonight, and wilt know tomorrow,
> This mark of my shame, this seal of my sorrow;
>   But vainly thou warrest
>   For this is alone in
>   Thy power to declare,
>   That in the dim forest
>   Thou heard'st a low moaning,
> And found'st a bright lady, surpassingly fair . . .

The power of the music here masks the complexity of the very peculiar statement being made.

The search for the source of Coleridge's 'new principle' of metre, following the clues, as I have done here, into the symbolic system of his personal myth, seems to have led to this preternatural, weirdly composite female. Is it possible to identify her any more closely?

I have touched on her association with the Shaman's Goddess of Life and Death, Mother of the animals, with the Anath behind Jehovah, with Hel and Alphitos, with Isis and the Nightmare. But at

---

* 'Christabel' Part II, which I will refer to here and there for convenience, simply makes this poem's relationship to 'The Ancient Mariner' more explicit. 'The Ancient Mariner' presented a portrait of the Mariner and the Nightmare Life-In-Death in a panoramic setting. As I described earlier, in 'Christabel' Part I Coleridge zooms into close-up, and reveals exactly what was going on between them. At this degree of magnification, the Mariner has separated into two people: Christabel (the ideal soul of his Christian Self) and her father, 'the aged knight, Sir Leoline' (his Christian Self's shell of moral and intellectual ego). The Nightmare Life-In-Death cried 'I've won!', and left the reader mystified. In 'Christabel' Parts I and II Coleridge presents the inside story, the full drama, behind that cry, and reveals just how the Serpent Woman overpowered the Mariner's susceptible soul as a first step to overpowering his moral and intellectual ego and thereby the whole man.

bottom, Coleridge's sacred constants are the Oak, the Serpent in the Oak, and the Woman in the Oak. If acorns were apples, this would be the famous group in the garden of Eden. Apart from the familiar one in Genesis, mythic interpretations of this situation sometimes portray the Serpent and the Woman as two aspects of the one Goddess, or as the Goddess (the Serpent) and her High Priestess (the Woman). Sometimes there are two women, and the possible permutations multiply. The Serpent can then be the God, and the women the two opposed aspects of the Goddess. This last reality lies behind the myth of Adam's two consorts: Eve and the Demon Lilith and the Serpent's mysterious relationship to both, which cannot have been unknown to Coleridge. Listening more closely, with an ear to the body-language behind this mythic lexicon, one can't help hearing, in the 'mingled measure', the two voices of his mother and the voices he later divided between his two Saras. One imagines (almost sees!) the Oak and all its ramifications as a contorted hologram in his brain-scan, every word making it shiver like lightning. And when he prays, one imagines the Snake that wreathed and kissed his heart as a violent, rippling displacement in the lower spikes of his electrocardiograph. In other words, one feels the biological reality of a mythos that projected, on the cave-wall, in hallucinatory fashion, the drama of his nightmares, convulsed his behaviour, alienated his friends and dissolved his career. And though in another perspective it can be read as a large-scale, brilliantly concise, diagnostic, luminous vision of England's spiritual/intellectual predicament, it was a predicament that left Coleridge himself hanging on a cross.

In every perspective, Geraldine's rape of Christabel is the most powerful image of the nuclear event, the germinal event, in Coleridge's poetic life. This revelatory act is shocking on several counts, not only because a woman first hypnotizes then rapes a woman, or because she does it with such mysterious purpose (emerging from nowhere to do it). Since Geraldine is raping the 'soul' of Coleridge's Christian Self she is actually raping Coleridge too. She is simultaneously raping both the woman in the man and the man in the woman. Coleridge, as his verses make clear, is as overawed as Christabel by her erotic power and beauty. But what is truly shocking (unforgettable, unfathomable) is that this great beauty reveals, with a horrible deliberation, a bosom which is ('this mark of my shame, this seal of my sorrow') indescribably repulsive. The words that Coleridge uses (in Part II) to describe it, 'old', 'cold', and even the words he cancelled (from Part I), 'hideous, deformed and foul of hue', and 'A vision foul', are nothing to the horror of evil that he manages to suggest. Yet this 'mark of . . . shame' is the very proof of just who she is. And the fact that this being has not only revealed herself to him, but has taken possession of the 'soul' of his Christian Self, in this irreversible enforced abasement and act of possession, as the 'Lord' of the 'truth' of his utterance, is – for Coleridge – the 'truth impossible to face'.

Geraldine's 'human' nature in 'Christabel' establishes her centre of gravity, but what counts, for a reader, is her whole aura of suggestion, and that is the sum of her manifestations throughout the development of the visionary poems. Her corpse-like and reptilian bosom identifies the *divine* beauty (Coleridge uses the word to describe her eyes, which are the next moment 'shrunken serpent's eyes') as the 'greater than Jehovah'. Everything that has stirred in her history – the Fury Form of the 'great, nameless and malignant Female', the submarine giver of food and Mother of sea-creatures, the Abyssinian damsel with a dulcimer and the corpse-eating Nidhogg in Hel, the woman wailing in the chasm for her demon lover and the slimy things that crawled with legs in the rotting sea, the Nightingale and the love-maddened alligator, the Nightmare Life-In-Death and the Maenads that sent Ebon Ebon Thalud to tear out Coleridge's eyeball, Alphitos the leprous-faced night-goblin Goddess and the world-encircling serpent filling the sea with its luminous coils, the waning moon embracing a star and the wary, wily old long-breathed witch Nature, tough-lived as a turtle, Heaven's Mother, the Great Goddess of the putrefying, oceanic grave and the radiant cauldron of abounding new life, the river of erotic song and the sacred word: all these have converged, with their metaphysical hinterworlds and dream-sargassos, into the coiled power of Geraldine. Like a Cleopatra/Cressida, from every 'joint and motive' of her paradoxical being she calls his Christian Self to surrender to her kind of love, the beauty of her truth and the fact of her lordship. This 'rape under hypnosis' is simply the ultimate form of her 'call'. It is the imperious seal of her possession, the *fait accompli*. And 'Christabel' Part I is her monumental poetic trophy, the final tableau of her triumphant will. At the close she reclines, satiated, like that snake wreathed around Coleridge's heart. And Christabel sleeps in her coils, helpless, violated and blissful.

Though it took some time for Coleridge to realize consciously what had happened, at bottom he understood instantly, and fled.

XXIII Lord of Utterance

What Geraldine is actually saying, in that incantatory declaration of her will and omnipotence, is that though Christabel is now aware of Geraldine's loathsome secret – namely, her reptilian and corpselike *body* – nevertheless it is a secret she can never divulge. This comes as a hypnotic command, instructing her to speak of Geraldine henceforth only as 'surpassingly fair'. In the creaky Gothic plot this enforced secrecy has a creaky function. In Part II, Geraldine will move on to the next stage of her plan, seducing Christabel's father as easily as she has seduced Christabel, and Christabel must tell no tales.

But as the personification of the sacred Alph, the river of Coleridge's poetic word, she is saying something else – and saying it to Coleridge. Here it is not so much a hypnotic command as a statement of fact. Though his vision of her is one of terror, he will speak of her only as 'surpassingly fair'. Though he sees her as the Goddess of Death and the rotting sea, as well as the Goddess of Life and of the effulgent sea of birth, he will worship her as the wholly beautiful. That is to say, like Job he will glorify her beauty 'though it slay me'. This is not a poetic or religious perversity. It is a commonplace of the mystical life. Perhaps of the life of the dedicated scientist also. It is a simple recognition of the natural and presumably biological law that whatever is perceived as reality emits a compelling fascination indistinguishable from beauty. And this

Female presented herself to Coleridge's unusual awareness as the ultimate reality, therefore the ultimate truth, therefore the ultimate beauty. The speech that expresses her reality, her truth, and so, inevitably (and as it were incidentally), her beauty, is therefore his 'sacred speech', his only genuine utterance.

That is how she comes to be sole 'lord' of his 'utterance'. And that is why his Christian Self, in its constant evasion of her and the dreadful life of her Oak Tree, has no sacred speech – only a Babel of intellectual tongues that plug Coleridge's ears from the 'call' of her truth, her reality, her beauty, and from any song out of the Oak.

When he rejects Geraldine and flees – he has renounced that speech. He is thereafter, from Geraldine's point of view, and from the point of view of his own 'sphere of acute feelings', speechless. However much he may talk and write, it is all non-language. Comparatively. His flight into Germany is therefore the third circle that he weaves around his Unleavened Self and Her.

This explains why his unique music is confined to so few poems: mainly the three visionary poems, with slight leakage into two or three others. It is confined to poems that deal with his myth – or rather with her myth. That core-like image cluster – woman/reptile/oak – brings the clockwork inevitability of its meanings and dynamics with it wherever it appears, along with its distinctive 'sacred' language. But that is simply characteristic of the mythic poet. In Wordsworth's verse, the mythic elements are at once less distinctly formulated and more discursively diffused through a more unified temperament: the unique medicinal gum can exude at any moment, in the most unpromising corners. But in Coleridge's verse, unless this woman or her oak is about to appear, or is present, one finds only the exclusive wavelength and language of his Christian intellectual Self. Now and again these make an admirable poem – when they are braced against her painful absence, as a lament ('Dejection', 'Work Without Hope'), or are suffused by her nearness ('This Lime-tree Bower', 'Frost at Midnight'). But such works are moulded of an utterly different stuff from the magical substance of the visionary poems, and Coleridge knew it, when he admitted to 'hating composition'. As the record proves, except for those few months of natural, blessed release, his efforts at 'composition' could find only the language of his Christian intellectual Self – the very language that denied him release.

But the myth could pick up unlikely masks – especially carnival masks. 'Fire, Famine and Slaughter' and 'The Devil's Thoughts' (which had the kind of impact on Byron and Shelley that 'The Knight's Tomb' had on Scott) give a hint of the Mephistophelian sprites that frisked around his Fairy Queen. Another jeu d'esprit, 'The Raven', in which one can feel a whole undeveloped oeuvre of inspired factotum doggerel (a huge loss), turns out to be centred solidly on the Oak. Apart from these, and one or two more muffled echoes, the only times we hear his Unleavened Self give voice are inadvertently and *sotto voce* in passages of his descriptive prose jottings, sketching the effects of light, leaves or water – where he slips through (tiptoes past his terrors) into a delicacy and impassioned *recitative* that has no equal before Hopkins.

But the most illuminating of these fragmentary glimpses into his myth is 'The Knight's Tomb'.

XXIV · On the Breast of Helvellyn

The Oak appears in 'The Knight's Tomb' – only to disappear. If 'The Raven' dramatizes the Unleavened Self's murderously vengeful rage over the demolition of the Oak, 'The Knight's Tomb' records Coleridge's mourning acceptance of the loss.

> Where is the grave of Sir Arthur O'Kellyn?
> Where may the grave of that good man be? –
> By the side of a spring, on the breast of Helvellyn,
> Under the twigs of a young birch tree!
> The oak that in summer was sweet to hear,
> And rustled its leaves in the fall of the year,
> And whistled and roar'd in the winter alone,
> Is gone, – and the birch in its stead is grown. –
> The Knight's bones are dust,

And his good sword rust; –
His soul is with the saints, I trust.

Here is another Paradise Mountain, a spring, and a tree. And under the tree something new – a dead man in his grave.

The Oak, that lived so sweetly and heroically through the seasons, has suddenly – without any explanation – gone. In its place, unqualified except by the qualitiless adjective 'young', is a Birch tree.

The man died and the Oak tree went. The logic is: they were one and the same. Or, the life of the one was dependent on the life of the other. Now it has gone and he is under the ground that its boughs shaded. And over his buried corpse, in its place, is a Birch.

The name Sir Arthur O'Kellyn is one of those odd compounds invented by Coleridge, like Sir Henry, Lord Falkland, in 'The Ballad of the Dark Ladie', and the Baron Sir Leoline, Christabel's father, and Sir Roland de Vaux of Tryermaine, the father of Geraldine. According to his carefully assembled name, Sir Arthur was a Warrior (Knight), Celtic (O'Kellyn), and Royal Brythonic (Arthur). He was a warrior chieftain from the obscure front line of the Pagan/Christian deadlock – belonging in some fashion to both sides. Behind him, perhaps, opens the 'preternatural' dimension of the mythos of the Grail, the only realm in which integration of those two worlds might occur.

Within Coleridge's more particular, personal mythos, this figure (a form of Thor – Ar-Thur) is a Knight of the Oak. He is loosely related, therefore, to Sir Leoline, who fell so easily into the power of Geraldine, his daughter's seducer and usurper. Also to Sir Henry ('Ballad of the Dark Ladie') who was something of a Demon Lover. Also to the Mariner, whose quest was a modified 'Excursion of Thor' and none the less knightly for being made on shipboard rather than on horseback.

He is the half-noble negotiator between the two worlds, who lived in the possibility that the two might co-exist: a man of two selves. As if he might be a Kubla Coleridge who could suspend the prejudice of his Christian Self and give audience to his Unleavened Self – even to the point of becoming temporarily possessed by the Unleavened Self.

The Coleridge who could, in a fascinated sort of way, allow the half-somnambulist (as if drugged) Christabel to be overpowered and seduced by the purposeful Geraldine (and could even, like Sir Leoline, himself succumb to Geraldine). The Coleridge who could, briefly, write the visionary poems as straight autobiography.

The fact that this person now lies in his grave, and that the oak has gone, tells us that the negotiating faculty has died in Coleridge, who has accordingly retreated into exclusive self-identification with his Christian Self. He has thereby 'lost' his Unleavened Self – with its woman, its serpent, and its Oak. Nothing remains but the Christian Self, which is represented, as now appears, by the Birch. The Oak, that shared Sir Arthur's life, has been replaced by the Birch, over his grave.

But why on Helvellyn? Wordsworth's very own mountain, one might have thought. In every way, the poem is close to Christabel, but (by its subject) comes later. Though Coleridge would recite it, he did not publish it until he assembled his *Complete Poems* which came out the year of his death, in 1834. But some who knew him put its composition as early as 1802, two years after Wordsworth delivered the fatal blow. It commemorates Coleridge's own words, after all: 'The poet is dead in me.' But buried on Helvellyn. Why Helvellyn, as if under Wordsworth's very threshold? Why not, as Sir Arthur might have preferred, Mount Abora? or some other mountain that could conceivably be a stand-in for Mount Abora?

But Helvellyn is just that. Coleridge's familiarity with the Norse Goddess of the Underworld could not have failed to prompt the association, during one of his regular walks across the top of this mountain, on his way from his own home in Keswick to Wordsworth's cottage in Grasmere and back. The mountain was sacred to all of them. Dorothy records how William, Coleridge and she had fantasized about building a house up there – a home for their poetic future. After the fateful three-day visit in October 1800 when Wordsworth, having raised Coleridge's hopes to the highest, with his first reception of the finished 'Christabel', suddenly reversed his opinion (perhaps not mincing his words, probably paraphrasing his lethal note about 'The Ancient Mariner' that Coleridge would not see till the volume was published), maybe Coleridge came back over Helvellyn. Whether he did or not, it would occur to him sooner or later, as the death-blow to his poetic hopes took effect, that the most fitting burial place would be the very site on which those hopes had dreamed of building their home. The mountain of Hel, no longer Hel the oracular Sybil but Hel the Goddess of death, was the appropriate grave-mound for the presiding poetic genius of the never-to-be-written 'Excursion of Thor'. Where he would lie in the coffin-ship of the Nightmare Life-In-Death herself. Moreover, it is likely enough that Coleridge had lit upon the Old Norse *vella*, to boil, and *vell*, a bubbling up, with their close links to old Scandinavian and English words for well-spring. That spring, beside which Sir Arthur lay, is in other words the fountain that boils up out of his Norse underworld from the roots of the great Tree. Closer than Mount Abora. The grimmer source within the 'mighty fountain' of the Alph.

But why was Thor's Oak replaced by a Birch Tree? Why a Birch?

xxv The White Birch and The Dark Ladie

Coleridge's many references to the Oak are countered, here and there, by his delight in the Birch. The airy, showering light of the silvery Birch is opposite, in obvious ways, to the Oak – and yet in his mythos, though it does not belong to that rooted 'strength' and truth of the heart's passions, it does offer a substitute happiness: the consoling pleasure of freedom from those passions: the promised pleasures of love not as it actually is, tragic and terrifying to him, but love as it ought to be – a nostalgia for an idealized love that might have been.

During the spring months in which he finished 'The Ancient Mariner' and composed Part I of 'Christabel', he was working on another 'Ballad' that was clearly striving to enter the same visionary freedom, intensity, depth – but failing. This was 'The Ballad of the Dark Ladie'.

Of this poem's narrative action Coleridge kept and published only a fragment – which has nevertheless an amputated kind of completeness. In one sense it is a code-book for the two long narratives, identifying the tight connections between them in simple terms.

It opens with the Dark Ladie weeping 'in silent pain' for her betrothed Knight to come to her 'over the hills'. This is a direct link to two of the five women in the three visionary poems: to the woman wailing for her demon lover in the holy chasm of the Alph's source, on the one hand, and to Christabel praying under the Oak for her lover 'that's far away'. These links become stronger as the poem develops.

The Dark Ladie is closer to the woman wailing for her demon lover in that she sits close to a brook that falls scattering down a rock face, and though not under a 'waning moon' she 'lingers' under a sun that is 'sloping down the sky' – towards the dark.

But she is closer to Christabel in that she is sitting on moss, under a tree. Though the tree above her is not the mistletoe-bunched, dragonish Oak, that brandished its many heads and tentacles over Christabel, but a Birch with 'silver bark', at least the moss from Christabel's Oak is here – beneath her. And it is the same moss, perhaps, that cushioned the knees of the Holy Hermit, in 'The Ancient Mariner', when he kneeled in prayer 'at morn, and noon, and eve', and that

> wholly hides
> The rotted old oak-stump.

As if the Holy Hermit, in spirit, might be there, with his invisible arm around her shoulder, and his protective voice in her ear. (It will turn out to be appropriate, too, that she seems to be sitting on Sir Arthur O'Kellyn's grave.)

According to these suggestions (from all three visionary poems), The Dark Ladie somehow incorporates the two women from the opposite ends of Coleridge's feminine spectrum: the pure-minded Christian virgin, like Christabel, and the reptilian siren from the abyss, like Geraldine. Everything about her that is silvery white expresses a Christabel, and everything about her that is dark conceals a Geraldine.

When her longed-for Knight comes over the hills, the stilted verses have prepared us for a stilted noble figure. But in the etymological tenacity of Coleridge's richly precise yet protean code of signs, that Griffin crest, the flying half-reptile, is ominous.

He turns out to be Lord Falkland. And even the homely Christian name Henry cannot quite domesticate the eponym – from the fringe of the Antarctic seas, the latitudes of the Albatross. The moment his name passes her lips:

> Lord Falkland, it is thou!

the Dark Ladie reveals her own identity, and his, more nakedly:

> She springs, she clasps him round the neck.

This accidental-seeming hint of the Albatross floats on through her declaration:

> My Henry, I have given thee much,
> I gave what I can ne'er recall,
> I gave my heart, I gave my peace,
> O Heaven! I gave thee all!

But it suddenly stiffens into solidity when having promised her the 'fairest' of his sire's 'Nine castles' (as if that might be the castle of the most desirable Muse) he suddenly asks her to:

> Wait only till the stars peep out . . .

> Wait only till the hand of eve
> Hath wholly closed yon western bars,
> And through the dark we two will steal
> Beneath the twinkling stars!

The Dark Ladie's wavering oscillation between a Crucifix-pure Christabel and a love-sick woman inwardly wailing for her demon lover now goes hard over to Christabel Militant and sticks there. She recoils from his proposal with:

> The dark? the dark? No! not the dark!
> The twinkling stars? How, Henry? How?

[448]

The only excuse for this outburst is that she is talking in mythic algebra – using the signs made more explicit in 'The Ancient Mariner'. The 'dark' is the same that came in 'one stride' after the Nightmare Life-In-Death's winning throw and triumphant cry: 'I've won!' The stars are the same that rushed out, at the same moment. In that starry dark the waning moon will soon rise and she will find herself transmogrified, like the werewolf, to the woman wailing for her Demon Lover who is, as is now evident, Lord Falkland. Carrying on with the same algebraic system, she retorts:

> Oh God! 'twas in the eye of noon
> He pledged his sacred vow!
>
> And in the eye of noon, my love
> Shall lead me from my mother's door,
> Sweet boys and girls all clothed in white
> Strewing flowers before:
>
> But first the nodding minstrels go . . .

This looks more and more like the Church Marriage Ceremony that went before the Feast – which the Mariner's spell-stopped listener found it impossible to join. And from which – burdened with the vision of the Goddess of rainbow sea-serpents and of the worms of the grave – he had to turn away. But the Dark Ladie goes brightly and blithely on with her wedding plans:

> With music meet for lordly bowers,
> The children next in snow-white vests,
> Strewing buds and flowers!
>
> And then my love and I shall pace,
> My jet black hair in pearly braids,
> Between our comely bachelors
> And blushing bridal maids.

In this evidently strained ritual (where Coleridge is struggling with the memory of his own forced marriage) the Christian Coleridge seems to be trying (speaking through the Dark Ladie) to persuade 'the betrothed knight' to do exactly as he did: remove the world of

[449]

the Unleavened Self, embrace the Christian moral law. The Dark Ladie, in her Christabel persona, is certainly trying to persuade him.

Lord Falkland, one imagines, is listening in dismay. Hoping to embrace a Geraldine, he finds his neck locked in the arms of a Christabel. His dream of converting her into an Abyssinian singing girl and going wild to her instrument, perhaps on the Susquehanna where the alligators roar, seems to have walked straight into a trap. We can assume this because after his first love-call ('Come into the dark') he is struck dumb by her reaction, and never speaks another word.

Perhaps he is figuring desperately how he can wake up the recessive Geraldine and excite her to throw off this dominant and domineering Christabel. Or maybe the alternative is flitting through his head – a premature grave on Helvellyn.

The verse never breaks through into poetry and in fact it rehearses the ritual assassination of the poetic gift in Coleridge: a monologue asphyxiation by the Christian Self. It dramatizes, in other words, the utter suppression of Geraldine, the 'lord of utterance'. She appears in this poem only by reflection in Lord Falkland's confident expectation and summons, and in the Dark Ladie's darkness (in one note, Coleridge calls her The Black Ladie), which is concentrated passively in her 'jet black hair', where it will submit (without protest, according to Christabel) to the birch-silver 'pearly braids' of Christabel's bridal crown, and to the silver-whiteness that dresses every aspect of her wedding, and that is epitomized, at the opening of the poem, in the Birch Tree under which she sits.

The Birch Tree that has replaced the Oak on Sir Arthur's grave.

But, for a moment there in passing, the Dark Ladie Christabel was also the Albatross, heavy around Lord Falkland's neck. Indeed, her whole oration about her perfect marriage is given while hanging around Lord Falkland's neck.

This is one of the clues to the place of the Albatross in the algebraic mythic system.

xxvi The Interplay of the Three Planes

In the particular interpretation that I have followed, the single Tragic Opera of the three poems (and the two subsidiary poems) tells the autobiographical story of the conflict between Coleridge's two selves, as it was precipitated and brought to a climax by the reptilian Female's 'call'.

This autobiographical aspect of the Three-Act Drama constitutes one plane or level – what might be called the upper and dramatically active level – of the vision.

On that level, I interpreted the shift, in 'The Ancient Mariner', from the loathsome 'dead' Universe to the blessed 'living' Universe, as an effect of a sudden shift in the Mariner's outlook. I described it as a shift from the outlook of his Christian Self to that of his Unleavened Self. It has been described elsewhere as a shift from a new religion to an older religion – a 'regression' from narrowly Protestant Christian to archaic Pagan. Coleridge experiences his Pagan 'regression' as a breakthrough to a vision of greater spiritual meaning: his vision of the beauty of the sea-snakes, which renews his (the Mariner's) spiritual being, and redeems all the horrors of his Christian adventure. Nevertheless, when Coleridge's habitually dominant Christian attitude reasserts itself, after this brief, mystical reversal, the returned Mariner's experience is recounted, and heard, not as a vision of greater spiritual meaning, a revelation of the divine glory of the total creation, but as something unspeakably dreadful, incomprehensibly ominous and disheartening, a tale too terrible to be told or heard, like a curse.

And on the autobiographical level, that is how the vision did operate on Coleridge, like a curse – destroying his life.

It became a 'curse', however, only in so far as he rejected it – only in so far as he refused the 'call'. The broken torso of Apollo commanded Rilke: 'You must change your life'. In Coleridge's case, to have accepted the vision and obeyed the 'call' would have meant renouncing Christianity (at least as completely as Goethe renounced it, re-adapting only what he needed to keep). What that conversion would have signified for Coleridge, simply in the way of social consequences, can be imagined. On the other hand, the traditional penalty for refusing the 'call' is death of some kind (which is why, in societies that observe such events closely, the 'call' itself is so much feared: no normal person wants either of the two options).

While the Three-Act Drama presents Coleridge's response to the 'call' on that autobiographical level, it also incorporates the archetypal, visionary world from which the 'call' emerges. This archetypal world constitutes a different, deeper level. Perhaps autobiographical factors gave it a distinctly Coleridgean aspect, or sensitized him to the particular form in which it revealed itself to him. At the same time it is clearly the same archetypal world that has revealed itself, in some not too dissimilar form, in all cultures, as one of the earliest, most profound, most intimately meaningful and all-embracing 'religious' truths. It is the world of the great Female of Life and Death, in whom the sexually irresistible 'bride' somehow embodies not only the animal and vegetable kingdoms, and the processes of the elements, but the extremes of the devouring grave and the maternal womb. These last two in particular, like her two selves fighting for dominance, do not so much alternate as coexist, each within the other.

On this deeper level, that shift from the loathsome 'dead' universe to the blessed 'living' universe, and from the leprous Aphrodite dicing with death to Mary Queen, Heaven's Mother, is not a shift from one religion to another. The whole vision exists firmly within a Pagan universe – a single universe. The shift is simply one pulse of the oscillation between those two extremes of the great Female's manifestation – a movement of the eyes with which her consort and son (the Mariner) encompasses her totality, in 'terror and adoration', as in Job.

The religious structure of that Pagan, archetypal level is therefore quite intact, beneath the equally intact structure of the protestant (Jehovan) level. The theological implication of this comes clear if it is put slightly differently. As sketched out above the negative pole of the Female's Universe has a different meaning on each level. On the deeper level, it is simply the dark half of her sacred completeness, a phase of her divinity. But on the upper level it is the disgusting and terrifying hell, which the Christian regards as evil and absolutely rejects. Likewise, the positive pole of the Female's Universe has a different meaning on each level, though less pronounced and not inverted – i.e. not contradictory or antithetical. On the upper level, if it can be accepted at all (and the subject of the poem, in one sense, is the difficulty of this acceptance) it is the benign Universe of Mary Queen, Heaven's Mother – that sole portion of the primitive, Pagan vision which one form of Christianity could assimilate. On the lower level it is the benign Universe of Mary Queen's historical pre-decessors, the same Goddess in non-Christian form, as it might be the benign Universe of a bountiful and forgiving Arnaquagssak.

This approach to full Pagan vision via something like Celtic Christian Catholicism, which the Protestant Mariner follows, casts light on Coleridge's occasional scattered remarks about Catholicism that qualify his usual severe reservations. It explains, maybe, why his Notebook pages about St Teresa suddenly blaze with a quite peculiar as if secretly infatuated intensity. As if his Christian Self, before it could surrender to the Serpentine Female (and all her works) in 'Christabel', had first to be immersed and softened in the Mariolatrous hyperaesthesia of 'The Ancient Mariner'.

In this way, his image of the upper Jehovan level and his image of the lower Pagan level are fused in a kind of pun. And the mechanism of this pun is not accidental or contrived, but true to historical reality.

What combines the two levels, in 'The Ancient Mariner', is a third level, which belongs to both: not so much a third level as a third plane, vertical to the horizontals of the other two and bisecting both. This is the shamanic plane, the plane along which the Mariner actually moves. Disabled by the conflict on the upper level, he is compelled to take to the shamanic plane and plunge himself in the healing wholeness of the lower level. Insofar as he brings back the vision of that wholeness and the first-hand experience of living within it, he heals us too, which is one reason why we value 'The Ancient Mariner' as we do.

XXVII Identikit of the Albatross

Wordsworth contributed the Albatross. Coleridge had played paranormal midwife for Wordsworth's creative psyche. Now Wordsworth proved that he could return the favour. He could smuggle at least one essential thing to Coleridge's awareness, out of Coleridge's hidden self, past Coleridge's self-censorship. But this is a common enough experience where two people share a wavelength of excitement.

So the white Albatross emerged from the Alph's nest of images – as if it might be the Alphatross. And however we look at it, the bird's rightness is uncanny.

In the most general sense, the Albatross in flight, and in friendly attendance on the ship, is the bird form of the 'call' – and as I mentioned earlier is therefore the bird-form of the great Female (like Vuokho), or in this case of the Nightmare Life-In-Death.

When the Mariner shoots it, the act is the Christian Self's declaration of war against the Unleavened Self and against the archetypal plane of the great Female which it represents.

At the same time, on the shamanic plane the bird is that Keeper of The Threshold – the animal form whose sacrificial death opens the spiritual vision.

But the more intricate meanings of the Albatross emerge most clearly with the help of 'The Ballad of the Dark Ladie', if the Albatross is regarded as the Dark Ladie herself. In this perspective, the significance of the Albatross is tightly linked to the plane of the autobiographical conflict.

The bird contains both of the Dark Ladie's selves – the Christabel Christian Self and the Geraldine Unleavened Self.

As it flies, and plays about the ship, it is the Dark Ladie *Geraldine*, wailing or weeping 'in silent pain' for her lover (in other words, uttering the 'call'). But as the bolt from the Mariner's Crucifix Crossbow penetrates it, the Geraldine spirit – i.e. the bird's *life* – is killed in it.

The falling bird then changes in mid-air. The dead Albatross that hits the deck is the living Dark Ladie *Christabel* – i.e. the bird's *death*

– stepping to her wedding, or at least insisting that the ceremony be 'white' and 'in the eye of noon'.

The Mariner has made his conscious decision to refuse the 'call'. He must now be taught how he has unconsciously made the opposite decision, and has, by that very killing surrendered to the 'call'. The Mariner has murdered the Albatross in his Christian life of the 'lie'. He will now be taught what that means in the Unleavened life of the 'truth', where what he thought was a murder is in fact a sacrifice.

The Female, who is all the elements and creatures of the wind and sea, sweeps him to the confrontation and judgement.

The process of judgement, punishment and correction begins in the 'silent sea', as a paralysis of Heaven and Earth. The water of feeling and of heartfelt utterance – the water of Alph, no less – is as if dried up, even though the ship sits on an ocean of it. Language itself dries up – the language of the Christian Self, that is (the prayer to Jehovah), and the tongue withers. The water, which should be life, now appears to be death, and actually rots.

This is how the great Female's universe appears to the Christian Self who could not accept it. The Christian Crossbow Self not only rejected it, but, by killing its messenger the Albatross, killed it too.

The Christian Crossbow Self has performed the role of 'a Death' – dealing apparent death.

Considering the situation as a game, one could say the Christian Crossbow Self has won the first round, and in winning has forced onto the bird and the sea of the Female (the waters of Alph) a state like death, and onto itself a life of horror, dumbly staring at the world of its own death-dealing rejection, a world that seems to putrefy.

At which point the Mariner finds the Albatross hanging round his neck.

In the general sense, the Albatross is now two things. It is the Mariner's Christian Crossbow Self, with its burden of 'agony', its 'cross', which is the consequence of being Coleridge's Christian self. And at the same time it is the Christian Self's victim – the dead emanation of the 'lifeless ocean' of the rejected great Female's 'call'.

But in the more particular and precise sense, the Albatross hanging around the Mariner's neck is identical to the Dark Ladie Christabel hanging around the neck of Lord Falkland in 'The Ballad of the Dark Ladie'.

In that poem, Christabel triumphs in the end. At Lord Falkland's mention of the 'dark' and the 'stars', she assumes total defensive possession of the Dark Ladie's body. Her monologue insistence on a birch-white wedding in 'the eye of noon' is like a two-way exorcism. As if while with her left arm she hung around Lord Falkland's neck, with her right hand she lifted the pearly crucifix from between her breasts and held it up between their mouths, interdicting his lustful kiss and simultaneously banishing the demon lover/Unleavened Self from him and the spirit of Geraldine from herself.

As I noted, Falkland stands dumb, as if his tongue were 'withered at the root', and the displaced Geraldine slumps inside Christabel like a dead bird. Dark Ladie Christabel hangs on Lord Falkland's neck, that is, like the death-dealing Crucifix Crossbow combined with the murdered Albatross: 'a Death' carrying its winnings.

In the unsuccessful, aborted 'Ballad of the Dark Ladie', the game ends there, with the Dark Ladie Christabel still a clear winner and Lord Falkland staring over her shoulder at the death of his world of Eros. Just as the Mariner stares over the shoulders of the dead Albatross at the putrefying sea. Just as Coleridge stared over the shoulders of his colder and colder wife he wanted to love but could not.

The pivotal event of 'The Ancient Mariner' is the Mariner's transformation from the Protestant Christian who cannot pray in his world of loathsome death, to the (quasi-Catholic) Pagan spontaneously blessing the Creation in his world of radiant life. This sudden overthrow of the Christian Self by the Unleavened Self can be followed as the overthrow of the Christabel Self by the suddenly reviving Geraldine Self within the Dark Ladie form of the Albatross.

The overthrow could not happen in 'The Ballad of the Dark Ladie', much as Lord Falkland wanted it to, but in 'The Ancient Mariner' it can and does. The game here is far from over. When the Mariner sees the dark bars fleck the setting sun, Geraldine comes awake in the body of the Albatross. When the Mariner bites his arm, she returns irresistibly to life (and the Mariner is able to speak).

The opposition of these two female players, and the state of play, within the Dark Ladie Albatross, is now projected into the 'spectre bark' – the Christabel Christian Self being represented by 'a Death' and the Unleavened Geraldine Self by a lunar, deathly, beautiful woman. And now it turns out that the Dark Ladie Christabel's winning throw was illusory, and her gains temporary. The blood-drinking, supernatural Female, coming fully to life, makes the winning throw that concludes the game. Her cry: 'I've won!' means 'It is all mine!' – i.e. Coleridge and the Universe. At once, the partial outlook of the 'lie' begins to fail and the revelation of the all-inclusive 'truth' to take over.

This transformation is also projected – onto the Christian crew, who now drop dead, and onto the heavens, where the 'dark' arrives, the stars 'rush out', and the waning moon rises. Gradually the curse in the eyes of the dead Christian crew – more terrible and damning than an orphan's curse – shrivels away (as in the eyes of the Dark Ladie Christabel, perhaps, as she still clings around Lord Falkland's neck), and gives place to the radiance of the moonlit sea, full of beautiful sea-creatures, teeming with holy life. As if Lord Falkland were to find, instead of censorious Christabel, Geraldine brilliantly alive in his arms, kissing him in the 'deep, romantic chasm', under the suddenly risen moon. Now that the sea-Female has absolutely won, and has returned to full possession of her own creation, the Mariner (part of her winnings) blesses what he sees in a rapture of recognition. At that point the Albatross, like the last vestige of his lethal Crossbow Christian Self, and the last weight of the now truly dead Dark Ladie Christabel, drops from his neck into the sea.

But again, one imagines the bird's mid-air falling corpse changing as before but in the opposite direction, and returning to what it was, to its true Geraldine-like life – if not to a living Albatross then to a sea-serpent of splendour and fluorescence, that plunges under and swirls away in flaring rainbow glories, among all the rejoicing sea-snakes.

Over this scene the waning moon with its star 'within the nether

[457]

tip' lifts the Goddess's archaic banner. The Mariner is the star. And Coleridge himself is up there, in the lap of the 'great, malignant, nameless Female' (the one young STC ran out into the 'dreadful, stormy night' to find), now more blessed than Heaven's Mother, and in fact he climbs through the abyss with her in a rapturous embrace.*

Briefly. And only in these poems. Before he wakes up to what has happened.

Postscript: The Snake in the Spine

The stark either/or of Coleridge's Christian dilemma, in the three visionary poems, came partly from the fact that his 'other God', the god of the alternative truth, the 'greater than Jehovah', took the form which in all orthodox Christian contexts is the very incarnation of Evil: the Snake.

The irruptive, 'preternatural' element of his revelatory experience could have conceivably taken on several different forms, any of which might have served as a workable expressive image. And one can't help wondering whether he wouldn't have found things easier, and his main problem more soluble, if only he had settled on a more evolved, less notoriously proscribed, less exacting symbol than the Snake – in the way that (confronting a conflict of broadly similar forces) Shakespeare and Eliot did.

---

* Remembering Pantisocracy's paradisal dream of life on the Susquehanna, in the American South, and drifting South still further, Coleridge might have recognized the tragic departure, on a raft of snakes, of the Mexican Redeemer god, Quetzalcoatl. After his intoxicated surrender to Xochiquetzal (the Aztec Anath), Quetzalcoatl rose to become the morning star (the star near the waning moon). Then instead of composing 'The Knight's Tomb', as elegy for his poetic genius, Coleridge might have transcribed Quetzalcoatl's own lament for himself:

> He made a lament, a song
> About his going. He sang:
> 'Our Mother
> The Goddess with her mantle of serpents
> Is taking me with her
> As her child.
> I weep.'

One thing that cannot be doubted about Coleridge is the hundred per cent authenticity of his instinctive high-minded 'goodness'. His inborn benevolence of heart, spirit and mind was, in its way, a passion that determined all his other passions. It can often be felt directly, almost as a selflessness, almost, at times, as a latent saintliness. It can be felt in the poems as pervasively as in the Notebooks – in his exalted absorption with the sea-snakes and with Geraldine's uncanny beauty as unmistakeably as in his persistent, costly humility of love towards his 'cruel' friends. It emanates convincingly from the whole man, not just from the vigilant piety of his Christian Self. Indeed, his Christian Self's narrow absolutism, occasionally sharpened to sectarian petulance (against Catholicism, for instance) by what he himself recognized, and regretted, as an intellectual vehemence that could resemble arrogance, was what most often displaced and obscured it. At the same time, it was most nakedly displayed in the poetry of his most intense visionary moments. Perhaps for many readers, this is still the paradox of the poems and of Coleridge the Christian moralist: the fact that the 'evil' (in 'The Ancient Mariner' the sea-reptiles, in 'Christabel' Geraldine's serpent self) is the bearer of the omnipotent 'preternatural' beauty – which transfigures in the first poem the Mariner and in the second Christabel herself. Or, to put it another way, while that mystical love of goodness pervaded his whole nature, yet his poems revealed, and in a sense proved, that for him it radiated, as from a nucleus, from what his Church held to be the very symbol of evil.

In the poems the Serpent is assimilated to the Woman. A post-Freudian could well give this Woman of Coleridge's a role that is in the circumstances just as negative, from the post-Freudian point of view, as the Serpent is from the Christian. That is to say, the demonized lover/singer of 'Kubla Khan', with 'his flashing eyes, his floating hair', could be suspected of having drunk the milk and honey-dew not of Paradise but simply of the womb.

Just so, in 'The Ancient Mariner', after the collapse of his Christian vision of the woman's ocean as a waterless hell of death, the Mariner suddenly accepts it as a dazzling paradise of love, and falls into a trance of sleep while his whole body drinks in bliss in the rocking womb or cradle of the ship. Again, Christabel the same, when she wakes ravished – wholly possessed – in the wreathing arms of Geraldine:

> O sorrow and shame! Can this be she,
> The lady, who knelt at the old oak tree?
> And lo! the worker of these harms,
> That holds the maiden in her arms,
> Seems to slumber still and mild,
> As a mother with her child.
>
> A star hath set, a star hath risen,
> O Geraldine! since arms of thine
> Have been the lovely lady's prison.
> O Geraldine! one hour was thine –
> Thou'st had thy will! By tairn and rill,
> The night-birds all that hour were still.
> But now they are jubilant anew,
> From cliff and tower, tu-whoo! tu-whoo!
> Tu-whoo! tu-whoo! from wood and fell!
>
> And see! the lady Christabel
> Gathers herself from out her trance;
> Her limbs relax, her countenance
> Grows sad and soft; the smooth thin lids
> Close o'er her eyes; and tears she sheds –
> Large tears that leave the lashes bright!
> And oft the while she seems to smile
> As infants at a sudden light!

Looked at in this way, the Snake Woman appears not only as the personification of the delusory, as-if-almighty glamour of evil, she can also be seen as a symptom of infantilism in Coleridge.

A defender of Coleridge has to shift everything into an altogether bigger arena, and to find a better word than the psychoanalyst's disparaging *infantilism*. Coleridge himself considered a certain child-heartedness to be an adult's highest human endowment. He derived this not from the spiritual and wisdom traditions of China and India, where it is a basic tenet, but from his own perception. He links it specifically with the physiology of language:

To trace the if not absolute birth yet the growth and endurance of Language from the Mother talking to the child at her Breast –

(Notebook)

and with unspoiled conciousness:

To carry on the feelings of childhood into the powers of manhood, to combine the child's sense of wonder and novelty with the familiar . . . , this is the character and priviledge of genius, and one of the marks which distinguish genius from talents.

(Essay xv, 'The Friend')

But his more esoteric blissful sense of the 'preternatural' Woman who is also a Serpent hearkens further back still, beyond his childhood and mother's womb.

In Pagan religions the Snake is almost without exception a positive figure, anything but evil, though sometimes 'terrible' – and often the highest deity.

Perhaps this seems to suggest that beneath his efforts to be a pure, whole-hearted Christian, Coleridge was in fact a pure, whole-hearted, genuine pagan, something like the regenerate Apuleius at the end of *The Golden Ass*. But things were obviously not so simple. Or perhaps they were much simpler. His attitude to the Serpent Woman had nothing fanciful about it, nothing nostalgic, no archaicizing in the bad sense. It was first hand, existential, peremptory, overwhelming and incomprehensible to him. In that case, one has to consider what might seem unlikely.

The Serpent and the Woman combined appear again, beyond 'paganism', in the spiritual asceticism of India. Fundamental to all forms of yoga is the ideal purpose of awakening *Kundalini*. In the curious biological apperception of Indian spirituality, this is 'the serpent power' that successful yogic practice awakens at the base of the spine and raises up, through the body, from station to station, via the spine, eventually to the crown of the head. As it ascends, this elemental, thaumaturgic energy awakens each successive centre of 'preternatural' faculties – culminating in a transfigured state of illumination regarded as union with the True Self, the highest 'divine' condition of Being attainable to human consciousness. The vast literature of Indian spirituality revolves around this first practical essential: the awakening of the dormant spinal power. When it does awaken, it is experienced in vision as a Serpent, and is always described as a Serpent, except when it is experienced and described as the 'Divine Mother'.

The 'awakening' of the serpent power is not confined to practising yogis. It may awaken of itself, to some degree, in any person of passionately concentrated inner life – as in the often experienced paranormal episodes that accompany intense love, or that may develop out of a suffering that is inescapable, acute and prolonged enough. According to the anecdotal biographic literature, wherever the person is unprepared (by the necessary psychic and physical training and guidance) the psychosomatic effects of the Serpent's ascent can be chaotic, terrifying, seemingly pathological, and may last for years. If opium and his struggle against it were not confusing the picture, Coleridge's extraordinary physical symptoms might well qualify. Even so, no matter what the external life, the serpent power becomes the bringer (the Mother), eventually, of some portion of spiritual gifts (healing powers etc.) if not of the ultimate illumination. There is a parallel to the sophisticated, assiduously-cultivated Indian phenomenon, as well as to the rough and ready commonplace, spontaneous one, in the experiences and arduous training initiations that produce traditional shamans, the *Angekoks*.

Setting Coleridge's vision in this *biological** context, one wonders whether it could have been induced by a spiritual awakening of that kind – spontaneously undergone by his *Unleavened Self*. The abnormal intensity and 'authority' of the vision suggests the possibility. His account of it, which engaged him in such moral struggle, could then be seen as the result of an over-crystallization of the imagery and an over-literal interpretation of it in Christian terms.

---

* 'Biological' in the sense that 'the serpent power' can be regarded as a usually dormant resource, the most primordial, fundamental, emergency resource, of our animal body, one that has, when aroused, seemingly supernatural, centralizing, unifying, intensifying effects on developed consciousness.

That would be inevitable from his Christian Self's point of view. In other words – historically deprived of any adequate symbolic (mythic) paradigms and conceptual categories, such as might represent the reality of that experience, his Protestant Christianity would mistranslate it, automatically, as evil Snake business. His artistic problem became: how can the revelation be expressed through a language of signs in which it can appear only as the opposite of itself? As the poems show, he solved the problem by shifting to another language. He relaxed from the protestant language in which the poems are framed, and thence dissolved through a Catholic into a wholly Pagan language in the core of the vision presented. Supposing as I say that the Serpent Power was his true subject, the Pagan mythos simply became his appropriate symbol of it.

If this supposition were true, if in his case the Serpent Power truly had awakened and moved, it would help to explain that apparent inconsistency: the coexistence, in him, of his benevolent, spiritu-alized potentially saintly passion of passions, and of the peculiar yet transcendent Snake and Snake Woman imagery in the great poems.

There is an Indian tradition that Christ spent his lost seventeen years in the Himalayas, among Kashmiri yogic adepts. His moun-tain top shrine is famous and still venerated. If that had been likewise an accepted Western tradition, known to Coleridge in all its circumstances (and as likely as any other), as it is to us now, we might find it easier to set the radical, primitive, extra-Christian inclusiveness of his religious feeling in a positive context. And easier to grant a positive value to what he glimpsed of the Snake and the Woman – on the far side of his Christian Self's busy ratiocinations. We might then be able to say: what opposed and challenged his defensive, orthodox Christianity was not so much an 'Unleavened Self' as a greater holistic revelation, more truly like Christ's own, more self-evidently that of a greater 'god of love'.

One imagines Coleridge's own mythos emanating from three octaves: the higher 'preternatural' octave, the middle Pagan octave, the lower womb-world octave. In the higher octave, the Kundalini power ascending resonates 'divine' illumination, the authority and actual presence of the 'divine', from the images of the Snake and the Great Female. In the middle octave, the 'song' of the Pagan double-natured Serpent Woman of Sexuality and death 'translates', incorporates and transmits the revelation and real power of the higher octave. In the lower octave, the 'symphony' of the earth-enfolding Serpent and Mother-womb accompanies in contrapuntal harmony and with rich chordal effects the 'song' of the middle octave. All three octaves are centred on the spinal 'tree' through which Kundalini climbs. In mythic narrative terms, Kundalini attempts to wholly take possession of Coleridge and so to transform him, which becomes the drama of 'the call'. His awareness of that produced the spontaneous musical vision for which he laboured to find the metrical/rhythmical expression.

It is in this sense that in rejecting 'the call', his Christian Self rejected the 'greater god'. Or rather, in this sense his Christian Self censored everything but a generalized mystical passion for 'goodness' and an incandescent religiosity – which remained as the staples of his existence.

These crumbs from the supper of the Great Snake and the Serpent Woman were all that he could bring into his daily life. Except for that brief period, when he returned with the three poems.

Note

While my remarks in this essay are based mainly on easily accessible material in Coleridge's Poems and Notebooks, Coleridge biography, J. L. Lowes's *Road to Xanadu*, and common knowledge about such things as Norse Myth, the King James Bible, the Ballads etc., I do draw heavily on two other sources that may be unfamiliar to many students of English poetry.

One of these is the history of the cult of the Female in religious tradition. In particular, I draw on one view of this history, in which it can be seen to illuminate aspects of mankind's psychological evolution – both as this evolution has been experienced (and expressed) in the long development of recorded human cultures, and as it is recapitulated (sometimes, as in Coleridge, with great self-awareness) in the psycho-biological life of individuals. For curious readers, a graphic overview of the vast lineaments of the subject can be found in Erich Neumann's *The Origins and History of Consciousness* (translated by R. F. C. Hull, Princeton/Bollingen, 1954) and *The Great Mother: An Analysis of the Archetype* (translated by Ralph Mannheim, Princeton/Bollingen, 1955) – especially in the latter. A more detailed account of the material itself is supplied by *The Myth of the Goddess*, by Anne Baring and Jules Cashford (Viking, 1991).

The other source to which I owe a good deal is the literature dealing with shamanism. The unchanging spontaneity and ubiquity of shamanic experience, its place in the history of both great and small artistic and spiritual traditions, and its direct connection with the manner and subject matter of certain kinds of poetry, is well worth looking into. The best known introduction to the phenomenon is Mircea Eliade's *Shamanism: Archaic Techniques of Ecstasy* (translated by Willard Trask, London: Routledge, 1964).

1993

Rhythms .

WINTER POLLEN
Occasional Prose
TED HUGHES

EDITED BY
WILLIAM SCAMMELL

faber and faber
LONDON · BOSTON

For Carol

First published in 1994
by Faber and Faber Limited
3 Queen Square London WC1N 3AU
This paperback edition first published in 1995

Set in Linotype Sabon
by Wilmaset Ltd, Birkenhead, Wirral
Printed in England by Clays Ltd, St Ives plc

A CIP record for this book
is available from the British Library.

ISBN 0-571-17426-4

2 4 6 8 10 9 7 5 3 1